P9-ECK-263

THE
LAW
BOOK

FROM HAMMURABI TO THE INTERNATIONAL CRIMINAL COURT,
250 MILESTONES IN THE HISTORY OF LAW

Michael H. Roffer

STERLING
New York

To Susan, Jillian, and Ben—my most important milestones—
and to the memory of my parents, Celia and Jerry

STERLING
New York

An Imprint of Sterling Publishing
1166 Avenue of the Americas
New York, NY 10036

ISBN 978-1-4549-0168-6

Distributed in Canada by Sterling Publishing
c/o Canadian Manda Group, 664 Annette Street
Toronto, Ontario, Canada M6S 2C8
Distributed in the United Kingdom by GMC Distribution Services
Castle Place, 166 High Street, Lewes, East Sussex, England BN7 1XU
Distributed in Australia by Capricorn Link (Australia) Pty. Ltd.
P.O. Box 704, Windsor, NSW 2756, Australia

For information about custom editions, special sales, and premium and corporate purchases,
please contact Sterling Special Sales at 800-805-5489 or specialsales@sterlingpublishing.com.

Manufactured in China

2 4 6 8 10 9 7 5 3 1

www.sterlingpublishing.com

Contents

Introduction 7

c. 2550 BCE The Oldest Written Will *10*

c. 2100 BCE The Code of Ur-Nammu *12*

c. 1792 BCE The Code of Hammurabi *14*

c. 1300 BCE The Ten Commandments *16*

621 BCE The Draconian Code *18*

594 BCE The Laws of Solon *20*

c. 480 BCE The Gortyn Code *22*

450 BCE The Twelve Tables *24*

399 BCE The Trial of Socrates *26*

c. 180 The Talmud *28*

c. 250 The First Law School *30*

c. 250 The Brehon Laws of Ireland *32*

529 The Justinian Code *34*

561 The Irish Copyright War *36*

624 The Tang Code *38*

652 The Quran *40*

1140 Canon Law and the *Decretum Gratiani* *42*

1166 The Assize of Clarendon *44*

c. 1200 *Lex Mercatoria* *46*

1215 The Magna Carta *48*

1275 The Statutes of Westminster *50*

c. 1350 The Star Chamber *52*

1431 The Trial of Joan of Arc *54*

1481 Littleton's *Tenures* *56*

1492 The Alhambra Decree *58*

1527 *Les Termes de la Ley* *60*

1601 An Act for the Relief of the Poor *62*

1616 Compulsory Education Laws *64*

1625 *On the Law of War and Peace* *66*

1629 The First Blue Laws *68*

1648 Peace of Westphalia *70*

1651 *Leviathan* *72*

1670 *Bushel's Case* *74*

1679 The Habeas Corpus Act of 1679 *76*

1685 The Black Code of Louis XIV *78*

1692 The Salem Witchcraft Trials *80*

1695 Lapse of the Licensing Act *82*

1710 The Statute of Anne *84*

1720 The Bubble Act *86*

1735 The Trial of John Peter Zenger *88*

1751 The Gin Act of 1751 *90*

1761 The Writs of Assistance Case *92*

1765 Blackstone's *Commentaries* *94*

1787 The U.S. Constitution *96*

1789 The Judiciary Act of 1789 *98*

1789 The Declaration of the Rights of Man *100*

1790 America's First Copyright Law *102*

1791 The Bill of Rights *104*

1792 The Coinage Act of 1792 *106*

1798 The Triple Assessment (Income Tax) *108*

1803 The Power of Judicial Review *110*

1804 The Napoleonic Code *112*

1805 The Superiority of Possession *114*

1819 The Supremacy of Federal Law *116*

1821 The Supremacy of Federal Courts *118*

1824 Congressional Regulation of Commerce *120*

1824 Administering Native Peoples *122*

1839 *The Amistad* *124*

1842 Recognition of Labor Unions *126*

1843 The M'Naghten Rule *128*

1848 The Field Code   *130*

1854 The Measure of Contract Damages   *132*

1857 The *Dred Scott* Decision   *134*

1861 The Government Printing Office   *136*

1863 The Emancipation Proclamation   *138*

1864 The Geneva Convention   *140*

1865 The Abolition of Slavery   *142*

1866 The Civil Rights Act of 1866   *144*

1868 Impeaching President Andrew Johnson   *146*

1868 The Fourteenth Amendment   *148*

1869 Prohibition of Racial Voter Discrimination   *150*

1870 The Law School Revolution   *152*

1872 Law Reporting and Legal Publishing   *154*

1873 Obscenity and the Comstock Act   *156*

1873 Admission of Women to the Bar   *158*

1876 Legal Aid Societies   *160*

1878 The Berne Convention   *162*

1881 The Insanity Defense   *164*

1882 The Chinese Exclusion Act   *166*

1883 The Civil Rights Cases   *168*

1886 Equal Protection Rights   *170*

1887 The Interstate Commerce Act   *172*

1888 The Brazilian Slave Emancipation Act   *174*

1890 The Right to Privacy   *176*

1890 The Sherman Antitrust Act   *178*

1893 New Zealand Women's Suffrage   *180*

1896 *Plessy v. Ferguson*: Separate but Equal   *182*

1897 Corporate Personhood and Liability   *184*

1900 The German Civil Code   *186*

1901 The Cuban Constitution of 1901   *188*

1908 Women in Factories   *190*

1909 Congressional Power to Tax Income   *192*

1910 The White-Slave Traffic Act   *194*

1910 Workers' Compensation Law   *196*

1911 Busting the Trusts   *198*

1911 The Triangle Shirtwaist Fire   *200*

1913 The Federal Reserve Act   *202*

1914 The Exclusionary Rule   *204*

1914 The Clayton Antitrust Act   *206*

1915 The Prohibition of Illegal Narcotics   *208*

1916 The Child Labor Act of 1916   *210*

1916 The Expansion of Consumer Rights   *212*

1918 Prohibition   *214*

1919 Women's Right to Vote   *216*

1919 Yelling "Fire!" in a Crowded Theater   *218*

1920 New York State Legalizes Boxing   *220*

1921 The Chicago "Black Sox" Trial   *222*

1921 Censorship and the Hays Office   *224*

1921 The Emergency Quota Act   *226*

1925 The Scopes "Monkey" Trial   *228*

1926 The United States Code   *230*

1928 The Danger Zone in Tort Law   *232*

1928 Wiretaps   *234*

1933 Hitler's Rise to Power   *236*

1933 Wall Street Regulation   *238*

1933 Censorship and *Ulysses*   *240*

1933 The Repeal of Prohibition   *242*

1934 The Federal Communications Act   *244*

1934 The Securities Exchange Act   *246*

1935 The National Labor Relations Act   *248*

1935 The Nuremberg Laws   *250*

1935 The Social Security Act   *252*

1936 The *Federal Register*   *254*

1937 FDR and the Court-Packing Plan   *256*

1937 Cameras in the Courts   *258*

1938 Rule 23 and Modern Class Action   *260*

1938 The Food, Drug, and Cosmetic Act   *262*

1938 The Fair Labor Standards Act   *264*

1939 Militias and the Right to Bear Arms   *266*

1940 The Alien Registration Act   *268*

1941 Strict Products Liability   *270*

1941 California's Anti-Okie Statute   *272*

1942 Internment of Japanese Americans   *274*

1944 The G.I. Bill   *276*

1945 The Nuremberg Trials   *278*

1946 Rent Control   *280*

1946 The Protection of Trademarks   *282*

1947 Colonialism and Postwar Independence   *284*

1948 General Agreement on Tariffs and Trade   *286*

1948 The U.N. Convention on Genocide   *288*

1948 The Hollywood Ten   *290*

1948 Universal Declaration of Human Rights   *292*

1948 The Displaced Persons Act   *294*

1951 Rejection of the Alien Registration Act   *296*

1951 The Rosenberg Trial   *298*

1951 The E.U. and the Treaty of Paris   *300*

1954 *Brown v. Board of Education*   *302*

1954 The Communist Control Act   *304*

1956 The Interstate Highway Act   *306*

1957 The Limits on Obscenity   *308*

1957 The Wolfenden Report and Gay Rights   *310*

1959 The European Court of Human Rights   *312*

1959 No Man's Land   *314*

1961 States and the Exclusionary Rule   *316*

1961 The Eichmann Trial   *318*

1963 The Trial of Nelson Mandela   *320*

1963 The Right to Counsel in State Court   *322*

1964 Limits on Libel Laws   *324*

1964 The Civil Rights Act of 1964   *326*

1965 The Voting Rights Act   *328*

1965 Conscientious Objection   *330*

1965 The Body and the Right of Privacy   *332*

1966 The Freedom of Information Act   *334*

1966 Miranda Warnings   *336*

1967 Interracial Marriage   *338*

1967 The Vietnam-Era Draft Laws   *340*

1969 No-Fault Divorce   *342*

1969 Free Speech and Threats of Violence   *344*

1969 The Fairness Doctrine   *346*

1970 The National Environmental Policy Act   *348*

1970 The Court-Martial of William Calley Jr.   *350*

1970 Public Health and Cigarettes   *352*

1970 The RICO Act   *354*

1970 Baseball's Reserve Clause   *356*

1970 The Occupational Safety and Health Act   *358*

1970 The Trial of Charles Manson   *360*

1971 Enfranchising Eighteen-Year-Olds   *362*

1971 The *Pentagon Papers*   *364*

1971 Employment Discrimination   *366*

1971 Court-Ordered School Busing   *368*

1972 Banning the Death Penalty   *370*

1972 The Equal Employment Opportunity Act   *372*

1972 The Equal Rights Amendment   *374*

1972 The Trail of Broken Treaties   *376*

1973 The Endangered Species Act   *378*

1973 The First Ban on Gay Marriage   *380*

1973 A New Obscenity Standard   *382*

1973 *Roe v. Wade*   *384*

1973 The War Powers Act of 1973   *386*

1974 Presidential Subpoena Compliance   *388*

1975 Attorneys' Fee Awards   *390*

1975 Restrictions on Involuntary Commitment   *392*

1975 Racism and U.N. Resolution 3379   *394*

1976 The Right to Die   *396*

1976 Health Care and the Duty to Warn   *398*

1976 The Copyright Act of 1976   *400*

1976 The Death Penalty Returns   *402*

1976 Palimony   *404*

1977 Attorney Advertising   *406*

1978 Affirmative Action   *408*

1978 The FCC and Filthy Words   *410*

1978 The Son of Sam Law   *412*

1978 The Entrapment Defense   *414*

1983 The McMartin Molestation Case   *416*

1984 First Mandatory Seat-Belt Law   *418*

1984 Administrative Agency Determinations   *420*

1984 Parody and the First Amendment   *422*

1984 Time-Shifting and Fair Use   *424*

1986 Peremptory Challenges to Jury Selection   *426*

1986 The First Evidentiary Use of DNA   *428*

1987 Pregnancy Discrimination   *430*

1987 Robert Bork's Supreme Court Nomination   *432*

1988 Surrogate Motherhood   *434*

1988 Women's Admission to Private Clubs   *436*

1989 The Fatwa against *The Satanic Verses*   *438*

1989 Celebrity Tax Prosecution   *440*

1989 The First Gay Marriage Laws   *442*

1990 The Americans with Disabilities Act   *444*

1990 The End of Apartheid   *446*

1991 Confirming Clarence Thomas   *448*

1991 The Trial of Manuel Noriega   *450*

1992 Smoking Litigation   *452*

1992 The Rio Conference   *454*

1993 Creation of the European Union   *456*

1994 The Hot Coffee Case   *458*

1995 Stem Cell and Cloning Legislation   *460*

1995 The O.J. Simpson Murder Trial   *462*

1996 Limits on Punitive Damages   *464*

1996 South Africa's Constitution   *466*

1996 Legalization of Marijuana   *468*

1997 Presidential Immunity   *470*

1997 The Communications Decency Act   *472*

1997 Physician-Assisted Suicide   *474*

1998 The Line-Item Veto   *476*

1998 Indictment of Augusto Pinochet   *478*

1999 Copyright in the Digital Age   *480*

2000 *Bush v. Gore*   *482*

2000 The Microsoft Monopoly   *484*

2001 Golf Carts on the PGA Tour   *486*

2001 Expanded Copyrights   *488*

2001 The USA PATRIOT Act   *490*

2002 The Sarbanes-Oxley Act   *492*

2002 The International Criminal Court   *494*

2005 Public Purpose and Eminent Domain   *496*

2008 The Legality of Gun Control   *498*

2010 Google Books and Fair Use   *500*

2010 Wall Street Reform   *502*

2012 The Future of Juvenile Punishment   *504*

2012 The Affordable Care Act   *506*

2015 The Legal Fight for Gay Marriage   *508*

Acknowledgments   *510*

Notes and Further Reading   *511*

Image Credits   *525*

Index   *526*

Introduction

The law surrounds us. It affects the food we eat, the water we drink, and the air we breathe. It travels with us. It defines our relationships with the people with whom we live, work, and share space. It affects our homes and schools, our offices and stores. The law touches every aspect of our lives and even our deaths. This book explains how much of that came to pass.

Historians trace the first formal compilation of laws to King Ur-Nammu of Sumer, circa 2100 BCE. Several centuries thereafter came King Hammurabi's better-known code, famous for its retributive "eye for an eye." Later notable laws include the Ten Commandments, the Laws of Solon, the Twelve Tables of Roman law, and the Justinian Code. English laws existed prior to the Norman Conquest in 1066, but their development in the context of modern law began with the Magna Carta in 1215 and its implementation through the Statutes of Westminster (I and II) in 1275 and 1285. Anglo-American law began to take shape in the American colonies in the early 1600s, which laid the foundation for the Constitution in 1787.

Over the centuries that followed, American law took root. As it developed and matured, two competing principles emerged: stability and change. The law provides stability in a changing world, and a world in flux changes the law to maintain stability. A hallmark of the American tradition, precedents typically serve as the basis for judicial decisions. As Supreme Court Justice Benjamin Cardozo observed, "What has once been settled by a precedent will not be unsettled overnight, for certainty and uniformity are gains not lightly to be sacrificed." Yet the law does change. Slavery was permitted and then outlawed; the death penalty was barred and then reinstated; books were banned and then constitutionally protected. Dramatic changes like these sometimes may seem inconsistent, but they embody legal scholar Roscoe Pound's aphorism that the "law must be stable, and yet it cannot stand still."

I've taken an eclectic approach in compiling the 250 milestones in this book. As you'll see, my choices fall predominantly within the American tradition, and the majority of the essays focus on the last two centuries, which intentionally reflects the law's steady expansion over time and more recent explosive growth. Some essays embody key court decisions while others examine important statutes. Many deal with events that have become a part of history—including infamous trials—and several speak to key texts that have shaped legal thought and theory.

Foundational texts, including the Assize of Clarendon and the Magna Carta, laid the historical groundwork for many of the procedural protections that safeguard against overzealous enforcement of laws and the encroachments of political power in the courtroom, or they proscribe various forms of discrimination. Slavery legislation evolved from a codification of practices in the Black Code of Louis XIV to worldwide abolition two centuries later. Women began their long, legal struggle for recognition and fairness first at the Illinois bar in the early 1870s, then in factories, at the voting booth, and in the courtroom, where they defended their right to bodily privacy and staved off social discrimination. The concept of a right to privacy originated in an 1890 law review article, evolving to encompass regulation of access to contraception and birth control and play a key role in the long-fought battle over gay marriage.

Copyright law emerged to protect the rights of authors and other creators and later defined the nature and limits of fair use. Laws regulating the nature of expression developed to permit seditious speech, to block words that incite danger, and to allow obscenity and indecency but also to allow the government to regulate the public exposure to obscenity and indecency.

In the realm of the workplace, labor unions gained legal recognition in 1842, but it took nearly a century for employees and unions to level the playing field with employers through collective bargaining. Congress also enacted legislation providing fair treatment and fair pay for workers along with additional workplace protections. In the overlapping sphere of finance, the law has played an important role in regulating money. Britain adopted history's first income tax statute in 1799, but not until 1913 did America's first permanent income tax hit the books. A decade and a half later, Wall Street crashed, triggering the Great Depression and a raft of regulations that Congress bolstered and amplified some seventy-five years later when the collapse of the subprime mortgage market prompted the Great Recession.

Many of the other milestones reflect laws aimed at protecting individuals from the conduct of others, but sometimes they aim to protect people from themselves. Blue laws existed in antiquity, but more recent legislation targeted gin, opium, alcohol in general, and tobacco.

Many laws spurred infamous trials, including the Salem Witchcraft Trials, the Communist witch hunt that led to the HUAC hearings of the Hollywood Ten, and the O. J. Simpson trial, which officially heralded the age of courtroom television.

· · ·

The law is all-inclusive and far-ranging. As such, I've tried to capture that breadth with a representative sampling of important topics with broad appeal. But these 250 milestones cannot be taken as *the* 250 landmarks of legal history. Reasonable minds will disagree on the importance of specific legal events and developments and their role in the pantheon of legal history, and milestones resonate differently in various places. But of these milestones, most have effected profound change—for good or for bad—and each reflects a new, historical structure or path on the legal landscape.

My goal wasn't just to introduce some of the most meaningful and influential steps in legal history but also to explain why a particular step became a milestone. Some will be obvious; others more subtle. I also aimed to supply a basic understanding of what have become fundamental legal principles and ultimately connect the dots between the principles and their relevant landmarks. These encounters all will be brief and none comprehensive. Indeed, most barely scratch the surface of issues to which judges and scholars have devoted and continue to devote a great deal of thought, energy, and writing. But hopefully the essays and their accompanying imagery will pique your curiosity and entice you to delve deeper into areas you find relevant or compelling.

Organizationally, the essays appear in chronological order and, given the interrelated nature of many legal principles, you will find helpful cross-references throughout. Although each essay is ascribed to a single year, many of the legal developments or events in this book fall within a range of possible dates. Dates for legislation all refer to date of enactment, which isn't necessarily the law's effective date.

A final and necessary caveat: None of these entries contains or offers legal advice.

The Oldest Written Will

Flinders Petrie (1853–1942)

On December 26, 1889, the *London Standard* broke the news of the discovery of the oldest known will. Flinders Petrie—a renowned English archaeologist and Egyptologist and regarded as a father of modern archaeology—found the papyrus in the ancient Egyptian town of Kahun, which lies in modern Al-Fayyūm, about sixty miles south of Cairo. The discovery "curiously illustrates the continuity of legal methods," according to the *London Standard* correspondent.

Prior to Petrie's findings, historians and legal scholars studied the existence and evolution of ancient wills only through succeeding stages of later civilization: discussions of Solon introducing wills to Ancient Greece during the sixth century BCE, the Roman law relating to wills appearing in the Twelve Tables of the fifth century BCE, and in the Justinian Code in the mid-sixth century of our own era. What made this ancient will even more remarkable, though, was its "singularly modern form." The *London Standard* article remarked "that it might almost be granted probate today."

Bearing an approximate date of 2548 BCE, the will appears to have been from someone identified as Sekhenren, devising to his wife, Teta, "all the property given him by his brother for life." It forbade her from "pulling down" the houses his brother built for him but authorizes her to give them to any of her children. The will bears an attestation clause indicating that two scribes witnessed its execution.

What surprised commentators most was the disposition of the husband's property to his wife at a time when women were thought not to have the right to acquire or exercise rights over property. The revelation also upended a belief in the long-standing patriarchal tradition of property passing to the eldest son. According to the article, "the whole history of the family becomes unsettled by this bold departure from what has been believed to be immemorial custom. . . . It seems to put the period of legal evolution some twenty centuries back."

SEE ALSO The Laws of Solon (594 BCE); The Twelve Tables (450 BCE); The Justinian Code (529).

A 1934 portrait, by Hungarian artist Philip Alexius de László, of Sir Flinders Petrie, who discovered the papyrus bearing the oldest known written will.

The Code of Ur-Nammu

Ur-Nammu (c. 2112–2095 BCE)

Mesopotamia, in what today includes Iraq, Syria, and southeastern Turkey, gave rise to the earliest known civilization. Ruled by King Sargon, the Akkadian Empire developed there first, circa 2350 BCE. Sometime thereafter, King Ur-Nammu united the Sumerians and Akkadians, founding the Third Dynasty of Ur, which lasted until approximately 2004 BCE.

Ur-Nammu's most important legacy is the Code of Ur-Nammu, which Klaas Veenhof, eminent scholar of Babylonia and Assyria, indicates influenced the codes of two subsequent kings, Lipit-Ishtar (c. 1930 BCE) and Hammurabi (c. 1792 BCE), and the Code of Eshnunna, a city in northern Mesopotamia (c. 1800 BCE). Unlike the Code of Hammurabi, we know very little about this code or the other two following because only small fragments remain. Judicial records survive from the twenty-fourth century BCE as do edicts of prior kings Emmetena and Urukagina, but Ur-Nammu's Code is, according to Veenhof, "The first truly legislative text." Nevertheless, archaeologists question whether Ur-Nammu himself issued the code or it resulted from the work of his son and successor, Shulgi.

Written in cuneiform, the Code consists of a prologue followed by paragraphs setting forth approximately forty conditional laws: "If X, then Y" where X represents conduct and Y represents the legal ramification. It thus presents a schedule of predetermined consequences for violating the rules of conduct governing the Akkadian and Sumerian people. The prologue suggests Ur-Nammu considered himself empowered by the gods to proclaim these laws and ends with "I made evil, violence, and the cry for justice disappear."

Unlike the retributive Code of Hammurabi, the Code of Ur-Nammu imposed monetary penalties for causing bodily injuries to others. For example, Ur-Nammu calls for a man who takes out the eye of another to "weigh out half a mina of silver." Other provisions cover perjury (15 shekels), deflowering another man's slave (5 shekels), breaking a bone of another (10 shekels), and divorcing a first wife (1 mina of silver). It also addressed criminal conduct more harshly than noncriminal offenses, punishing murder and rape with death, and kidnapping with imprisonment and a fine. In the surviving text, kidnapping is the only crime for which imprisonment was imposed.

SEE ALSO The Code of Hammurabi (c. 1792 BCE); The Draconian Code (621 BCE); The Twelve Tables (450 BCE).

The hymn on this Neo-Sumerian tablet from the reign of Ur-Nammu praises the king and his divine provenance.

The Code of Hammurabi

Hammurabi (c.1810–c.1750), **Gustave Jéquier** (1868–1946)

It may be impossible to identify mankind's true first legal code, but legal scholars and historians point to the Code of Hammurabi as among the oldest and most complete written collections of laws in existence.

Between December 1901 and January 1902, a French archaeological expedition was excavating the acropolis at Susa, a city in the ancient empire of Elam, now Shush in the Khuzestan region of Iran. One of the men, Gustave Jéquier, uncovered a block of black diorite more than seven feet high.

Engraved in the stone is the most complete known copy of the Code of Hammurabi, the the sixth king of Babylon, known as the "Law Giver." The top of the stela depicts Shamash, the Babylonian god of justice, delivering the laws to Hammurabi so he can issue them to his people. A prologue to the Code expresses Hammurabi's overarching purpose: "that the strong might not oppress the weak, that justice be given the orphan and the widow."

The Code itself consists of 282 separate provisions arranged by subject: procedure, property, military, debts, family law, personal injury, and so on. Punishments proscribed for violations differ according to the social status of both offender and victim, and the Code accordingly recognizes three classes of people: wealthy, upper-class property owners; paupers and serfs; and slaves.

The best-known provisions of the Code contain a fundamental principle: "If a man destroy the eye of another man, they shall destroy his eye. If a man breaks another man's bone, they shall break his bone. . . . If a man knock out a tooth of a man of his own rank, they shall knock out his tooth." Although this retributive approach to justice stood as a powerful doctrine in early civilizations, it no longer functions as the controlling paradigm in modern legal systems. Advocates for the death penalty often invoke it as a justification for capital punishment, however.

In an epilogue to the Code, Hammurabi curses all future rulers who fail to heed his words and judgments. The stela now stands in the Louvre in Paris.

SEE ALSO The Code of Ur-Nammu (c. 2100 BCE); The Twelve Tables (450 BCE), The Justinian Code (529); The Death Penalty Returns (1976).

Detail of the seven-foot-four-inch-tall stela containing the Code of Hammurabi in Akkadian cuneiform script.

The Ten Commandments

c. 1300 BCE

Controversy often lies where law and religion intersect, yet they intertwine inextricably. We have no better example of this principle than the Ten Commandments. Other rules governing human conduct may have preceded them, but for many, particularly in Judeo-Christian nations, the Commandments serve as a foundation to all subsequent law. For example, on the east (courtyard-facing) side of the U.S. Supreme Court Building, the pediment features at its center Moses holding the Ten Commandments; the great oak doors to the courtroom each display them; and carved within the South Courtroom itself, among seventeen other key lawgivers, Moses also holds them.

According to religious tradition, Moses, a Hebrew leader believed to have communicated directly with the god of Israel, ascended Mount Sinai where he received ten divinely sanctioned rules engraved on two stone tablets. He also received instruction to give these rules to his people, who were to use them as standards for moral and just living. As such, Sir Edward Coke—celebrated English jurist, chief justice of the Court of Common Pleas, and chief justice of the King's Bench—called Moses "the first reporter or writer of law in the world."

Each of the Commandments falls into one of two categories: the purely religious or those of secular significance. Within the latter category fall the commandments forbidding theft (a cornerstone of modern property law), forbidding killing (often interpreted to forbid unjustified killing, which is still punished severely today), and forbidding perjury. Just these few examples show the perseverance of the principles set forth in the Ten Commandments millennia ago.

Ironically, the legal question concerning the proper place of the Ten Commandments in public places has proved vexing for the Supreme Court itself. In two cases decided on the same day in 2005, the Court reached different conclusions (each time in 5–4 decisions) as to the circumstances under which a state may lawfully display a representation of the Ten Commandments without violating the Constitution's establishment clause.

SEE ALSO The Talmud (c.180); The Quran (652).

A stained-glass window depicting Moses holding the Ten Commandments, which have been described as among "the most famous laws in all human history."

The Draconian Code

Draco (c. 650–c. 600 BCE)

Before the advent of written laws, people depended on memory and oral tradition for the knowledge and transmission of customs or laws from generation to generation. Legal historian and scholar William Seagle has described the law as "the science that lives by the written word," in which the "words themselves are the subject of the science, the words *are* the law." Draco, an Athenian statesman and archon, or magistrate, introduced what some consider the first written laws to Athens and the Ancient Greeks in 621 BCE.

History records little of Draco beyond the laws that he memorialized and, in particular, their severity. Greek biographer and historian Plutarch noted that the penalty for almost all offenses covered by Draco's laws was death, and earlier the orator Demades is said to have remarked that Draco's laws were written in blood, not ink. Numerous accounts speak of Draco, when asked why he imposed the penalty of death on small offenses, replying: "The smallest of them deserve death, and there is no greater punishment I can find for the greater crimes."

Draco's laws resulted in part from a growing sense of the lower classes (among freeborn, native, landholding men) that the law ought to be open and accessible to all. Until this time, as Professor Rene Albert Wormser explains, the laws "reposed in the convenient memories of the aristocrats and their priests, and it was therefore impossible for an ordinary citizen to point to a page and paragraph and say, 'There are my rights.'" The most famous of Draco's laws made a distinction between intentional and unintentional homicide—an early precursor to contemporary manslaughter legislation—and provided a punishment of exile, in place of personal revenge, for the lesser crime.

Although the term *draconian* has come to characterize laws or punishments excessively severe in their reach or which call for brutal, harsh punishment, some experts recognize that Draco didn't necessarily generate all of those laws. He was, however, responsible for committing them to writing, and the epithet remains his legacy.

SEE ALSO The Laws of Solon (594 BCE); The Twelve Tables (450 BCE); The Justinian Code (529).

Greek statesmen of the Areopagite Council, founded by Draco c. 621 BCE, gather atop Ares' Hill.

The Laws of Solon

Draco (c. 650–c. 600 BCE), **Solon** (c. 638–c. 558 BCE)

Nearly thirty years after Draco first codified the laws of Greece, Attica, the larger region encompassing Athens, continued facing unrest and the prospect of civil war. In hopes of reconciling the discord between the aristocracy and the commoners, middle-class merchants and tradesmen turned to the statesman Solon, a man they sought to achieve reform. Despite his noble birth, Solon's character and reputation earned him the trust and confidence of commoners and nobles alike. Plutarch said of him that the "upper class consented to his appointment because he was wealthy and the poor because they knew he was honest." In 594 BCE, Solon was appointed archon, or magistrate, of Athens.

Although Solon abolished most of Draco's harsh laws, his most significant contributions lay in his new approach to law for Greek society and in his enactment of laws that broke from tradition. Believing that "equality bred no war," Solon introduced a new balance of power between the nobles and commoners. He canceled farmers' debts and eliminated slavery as a "remedy" for debt. He made justice more accessible by allowing all citizens to prosecute claims for injuries that they or others had suffered as well as by establishing a right of appeal for decisions of magistrates. Within the citizen assembly known as the *ecclesia*, the supreme court, the *Heliaea*, heard appeals. Solon also created the *boule*, a council of representatives from different classes that debated legislation before the ecclesia voted on it. Most historians see in Solon's efforts and accomplishments the early foundations of Greek democracy, particularly his liberalization of eligibility requirements for office that enabled commoners to participate.

Solon's laws were inscribed on revolving wooden tablets called *axones* and on stone pillars known as *kyrbeis*; the latter were erected in public places, making them accessible to everyone. Most of Solon's laws remained the laws of Athens for five centuries and served as the legislative model for other Ancient Greek city-states.

SEE ALSO The Draconian Code (621 BCE); The Twelve Tables (450 BCE); The Justinian Code (529).

Solon, one of the Seven Wise Greek Men *statues, stands in the Library of Congress in Washington, D.C.*

The Gortyn Code

Gortyn, located near modern-day Heraklion, had been one of the most powerful cities in Crete prior to the Roman conquest of Greece in 67 BCE. In the 1850s, archaeologists working there began discovering limestone blocks in and around a stream. Doric inscriptions on the blocks, dating to between 480 and 460 BCE, contained a list of laws now known as the Gortyn Code. The full Code, approximately six hundred lines of text, was inscribed on twelve large columns that formed part of a circular wall of a building believed to have been a court.

The Code notably contained old laws, amended laws, and new ones, reflecting the adaptation of legislation over time, and it dealt primarily with family law. It addressed marriage; property rights, including those of a divorced wife and the sale of family property; children of mixed marriages; adoption; inheritance through succession (though not testamentary succession); rape, seduction, and adultery; ownership of slaves and slave marriages; and the marriage and inheritance of heiresses (those women who were the sole descendant of a deceased father).

As in the Code of Hammurabi more than a thousand years earlier, the Gortyn Code distinguished among three different social classes: free citizens, unprivileged persons (freed slaves and others without political rights), and slaves. Fines varied according to class, with slaves receiving the lowest. Evidentiary requirements also differed proportionately to class. A free person required corroborating testimony from four witnesses; the unprivileged needed just two; and a slave needed that of his master and one other. The code also made distinctions based on gender and age: Males were categorized as ungrown, grown, or "runner," while females were classified as either ungrown or grown. Puberty demarcated the grown stage for both males and females, and men became "runners" once they acquired the right to exercise in the public gymnasium, generally between the ages of seventeen and twenty. Ronald Willetts, a scholar of Cretan studies, called the Code unique "in its magnitude, its precision, its ordering of so many aspects of social life under the sanction of law."

SEE ALSO The Draconian Code (621 BCE); The Laws of Solon (594 BCE); The Twelve Tables (450 BCE).

This limestone wall displays the laws of the Gortyn Code, which set the legal bounds for many aspects of Cretan life in the fifth century BCE.

ΝΕ ... ΟΣ ... ΑΙ ΚΑΚ ΑΜΑΤΟ ΤΟ ... ΕΝ Τ Ε
ΑΤ ... ΘΕΡΘΟ ... ΓΤΟΑΜΝΑΣ ... ΑΤΑ ... ΑΙ ΕΤ
ΣΑ ... Ο ΔΕΚΑΣ ΚΑΚΣ ΑΚΣ ΑΚΑΤΟ ΑΝΑ ... ΕΟ
ΔΣ ... ΣΛΕΡΣ ... ΜΣ ΑΜΕΡΑΣ ΑΝ ...
ΡΑ ... ΕΝΤΣ ... ΑΜΕΣ ΚΑ ... ΚΑΚΛΑ ΤΟΙ ... Ο ΜΕΝ ... Ι
ΑΝ ... ΑΙ Μ ... ΕΝΟΘΕΡΟΝ ΤΑ ΤΕΡΑ Τ Ο ΛΟΙΣ ... ΚΝ
ΝΕ ... ΕΙΕΝΟΘΕΡΟ ... ΑΜ ... ΕΡΑΝΕΡΑΝ ΚΜ Τ ... Ι ... ΟΜΕΝ ... Α Α
ΑΔ ... Α ΑΓΕΚΑ ... ΑΑ ... ΟΝΟ ... Α Ι Λ ΘΩ ... Τ
... Α ΛΜΕΣ ΤΟ ΔΕ ΚΡΟΝΟ ΤΟ ΛΟ ... ΤΩ
ΕΝ ... ΜΥ ΥΤ ΑΚ ΡΣ ΥΕΝ ... Α Σ ... ΑΝΝΣΟΣ ΤΟ ... Ω Α ... ΚΕ
ΕΚ ... ΜΜΟΝ ΑΤΑΝΟΑΜ ... ΑΝΟ Τ ... ΤΜ Ν
ΜΣ ... Ν Ε Υ ΑΣ Ω ΕΑ ΤΟ ΟΝΣΟΣ ... ΑΣ Τ ΥΜ ... ΑΚ ... ΝΟ
ΤΧ ... ΕΝ ... ΔΕΣ ΟΜ ΕΝ Ε Ε Υ Θ ... ΟΝ
ΑΤ ... ΙΑΣ ΔΕΚΑ ΑΝΟΡΕΣΟΜΕΝ ... ΕΝ ... ΝΟΑ
ΤΟ ... Ο ΤΟΙ ΚΑΡΤΟΝ ΑΜ ΑΜ ΕΝ ΕΝ
Ε ... ΤΕΙ ΕΥ ... ΘΕΡΟΝΑΣΣΟ ΣΩ ... ΑΝ
ΕΧΕ ... ΤΣ Α ΣΔΕΚΑΝ Ψ ΣΔΟΤΟΑ Σ ΣΩ ΤΟΙ ΣΟ ... ΝΤΣ
ΤΕ ... ΟΣΟΙ ΤΕΜΦΟΝ Ε ΚΑ ΤΕ ΡΟ ΜΕΝΝ
ΜΑΝ ... ΕΜΑΣ Ω ΕΝ ΚΑΜ ΑΣΤΥ ΜΑΤΟ ΣΟΜ Ε ... Κ ... Κ ... ΡΑΛ
ΡΑΛ ... ΑΝ ... ΑΤΑ ΤΟ Ι ΖΑ ΜΝ Ο ... ΑΤΑ ... Τ ΜΑ
ΟΝ ... ΔΕΚΑ ΟΙ ΤΕΡΟΣ ΜΑ ΟΟ ΟΝ ΣΟΙ ΙΣ ... Γ ... ΤΜΟ
ΟΝ ... ΟΝΕ ΑΤΕΡΟΣ ΤΟΝ Α ΣΚΑΤΑΝΟ
ΝΝΝ ... ΥΥ ΤΑ ΚΡΣ ΥΕΝ ΟΥΕΕ ΚΑΝ ΣΚ ... Γ ΣΟ
ΝΑΛ ... ΝΟ ... Ο ... ΟΛΝ ΜΕΝ ΕΙ ΕΥΘ ΕΡΟΝ ... Α Σ ... ΟΕ
... ΑΜ ΑΣ ΤΑΝ Ε Λ ... ΑΜ ΕΡΑΝ ΤΟ ... ΑΝ ... Δ
... ΣΕ ΑΤΕΙ ΝΟ ... Σ ... Ο ... Ο ΤΟ Ι Τ ... Σ ΔΕ
ΚΑΜ ΕΤΑ ΜΑ Μ Ε ΣΕΜ ΕΑ ΟΣ ΔΟ ΣΟ ΣΣ ΚΑΚ
ΤΑ ΝΟ ΘΕΡΟ ... Σ ΚΕ ΝΤΟ ΜΕ ΝΕ Ι ΕΥ ΘΕΡΟ ... Α Μ
... Σ ΕΝ ΤΕΚΟΝ ΤΑ Μ ΤΑΤ Ε ΡΑ Μ ΜΚΑΣ Μ
... ΤΑ ΤΕ ΡΑ ΤΑ ΜΑ ΜΕΡΑ Μ ΓΕ ΚΑ ... Τ
Η ... ΑΜ ΦΡΣ ΥΚΑΤΑ Λ ΑΜΕΣ ΤΟ ΔΕΟ ΤΟ ... ΜΑ ... Η
... ΔΕ ΚΑ Π ΑΤΕΡΑ Ν ΑΚΑΣ ΔΥ Ρ ΚΝΑΝ
... ΤΑ ΜΑΜ ΕΡΑ Μ ΓΕ ΚΑ Α ΤΑ Μ ΑΚΕΙ Μ ΑΜ ΦΡΣ ΥΚΑ
... Σ Ο ΔΟ ΣΕ Μ ΚΕ ΡΑ Ν Μ ΕΔΕ ΚΑ ΚΑΤΑ Σ
... ΚΑΙ Μ ΕΣΟ Ι Σ ΚΑ Μ ΤΑ ΚΛ ΔΟ Σ ΤΥ ΑΥ ΝΕ ... Λ ... Ο ΣΣ
ΝΟ ... ΡΑ ΔΔΕΘ ΘΑ Τ Ζ Α Τ ΡΣ Τ ΡΑ Ε Μ Ε Σ Ω
... ΣΟΝ Α Ε Μ ΕΤΟ Ε ΚΡΟΝΟ Τ ΟΝΟ Σ
... ΤΑ ΝΟ ΑΝ Ν Ν ΥΤ ΑΚ ΡΣ Υ ΕΝ Ε ΝΑ Μ Α Σ
ΚΑ Μ Α Ε Υ Ε Σ Ο ΔΟ Λ Ο Ι Ω Ο ΚΑ Ν ΣΚΑΘΕ
... ΣΚΑ Ι ΣΟΜ ΑΝ ΤΣ Μ Α ΣΤΥ ΡΟ Ν ΑΔΟΝ Α
ΡΩ Μ ΕΩ ΝΕ Υ Ε ΘΕΡΩ ΛΑΣΟ ΝΑ Σ Ο Ε Σ Κ Μ ΑΤ

The Twelve Tables

As in other civilizations of the ancient world, Roman law began in an oral tradition of customs passed down over time. In the mid-fifth century BCE, the nobles and commoners of Rome consented to a commission of ten jurists, the decemviri, to consolidate and codify the laws. The first written Roman laws, the Twelve Tables, resulted.

The ongoing conflict between Rome's patrician and plebeian classes provided the impetus for the Twelve Tables because the plebeians objected to what they perceived as the patricians' arbitrary interpretation and enforcement of the law, believing a written code would temper if not end those practices. The laws were recorded on twelve wooden or bronze (historians disagree) tablets and displayed publicly in the forum. Noted legal historian Sir Henry Maine suggests that the value of the Twelve Tables lies not in their classifications or their "terseness and clearness of expression but in their publicity and in the knowledge which they furnished to everybody as to what he was to do and what not to do."

The Twelve Tables covered both substantive and procedural law. The procedural rules dealt with commencing legal action by oral summons, handling witnesses, and providing for executions on judgments, among other topics. Substantive matters included validation (negating Solon's elimination) of the customary principle that allowed enslavement for unpaid debts as well as penalties for both intentional and unintentional murder. (In the case of intentional murder, the victim's family determined the punishment, which could include avenging the death.) The Tables also addressed compensation for personal injuries and property damage. Only three crimes in the Twelve Tables warranted the death penalty: bribery, treason, and defamation.

Romans venerated the Twelve Tables. William Blackstone in his *Commentaries* speaks of Cicero's oft-cited remark that "boys were obliged to learn the twelve tables by heart, as a *carmen necessarium*, or indispensable lesson, to imprint on their tender minds an early knowledge of the laws and constitution of their country." Those laws had a solid influence that lasted for hundreds of years.

SEE ALSO The Draconian Code (621 BCE); The Laws of Solon (594 BCE); The Justinian Code (529).

A photograph (c. 1895) of the ruins of the Temple of Saturn (left) and the Triumphal Arch of Septimius Severus (right) in the Roman Forum. In the foreground are the remnants of the rostrum, or speakers' platform, on which the engraved tablets of the Twelve Tables were mounted.

The Trial of Socrates

Socrates (c. 470–399 BCE)

The trial of Socrates pitted a "squat, ugly, barefoot man . . . with bulging eyes, prominent lips, and a pot belly" against the precepts of Athenian democracy. The renowned teacher and philosopher stood accused of "impiety," failing to recognize the Athenian gods, introducing new deities, corrupting the youth, and endangering the state.

Socrates had always been a gadfly, but the citizens of Athens were growing less patient with his disdainful views of democracy. (He believed that only the wise, meaning philosophers of course, were capable of governing.) Disapprobation fell on Socrates after two of his former pupils, Alcibiades and Critias, undermined Athens. In 411, after helping plan an expedition to Syracuse to conquer Sicily, Alcibiades switched loyalties, ensuring Sparta's victory and Athenian enmity toward him and his mentor. Several years later, Critias, a leader of the Thirty Tyrants oligarchy, led a revolt that Socrates made no effort to oppose.

Athenian law permitted citizens to initiate criminal proceedings, and Socrates soon stood accused. His trial took place in the public square with no lawyers or judges. A jury of 501 volunteers—male citizens over the age of thirty, chosen by lot—determined his fate. His accusers spoke for three hours, and Socrates was afforded the same time to respond. But he offered not a defense but a reaffirmation of his views and teachings.

The verdict: 281 guilty votes; not guilty, 220. He was sentenced to death but allowed the alternative of exile, which he rejected, not wanting to live a life other than what he had chosen. In an eloquent speech to the jury, Socrates acknowledged there were "ways of escaping death, if a man is willing to say and do anything." But for him, the issue was "not to avoid death, but to avoid unrighteousness."

The verdict, however unjust in retrospect, represented the lawful decision of the court. Evading that, Socrates reasoned, would constitute its own transgression against the state. Socrates stepped into a last bath and bade his farewells. A jailer appeared with a cup of hemlock, which Socrates stoically drained as tearful friends looked on. His last act was obedience to the laws of the state that governed him despite his disagreement with them.

SEE ALSO The Draconian Code (621 BCE); The Laws of Solon (594 BCE); The Death Penalty Returns (1976).

The Death of Socrates (1787) by French neoclassical painter Jacques-Louis David depicts Socrates about to drink the cup of hemlock, choosing execution over exile.

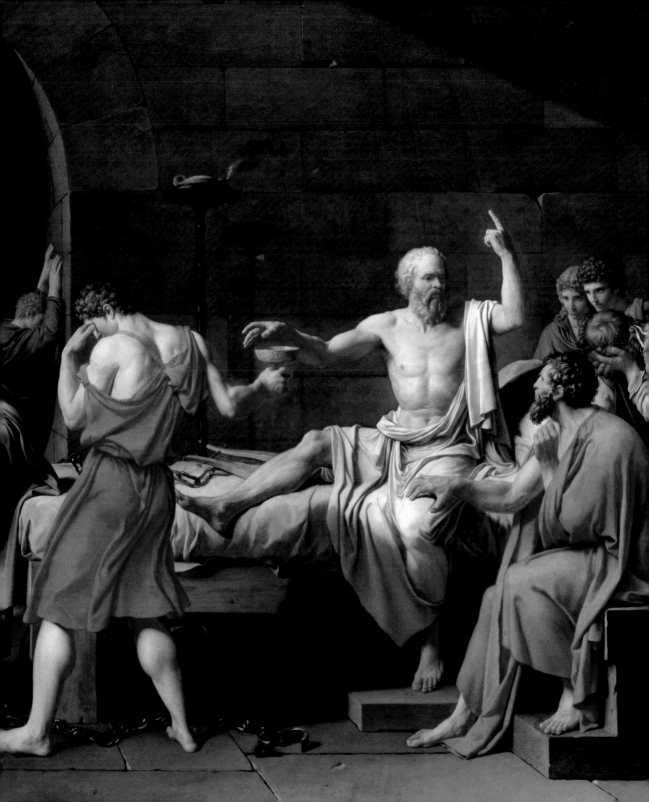

The Talmud

The foundations of Jewish law lie in the Torah, the first five books of the Hebrew Bible: Genesis, Exodus, Leviticus, Numbers, and Deuteronomy. Until the sixth century BCE, Jews reflected on and discussed the Torah and its teachings, generating and perpetuating an oral tradition that accompanied the written word. Then began a long period of Jewish subjugation and exile, first at the hands of the Babylonians and eventually the Romans. As a continued oral tradition became more precarious, sages and scholars recorded it, ultimately producing the Talmud.

The recorded oral tradition constitutes the Mishnah, the compilation of which began around 70 CE and continued until approximately 200. Analysis, interpretation, and teaching of the Mishnah continued for centuries, much of it committed to writing. During the fifth century of our era, this exposition of and commentary on the Mishnah became the Talmud, or the Gemara. Over time, two versions of the Talmud appeared: the Jerusalem Talmud and, one or two centuries later, the Babylonian Talmud. The latter is considered less obscure, more comprehensive, and therefore more authoritative. Talmudic scholar Adin Steinsaltz describes the Talmud as

> a conglomerate of law, legend, and philosophy, a blend of unique logic and shrewd pragmatism, of history and science, anecdotes, and humor. It is a collection of paradoxes: its framework is orderly and logical, every word and term subjected to meticulous editing, completed centuries after the actual work of composition came to an end; yet it is still based on free association, on a harnessing together of diverse ideas reminiscent of the modern stream-of-consciousness novel.

In discussing the origins and history of law, historian Robert Shaffern observes that the "law of the Hebrews/Israelites has passed into the religio-cultural inheritance of today's Jews and Christians" and that "even many secularized peoples of the modern world can trace their basic legal principles to ancient Israel." Those laws, he suggests, "may well be the most important and influential collection of legal materials in world history."

SEE ALSO The Ten Commandments (c. 1300 BCE); The Quran (652).

The Talmud Hour (c. 1900) by German painter J. Scheich captures the essence of Talmudic learning and teaching: reading, studying, discussing, and questioning.

The First Law School

Centuries before the first Western law school opened its doors at the University of Bologna (circa 1088) and the first American law school in Litchfield, Connecticut (1784), began classes, formal legal education flourished at the law school of Berytus in the Roman province of Syria (today Beirut, Lebanon). Classics and legal scholar Anton-Hermann Chroust identifies the institution as the leading Roman law school from the period of Diocletian (284–305) to that of Justinian (527–565)—the latter emperor calling it "the midwife of all laws"—though Rome and Constantinople (after 425) had their own law schools as well. In 534, Justinian barred the teaching of law except at these three schools, which he elevated to the status of imperial law schools.

The course of study at Berytus lasted five years, and graduates had no difficulty finding employment. Students attended lectures on the four books of Gaius's *Institutes* and on compiled works relating to dowries, guardianships, wills, and legacies. After publication of Justinian's Code in 533, the curriculum changed considerably. In addition to the *Institutes*, first-year lectures now covered the first four books of Justinian's *Digest*, while the next three years encompassed the remaining books. During the final year, pupils studied the imperial constitutions and statutes of the Code. Instruction originally took place in Latin, but by the fifth century it had switched to Greek. The fifth century also ushered in a shift in the teaching approach itself. Pedagogical focus changed from case studies and exposition to reading translated indexes and preparing commentaries.

Berytus attracted students from more than twenty provinces, "from Iberia to Armenia," according to classics scholar Kathleen McNamee. Then in 551 a massive earthquake destroyed the school and killed tens of thousands of the city's residents. The school reopened in Sidon, a Phoenician city twenty-five miles south of Berytus, but it never regained its earlier prominence.

SEE ALSO The Laws of Solon (594 BCE); The Twelve Tables (450 BCE); The Justinian Code (529); The Law School Revolution (1870).

These Ancient Roman ruins are near the original site of the law school of Berytus in present-day Beirut, Lebanon.

The Brehon Laws of Ireland

King Cormac mac Airt (c. 227–266), **St. Patrick** (c. 400–c. 450)

Noted legal historian and jurist Sir Henry Maine described the Brehon laws, the laws governing Ireland for more than 1,200 years, as "a very remarkable body of archaic law, unusually pure from its origin." The code consisted not of legislative enactments but rather the rendered judgments of Brehons, who served as arbitrators when called to resolve disputes based on customary law. Legal scholar Josiah H. Blackmore II has described them as more than judges—they were "legislators, teachers of the customary law of the land, expositors, interpreters and keepers of legal traditions."

The laws developed over centuries and passed from generation to generation through oral tradition prior to the widespread development of writing. To facilitate memorization and continuity (verse being less amenable to alteration than prose), the laws were formulated in rhythmic verse. The first written versions of the laws and their compilation into a code emerged around 250 during the reign of King Cormac. Two centuries later, St. Patrick commissioned nine men to revise the Brehon laws to conform with Christian doctrine. In 441, their efforts yielded the *Senchas Már* ("Great Book of Irish Law"), a revised recodification that remained in effect until the seventeenth century when English law fully supplanted it.

An article on Irish law published in the *Law Society Journal* explains that "honorable action was the keynote of the Brehon laws. . . . Once the law was proclaimed, it was accepted by all as the law of the land to be followed implicitly thereafter." The essence of the laws was compensation for wrongs, and any wrong—a tort, breach of contract, outright crime—was called an offense, the remedy for which was payment of a mulct in an amount determined by the Brehon and which also included the Brehon's fee. No officials enforced Brehons' judgments. Instead, distraint allowed for the seizure of the judgment debtor's property pending payment of the mulct. Hugh A. Carney, in a 1930s article in the *Law Society Journal*, notes that as a practical matter, "Brehon judgments were irresistible in execution because the full power of public opinion was behind them. . . . The only way to evade the law was to run away."

SEE ALSO The Irish Copyright War (561).

Irish Brehons are depicted in this 1821 illustration from The Costume of the Original Inhabitants of the British Islands *by Samuel Rush Meyrick and Charles Hamilton Smith.*

C.H.S. del.^t

Aquatinted by R. Havell.

Irish   *Brehons.*

Published June 1, 1815, by R. Havell, 3, Chapel Street, London.

The Justinian Code

Justinian I (483–565), **Tribonian** (c. 485–545)

Although the first written Roman laws appeared in the Twelve Tables, later state-issued legal publications took on increasing importance. As John Hessler, a research specialist at the Library of Congress, notes, the Justinian Code "is certainly the most important and influential collection of civil and secular law that has come down to us from antiquity. This collection of legal texts, which in the sixth century gathered together in one place nearly the entire history of surviving Roman law, has been seen by many scholars as the seed from which sprouted all later Western systems of jurisprudence."

Justinian ruled as Byzantine emperor from 527 until his death in 565. He wanted to reclaim the lost western half of the Roman Empire, which had fallen to the Goths in 476, as well as restore the Roman legal system after centuries of neglect. Justinian sought to boil down the great mass of materials; remove what was outdated, superfluous, or inscrutable; and systematize the remaining principles. By doing so, he sought to compile the empire's many scattered laws into a single official body of work readily available to all who needed it.

Managed by the jurist Tribonian and published from 528 to 534, the *Corpus Juris Civilis*, its official name in Latin, consists of four major parts: (i) the Code, comprising twelve books containing a collection of imperial laws and constitutions; (ii) the Digest, later considered the most important element, which contains within its fifty books much of the historic works of Roman jurists, along with the compilers' commentary on the law, distilling the most valuable learning; (iii) the Institutes, which functioned as an introductory legal textbook on Roman law but which was itself enacted into law; and (iv) the Novels, which included amendments or new laws Justinian added after completion of the *Corpus* itself.

The authority of the Code survived in the East for several centuries until new Byzantine laws eventually overwhelmed it. It largely disappeared in the West until the Digest in particular became the foundation for the teaching of law that blossomed in Bologna and the rest of Europe during the eleventh and twelfth centuries.

SEE ALSO The Draconian Code (621 BCE); The Laws of Solon (594 BCE); The Twelve Tables (450 BCE); The First Law School (c. 250).

This mosaic portrait of Justinian I stands in the Basilica of Sant'Apollinare Nuovo in Ravenna, Italy.

The Irish Copyright War

St. Columba (521–597), Finnian of Moville (495–589)

King Diarmait mac Cerbaill of Tara issued the first known ruling of what today we call copyright infringement. The dispute arose after Colm Cille, an Irish monk later known as St. Columba, surreptitiously copied a psalter, or book of psalms, while visiting Abbot Finnian of Moville, his former tutor and mentor. Columba was widely respected as a missionary, collector of manuscripts, and prolific scribe who often copied the works of scholars he visited. When Finnian learned what Columba had done, the abbot demanded the copy, insisting that it belonged to him as much as the original. Columba refused.

The argument went before the king, who ruled for Finnian under Brehon law. Diarmait's decision is best known for the aphorism it coined: "To every cow her calf, so to every book its copy," the first half of which became a popular Irish proverb (*Le gach boin a boinìn*). But the ruling also presaged modern copyright laws and the limits on copying original works. The decision stunned Columba, who protested it as an unjust sentence and vowed revenge. He left Tara and enlisted the aid of his clan from the north. They returned with him in 561 to launch the Battle of Cul Dreimhne (also known as the Battle of the Book), which deposed the king and left three thousand dead. Columba won the battle, but his actions disturbed other churchmen, who excommunicated him. The expulsion was overturned eventually, but Columba left Ireland for Iona in Scotland, where he founded his famous abbey and worked with great success to spread Christianity to the Scottish Picts.

The Royal Irish Academy in Dublin holds what is believed to be Columba's copy of the psalter, also known as the *Cathach*, meaning fighter or battler. The academy describes the book's fifty-eight leaves, covering psalms 31 to 106, as "the oldest extant Irish manuscript of the Psalter and the earliest example of Irish writing."

SEE ALSO The Brehon Laws of Ireland (c. 250); The Statute of Anne (1710); The Berne Convention (1878); Google Books and Fair Use (2010).

St. Columba triggered history's first copyright infringement ruling and a clan war known as the Battle of the Book.

Columbkille

Derry

The Tang Code

The history of China, one of the world's oldest civilizations, cascades through a succession of dynasties that began almost four thousand years ago and ended in the early twentieth century. Among the most important periods of Chinese history was the Tang dynasty (619–906), credited with securing for China a sustained period of political and cultural supremacy. That dynasty also produced the Tang Code, which Wallace Johnson—a highly regarded scholar of East Asian languages and cultures and one of the first to translate the Tang Code into English—describes as "certainly the most seminal legal work to have appeared in the whole of East Asian history."

The Tang Code consists of 502 articles in two parts. The first sets forth general principles of criminal law while the second enunciates specific offenses and their punishments. One of the Code's core objectives was to help maintain social order, amid perceived declining morality, through deterrence of unacceptable behavior. Han philosopher Tung Chung-shu, who viewed the human and natural worlds as linked, greatly influenced the development of the Code. The essence of the code holds that an offense disrupted society, the proper balance of which could be restored by the proper punishment or, in certain cases, by confession and restitution. The Code focuses on an individual's status or position in determining punishment, setting forth specific reductions for specific offenses, but it also recognizes mitigating factors, taking into account age, gender, and mental and physical condition as the basis for reduced punishment in appropriate cases.

The Tang Code directly influenced China for a millennium during at least three succeeding dynasties—the Sung (960–1270), the Yuan (1279–1368), and the Ming (1368–1644)—but its impact is widely acknowledged to have extended to foreign lands, affecting the criminal laws of other countries including Japan, Korea, and Vietnam. As Professor Johnson writes: "The Code has been the single most influential piece of legislation to appear in East Asia."

The Tang Code enumerates five kinds of corporal punishment: flogging, caning, imprisonment, exile, and death, the last of which is depicted in this 1864 lithograph, by illustrator Émile Bayard, published in the French magazine Le Tour du Monde.

The Quran

Muhammad (c. 570–632)

Islamic law, known as Sharia, begins with the sacred scripture of Islam. According to religious tradition, the prophet Muhammad received his first revelation near Mecca in 610 and continued receiving them until his death. His disciples committed his words and deeds to memory, and after his death scribes compiled them into what became the Quran.

The Quran contains approximately five hundred legal injunctions from God about how individuals should conduct themselves. It also contains Sunnah, the tradition of what the prophet did, said, and taught. When recorded, these traditions became known as Hadith. Together, the Quran and Sunnah comprise Sharia.

Sharia has five categories of what Islam scholar Wael Hallaq calls *moral-legal commandments*. First is the forbidden, with punishment for committing prohibited acts, including breach of contract and theft. Second is the obligatory, where punishment applies to failure to do something necessary such as prayer or the payment of debts. The third is the recommended category, which includes meritorious acts such as aiding the poor, visiting neighbors and friends, and offering a traditional Islamic greeting. The last two categories are the neutral and the disapproved. Although no punishment pertains for failure to do the recommended or undertaking the disapproved, those who act in such ways are understood to be judged in the future, presumably the hereafter.

During Islamic law's early development, a mufti, or learned jurist, provided answers to questions from citizens as well as judges about the application of law to specific cases. The mufti issued his answer, a legal opinion, in the form of a fatwa (today associated with the edicts of religious leaders). Fatwas served as the early foundations for a developing body of law, much the way court opinions function in common-law legal systems. While the word *Sharia* connotes the divine origins and quality of the law, scholarship, discussion, and debate about Sharia are called *fiqh*, meaning the human understanding and expression of Sharia.

For most Muslim-majority nations today, Sharia has become a foundation of secular laws, rather than a controlling doctrine, or is applied only in particular areas, for example: family matters relating to marriage, divorce, and inheritance. Nations where Sharia plays a dominant role include Iran, Northern Nigeria, Saudi Arabia, and Sudan.

SEE ALSO The Ten Commandments (c. 1300 BCE); The Talmud (c. 180); The Fatwa against *The Satanic Verses* (1988).

An excerpt from a thirteenth-century Arabic Quran, which contains the foundations of Islamic law.

ثُمَّ اصْبُوا ... قُوا ... أَنْتَ ... الْعَذ

... تَمُرُّونَ ... بِهِ

فِي جَنَّاتٍ وَنَعِيمٍ

... مُتَقَلِّبِينَ ... قَلِيلٍ ... كَعَالَهُ

يُدْعَوْنَ فِيهَا ...

Canon Law and the *Decretum Gratiani*

Gratian (c.1110–c. 1158)

Most people likely think of canon law as religious both in origin and nature and initiating with the Catholic Church. While canon law certainly does address worship, the clergy, and the Church, it also has a broader secular legal significance. Indeed, legal historians have extolled it as a vital part of the Western legal tradition.

Beginning in the late eleventh and early twelfth centuries, much of Europe functioned under two legal systems: Roman law and canon law. The former influenced the latter, and the two systems competed against but also complemented each other. Canon law's origins lay initially in ecclesiastical principles and Church teachings but gradually came to include secular issues as well.

In 1140, a Benedictine monk in Bologna named Gratian completed a compilation of approximately 3,800 canonical texts, which contain significant substantive analysis of doctrine. Gratian undertook to reconcile incongruities, discordances, and downright contradictions that appeared as various doctrines developed over time and through different sources. The work's formal title is *Concordia Discordantium Canonum* (*Concordance of Discordant Canons*), known familiarly as the *Decretum Gratiani* or *Gratian's Decree*. Legal scholar Harold J. Berman describes it as "the first comprehensive and systematic legal treatise in the history of the West, and perhaps in the history of mankind."

Although the *Decretum* wasn't an official Church publication, legal scholar William W. Bassett writes that it nonetheless "became the fundamental and universally consulted canonistic collection, upon which all subsequent development of canon law depended." Indeed, it became the authoritative canon law text in universities throughout Europe. Its significance lays in its organization and analysis of existing legal principles and the creation of a hierarchy among the three sources of law: divine law, or the revealed will of God; natural law, which discerned God's will through human reason or conscience; and positive, or man-made, law. That approach resulted in what Bassett describes as "a system of law that first articulated many of the principles of modern law and of the democratic institutions of modern government."

SEE ALSO The Ten Commandments (c. 1300 BCE); The Talmud (c. 180); The Quran (652).

This illuminated table of affinity—from a French edition of the Decretum Gratiani, *c. 1170–1180—shows interfamilial relationships. Such tables helped the Church determine issues of inheritance and the legality of marriages.*

The Assize of Clarendon

Henry II (1133–1189)

Historians trace the genealogy of the modern-day grand jury to a royal hunting lodge in twelfth-century England. In Clarendon Palace in Wiltshire, King Henry II promulgated the Assize of Clarendon, providing the blueprint for one of the most significant procedural components of criminal law.

Traditionally, anyone could charge a person in England with a crime, although typically the crime's victim pursued the charges. That changed in 1166, when Henry II created the Assize of Clarendon to enhance the crown's power by supplanting the role of ecclesiastical courts. The Assize—which translates loosely as "to settle" or "to assess"—required twelve men from each locality to announce publicly and under oath those they suspected of crimes including murder, robbery, larceny, or harboring anyone who had committed those transgressions. The accused was then subjected to trial by ordeal, which usually ended in death. Ten years later, the Assize of Northampton expanded the list of crimes by adding forgery and arson. Over time, almost all serious crimes were included.

During the fourteenth century, the procedure underwent modification. Now a group of twenty-four knights selected by the county sheriff—a body known as *le grande inquest*—initiated prosecutions. The original group of twelve local men, however, had a new purpose; they became known as the petit jury, and they assumed responsibility for determining guilt or innocence after a trial. In the late eighteenth century, William Blackstone wrote in his *Commentaries* that the Magna Carta required a grand jury determination of probable cause and a vote by a petit jury at trial on whether there was sufficient evidence for conviction.

The role of the grand jury continued to evolve, and by the seventeenth century it had ceased to function as an enforcer for the crown and became instead a safeguard against arbitrary prosecutions. By the mid-seventeenth century, the English grand jury made its way to the American colonies, where it soon found a hallowed place in the Bill of Rights.

SEE ALSO The Magna Carta (1215); The Star Chamber (c. 1350); *Bushel's Case* (1670); The Trial of John Peter Zenger (1735); The Bill of Rights (1791); Peremptory Challenges to Jury Selection (1986).

Sculpted here on Canterbury Cathedral, King Henry II of England issued the Assize of Clarendon.

HENRICVS II REX

Lex Mercatoria

In the thirteenth century, as the Renaissance spread from southern Europe, trade increased and commerce flourished. As business expanded, merchants fashioned an informal body of rules based on their own commercial customs and practices. These rules—collectively the *lex mercatoria*, or merchant law—became the governing doctrine for resolving commercial disputes in merchant courts that arose along major trading routes. As one of its principal advantages, uniform rules reduced uncertainty among foreign merchants doing business locally.

Although present throughout Europe, lex mercatoria grew quickly in England, where commerce was thriving in part due to the Magna Carta. The Great Charter commanded that all merchants have "safety and security in coming into England and in staying and traveling through England" and "to buy and sell without any unjust exactions." As was the case throughout Europe, England also benefited from an abundance of annual markets and fairs throughout the country. Because those events generated significant revenues for the crown in the form of franchise fees, it was particularly important to afford merchants an avenue for the expeditious resolution of any commercial disputes. Instead of common-law courts, merchants turned to Courts of Piepowders and Courts of the Staple—the former from *pieds poudrés*, meaning dusty feet, in reference to the traders traveling from market to market; the latter from the Statute of the Staple, which in 1353 created regional centers (called staples from an Old French word for market) for trade in certain goods. That statute also directed that a merchant preside as judge to apply lex mercatoria.

The Uniform Commercial Code, introduced in 1952, today governs all contracts for the sale of goods in the U.S. and defines an agreement between contracting parties in part as "including . . . course of dealing or usage of trade," a practice that derives directly from merchant law. Lex mercatoria also retains a role in modern jurisprudence among scholars engaged in the study of international law and the structure of commercial transactions in an increasingly globalized economy. Indeed, the preamble to the UNIDROIT Principles of International Commercial Contracts makes explicit reference to it.

SEE ALSO The Magna Carta (1215); Congressional Regulation of Commerce (1824); General Agreement on Tariffs and Trade (1948).

This painting by Fritz Wagner (1872–1967) depicts merchants in a Dutch tavern.

The Magna Carta

Henry I (c. 1069–1135), **King John** (1167–1216), **Stephen Langton** (c. 1150–1228), **Edward I** (1239–1307)

On inheriting the throne in 1100, King Henry I of England issued (and then largely ignored) the Charter of Liberties, or Coronation Charter, which redressed abuses of power by his brother William II by establishing royal directives concerning the barons of the realm and church offices, among other points.

A century later, Henry's great-grandson John had lost most of his French territories and a lot of money in trying to regain them. In 1214, he taxed the barons to finance an ultimately unsuccessful military campaign in France. The next year a group of barons, angry at John's repeated violations of feudal and common law, rebelled. At Runnymede, between Windsor and the rebels' camp at Staines, the king agreed to sign the Magna Carta ("great charter").

Drafted by intercessor Stephen Langton, the archbishop of Canterbury, the Magna Carta and its sixty-three clauses became a symbol of the supremacy of constitution over king, guaranteeing a barons council, church rights, protection from illegal imprisonment, swift justice, and tax limitations. In Chapter 39, its best-known provision, the king pledged that "no freed man shall be taken, imprisoned, disseised, outlawed, banished, or in any way destroyed, nor will We proceed against him, except by the lawful judgment of his peers and by the LAW OF THE LAND." That simple but sweeping prohibition ultimately serves as the foundation for due process of law. According to legal journalist James Podgers, "that King John agreed to sign a document affirming the principle that no one, not even a monarch, is above the law was historic." Legal scholar A. E. Dick Howard notes that the document had "enormous significance in the development of one of our most precious ideals: the rule of law, a government of laws and not of men."

But neither king nor barons ultimately obeyed it, and Pope Innocent III voided its legality, which triggered the First Barons' War. Subsequent kings issued, ignored, and reissued the arrangement until Edward I confirmed it as a permanent statute in 1297, from which point it became the living cornerstone of Anglo-American constitutional law, explicitly invoked even eight centuries after its creation by the U.S. Supreme Court in rulings involving enemy combatants (2008) and petitioning the government (2011).

SEE ALSO *Bushel's Case* (1670); The Habeas Corpus Act of 1679; Blackstone's *Commentaries* (1765); The U.S. Constitution (1787); The Bill of Rights (1791); Universal Declaration of Human Rights (1948).

This 1937 painting of King John and the Magna Carta by Boardman Robinson hangs in the Department of Justice building in Washington, D.C.

The Statutes of Westminster

Edward I (1239–1307)

Today we use the word *statute* to mean an act or, in the words of *Black's Law Dictionary*, "A law passed by a legislative body." But as English historians H. G. Richardson and George Sayles explain, that word didn't come into common use until the end of the thirteenth century. Until then, enactments were called provisions or *établissements*.

Shortly after returning from the Ninth Crusade and ascending to the throne, King Edward I convened his first parliament at Westminster in 1275, which produced the first Statute of Westminster, its fifty-one clauses in Anglo-Norman (Old French) covering a full range of substantive legal areas as well as the administration of justice. In 1877, English historian William Stubbs called the statute "almost a code by itself" because it provided common rights to all and free elections. Around that same time, law historian George Crabb praised Edward I for his efforts, dubbing him "the English Justinian."

A second Statute of Westminster (II), enacted in 1285, contained fifty clauses and is best known for the establishment of two important doctrines: the estate "tail" in land (a device limiting succession in land ownership to the heirs of the original owner, thereby ensuring continued family ownership through succeeding generations); and the "action on the case," a means of providing a remedy for wrongs not expressly recognized by the common law or for which there was no other known cause of action to provide redress. The third Statute of Westminster (III), enacted in 1290, proscribed subinfeudation, a practice by which feudal tenants leased part of their lands to others and collected payments from them to the detriment of the feudal tenant's lord and successors.

The original Statute of Westminster continues to have relevance even today. In 2009, the New York Court of Appeals invoked one of its provisions for interpretive aid in a case concerning attorney deceit upon the court, noting that in a 1787 law the New York Legislature adopted language strikingly similar to the medieval enactment.

SEE ALSO The Justinian Code (529); The Assize of Clarendon (1166); The Magna Carta (1215); The U.S. Constitution (1787).

The Palace of Westminster, where the Parliament of England and later Great Britain has convened since the reign of Edward I, sits on the banks of the River Thames.

The Star Chamber

Legal scholar Elizabeth G. Thornburg writes that "to label a case a 'Star Chamber proceeding' today is a terrible insult—an accusation of gross procedural unfairness and abuse of power. But the story of the real Court of Star Chamber is considerably more complicated." Historians trace the origins of the Court of Star Chamber to the latter half of the fourteenth century and its name—according to the leading theory—to the chamber's ceiling, decorated in the medieval style with stars painted in gold.

The Court of Star Chamber began as an extension of the King's Council, by which citizens sought legal help unavailable in the existing courts, thereby enabling the less fortunate to pursue claims against the wealthy. In 1487, Henry VII formalized the structure of the court, which had separated from the King's Council, to consist of seven men: a bishop, the chancellor, two justices, the keeper of the Privy Seal, a lord, and the treasurer. As the Star Chamber evolved, however, and because it represented an extension of the crown, it came to create new laws. For example, it made crimes of libel, perjury, and conspiracy. However appropriate or necessary such laws were, the process inhibited political dissent and criminalized the expression of certain opinions. Proceedings in the Star Chamber generally deprived defendants of sufficient procedural rights, including trial by jury.

By the early 1600s, the Court of Star Chamber had ceased to function as an honorable institution of justice. Instead, it had become a political club wielded by the king to suppress opposition and punish dissent. The Long Parliament—the first gathering of that body since Charles I had dissolved the previous one eleven years earlier—abolished the Court of Star Chamber with the Habeas Corpus Act of 1640.

The physical court itself stood at the Palace of Westminster (better known in America as the Houses of Parliament) until 1806, when it was demolished. The ceiling that gave the chamber its name now hangs in Leasowe Castle in Cheshire, but its reputation remains in place, far and wide, as a metaphor for harsh and seemingly arbitrary legal or governmental decisions made in private.

SEE ALSO The Assize of Clarendon (1166); *Bushel's Case* (1670); The Habeas Corpus Act of 1679; Legal Aid Societies (1876); The Right to Counsel in State Court (1963).

The ceiling that gave the Star Chamber its name now hangs in Leasowe Castle.

The Trial of Joan of Arc

Jeanne d'Arc (1412–1431), **Pierre Cauchon** (1371–1442), **Callixtus III** (1378–1458)

By the time Jeanne d'Arc was twelve years old, she claimed to have seen visions of saints who encouraged her to help end the bloody Hundred Years' War that already had been raging for decades between Plantagenet England and Valois France for dynastic control of the latter kingdom. At age sixteen, she began petitioning for a role in the military. The surviving historical record remains silent as to her leadership on the battlefield, but her dramatic presence helped reverse the tide of the war in favor of the French. Nevertheless, a series of military setbacks eventually led to her capture and prosecution for heresy by an English-supported church in Rouen, France, led by Pierre Cauchon, the bishop of Beauvais.

During her trial, church investigators suspected Joan of being a witch or sorceress because of her masculine tendencies and rebellious refusal to answer questions. Despite little evidence to support charges of heresy, Joan's few recollections of her visions and her reluctance to wear women's clothing—probably to avoid being raped in prison— sufficiently convinced Church officials that she was possessed of an immoral character. The legal failings of her trial were many: She faced a biased court conducting a private trial. She never heard the accusations against her, nor did she face the opposing witnesses. She couldn't call her own witnesses or have counsel for her defense, and she was denied any right of appeal.

At the conclusion of the trial, which legal scholars have described as a travesty of justice, she was sentenced to death and burned at the stake on May 30, 1431, for contravening Deuteronomy 22:5, "The woman shall not wear that which pertaineth unto a man . . . for all that do so are abomination unto the LORD thy God."

A quarter of a century later, after calls to overturn the verdict, Pope Callixtus III directed a new trial. In the end, the Church recognized its failure, and in 1456 the appellate ecclesiastical court declared her innocent by the same evidence that had led to her execution. Pope Benedict XV canonized her as a saint in 1920.

SEE ALSO The Trial of Socrates (399 BCE); The Salem Witchcraft Trials (1692).

Later canonized by the Catholic Church, Joan of Arc—depicted in this 1898 painting from the side altar in the Cathedral of Our Lady in Antwerp, Belgium—is one of the best-known victims of religious persecution.

Littleton's *Tenures*

Thomas de Littleton (c.1422–1481)

The advent of the printing press in the mid-fifteenth century wrought revolutionary changes across all aspects of European culture and society. The ability to disseminate printed material—from one-page pamphlets to multivolume books, all brimming with knowledge to be spread and acquired—laid the groundwork for many profound advances that accreted over the centuries. The legal realm felt those revolutionary changes as well, although it did manifest an initial resistance to textbooks.

Two icons of English jurisprudence had authored significant legal texts long before the coming of the printing press. Ranulf de Glanville, chief justiciar during the reign of Henry II, wrote *Treatise on the Laws and Customs of the Kingdom of England*, the first work on English laws. Around 1235, Henry de Bracton, an English jurist, wrote *On the Laws and Customs of England*, establishing guidelines on criminal intent and the legitimate rule of kings. But legal historians identify the 1481 publication of *Treatise on Tenures* by Thomas de Littleton as the first true legal textbook, meaning that it contains narrative exposition and analysis rather than merely compiling primary materials on the subject. Littleton's *Tenures* garnered enormous acclaim. English jurist Lord Edward Coke, whose 1628 *Commentary on Littleton* itself became a standard, described the book as "the ornament of the common law, and the most perfect and absolute work that was ever written in any human science." Nineteenth-century legal historian F. W. Maitland said of Littleton's *Tenures*, "I don't know any book which puts the outlines of the classical common law in so clear a shape."

Littleton established a model that future scholars emulated in their own treatises. By providing a comprehensive and authoritative exposition of legal doctrine, they supplied organization and meaning to the law, particularly as the number of cases and statutes multiplied.

SEE ALSO *Les Termes de la Ley* (1527); Blackstone's *Commentaries* (1765); The Field Code (1848); Law Reporting and Legal Publishing (1872).

Sir Thomas de Littleton authored the first legal textbook, Treatise on Tenures.

Vng Dieu et Vng Roy

The true portraiture of Iudge Littleton the famous English Lawyer

Ferdinand II of Aragon (1452–1516), Isabella of Castile (1451–1504), Juan Carlos of Spain (b. 1938)

Ferdinand and Isabella are best known today for commissioning Christopher Columbus's venture to seek a western trade route to the Orient. The Genovese man famously set sail from Spain on August 3, 1492, but only months earlier his royal patrons had issued the Edict of Expulsion, otherwise known as the Alhambra Decree commanding "all Jews and Jewesses of whatever age they may be" either to accept baptism and conversion to Christianity or leave to the country.

A new wave of anti-Semitism had been smoldering over the fifteenth century. Many Spanish Jews had converted to Christianity to avoid persecution and be allowed to engage in proscribed activities. As a group, the *conversos* flourished in business and the universities, but their success bred anger and resentment. In 1478, Ferdinand and Isabella established the Congregation of the Holy Roman and Universal Inquisition Holy Office but better known as the Spanish Inquisition—under their own control, rather than the pope's, to expose and punish conversos who they believed had retained their Jewish faith in secret. Led by Tomás de Torquemada, the Spanish Inquisition fanned the flames of anti-Semitism, leading inexorably to the Edict of Expulsion.

Scholars disagree over the number of Jews who fled Spain in the wake of the edict but generally it's thought to be one hundred thousand of a population of about one million. The last Jews left Spain on August 2, 1492, on ships described as a "fleet of woe." The next day Columbus departed with his three ships on a very different voyage. Historians have noted with sad irony the important role that financially influential conversos played in persuading Ferdinand and Isabella to support Columbus's enterprise as well as his reliance on nautical instruments and astronomical tables supplied by them.

In 1968, military dictator Francisco Franco's fascist government symbolically declared the Alhambra Decree void. In 1992, five hundred years after its issuance, Juan Carlos formally rescinded his ancestors' decree, and in 2014, several months before he abdicated the throne, his government offered citizenship to the descendants of Jews expelled by the decree.

SEE ALSO The Chinese Exclusion Act (1882); Hitler's Rise to Power (1933); The Nuremberg Laws (1935)

The 1889 painting by Emilio Sala (1850–1910) shows Torquemada offering the Edict of Expulsion to Ferdinand

Les Termes de la Ley

John Rastell (c. 1475–1536)

While reading this book, you might need a dictionary to understand the meaning of an unfamiliar word. Dictionaries allow people to increase their knowledge of a language or specific subjects and thereby their ability to comprehend thoughts and ideas. We largely take that ability for granted today. Imagine a world before dictionaries existed; to what sources could a reader turn for the meanings of words newly encountered?

In 1527, John Rastell, an English lawyer and author, published the first law dictionary in England: *Expositiones Terminorum Legum Anglorum*, later known as *Les Termes de la Ley*. The dictionary included 208 entries laid out alphabetically in parallel columns, one in Latin and the other in Law French, known as Anglo-Norman. A second edition, issued in 1530, added English translations. Rastell's work wasn't just the first law dictionary; it was the first English-language dictionary of any kind. It preceded the arrival of *The Dictionary of Syr Thomas Eliot Knyght* by more than a decade and Robert Cawdrey's *Table Alphabeticall* by seventy-five years. Samuel Johnson's *Dictionary of the English Language* didn't appear for another two centuries.

Rastell intended his dictionary to serve an educational function. Beyond lawyers and students, Rastell hoped to inform and educate ordinary citizens. In his view, only an informed citizenry could bring about the ultimate social purposes of the law.

Rastell's dictionary appeared in twenty-nine subsequent editions between 1527 and 1819, despite facing competition from the 1729 publication of Giles Jacob's *New Law-Dictionary*, which moved the form of the legal dictionary in the direction of an encyclopedia. Bibliographer Howard Jay Graham describes *Termes de la Ley* as "the ultimate ancestor of every Anglo-American law dictionary and legal encyclopedia," and observes that it "probably has exercised as nearly permanent and decisive an influence as any lawbook in English history."

SEE ALSO Littleton's *Tenures* (1481); Blackstone's *Commentaries* (1765); The Field Code (1848); Law Reporting and Legal Publishing (1872).

This title page is from a seventeenth-century edition of the seminal text.

LES TERMES DE LA LEY:

OR

Certaine difficult and obscure Words and Termes of the Common
Lawes and Statutes of this Realme now in vse
expounded and explained.

Newly imprinted, and much in-
larged and augmented.

With a new Addition of
aboue two hundred and fifty words.

HOR: *Multa renascentur quæ jam cecidere, cadentque*
Quæ nunc sunt in honore vocabula, si volet vsus.

LONDON;
Printed by the Assignes of Iohn More
Esquire. 1636.

An Act for the Relief of the Poor

Henry VIII (1491–1547), Elizabeth I (1533–1603)

Although the law generally doesn't distinguish between rich and poor, in some instances it makes provisions for the poor, reflecting the state's recognition of its responsibility to provide for the welfare of its constituents. If not the product of innate altruism, that recognition usually derives from religious custom or indoctrination. Through the end of the sixteenth century in England, the Church largely cared for the poor, particularly through monasteries and parish priests. The necessary resources came from the generosity and tithes of parishioners. In 1535, Parliament passed an act punishing vagabonds and beggars, and the next year Henry VIII began his infamous Dissolution of the Monasteries, which greatly diminished parochial resources, resulting in a dramatic increase in poverty.

In 1601, a few years before the death of Queen Elizabeth I, Parliament enacted the first comprehensive law designed specifically to address the economic needs of the indigent—rather than just punishing them—by passing the Act for the Relief of the Poor. Known as the Elizabethan Poor Law, it built on the legislation enacted under Henry VIII, and its hallmark was changing the mechanism of administration from ecclesiastical to secular. Charity no longer came through voluntary parish contributions but rather through compulsory, state-enforced taxes. The law also implemented a formal categorization of the types of poor and their respective treatment. The "impotent poor," those unable to work, were entitled to direct relief, paid with monies collected through taxation. The able-bodied, employable poor were put to work, usually in manufacturing, under the auspices of overseers. The "idle poor," the able-bodied who refused to work, were incarcerated. Poor children were put to work as apprentices. One additional feature imposed on parents, grandparents, and children the obligation to accept financial responsibility for one another.

According to political scientist and former chairman of the California State Social Welfare Board Jacobus tenBroek, the act "fixed the character of poor relief for three centuries not only in England but in America as well. Today its principal features linger in the welfare programs of all of our states."

SEE ALSO The Star Chamber (c. 1350); Legal Aid Societies (1876); Congressional Power to Tax Income (1909); The Social Security Act (1935).

Queen Elizabeth I presided over the first comprehensive law that addressed the economic needs of the impoverished.

Compulsory Education Laws

Mark Twain reportedly said that he never let his schooling interfere with his education. But as nations have developed, they've recognized the profound importance of formal education, adopting compulsory education laws to ensure its provision.

In 1616, Scotland became the first country to implement comprehensive compulsory education with the Privy Council's School Establishment Act. An earlier Education Act of 1496 had directed all sons of barons and freeholders of means to attend grammar schools, but the 1616 act mandated that every parish establish a publicly funded, Church-supervised school, meant to emphasize Protestantism and obliterate Scottish Gaelic. The act found little success, though, until the Education Acts of 1633 and 1646, which authorized bishops to tax landowners to support the schools.

More than a century later, King Frederick William I of Prussia mandated that all children "not otherwise provided with instruction"—which excluded those with private tutors or attending the gymnasium—attend village schools. His son and successor, Frederick the Great, continued the policy and issued a 1763 directive known as the General Regulations for Village Schools.

American compulsory education laws date back to the colonial era, but those dealt only with the establishment and maintenance of free public schools; attendance remained voluntary. The first state to enact a true compulsory education law was Massachusetts, which did so with the 1852 Compulsory Attendance Act, requiring children between the ages of eight and fourteen to attend school for at least three months each year, including at least six consecutive weeks.

Compulsory school attendance didn't emerge in the U.K. or France until the late nineteenth century. In Britain, a powerful upper class didn't want to give the working classes ready means to escape their station, delaying its adoption until 1880. In France, a clash between religious and secular authorities provided the stumbling block. In 1880, Jules Ferry, then the minister of public education, shepherded through the legislature two bills calling for the establishment of free and compulsory primary education for all children. Free primary education became law in 1881, and compulsory primary education, which eliminated religious instruction or presence in public schools, became law in early 1882.

SEE ALSO The G.I. Bill (1944).

John Knox (c. 1514–1572) led the Protestant Reformation in Scotland, and his Book of Discipline *inspired the* School Establishment Act *of 1616.*

On the Law of War and Peace

Hugo Grotius (1583–1645)

Unremitting advances in technology, communication, and transportation continue to bring the nations and peoples of the world closer together, making a workable system of international law even more important. The earliest foundations of international law began to appear shortly after the fall of the Roman Empire in the fifth century, but not until the early to mid-seventeenth century and the devastation of the Thirty Years' War did formal doctrines and theories begin to emerge.

The most influential thinker on the subject was Dutch scholar and jurist Hugo Grotius. In 1625, Nicolas Buon published Grotius's classic of legal literature, *De Jure Belli ac Pacis* (*On the Law of War and Peace*). Some modern scholars question whether Grotius's reputation as the father of international law is overstated, but no one can assail his impact as a theorist. "There is little doubt that the seeds of both the contemporary international human rights movement and modern Bills of Rights can be traced to Grotius's magnum opus," according to legal scholar John Dugard.

Grotius receives credit for developing a modern theory of natural law, divorced from religion or divine law. Importantly, he believed that nations were subject to the same laws as individuals. Therefore he recognized the equality, independence, and sovereignty of states. He developed a system of principles by which nations ought to abide in their conduct toward one another whether at war or in times of peace. Indeed, Professor Dugard attributes the enduring appeal of *De Jure Belli ac Pacis* to its "rejection of *raison d'état* [state interest] as the basic premise of international relations and from its attempt to inject morality, justice, and idealism into the international legal order."

For Grotius, only wars for just causes—defending or recovering property, for example—were proper, and he squarely rejected the propriety of preemptive war. Military aggression could be undertaken only to enforce rights and had to be carried out in good faith and within the bounds of law, thereby making war a moral enterprise on the international level.

SEE ALSO Canon Law and the *Decretum Gratiani* (1140); The Peace of Westphalia (1648); The Bill of Rights (1791); The Geneva Convention (1864); Colonialism and Postwar Independence (1947).

This 1886 statue of Hugo Grotius, by the Dutch sculptor Franciscus Leonardus Stracké, stands in the central market square of Delft in the Netherlands.

The First Blue Laws

Constantine the Great (c. 272–337), **Samuel Peters** (1735–1826),
J. Hammond Trumbull (1821–1897)

Laws that prohibit specified secular activities on days of worship existed in the ancient world, but their colorful name appeared more recently. Commentators point to Roman emperor Constantine the Great—whose edict in 321 commanded city residents to rest "on the venerable day of the sun"—as having promulgated the first Sunday Closing Law. Virginia's House of Burgesses enacted America's first Sunday Closing Law in 1629, ordering "that the Sabath day be not ordinarily profaned by workeing in any imployments or by journeying from place to place."

But etymologists ascribe the first usage of the phrase "blue laws" to a satire of Connecticut Congregationalists in the March 3, 1755, issue of the *New-York Mercury*: "Since . . . the Revival of our old Blue Laws, we have the Pleasure to see the Lord's Work go on with Success." Reverend Samuel Peters, an Anglican critic of those same Congregationalists, further popularized the term in his hostile *General History of Connecticut*. Peters held that lawgivers in the colony of New Haven "betrayed such an extreme degree of wanton cruelty and oppression, that even the rigid fanatics of Boston, and the mad zealots of Hertford, put to the blush, christened them the Blue Laws." Peters suggested that "blue" served as a euphemism for "bloody"—descriptive of a violator's condition after punishment for disobedience and still considered an expletive in the U.K. today—but his position lacked historical support. In 1876, Connecticut historian J. Hammond Trumbull offered another plausible etymology: "true blue" never faded, serving as a symbol of constancy and fidelity. "After the Restoration," Trumbull wrote, "Nothing could be more unpopular . . . than constancy in virtue and adherence to convictions of duty. 'True blue' became a term of reproach, reserved for puritans. . . . To be 'blue' was to be 'puritanic,' precise in the observance of legal and religious obligations."

Nearly every state in the Union has had some type of blue law, but as commerce and competition expanded, courts carved out exceptions to blue laws, sometimes to the point of obliterating the rule. By the twentieth century, the laws became increasingly unpopular, and most legislatures eliminated them, though some do remain.

SEE ALSO Canon Law and the *Decretum Gratiani* (1140); The Prohibition of Illegal Narcotics (1915); Prohibition (1918); The Repeal of Prohibition (1933); Legalization of Marijuana (1996).

This 1895 political cartoon illustrates the restrictions imposed by Blue Laws.

Peace of Westphalia

The Peace of Westphalia consists of three treaties executed in 1648 in the Westphalian towns of Münster and Osnabrück. The Peace of Münster ended the Eighty Years' War between Spain and the Netherlands, establishing the Dutch Republic's independence. The Treaty of Münster and the Treaty of Osnabrück ended the Thirty Years' War among the Holy Roman Empire, France, Sweden, and their respective allies, waged principally in what is now Germany and resulting from religious conflict and a common thirst for territorial expansion.

Leo Gross, scholar of international law and relations, likened the Peace of Westphalia to the United Nations Charter because it tried "to establish something resembling world unity on the basis of states exercising untrammeled sovereignty over certain territories and subordinated to no earthly authority." Historians point to the Peace of Westphalia as the beginning of a system of sovereignty independent from Church authority or secular monarchy founded on divine right. This secularization had little immediate impact, but over time it fostered republican forms of government, eventually leading to the political theory of sovereignty deriving from the people.

The critical principle of this new theory held that each state was equal in its respective sovereign rights, allowing for a balance of power among nations, which forms what international law scholar Ian Brownlie calls "the basic constitutional doctrine of the law of nations."

Reality demonstrated otherwise, however. Historian Herbert Rowen notes that, although the Peace seemingly ended wars of religion, they yielded to "an interval of non-ideological wars, when aggrandizement and power-seeking ordinarily paraded naked before men." The inequality in real strength among nations meant that "the Peace of Westphalia could only be a truce and the diplomats' compromises were ultimately as impermanent as generals' victories."

The next year, Tsar Alexis I, who had supported Sweden against the Holy Roman Empire in the Thirty Years' War, issued the *Sobornoe Ulozhenie*, the Russian legal code, which William Butler, an authority on the law of Russia, called "a watershed in Russian legal history, as consequential as the Peace of Westphalia was for European diplomacy and the law of nations."

SEE ALSO *On the Law of War and Peace* (1625); *Leviathan* (1651); The E.U. and the Treaty of Paris (1951).

This 1648 painting by Gerard ter Borch shows the ratification of the Peace of Münster between the kingdom of Spain and the Dutch Republic on May 15, 1648.

Leviathan

Thomas Hobbes (1588–1679)

What makes a book revolutionary often isn't its thought-provoking content but the context from which that content springs. Such was the case with the publication of Thomas Hobbes's *Leviathan* in 1651. At the time, England was nearing the end of its civil war, which had lasted for nine bloody years. Unrest had become the social and political norm; law was a morass, a tangle of theories with little cohesion. Despite this chaos, according to political scientist Gary McDowell, one overarching framework stood above all: "the powerful and pervasive influence of Christianity." *Leviathan* made waves by calling into question traditional Christian notions of man, law, and government, marking a major turning point in legal theory and laying an important cornerstone for the development of law over the next century.

The title of the book comes from the Hebrew word for "coiled" or "twisted," used to describe a sea monster in the Hebrew Bible. Hobbes argues that, for a commonwealth to remain free from fear and the violence inherent in human nature, it has to enter into a contract with a sovereign whereby it obeys manmade laws in exchange for the sovereign's protection from the naturally violent state of man. Hobbes's model of exchange between the sovereign and the people formed the basis of social contract theory, which explains the rationale behind law and government.

Leviathan met with a harsh reception. Some of Hobbes's contemporaries accused him of misconstruing human nature as naturally evil, a bold contradiction of the benevolent Christian god who created man in His image. Hobbes's theory on the establishment of law, which stems from man's will to contract with the sovereign and not from divine proclamation, further antagonized his Christian audiences. Despite this early negative reception, however, the principles set forth in *Leviathan* have withstood the test of time. As Loreta Medina writes in *The Creation of the U.S. Constitution*, from Hobbes, America's founding fathers "learned the doctrine of the sovereignty of the people that made a government dependent on the consent of the governed," and today many scholars consider Hobbes a pillar of modern constitutionalism.

SEE ALSO *On the Law of War and Peace* (1625); The U.S. Constitution (1787); The Declaration of the Rights of Man (1789); Universal Declaration of Human Rights (1948).

This detail of the frontispiece to Leviathan, *illustrated by French artist Abraham Bosse, shows a sovereign— modeled after the recently beheaded King Charles I—consisting of, and therefore deriving his power to govern directly from, the people.*

Bushel's Case

King v. Penn and Mead, **William Penn** (1644–1718), **John Vaughan** (1603–1674)

> *A court is only as sound as its jury, and a jury is only as sound as the men who make it up.*
>
> —Harper Lee, *To Kill a Mockingbird*

In August 1670, William Penn—who later founded the Colony and the Commonwealth of Pennsylvania—and William Mead were charged with "unlawfully and tumultuously" assembling to preach and speak as they led a Quaker worship session on London's Gracechurch Street. At the conclusion of *King v. Penn and Mead* at the Old Bailey (the Central Criminal Court of England and Wales), the jury found Mead not guilty and Penn guilty. The infuriated judges refused to accept the verdict and instructed the jurors to continue deliberating. When the jury returned a similar verdict, they were sent back again with the warning that "you shall not be dismissed till we have a verdict that the court will accept; and you shall be locked up, without meat, drink, fire, and tobacco. . . . We will have a verdict, by the help of God, or you shall starve for it."

Two days later, the jury returned, this time finding both defendants not guilty. The court immediately imprisoned all twelve jurors for contempt. Edward Bushel, one of the jurors, refused to pay the fine set for release. Instead, he sought a writ of habeas corpus from the Court of Common Pleas challenging the lawfulness of his imprisonment. The court granted the writ, and he was released two months later.

Bushel's Case prompted a landmark decision on the role of juries. Lord Chief Justice Vaughan declared the imposed fines and imprisonment unlawful and held that a jury couldn't be punished for its verdict, thereby ending judges' ability to control verdicts according to political whim and also establishing the independent power of the jury, which Blackstone calls "the sacred bulwark of our liberties." *Bushel's Case* became the foundation for the concept of jury nullification, by which a jury nullifies a law it thinks improper by finding a defendant not guilty regardless of its belief in the defendant's guilt strictly by the letter of the law.

SEE ALSO The Assize of Clarendon (1166); The Habeas Corpus Act of 1679; The Trial of John Peter Zenger (1735); Peremptory Challenges to Jury Selection (1986).

The Birth of Pennsylvania 1680 by Jean Leon Gerome Ferris (1863–1930) shows King Charles II giving a land charter to William Penn in the Palace of Whitehall.

The Habeas Corpus Act of 1679

The common-law writ of habeas corpus—the "Great Writ"—first appeared in England in the twelfth century in the Assize of Clarendon in order to deliver a person to court. Literally translated, "habeas corpus" means "you may have the body." Known as a high prerogative writ, originally only the king could grant it.

Gradually the writ evolved into enabling a prisoner to challenge the lawfulness of his or her confinement, although initially it proved ineffective. As historian Helen Nutting explains, "delays and evasions almost negated the effect of the writ" because "courts had no means of forcing obedience to the first writ" and penalties "only accompanied the third . . . so that a jailer was perfectly within the limits of accepted procedure in not . . . bringing the prisoner to court until he received the third writ." Hoping to remedy that messy situation, Parliament passed the Habeas Corpus Act of 1679.

Political scientist Neil Douglas McFeeley described this new writ as "the most effective weapon yet devised for the protection of . . . liberty," providing for "a speedy judicial inquiry into the validity of any imprisonment on a criminal charge and for a speedy trial of prisoners incarcerated while awaiting trials." It required a prisoner to be produced within three days and that unless the prisoner was shown to be "detained upon a legal process, order or warrant, out of some court that hath jurisdiction of criminal matters," he or she was to be released. Notably, the writ expressly didn't apply to those imprisoned on a criminal conviction.

The 1679 statute didn't extend to the American colonies, but English common law did, and many of the colonies embedded the writ in their own constitutions. Indeed, the writ was so important that the Constitutional Convention delegates included it—with little debate and no dissent—in Article I of the U.S. Constitution: "the privilege of the writ of habeas corpus shall not be suspended, unless when in cases of rebellion or invasion the public safety may require it." As legal historian G. Edward White notes, "the framers sought to make it clear that incarcerated persons would continue to be able to challenge their confinement."

SEE ALSO The Assize of Clarendon (1166); *Bushel's Case* (1670); The U.S. Constitution (1787).

King Charles II of England, shown in this c. 1683 portrait by John Reilly (1646–1691), presided over the passage of the Habeas Corpus Act.

The Black Code of Louis XIV

Louis X (1289–1316), **Louis XIV** (1638–1715), **Maximilien Robespierre** (1758–1794), **Napoléon Bonaparte** (1769–1821)

Although Louis X abolished slavery in France in 1315, his proclamation didn't apply to French colonies established several centuries later. Columbus and others who followed him enslaved indigenous Americans initially to serve as interpreters but ultimately to labor alongside African slaves in the West Indies. As the decades passed, many European nations came to depend on slavery's enormous economic value. The French established their first permanent Caribbean settlement on St. Kitts in 1625; two years later, African slaves began to arrive. By 1685, slavery had proliferated throughout the French colonies, which now included Martinique, Guadeloupe, St. Domingue (Haiti), and other islands. That year, Louis XIV signed the Code Noir, the Black Code, one of the most important documents in the gruesome history of slavery.

Its articles embraced civil law, criminal law, and religion and laid out the legal relationship between masters and slaves. Slaves were to be baptized and indoctrinated into Catholicism, a consequence of Louis XIV's staunch religious convictions and a primary motivation for the code. Slaves were defined as the personal property of their masters, which prohibited them from owning property themselves and dissociated them from other civil rights. But the code required masters to provide for and in some cases protect their slaves. Food and clothing allowances were detailed, and masters had to pay for slaves' medical care. Torture was prohibited, as was forced marriage. Interracial marriage was permitted, and, if a master married a slave, the slave and her children became free.

The Black Code helped improve conditions, but as the Age of Enlightenment progressed the nations of Europe increasingly recognized the cruelty and hypocrisy of the institution. Maximilien Robespierre's First Republic abolished slavery throughout the French colonies in 1794. Less than a decade later, Napoléon reestablished it. But the spirit and many provisions of the Code endured in French Louisiana, where it had been implemented by edict, and other American colonies under French influence, including Arkansas and Missouri, where the Code served as a blueprint for slave laws enacted after the Louisiana Purchase.

SEE ALSO *The Amistad* (1839); The *Dred Scott* Decision (1857); The Emancipation Proclamation (1863); The Abolition of Slavery (1865); The Brazilian Slave Emancipation Act (1888).

Louis XIV ruled France for more than seventy years.

The Salem Witchcraft Trials

William Phips (1651–1695), Cotton Mather (1663–1728)

The law doesn't always perform admirably. The Salem witchcraft trials reflect one of the most egregious instances of law overtaken by mass hysteria, resulting in a complete failure of impartial justice.

In colonial Salem, Massachusetts, more than two hundred people stood accused of practicing witchcraft and were subject to court-ordered torture, lengthy prison terms, or execution. The cases began in January 1692, when a local minister's daughters began having fits, uttering strange sounds and contorting their bodies. A town doctor "diagnosed" the malady as witchcraft. Soon other young girls began having outbursts, accusing certain women of cursing them. Dozens of women and men were brought in for questioning.

By May 1692, with fear and paranoia rampant, Governor William Phips established the Court of Oyer and Terminer for cases alleging witchcraft. None of the appointed judges, however, had had any legal training. In the first case, brought against an older town gossip named Bridget Bishop, the defendant was found guilty despite scant evidence. An account of the case from preacher Cotton Mather demonstrates how cursory the proceeding was: "There was little occasion to prove the witchcraft, it being evident and notorious to all beholders."

By the fall of 1692, many in the community were growing concerned and started questioning the legitimacy of the court's rulings. When Lady Phips, the governor's wife, came under suspicion, the governor called a halt to the hysteria, banning further arrests and dissolving the Court of Oyer and Terminer. In 1693, he pardoned all who had been charged with witchcraft. Whatever the underlying causes, the unjust persecutions of those considered "different" in the town of Salem reflected a legal system's failure to protect its constituents from hysteria-driven prosecution. Three centuries later, on August 5, 1992, Salem dedicated the Witchcraft Victims' Memorial to honor those accused and executed. In 2001, the Massachusetts legislature passed An Act Relative to the Witchcraft Trial of 1692, further extending an earlier formal exoneration.

SEE ALSO The Trial of Socrates (399 BCE); The Trial of Joan of Arc (1431).

This 1892 lithograph by Joseph E. Baker (1837–1914) dramatically depicts one of the witchcraft trials held in Salem, Massachusetts.

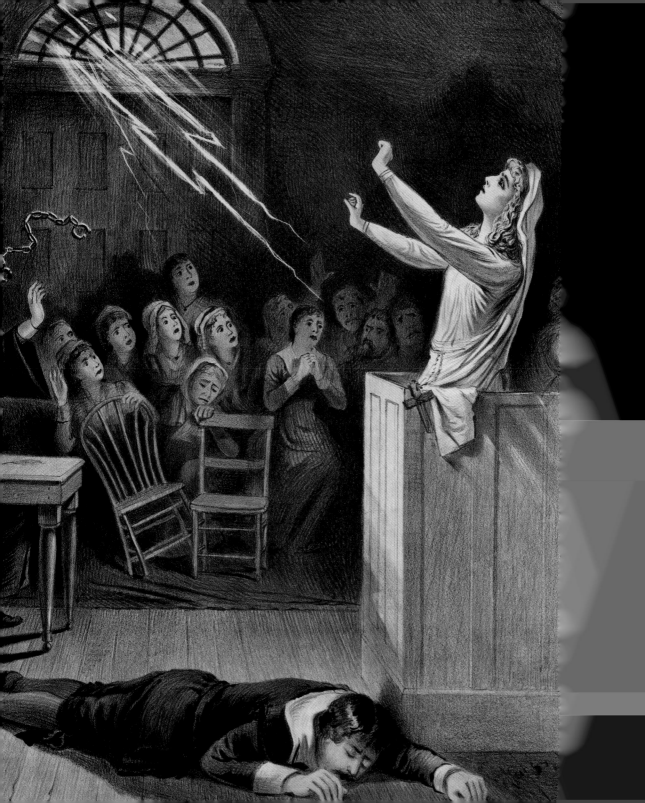

Lapse of the Licensing Act

Johannes Gutenberg (c. 1398–1468), **John Locke** (1632–1704)

Gutenberg's invention of movable type in the mid-fifteenth century presented Europe with a new concern: controlling the printed word. The new technology came to England in 1476 when William Caxton set up a press at Westminster, but it advanced slowly. In 1557, Mary I granted a royal charter—and a consequent monopoly over printing—to the Stationers' Company. In 1586, her sister, Elizabeth I, issued the Star Chamber Decree on printing, which severely restricted printing. Half a century later, in 1637, Charles I issued a second Star Chamber Decree on printing, and additional acts and orders restrained the activity over the years.

In 1662, Parliament passed the Licensing Act, formally "An Act for preventing the frequent Abuses in printing seditious, treasonable and unlicensed Books and Pamphlets, and for regulating of Printing and printing Presses." The statute regulated who could print, import, and sell materials; specified what couldn't be printed; and established the requirements for permissibly printed items. Only the existing master printers of the Stationers' Company and two university printers had the authority to print, and restrictions governed the admission of any new master printers. That monopoly afforded to the Stationers' Company provided the impetus for change.

When the Licensing Act came up for renewal in 1695, opposition in the House of Commons to the Stationers' monopoly, combined with the Stationers' own intransigence, led to a stalemate and thus lapse of the statute. One of the most persuasive voices opposing renewal was that of John Locke, who provided a memorandum to the House of Commons in which he railed against the Stationers' abuse of their monopoly. Ironically the debate never addressed freedom of speech or the press. In his history of free speech, *The First Freedom*, Robert Hargreaves observes that "freedom of the press had crept into England all but incidentally to the elimination of a commercial monopoly." Nevertheless, the "powers of the crown to control the press had gone forever, as had censorship and prior restraints on publication." Soon a profusion of newspapers erupted in London, in particular England's first daily, the *Daily Courant*, in 1702.

SEE ALSO The Star Chamber (c. 1350); The Statute of Anne (1710); America's First Copyright Law (1790); The Berne Convention (1878); The Copyright Act of 1976; Expanded Copyrights (2001).

English scholar and poet John Milton (1608–1674), as painted by Solomon Alexander Hart (1806–1881), wrote the polemical tract Areopagitica *(1644) to protest the Licensing Order of 1643, which ultimately expired in 1695.*

The Statute of Anne

Queen Anne (1665–1714)

As a general rule, the right of ownership in a creative work—otherwise known as the right to copy it or copyright—belongs legally to its author or creator, although he or she can assign, license, or sell that right.

But authors and other creators haven't always enjoyed formal protection of their works. Prior to Gutenberg's movable type and the printing press, monks, acting as scribes for the Church, typically reproduced texts by hand. As Daniel Boorstin, former librarian of Congress, put it: "the age of 'authorship' had not yet arrived." Following the advent of commercial printing in England, Mary I issued a royal charter in 1557 to the Stationers' Company, a long-standing trade guild, granting it a publishing monopoly. The law recognized individual printers of the Stationers' Company, not the authors of the books it printed, as the rights-holders in the works.

It wasn't until 1710 that Parliament enacted the first statute to protect the rights of authors. The Statute of Anne—formally An Act for the Encouragement of Learning by Vesting the Copies of Printed Books in the Authors or Purchasers of such Copies, during the Times therein mentioned—afforded authors significant rights for the first time and importantly granted them the exclusive right to reproduce their works, rather than automatically vesting those rights in printers or booksellers.

These original copyrights weren't unlimited, however. The protections of the statute, limited to books, lasted no more than twenty-eight years (one fourteen-year term that could be renewed), and authors had to donate nine copies of each work to the Royal Library and a number of university libraries, including Oxford and Cambridge. The statute additionally required, prior to publication, the registration of the title of a copyrighted work with the Stationers' Company if the owner wanted to seek penalties from an alleged violator. Eventually the statute also required placement of a notice in each copy of a book that it had been registered with the Stationers' Company.

It's no exaggeration to say that the statute laid the cornerstone for all subsequent copyright law in Great Britain (formed three years prior by the Act of Union, which joined the kingdoms of England and Scotland), America, and the rest of the world.

SEE ALSO America's First Copyright Law (1790); The Berne Convention (1878); The Copyright Act of 1976; Expanded Copyrights (2001).

Under Queen Anne, the Act of Union joined the kingdoms of England and Scotland, and the statute that bears her name established the first copyright law.

The Bubble Act

Financial crises don't belong exclusively to one particular economic or financial system, but they all ultimately derive from human avarice.

England's and then Great Britain's involvement in the War of the Spanish Succession (1701–1714)—a conflict principally among England, the Dutch Republic, and France over succession to the Spanish throne and rights to valuable trade opportunities in the Spanish colonies—had proved costly, and Parliament needed to raise funds. One way it did so was by selling its debt to merchants. In 1711, a group of investors incorporated the South Sea Company as a joint-stock company with transferrable shares, and Parliament issued its charter. In exchange for assuming war debt, the company was promised a trade monopoly on the Spanish colonies in the Caribbean and South America.

When the war ended for Great Britain in 1713, the South Sea Company found little value in its monopoly because Spain retained sovereignty over those colonies. It remains questionable whether trade was the company's true intent because it quickly excelled in exchanging shares of its stock with those holding government debt securities. Its new stockholders more than happily took possession of shares in what they believed was a thriving company.

In 1719, Parliament authorized the company to assume even more national debt, which it did through additional swaps of its own shares, which were quickly appreciating in value due to speculation—stirred up by the company itself, of course—about trading opportunities and successes in the South Seas. They had created the South Sea Bubble, a boom in trading South Sea shares, and the bubble was growing.

At the height of the bubble, Parliament enacted what became known as the Bubble Act of 1720, which required all joint-stock companies to have a royal charter. Historians remain uncertain about whether the intention was to protect unwary investors from stock-trading swindlers or whether the South Sea Company itself finessed the legislation to obstruct investment in other "bubble companies," thereby leaving more money for purchasing South Sea shares. Either way, the ensuing burst of the bubble caused the value of South Sea stock to plummet, resulting in one of the worst market crashes in financial history and a long-term erosion in investor confidence.

SEE ALSO Wall Street Regulation (1933); The Securities Exchange Act (1934); The Sarbanes-Oxley Act (2002); Wall Street Reform (2010).

James Carter's engraving of Edward Matthew Ward's painting of London's Exchange Alley captures the speculative excitement created by the South Sea Bubble.

The Trial of John Peter Zenger

John Peter Zenger (1697–1746), **William Cosby** (1690–1736), **Andrew Hamilton** (c. 1676–1741)

New York Governor William Cosby, a corrupt and greedy thief, controlled the only established New York newspaper, which of course defended him against his detractors. An opposition leader engaged printer John Peter Zenger to publish a new paper in which they could express their outrage. Thus was born the *Weekly Journal*, its first editorials seeking to expose the governor's political corruption. Cosby, determined to shutter the upstart paper, ordered all copies burned. Then he had Zenger arrested and charged with seditious libels for his attacks on the government.

Colonial law viewed defamation as libelous regardless of whether the words were true, and a judge decided what qualified as defamatory. The jury's duty in the matter was to determine whether the defendant published them, which Zenger never denied. Andrew Hamilton, a renowned Philadelphia trial attorney, represented Zenger at trial. Hamilton delivered a masterful, eloquent summation in which he convinced the jurors of their own power to determine the nature of liberty itself.

> The question may . . . in its consequence affect every free man that lives . . . on the main of America. . . . It is the cause of liberty. . . . Every man who prefers freedom to a life of slavery will bless and honor you as men who have baffled the attempt of tyranny, and . . . have laid a noble foundation for securing . . . a right to liberty of both exposing and opposing arbitrary power . . . by speaking and writing truth.

Against all odds, the jury found Zenger not guilty, underscoring the remarkable power of jurors to change the fate of individuals and society at large. The twelve men who freed Zenger laid the foundations for the rights to free speech and a free press that, fifty years later, found formal and lasting expression in the Bill of Rights. Indeed, Gouverneur Morris, one of the Founding Fathers and an author of the Constitution, described the case as "the germ of American freedom, the morning star of that liberty which subsequently revolutionized America."

SEE ALSO The Bill of Rights (1791); Limits on Libel Laws (1964).

British colonists publicly burned copies of John Peter Zenger's Weekly Journal *in 1733.*

The Gin Act of 1751

William Hogarth (1697–1764)

Gin is the anglicized, shortened form of *genever*, the Dutch word for the juniper berry and the spirit's principal flavoring agent. This clear liquor came to London in the late 1600s in the packs of English soldiers returning from war on the continent. It became an immediate hit, and exports from Holland approached ten million gallons by the 1680s. Then, in 1689, England banned the importation of all spirits to encourage their production at home. Incentives for domestic distillers made gin cheap and plentiful, transforming the drinking habits of the kingdom. Gin replaced beer and ale, becoming the most accessible of the few available social pleasures, and the working classes took to it with gusto.

By the 1720s, gin was taking its toll: London witnessed increasing crime, higher death rates, and lower birth rates. Parliament tried unsuccessfully to address the problem with the Gin Acts of 1729, 1733, and 1747, imposing taxes and licensing fees on the dram shops that sold it. Industry pressure and riotous protests from the "drinking poor" led to repeal each time, followed by even more prodigious drinking throughout the city. English engraver William Hogarth famously captured the turmoil in his *Gin Lane* lithograph, which included a sign above a gin cellar that read: "Drunk for a penny / Dead drunk for two pence / Clean straw for nothing."

By 1750, London faced a true epidemic. Parliament's response, the Gin Act of 1751, achieved the success that previous efforts hadn't. In addition to taxes and fees, distillers no longer could sell at the retail level and could supply only licensed buyers, thus eliminating virtually all the small dram shops. For the first time, this law also imposed severe penalties for noncompliance, including whipping, imprisonment, and even deportation. The result was remarkable. By one estimate, national gin consumption decreased from eight million gallons in the early 1750s to fewer than two million gallons by 1760.

Historian M. Dorothy George called the 1751 act a "turning point in the social history of London." Others have disputed whether the act alone diminished idleness, crime, and social unrest, but the act stands as one of the few successful instances of legislation prohibiting alcohol to curb civil strife.

SEE ALSO Prohibition (1918); The Repeal of Prohibition (1933).

William Hogarth's engraving Gin Lane *depicts the ills that befell Londoners from the unrestricted sale of gin in the eighteenth century.*

The Writs of Assistance Case

George II (1683–1760), James Otis Jr. (1725–1783)

More than thirty years before the Fourth Amendment to the Constitution prohibited unreasonable searches and seizures, Americans were objecting to the British government's seemingly unbridled authority to search private property by means of writs of assistance. Resistance to those writs helped lead to the Revolutionary War.

After the French and Indian War—the North American theater of the Seven Years' War—Britain grew concerned with the colonies' commercial trade with other countries. To prevent smuggling, the British turned to writs of assistance, similar to general warrants. Once issued, a writ allowed a customs officer almost entirely free reign to search ships, warehouses, shops, and homes. Writs could be executed repeatedly, and only the life span of the monarch under whom they were issued limited their term. Nor did they contain any particularity requirement, thereby enabling officers to search for any import on which a duty hadn't been paid.

The death of King George II in October 1760 set the stage for the colonists to challenge the writs. The British applied to the Massachusetts Superior Court for renewal of writs set to expire six months after the king's death. Among the writs eligible for renewal was one for Charles Paxton, surveyor of the Port of Boston. A number of merchants retained prominent Boston attorney James Otis Jr. to represent them in opposing the writs. Otis's final argument to the court lasted over four hours. He challenged the writs as inconsistent with the Magna Carta itself, describing them as "the worst instrument of arbitrary power, the most destructive of English liberty and the fundamental principles of law, that ever was found in an English law book."

The court withheld decision until it could obtain an opinion on how the writs functioned in England. After receiving an opinion as to the writs' legality, the court issued new writs ten months later. Although Otis lost the case, he won the favor of John Adams, who had observed his argument and later wrote: "Then and there was the first scene of the first act of opposition to the arbitrary claims of Great Britain. Then and there the child Independence was born."

SEE ALSO The Magna Carta (1215); The U.S. Constitution (1787); The Bill of Rights (1791).

This c. 1750 painting depicts King George II of Great Britain and Ireland, whose death prompted the Writs of Assistance case.

Blackstone's *Commentaries*

William Blackstone (1723–1780)

Although William Blackstone had a varied career—attorney, college administrator, chaired professor at Oxford University, member of Parliament, solicitor general to the queen, judge on the Court of King's Bench and the Court of Common Pleas—his most lasting contribution and the source of his enduring renown lies in his *Commentaries on the Laws of England.*

The Clarendon Press at Oxford published the four volumes of his masterwork from 1765 to 1769. It divided all of English common law into four categories: (i) the rights of persons (domestic relations, master and servant, parent and child, guardian and ward, infants); (ii) the rights of things (the law of property); (iii) private wrongs (torts, including assault, defamation, false imprisonment, wrongful death); and (iv) public wrongs (criminal law). The work derived from Blackstone's earlier lectures at Oxford, which one writer described as "marked as much by the skill of the man of letters as by the learning of the lawyer," adding that "his work became a feature of Oxford life." As Barry Yelverton, Chief Baron of the Irish Court of Exchequer, said of Blackstone: "He it was who first gave to the law the air of a science. He found it a skeleton and clothed it with life, colour, and complexion. He embraced the cold statue and by his touch, it grew into youth, health and beauty." Blackstone's purpose was to write a treatise for both laymen and law students. His success was immediate and sustained.

"In the history of American institutions, no other book—except the Bible—has played so great a role," according to former librarian of Congress Daniel Boorstin. The *Commentaries* quickly became a required resource for practicing lawyers, but Boorstin wrote that "in the first century of American independence, the *Commentaries* were not merely an approach to the study of law; for most lawyers they constituted all there was of the law."

The *Commentaries* played a significant role in laying the foundations of American law throughout the later nineteenth and early twentieth centuries. A new edition for students was published in England after World War II, and the *Commentaries* continue to be cited in the U.S. Supreme Court's opinions (including through its 2013–2014 term).

SEE ALSO The Law School Revolution (1870); Law Reporting and Legal Publishing (1872).

This portrait (c. 1755) of Sir William Blackstone hangs in London's National Portrait Gallery.

The U.S. Constitution

Although most American law isn't founded on the Constitution, America itself is. In the years immediately following independence from Britain—the first group of colonies to do so successfully—the thirteen American states created a governing structure under the Articles of Confederation. Completed in 1777 and ratified by the last of the thirteen states in 1781, the Articles proved ineffectual in establishing a strong national government. However, they did provide a framework for what followed.

In an effort to address the perceived weaknesses of the Articles, Alexander Hamilton and James Madison called in the fall of 1786 for a convention "to render the constitution of government adequate to the exigencies of the Union." Although the convention originally was authorized to propose amendments to the Articles of Confederation, the fifty-five delegates from twelve of the thirteen states almost immediately began to discuss and propose a new constitution.

On September 17, 1787, four months after first convening in Philadelphia, the delegates completed their work, affixing their signatures to a document consisting of four thousand words on four pages of parchment. This document, which soon became the U.S. Constitution, created a new government with separate legislative, executive, and judicial branches. The "Great Compromise" resolved debates over the issue of state representation: In the upper legislative chamber (the Senate), each state had an equal vote through two senators; in the lower chamber (the House of Representatives), each state had apportioned representation based on its population. Importantly, the Constitution provided an amendment process—but with a bar set intentionally high. Since the 1791 ratification of the first ten amendments, known collectively as the Bill of Rights, only seventeen other amendments have taken place.

The Constitution went into force on March 4, 1789, after ratification by eleven of the thirteen states, setting in motion a unique system of dual sovereignty between state and national governments. Constitutional scholar Richard Bernstein writes that its history "in many ways was and is the history of the United States since American national identity was a matter of political choice and political principle that the Constitution both exemplified and codified."

SEE ALSO The Magna Carta (1215); The Bill of Rights (1791); The Power of Judicial Review (1803).

The first of the four pieces of parchment that contain the U.S. Constitution.

We the People

of the United States, in Order to form a more perfect Union, establish Justice, insure domestic Tranquility, provide for the common defence, promote the general Welfare, and secure the Blessings of Liberty to ourselves and our Posterity, do ordain and establish this Constitution for the United States of America.

Article. 1.

Section. 1. All legislative Powers herein granted shall be vested in a Congress of the United States, which shall consist of a Senate and House of Representatives.

Section. 2. The House of Representatives shall be composed of Members chosen every second Year by the People of the several States, and the Electors in each State shall have the Qualifications requisite for Electors of the most numerous Branch of the State Legislature.

No Person shall be a Representative who shall not have attained to the Age of twenty five Years, and been seven Years a Citizen of the United States, and who shall not, when elected, be an Inhabitant of that State in which he shall be chosen.

Representatives and direct Taxes shall be apportioned among the several States which may be included within this Union, according to their respective Numbers, which shall be determined by adding to the whole Number of free Persons, including those bound to Service for a Term of Years, and excluding Indians not taxed, three fifths of all other Persons. The actual Enumeration shall be made within three Years after the first Meeting of the Congress of the United States, and within every subsequent Term of ten Years, in such Manner as they shall by Law direct. The Number of Representatives shall not exceed one for every thirty thousand, but each State shall have at Least one Representative; and until such enumeration shall be made, the State of New Hampshire shall be entitled to chuse three, Massachusetts eight, Rhode-Island and Providence Plantations one, Connecticut five, New-York six, New Jersey four, Pennsylvania eight, Delaware one, Maryland six, Virginia ten, North Carolina five, South Carolina five, and Georgia three.

When vacancies happen in the Representation from any State, the Executive Authority thereof shall issue Writs of Election to fill such Vacancies.

The House of Representatives shall chuse their Speaker and other Officers; and shall have the sole Power of Impeachment.

Section. 3. The Senate of the United States shall be composed of two Senators from each State, chosen by the Legislature thereof, for six Years; and each Senator shall have one Vote.

Immediately after they shall be assembled in Consequence of the first Election, they shall be divided as equally as may be into three Classes. The Seats of the Senators of the first Class shall be vacated at the Expiration of the second Year, of the second Class at the Expiration of the fourth Year, and of the third Class at the Expiration of the sixth Year, so that one third may be chosen every second Year; and if Vacancies happen by Resignation, or otherwise, during the Recess of the Legislature of any State, the Executive thereof may make temporary Appointments until the next Meeting of the Legislature, which shall then fill such Vacancies.

No Person shall be a Senator who shall not have attained to the Age of thirty Years, and been nine Years a Citizen of the United States, and who shall not, when elected, be an Inhabitant of that State for which he shall be chosen.

The Vice President of the United States shall be President of the Senate, but shall have no Vote, unless they be equally divided.

The Senate shall chuse their other Officers, and also a President pro tempore, in the Absence of the Vice President, or when he shall exercise the Office of President of the United States.

The Senate shall have the sole Power to try all Impeachments. When sitting for that Purpose, they shall be on Oath or Affirmation. When the President of the United States is tried, the Chief Justice shall preside: And no Person shall be convicted without the Concurrence of two thirds of the Members present.

Judgment in Cases of Impeachment shall not extend further than to removal from Office, and disqualification to hold and enjoy any Office of honor, Trust or Profit under the United States: but the Party convicted shall nevertheless be liable and subject to Indictment, Trial, Judgment and Punishment, according to Law.

Section. 4. The Times, Places and Manner of holding Elections for Senators and Representatives, shall be prescribed in each State by the Legislature thereof; but the Congress may at any time by Law make or alter such Regulations, except as to the Places of chusing Senators.

The Congress shall assemble at least once in every Year, and such Meeting shall be on the first Monday in December, unless they shall by Law appoint a different Day.

Section. 5. Each House shall be the Judge of the Elections, Returns and Qualifications of its own Members, and a Majority of each shall constitute a Quorum to do Business; but a smaller Number may adjourn from day to day, and may be authorized to compel the Attendance of absent Members, in such Manner, and under such Penalties as each House may provide.

Each House may determine the Rules of its Proceedings, punish its Members for disorderly Behaviour, and, with the Concurrence of two thirds, expel a Member.

Each House shall keep a Journal of its Proceedings, and from time to time publish the same, excepting such Parts as may in their Judgment require Secrecy; and the Yeas and Nays of the Members of either House on any question shall, at the Desire of one fifth of those Present, be entered on the Journal.

Neither House, during the Session of Congress, shall, without the Consent of the other, adjourn for more than three days, nor to any other Place than that in which the two Houses shall be sitting.

Section. 6. The Senators and Representatives shall receive a Compensation for their Services, to be ascertained by Law, and paid out of the Treasury of the United States. They shall in all Cases, except Treason, Felony and Breach of the Peace, be privileged from Arrest during their Attendance at the Session of their respective Houses, and in going to and returning from the same; and for any Speech or Debate in either House, they shall not be questioned in any other Place.

No Senator or Representative shall, during the Time for which he was elected, be appointed to any civil Office under the Authority of the United States, which shall have been created, or the Emoluments whereof shall have been increased during such time; and no Person holding any Office under the United States, shall be a Member of either House during his Continuance in Office.

Section. 7. All Bills for raising Revenue shall originate in the House of Representatives; but the Senate may propose or concur with Amendments as on other Bills. Every Bill which shall have passed the House of Representatives and the Senate, shall, before it become a Law, be presented to the President of the

The Judiciary Act of 1789

George Washington (1731–1799)

The American legal system rests on a foundation of common law, as opposed to civil law, meaning that its principles derive from precedents of cases previously decided. Behind those precedents sit the judges who author them and the courts in which those judges rule. But at the nation's founding, federal courts had to be established and judges appointed.

During the 1787 Constitutional Convention in Philadelphia, delegates agreed on the need for a national judiciary, but they lacked consensus on its form. As Alexander Hamilton wrote in *The Federalist Papers*, "Laws are a dead letter without courts to expound and define their true meaning and operation." The Constitution created the outline of a federal court system in Article III but delegated to the new Congress the task of shaping it: "The judicial Power of the United States, shall be vested in one supreme Court, and in such inferior Courts as the Congress may from time to time ordain and establish." The jurisdiction of the courts extended "to all Cases . . . arising under this Constitution, [and] the Laws of the United States."

Congress acted quickly. The first bill introduced in the new Senate, An Act to Establish the Federal Courts of the United States, today is known as the Judiciary Act of 1789. When President Washington signed it into law, it established the three-tiered federal court system that exists (in slightly different form) today: the Supreme Court, the circuit courts of appeals, and the district courts.

The jurisdiction of the district courts conformed to state boundaries, still the case today. The three original circuit courts each covered a wider geographic area. These courts consisted not of separate circuit judges but a single district court judge and two Supreme Court justices who traveled to hear cases by "riding circuit." The circuit courts also served as trial courts for cases between citizens of different states involving disputes of more than $500. The Act confirmed the Supreme Court's constitutional jurisdiction and also authorized it to hear appeals from the highest court in each state in cases raising questions of federal or constitutional law.

SEE ALSO The U.S. Constitution (1787); The Bill of Rights (1791); The Power of Judicial Review (1803).

Inside the East Courtroom of the Howard M. Metzenbaum U.S. Courthouse in Cleveland, Ohio—one of the federal courts created as a result of the Judiciary Act.

The Declaration of the Rights of Man

Benjamin Franklin (1706–1790), **Thomas Jefferson** (1743–1826), **Gilbert du Motier, marquis de Lafayette** (1757–1834)

In August 1789, the French National Assembly adopted the Declaration of the Rights of Man and of the Citizen, which served as the preamble to a new French constitution and helped define the rights of people in relation to the state. The first and most important clause reads: "Men are born and remain free and equal in rights," a core principle that inspired the burgeoning French Revolution. Other Articles provided for freedom of expression, freedom of religious opinions, equality under the law, a presumption of innocence prior to conviction, and an "inviolable and sacred" right to one's property.

Meanwhile, across the Atlantic, the Federalists, who had promised to amend America's nascent Constitution to include protections of civil liberties, were drafting the ten amendments that would become America's Bill of Rights in 1791. A remarkable similarity exists between the Declaration and the Bill of Rights in both content and language. Differing explanations account for which document influenced the other, but all agree that the writings of many Enlightenment philosophers—including Rousseau, Montesquieu, Spinoza, Locke, and Voltaire—influenced both documents. The marquis de Lafayette discussed his draft of the Declaration with Thomas Jefferson.

Both legal instruments find common heritage in the provisions of a number of state constitutions—with their own bills of rights—already in place in the American colonies. Benjamin Franklin, envoy and then minister to France from 1776 to 1785, brought these constitutions to France, where they were translated and circulated widely.

As part of a 1989 bicentennial commemoration of both the Declaration and the Bill of Rights—which marked what Senator Claiborne Pell called the "opening chapter of the French Revolution and the closing chapter of the American Revolution"—historian Crane Brinton noted the Declaration's enduring importance as "the inspiration of most nineteenth-century bills of rights in Europe." It served as a source document for bills of rights in Prussia and the Weimar Republic as well as the Soviet Declaration of the Rights of Workers and Exploited Peoples, and, like the American Bill of Rights, it remains in effect for the French Republic today.

SEE ALSO The U.S. Constitution (1787); The Bill of Rights (1791); Universal Declaration of Human Rights (1948).

The seventeen articles of the Declaration of the Rights of Man and of the Citizen played an instrumental role in defining the universal, equal rights of free citizens.

DÉCLARATION
DES DROITS DE L'HOMME
ET DU CITOYEN
Décretés par l'Assemblée Nationale dans les séances des 20, 21
23, 24 et 26 août 1789, acceptés par le Roi

PRÉAMBULE

LES représentans du peuple François, constitués en assemblée nationale, considérant que l'ignorance, l'oubli ou le mépris des droits de l'homme sont les seules causes des malheurs publics et de la corruption des gouvernemens ont résolu d'exposer dans une déclaration solemnelle, les droits naturels, inaliénables et sacrés de l'homme: afin que cette décla ration, constamment présente à tous les membres du corps social, leur rappelle sans cesse leurs droits et leurs devoirs, afin que les actes du pouvoir législatif et ceux du pouvoir exé cutif, pouvant être à chaque instant comparés avec le but de toute institution politique, en soient plus respectés: afin que les reclamations des citoyens, fondées désormais sur des princi pes simples et incontestables, tournent toujours au maintien de la constitution et du bonheur de tous.

EN conséquence, l'assemblée nationale reconnoit et déclare, en présence et sous les auspices de l'Etre suprême les droits suivans de l'homme et du citoyen.

ARTICLE PREMIER

LES hommes naissent et demeurent libres et égaux en droits, les distinctions sociales ne peuvent être fondées que sur l'utilité commune.

II.

LE but de toute association politique est la conservation des droits naturels et imprescriptibles de l'homme: ces droits sont la liberté, la propriété, la sureté, et la résistance à l'oppression.

III.

LE principe de toute souveraineté réside essentiellement dans la nation, nul corps, nul individu ne peut exercer d'autorité qui n'en émane expressément.

IV.

LA liberté consiste à pouvoir faire tout ce qui ne nuit pas à autrui Ainsi, l'exercice des droits naturels de chaque homme, n'a de bor nes que celles qui assurent aux autres membres de la société la jouissance de ces mêmes droits; ces bornes ne peuvent être déterminées que par la loi.

V.

LA loi n'a le droit de défendre que les actions nuisibles à la société. Tout ce qui n'est pas défendu par la loi ne peut être empêché, et nul ne peut être contraint à faire ce qu'elle n'or donne pas.

VI.

LA loi est l'expression de la volonté générale; tous les citoyens ont droit de concourir personnellement, ou par leurs représentans, à sa formation; elle doit être la même pour tous, soit qu'elle protege, soit qu'elle punisse, Tous les cito yens étant égaux à ses yeux, sont également admissibles à toutes dignités, places et emplois publics, selon leur capacité, et sans autres distinction que celles de leurs vertus et de leurs talens

VII.

NUL homme ne peut être accusé, arreté, ni détenu que dans les cas déterminés par la loi, et selon les formes qu'elle a prescrites, ceux qui solli citent, expédient, exécutent ou font exécuter des ordres ar bitraires, doivent être punis; mais tout citoyen appelé ou saisi en vertu de la loi, doit obéir à l'instant, il se rend coupable par la résistance.

VIII.

LA loi ne doit établir que des peines strictement et évidem ment nécessaire, et nul ne peut être puni qu'en vertu d'une loi établie et promulguée antérieurement au délit, et légale ment appliquée.

IX.

TOUT homme étant présumé innocent jusqu'à ce qu'il ait été déclaré coupable, s'il est jugé indispensable de l'arrêter, toute rigueur qui ne serait pas nécessaire pour s'assurer de sa personne doit être sévèrement réprimée par la loi.

X.

NUL ne doit être inquieté pour ses opinions, mêmes religi euses pourvu que leur manifestation ne trouble pas l'ordre public établi par la loi.

XI.

LA libre communication des pensées et des opinions est un des droits les plus precieux de l'homme; tout citoyen peut donc parler écrire, imprimer librement; sauf à ré pondre de l'abus de cette liberté dans les cas déterminés par la loi.

XII.

LA garantie des droits de l'homme et du citoyen nécessite une force publique; cette force est donc instituée pour l'avan tage de tous, et non pour l'utilité particuliere de ceux a qui elle est confiée.

XIII.

POUR l'entretien de la force publique, et pour les dépenses d'administration, une contribution commune est indispen sable; elle doit être également répartie entre les citoyens en raison de leurs facultés.

XIV.

LES citoyens ont le droit de constater par eux même ou par leurs représentans, la nécessité de la contribution pub lique, de la consentir librement, d'en suivre l'emploi, et d'en déterminer la quotité, l'assiette, le recouvrement et la durée.

XV.

LA société a le droit de demander compte à tout agent public de son administration.

XVI.

TOUTE société, dans laquelle la garantie des droits n'est pas assurée, ni la séparation des pouvoirs déterminée, n'a point de constitution.

XVII.

LES propriétés étant un droit inviolable et sacré, nul ne peut en être privé, si ce n'est lorsque la nécessité publique, légalement constatée, l'exige evidemment, et sous la condi tion d'une juste et préalable indemnité.

AUX REPRÉSENTANS DU PEUPLE FRANÇOIS

America's First Copyright Law

George Washington (1732–1799)

In America, the right to copyright originates in the Constitution itself, though its lineage traces back to Britain's 1710 Statute of Anne.

During the latter half of the eighteenth century, several of the colonies enacted copyright laws patterned after the Statute of Anne. During the Constitutional Convention in 1787, delegates considered a handful of proposals addressing the same issue. They enshrined the clause on which they ultimately agreed in Article I, Sec. 8, Cl. 8 of the U.S. Constitution: "The Congress shall have Power . . . To promote the Progress of Science and useful Arts, by securing for limited Times to Authors and Inventors the exclusive Right to their respective Writings and Discoveries."

Enactment of statutory copyright protection became an important priority for President Washington. Delivering his State of the Union Address to the second session of America's First Congress in January 1790, he remarked that "nothing . . . can better deserve your patronage than the promotion of science and literature." The House and Senate both responded favorably, agreeing with the president's sentiment that "the promotion of science and literature will contribute to the security of a free Government" and committing not to "lose sight of objects so worthy of our regard."

The country's first national copyright law followed: An Act for the Encouragement of Learning, which paralleled the Statute of Anne by granting authors the exclusive right to "print, reprint, publish or vend" their works for up to twenty-eight years. President Washington signed it into law on May 31, 1790. Nine days later, the nation's first copyrighted work, *The Philadelphia Spelling Book* by John Barry, was registered with the clerk's office for the U.S. District Court in Pennsylvania in accordance with statutory requirements.

SEE ALSO The Statute of Anne (1710); The Berne Convention (1878); The Copyright Act of 1976; Expanded Copyrights (2001).

Just nine days after enactment of America's first copyright law, John Barry of Philadelphia received the first copyright of the United States on his Philadelphia Spelling Book.

THE

PHILADELPHIA
SPELLING BOOK,

ARRANGED UPON A PLAN ENTIRELY NEW,

ADAPTED TO THE CAPACITIES OF CHILDREN,

AND DESIGNED

AS AN IMMEDIATE IMPROVEMENT IN

SPELLING AND READING

THE

ENGLISH LANGUAGE.

The whole being recommended by several eminent Teachers, as the moſt uſeful performance
to expedite the inſtruction of youth.

By JOHN BARRY, *Maſter of the Free
School of the Proteſtant Epiſcopal Church.*

PHILADELPHIA:

PRINTED BY *JOSEPH JAMES*

M,DCC,XC.

The Bill of Rights

Thomas Jefferson (1743–1826), James Madison (1751–1836)

The Constitution proper focuses on the organization and structure of the government but makes scant provision for individuals, saying little about personal liberties or equality. In fact, the word "equal" appears in the Constitution only in regard to each state's number of senators.

The absence of a bill of rights caused one of the largest stumbling blocks that Constitutional Convention delegates faced. Among the many compromises essential in forging and ratifying the Constitution was agreement that individual rights and liberties find express protection. The Federalists argued that a bill of rights was unnecessary because the government they wanted to create would have limited powers and not find itself in a position to violate citizens' rights. They also viewed such protections as redundant in light of rights provisions already extant in states' constitutions. Thomas Jefferson, then serving as ambassador to France, expressed dismay over the lack of a bill of rights, which would provide "fetters against doing evil, which no honest government should decline."

In drafting the Bill of Rights during the First Congress, James Madison largely relied on the Virginia Constitution's Declaration of Rights, itself drawn from the Magna Carta and the English Bill of Rights of 1689 (which followed the Glorious Revolution of 1688 and by which Parliament replaced James II in favor of his daughter Mary II and her husband, William III). The states quickly ratified the ten amendments that Madison crafted, which embody what's often called the "popular Constitution," or subjects of everyday attention and discourse. For example: freedom of speech and religion (First Amendment); gun control and the right to bear arms (Second); illegal searches and seizures (Fourth); due process of law (Fifth); a criminal defendant's right to counsel (Sixth); the right to a jury trial (Seventh); cruel and unusual punishment and the death penalty (Eighth).

Supreme Court Justice Lewis F. Powell Jr. described the Bill of Rights as "one of the greatest documents of western Civilization," containing "broadly-worded, forward-looking guarantees" that became "more than a symbol of American freedom; it became a powerful instrument in achieving and preserving it."

SEE ALSO The Magna Carta (1215); The U.S. Constitution (1787); The Equal Rights Amendment (1972).

The Bill of Rights is on display in the Rotunda for the Charters of Freedom in the National Archives and Records Administration building in Washington, D.C.

Congress of the United States,

begun and held at the City of New-York, on

Wednesday the fourth of March, one thousand seven hundred and eighty-nine.

THE Conventions of a number of the States, having at the time of their adopting the Constitution, expressed a desire, in order to prevent misconstruction or abuse of its powers, that further declaratory and restrictive clauses should be added: And as extending the ground of public confidence in the Government, will best ensure the beneficent ends of its institution.

RESOLVED by the Senate and House of Representatives of the United States of America, in Congress assembled, two thirds of both Houses concurring, that the following Articles be proposed to the Legislatures of the several States, as amendments to the Constitution of the United States, all, or any of which Articles, when ratified by three fourths of the said Legislatures, to be valid to all intents and purposes, as part of the said Constitution; viz.

ARTICLES in addition to, and Amendment of the Constitution of the United States of America, proposed by Congress, and ratified by the several States, pursuant to the fifth Article of the original Constitution.

first.   After the first enumeration required by the first Article of the Constitution, there shall be one Representative for every thirty thousand, until the number shall amount to one hundred, after which, the proportion shall be so regulated by Congress, that there shall be not less than one hundred Representatives, nor less than one Representative for every forty thousand persons, until the number of Representatives shall amount to two hundred, after which the proportion shall be so regulated by Congress, that there shall not be less than two hundred Representatives, nor more than one Representative for every fifty thousand persons.

second.   No law, varying the compensation for the services of the Senators and Representatives, shall take effect, until an election of Representatives shall have intervened.

third.   Congress shall make no law respecting an establishment of religion, or prohibiting the free exercise thereof; or abridging the freedom of speech, or of the press; or the right of the people peaceably to assemble, and to petition the Government for a redress of grievances.

fourth.   A well regulated Militia, being necessary to the security of a free State, the right of the people to keep and bear arms, shall not be infringed.

fifth.   No Soldier shall, in time of peace be quartered in any house, without the consent of the Owner, nor in time of war, but in a manner to be prescribed by law.

sixth.   The right of the people to be secure in their persons, houses, papers, and effects, against unreasonable searches and seizures, shall not be violated, and no Warrants shall issue, but upon probable cause, supported by oath or affirmation, and particularly describing the place to be searched, and the persons or things to be seized.

seventh.   No person shall be held to answer for a capital, or otherwise infamous crime, unless on a presentment or indictment of a Grand Jury, except in cases arising in the land or naval forces, or in the Militia, when in actual service in time of War or public danger; nor shall any person be subject for the same offence to be twice put in jeopardy of life or limb; nor shall be compelled in any criminal case to be a witness against himself, nor be deprived of life, liberty, or property, without due process of law; nor shall private property be taken for public use, without just compensation.

eighth.   In all criminal prosecutions, the accused shall enjoy the right to a speedy and public trial, by an impartial jury of the State and district wherein the crime shall have been committed, which district shall have been previously ascertained by law, and to be informed of the nature and cause of the accusation; to be confronted with the witnesses against him; to have compulsory process for obtaining witnesses in his favor, and to have the assistance of counsel for his defence.

the ninth.   In suits at common law, where the value in controversy shall exceed twenty dollars, the right of trial by jury shall be preserved, and no fact tried by a jury, shall be otherwise re-examined in any Court of the United States, than according to the rules of the common law.

tenth.   Excessive bail shall not be required, nor excessive fines imposed, nor cruel and unusual punishments inflicted.

eleventh.   The enumeration in the Constitution, of certain rights, shall not be construed to deny or disparage others retained by the people.

twelfth.   The powers not delegated to the United States by the Constitution, nor prohibited by it to the States, are reserved to the States respectively, or to the people.

Frederick Augustus Muhlenberg, Speaker of the House of Representatives.

John Adams, Vice President of the United States, and President of the Senate.

ATTEST,

John Beckley, Clerk of the House of Representatives.

Sam. A. Otis, Secretary of the Senate.

The Coinage Act of 1792

Alexander Hamilton (c. 1755–1804), **George Washington** (1732–1799)

The coins you used for your last vending machine purchase, dropped into a parking meter, or tossed into the Trevi Fountain in Rome owe their existence to the Coinage Act of 1792.

For nearly two thousand years in England, coins had been the dominant form of currency, but early colonists in America didn't have their own coins or the metal with which to make them. Instead, they relied on foreign coins and barter, including the use of wampum (beads) for trade in New England and tobacco in the South. The 1777 Articles of Confederation authorized the individual states as well as Congress to coin money, although they reserved to Congress the power to regulate its value. A decade later the Constitution vested in Congress the exclusive power to coin money.

In 1789, after formation of the new government and his inauguration, President Washington appointed Alexander Hamilton as the first secretary of the Treasury. In early 1791, he outlined to Congress the creation of a mint and a national system of coinage using the dollar unit, already widely in use in the states, as a measure of value. Congress accepted most of Hamilton's recommendations, and President Washington signed the resolution on April 2, 1792, passing the nation's first coinage act.

The act provided that "the money of account of the United States shall be expressed in dollars, dismes or tenths, cents or hundredths" using gold, silver, and copper. The Senate had pushed that the minted coins bear the image of President Washington, but the House as well as Washington himself found that idea too reminiscent of British coins bearing the face of a monarch. Congress instead chose to display Liberty personified on one side and the American eagle, already incorporated into the Great Seal of the United States, on the other. The eagle still appears on quarters, half dollars, and dollar coins, but Liberty yielded her place on the Roosevelt dime in 1946 in favor of her torch.

SEE ALSO The Triple Assessment (Income Tax) (1798); Congressional Right to Income Tax (1909); The Federal Reserve Act (1913).

The 1792 Coinage Act authorized the production of the Half Eagle gold coin, the first gold coin minted by the United States. It has a face value of five dollars and circulated between 1795 and 1929.

The Triple Assessment (Income Tax)

William Pitt the Younger (1759–1806)

Supreme Court Justice Oliver Wendell Holmes Jr. once wrote: "Taxes are what we pay for civilized society." But how society imposes taxes—who pays what in what proportion—has always posed a challenge.

Prior to the development of money, taxes were paid in-kind with labor, grain, cattle, or the like. Thereafter, assessments on land—the forerunner to property taxes—as well as tolls and customs duties on imports and exports became the principal sources of revenue for a state or its ruler. Not until 1798 did taxation of income become the subject of a government's affection.

During most of the eighteenth century, Great Britain relied on taxation of expenditures for revenue. Akin to a modern-day sales tax, the British system assessed what legal scholars Bernhard Grossfeld and James Bryce call "visible signs of wealth, be it carriages, servants, horses, dogs, clerks, watches, silverware, or windows." As the century's end neared, fighting Napoléon Bonaparte's armies drained Britain's treasury. Prime Minister William Pitt the Younger proposed legislation that became the Aid and Contribution Act of 1798. Known as the Triple Assessment, it required payment of thrice the amount a subject had paid in expenditure taxes in the preceding year.

The Triple Assessment gave way almost immediately to Pitt's proposal "that a general tax shall be imposed upon all the leading branches of income." In January 1799, the first income tax statute in history called for a progressive tax rate on annual income above £60, beginning at less than 1 percent and increasing to 10 percent on income over £200. Unsurprisingly, Pitt's tax was poorly received. Among other descriptions, it was called "a monstrous proposition" and "an indiscriminate rapine." Grossfeld and Bryce write that "from the very beginning . . . it had been accepted by the public with disdain and distrust."

Although Pitt's tax was repealed in 1802, the die had been cast. The following year, Parliament enacted a new income tax, which became the foundation for Britain's future tax policy as well as those that would be adopted thereafter in Germany and America.

SEE ALSO Congressional Power to Tax Income (1909); The Federal Reserve Act (1913).

An 1806 portrait of William Pitt the Younger, prime minister of Britain, who proposed legislation in 1798 to tax English citizens "upon all the leading branches of income," which became the first income tax in history.

The Power of Judicial Review

John Adams (1735–1826), **William Marbury** (1762–1835), **Thomas Jefferson** (1743–1826), **James Madison** (1751–1836), **John Marshall** (1755–1835)

Marbury v. Madison remains one of the most important decisions that the U.S. Supreme Court ever rendered. In it, the Court established its unequivocal power of judicial review over acts of Congress—nothing less than the power to determine whether congressional legislation comports with the Constitution.

After losing the 1800 presidential election to Thomas Jefferson, but before his term officially ended, President John Adams hurriedly worked to pack the courts with Federalist judges and appointed several justices of the peace, including William Marbury. The Senate duly confirmed those appointments on Adams's last day in office, allowing Adams to sign and deliver the official Commissions of Appointment that evening, earning them the sobriquet of "midnight judges." Marbury's commission and three others', however, remained undelivered, so President Jefferson refused to appoint them.

Marbury sought a writ of mandamus—a court order directing a public official to perform or refrain from performing a given act—from the Supreme Court ordering James Madison, Jefferson's secretary of State, to deliver the commissions.

In announcing the Court's unanimous opinion, Marshall noted first that Marbury had a legal right to his commission. The Senate had confirmed him; the president then signed his commission, completing the appointment. That last act necessarily made Marbury a judge; to rule otherwise implied a presidential power over constitutionally independent judges. Marshall found inescapable the conclusion that Marbury was entitled to a remedy. The only question was whether the remedy could be sought directly in the Supreme Court. The Judiciary Act of 1789 appeared to permit it, but Marshall ruled that statute unconstitutional; the Supreme Court didn't have the constitutional authority to function as a trial court except in cases involving states or ambassadors, and Congress couldn't expand the Court's original jurisdiction.

The decision established the Supreme Court's power of judicial review over congressional legislation as an immutable constitutional principle.

SEE ALSO The U.S. Constitution (1787); The Judiciary Act of 1789; The Supremacy of Federal Courts (1821).

John Vanderlyn painted this 1816 portrait of James Madison, President Jefferson's secretary of State and the fourth president of the United States.

The Napoleonic Code

Napoléon Bonaparte (1769–1821)

It's impossible to minimize the significance of the *Code Napoléon*. It represents Bonaparte's greatest legacy and has influenced the legal codes of virtually all of Western Europe as well as large parts of Central and South America.

Prior to the French Revolution, the laws of France formed a patchwork quilt. At least since the sixteenth century the dictates of Roman law governed life in the South, while the North relied upon traditional, Germanic-influenced customary law, a remnant of its Frankish past. Canon law continued to dominate the sphere of family and marriage, and local customs and feudal decrees continued their influence as well. For at least two centuries, leading Frenchmen had endeavored to bring order through codification to the jumble of laws—unsuccessfully.

When Bonaparte seized power in 1799, he recognized the need for codification and appointed a commission of the ablest men in the country without regard to political affiliation or other considerations. He insisted upon an "expeditious" draft, which was presented after just three months. It then went to the judiciary for review. After additional reviews in the Council of State, Bonaparte himself participated in revisions, a critic describing his contributions as "always stamped with the mark of genius." After legislative debate, the National Legislature approved and promulgated the code on March 21, 1804.

At the heart of the Napoleonic Code lie notions of equality and justice. It eliminated the feudal rule of primogeniture, nobility by birth, and privileges of class. No longer could the Church interfere in civil institutions. Individual freedom and the sanctity of private property became cardinal principles. The Code came to be venerated across the world for its clarity, concision, and simplicity. It remains the basis for modern French law, and, as a testament to its strength and endurance, parts of it remain in effect in Louisiana, which Bonaparte sold to America the year *before* the Code went into effect.

In the last year of his life, exiled to the island of St. Helena in the South Atlantic, Bonaparte reflected: "My glory is not to have won forty battles, for Waterloo's defeat will destroy the memory of as many victories. But what nothing will destroy, what will live eternally, is my Civil Code."

SEE ALSO The Justinian Code (529); The Declaration of the Rights of Man (1789).

Napoléon Crossing the Alps *(1801) by Jacques-Louis David.*

The Superiority of Possession

Pierson v. Post (1805), *Popov v. Hayashi* (2002)

In his 1690 *Second Treatise of Civil Government*, philosopher John Locke noted that "the great and chief end, therefore, of men's uniting into commonwealths, and putting themselves under government, is the preservation of their property," but it's a court decision from more than a century later that marks the relevant boundaries of property law.

In the summer of 1800, Southampton, New York, resident Ludowick Post was foxhunting. He claimed that, while he was in close pursuit of a fox along the beach, Jesse Pierson, another Southamptonian, killed the fox and stole it. Pierson told a different version: He saw a fox run from the beach to a nearby well and killed it there. The differing locations were significant. Post claimed that the beach represented "wild, uninhabited, and unpossessed land," which entitled him to the fox. By Pierson's version, he shot the fox on common land shared by his and other local farming families.

Post successfully sued Pierson for the value of the fox, but an appellate court reversed the ruling. The court assumed Post's version of events—that the fox was shot on uninhabited, unpossessed ground—and announced a bright-line rule "for the sake of certainty, and preserving peace and order in society." Ownership required possession, and "mere pursuit gave Post no legal right to the fox." Courts have used a variant of the *Pierson* holding, in which ultimate physical possession matters less than when possession took place. Thus, as a general rule, the first to possess property acquires presumptively superior title to it.

But questions inevitably arise about the meaning of possession: Does it require total dominion and control, or can it be achieved through intent to take control coupled with significant, active efforts to establish that control? A fascinating exposition of this issue occurred in the 2002 California Superior Court decision of *Popov v. Hayashi*, in which two baseball fans claimed possession of the Barry Bonds asterisked, record-breaking home run ball. One fan caught the ball but, before securing it, the surging crowd knocked it from his glove to the ground, where another fan claimed it.

SEE ALSO Public Purpose and Eminent Domain (2005).

A Fox Hunt (c. 1735) by English painter John Wootton.

The Supremacy of Federal Law

McCulloch v. Maryland, John Marshall (1755–1835)

In 1816, Congress chartered the Second Bank of the United States. When officers of the Baltimore branch made large loans to themselves without sufficient security, investors lost millions of dollars. Responding to this and other banking misdeeds, Maryland enacted legislation that essentially imposed a tax on foreign banks operating in the state.

In February 1818, the state successfully sued James W. McCulloch, the bank's cashier, for failure to pay the required taxes. In a unanimous opinion authored by Chief Justice John Marshall, the U.S. Supreme Court reversed the Maryland courts' findings against McCulloch, issuing what became one of the Court's landmark decisions and establishing two fundamental principles.

First, it found that the Constitution's failure to authorize Congress to create corporations or national banks didn't mean that Congress lacked that power. Chief Justice Marshall located that power in the necessary-and-proper clause of Article I, which granted Congress, in addition to its enumerated powers, authority to make "all laws which shall be necessary and proper for carrying into execution the foregoing powers." The only limitation: Congress couldn't invoke these implied powers to legislate in areas unrelated to its enumerated powers.

Second, the Court rejected the right of states to impose taxes on federal institutions like the Second Bank. In Chief Justice Marshall's oft-quoted words, "The power to tax involves the power to destroy." Were Maryland legislators permitted to "tax one instrument, employed by the government in the execution of its powers," he wrote, "they may tax any and every other instrument . . . which would defeat all the ends of government. This was not intended by the American people. They did not design to make their government dependent on the states."

Legal historian Maxwell Bloomfield writes that *McCulloch v. Maryland* "later played an essential role in redefining the scope of national power and justifying the emergence of the modern welfare state," noting that it was invoked "to sustain the regulatory programs of the New Deal" and to sustain "decisions validating the Voting Rights Act of 1965 and the public accommodations provisions of the 1964 Civil Rights Act."

SEE ALSO The Power of Judicial Review (1803); Congressional Regulation of Commerce (1824); The Civil Rights Act of 1964; The Voting Rights Act (1965).

The Old Supreme Court Chamber, where Chief Justice John Marshall presided. The North Wing is pictured here in 1800.

The Supremacy of Federal Courts

Cohens v. Virginia, John Marshall (1755–1835)

In a federalist political system, which recognizes the dual sovereignty of both federal and state governments, disagreements can arise as to which sovereign is "supreme" in certain areas of policy and law. The U.S. Supreme Court first addressed that issue in *McCulloch v. Maryland*. Some states, however, repudiated *McCulloch* as antithetical to states' rights. Two years later, the Supreme Court decided a related issue: Who was to be final arbiter of disputes over the Constitution, federal laws, and the powers of the federal government?

After Congress authorized the District of Columbia to sell Grand National Lottery tickets, brothers Mendes and Philip Cohen attempted to sell tickets for that lottery in their home state of Virginia. Despite arguing that they couldn't be prosecuted for selling lottery tickets authorized under federal law, the Cohens were convicted of violating a Virginia law proscribing the sale of out-of-state lottery tickets. Their appeal provided Chief Justice Marshall and a unanimous Supreme Court the opportunity to reaffirm and extend the principles of federal supremacy.

Marshall rejected Virginia's argument that this dispute concerned a state and one of its citizens and therefore lay beyond the Supreme Court's jurisdiction. He also rejected Virginia's assertion of sovereign immunity under the Constitution's Eleventh Amendment because the case didn't involve "a suit against a state." Historian Richard Ellis describes Marshall's decision as "a particularly eloquent restatement and elaboration of the basic principles of constitutional nationalism." The Constitution, Marshall wrote, "marks, with lines too strong to be mistaken, the characteristic distinction between the government of the Union and those of the states. The general government, though limited as to its objects, is supreme with respect to those objects."

Despite its importance in solidifying principles of federalism and judicial review, the decision didn't represent a victory for the Cohens. The Court affirmed their convictions after finding that in creating the Grand National Lottery, Congress didn't intend to create a true national lottery but only a local one. Thus, the convictions under Virginia law didn't contravene federal law.

SEE ALSO The Power of Judicial Review (1803); The Supremacy of Federal Law (1819); Congressional Regulation of Commerce (1824).

Chief Justice John Marshall—one of the most important figures in the history of the judiciary—depicted in an 1862 engraving by Alonzo Chappel.

Congressional Regulation of Commerce

Gibbons v. Ogden, **Thomas Gibbons** (1757–1826), **Aaron Ogden** (1756–1839), **John Marshall** (1755–1835)

In the summer of 1787, delegates meeting in Philadelphia for the Constitutional Convention encountered one of the new steamboats operating along the Delaware River. But a quarter of a century later another steamboat would cross paths with a product of that Philadelphia summer.

Article I, Section 8 of the Constitution declares that "Congress shall have the Power . . . To regulate Commerce with foreign Nations, and among the several states." The genesis of this commerce clause lay in the colonists' experience under the Articles of Confederation. Alexander Hamilton—who wrote in "Federalist No. 22" of "animosity and discord" stemming from the "interfering and unneighborly regulations of some States"— believed that the commerce clause would remove "obstacles to a uniformity of measure."

In 1808, the New York legislature granted an exclusive statutory license to Robert Livingston and Robert Fulton to navigate New York's waterways "with boats moved by fire or steam." In 1817, Aaron Ogden, who had purchased those rights from Fulton and Livingston, arranged with Thomas Gibbons to run a ferry service between New York City and Elizabethtown, New Jersey. Gibbons had secured a federal license from Congress pursuant to a 1793 statute under which he operated other boats as well. Ogden sought to enjoin Gibbons from operating those other boats based on his exclusive right to the New York waterways.

When the case reached the Supreme Court in 1824, Chief Justice John Marshall construed the commerce clause expansively. He held that Congress could regulate "any commerce which concerns more states than one," including navigation, as long as the regulation involved a commercial aspect. In light of Congress's plenary power over commerce, Marshall invoked the Constitution's supremacy clause—which declares all laws enacted by Congress the "supreme Law of the Land"—in finding that the New York statute granting Ogden's license conflicted with the federal law under which Gibbons held his. Signaling a new era in federalism, the decision laid the groundwork for national regulation of commercial affairs.

SEE ALSO The U.S. Constitution (1787); The Power of Judicial Review (1803); The Interstate Commerce Act (1887).

Daniel Webster, pictured in this c. 1851 photograph, argued the case on behalf of Thomas Gibbons in the U.S. Supreme Court.

Administering Native Peoples

John Marshall (1755–1835), **James Monroe** (1758–1831)

After the Revolution, congressional legislation vested the power to purchase native lands exclusively in the new federal government. In 1823, the U.S. Supreme Court rendered its seminal native-land acquisition decision, *Johnson v. M'Intosh*, in which Chief Justice John Marshall adopted the long-venerated European principle that allowed conquering powers to exercise sovereignty over new lands merely by virtue of finding them: Native Americans didn't own the lands that Europeans had discovered; they simply retained a right of occupation.

The Constitution empowers the president, with the advice and consent of the Senate, to regulate commerce with "Indian Tribes." The treaties that do so are the supreme law of the land and prevail over any conflicting state laws or constitutional provisions. They also must be construed liberally in favor of the Native Americans under long-standing U.S. Supreme Court doctrine. Despite this privileged status, these treaties haven't always been to the native peoples' benefit, and those that were weren't always honored.

By the early 1820s, a growing American population required more land. In the Removal Act of 1830, Congress granted the president vast authority and discretion. President Andrew Jackson exercised both to relocate almost all tribes east of the Mississippi River "voluntarily" to territory west of the river. The relocation effort itself fell to the Office of Indian Affairs, which President James Monroe had established in the Department of War in 1824. The forced relocations resulted in the deaths of thousands. The Trail of Tears, one of the most infamous, marched the Cherokee, Seminole, and three other tribes in the South to what is now Oklahoma over the course of seven years, 1831–1838. The Office of Indian Affairs became a bureau in 1834, and in 1849, when almost no tribes remained in the East, it moved to the Department of the Interior, where it remains.

The Doctrine of Aboriginal Title and the Discovery Doctrine remain legally valid today and have influenced the jurisprudence of other former British colonies, including Australia, Canada, and New Zealand. In 1992, the High Court of Australia cited *Johnson v. M'Intosh* in *Mabo v. Queensland*, a historic decision involving the land ownership rights of indigenous Australians.

SEE ALSO Colonialism and Postwar Independence (1947); The Trail of Broken Treaties (1972).

This 1939 mural, Indian & Soldier *by Maynard Dixon, adorns a wall of the Bureau of Indian Affairs at the Department of the Interior in Washington, D.C.*

1839

The Amistad

The scourge of slavery, which divided Americans and inexorably propelled the nation to war, wasn't unique to nineteenth-century America. The legal ramifications of slavery's international dimension famously presented themselves in the case of *The Amistad*.

In July 1839, the Spanish schooner *La Amistad* left Havana for another Cuban port, carrying fifty-three African slaves recently purchased by Spaniards José Ruiz and Pedro Montez. Four days into the journey, the slaves revolted, killing the captain and a crewmember and directing Ruiz and Montez to steer them back home to Sierra Leone. Instead, the Spaniards deceitfully navigated the ship north. The USS *Washington* of the Revenue Cutter Service (later the Coast Guard) spotted the *Amistad* off Montauk—the northeast point of Long Island in New York, where slavery was illegal—took control of the ship, and sailed it to New London, Connecticut—where slavery remained legal—to try the slaves for piracy and murder.

The seizure quickly yielded competing claims. The commander of the *Washington* claimed the *Amistad* and all of its cargo as salvage. The United States asserted claims on behalf of the government of Queen Isabella II of Spain. Ruiz and Montez sought the return of their slaves.

But a committee of abolitionists defended the slaves, insisting that U.S. courts had no jurisdiction over alleged crimes in Spanish territory, and they retained former president John Quincy Adams to argue before the U.S. Supreme Court. In a 7–1 decision, the Court concluded that the *Amistad* captives hadn't been enslaved legally because they were brought to Cuba in violation of a treaty banning the importation of slaves. Since they weren't slaves, Ruiz and Montez couldn't demand their return as their property. Furthermore, the captives were acting in self-defense when they killed the captain and crewmember and commandeered the ship and therefore were not guilty of mutiny or murder.

Despite setting the *Amistad* captives free, the decision didn't repudiate the institution of slavery. Nonetheless, as law scholar Douglas Linder notes, the *Amistad* case "energized the fledgling abolitionist movement and intensified conflict over slavery" and at the same time "soured diplomatic relations between the United States and Spain for a generation."

SEE ALSO The *Dred Scott* Decision (1857); The Emancipation Proclamation (1863); The Abolition of Slavery (1865);The Brazilian Slave Emancipation Act (1888).

Cinqué, chief of the Amistad *captives.*

Engraved by J. Sartain

Cinque

(Fac simile of the original Autograph.)

The Chief of the Amistad Captives

After the original Picture from Life by N. Jocelyn, New Haven, in the possession of Robt. Purvis Esqr. Philadelphia

Recognition of Labor Unions

Commonwealth v. Hunt, Lemuel Shaw (1781–1861)

Labor unions have played a large and powerful role in America's economic and political culture. They have drawn staunch supporters and zealous critics alike, but in their early days the groups themselves were illegal and their members often subject to criminal penalties. It wasn't until 1842 that unions were recognized formally as legitimate entities.

One of the first decisions resulting in criminal sanctions was the 1806 Philadelphia cordwainers case. A group of journeymen cordwainers, or shoemakers, went on strike, seeking a wage increase. They were arrested, prosecuted, and convicted for conspiracy. The law viewed bargaining over wages as proper only between individuals; group or concerted action for higher wages might result in increased wages across an entire trade or industry, thereby interfering with the rights of individuals willing to work for less. Business owners worried that higher costs would injure their ability to compete in the market.

In 1840, seven leaders of the Boston Journeymen Bootmakers' Society were prosecuted based on a complaint to the district attorney from a disaffected member who refused to recognize a Society disciplinary measure. The indictment charged the union as a criminal conspiracy because its members agreed not to work for anyone who employed non-union workers or those who had broken union rules and refused to pay their resulting fines.

The trial and conviction of these defendants unfolded in the celebrated case of *Commonwealth v. Hunt*. Chief Justice Lemuel Shaw, writing for the Supreme Judicial Court of Massachusetts, rejected the prevailing notion that a labor organization necessarily constituted a criminal conspiracy, radically reversing a presumption of illegality in concerted labor action. The rule he devised required examining the union's intentions and the means it employed to achieve its intentions. If neither was illegal, a conviction could not be sustained. A conspiracy, he wrote, "must be a combination of two or more persons, by some concerted action, to accomplish some criminal or unlawful purpose, or to accomplish some purpose, not in itself criminal or unlawful, by criminal or unlawful means."

SEE ALSO The National Labor Relations Act (1935); The Fair Labor Standards Act (1938).

Chief Justice Shaw rebuffed the standing view of labor organizations as criminal conspiracies.

The M'Naghten Rule

Daniel M'Naghten (1813–1865), **Edward Drummond** (1792–1843),
Nicholas Conyngham Tindal (1776–1846), **Queen Victoria** (1819–1901)

In January 1843, Daniel M'Naghten shot and killed Edward Drummond, personal secretary to Prime Minister Robert Peel. Charged with murder, M'Naghten stood trial at the Old Bailey. He pleaded not guilty, insisting "I was driven to desperation by persecution." Presenting an insanity defense through the testimony of nine medical witnesses, counsel established that M'Naghten had been delusional at the time of the shooting and that his delusions of persecution prevented him from exercising control over his conduct.

At the conclusion of the evidence, Lord Chief Justice Nicholas Conyngham Tindal all but instructed the jury to find M'Naghten not guilty on the ground of insanity. The jury acquiesced. M'Naghten was taken to Bethlem Royal Hospital (known colloquially as "Bedlam"), where he remained for twenty-one years. He was transferred to Broadmoor Asylum in 1864, where he died one year later.

The verdict outraged the public at large and Queen Victoria—herself the eventual target of eight assassination attempts—in particular. She requested legislation setting forth the correct legal rules for judging guilt against insanity. The House of Lords summoned all the judges of the common-law courts and put to them five questions of law. As Chief Judge John Biggs Jr. writes in *The Guilty Mind*, the judges "were under pressure from the Crown, the lords, and the press and were in a very difficult situation."

Their answers to those questions provided the formulation for the insanity defense, known as the M'Naghten Rule, that prevailed in England and America for more than a century: "It must be clearly proved that, at the time of the committing of the act, the party accused was laboring under such a defect of reason, from disease of the mind, as not to know the nature and quality of the act he was doing or, if he did know it, that he did not know he was doing what was wrong."

SEE ALSO The Insanity Defense (1881).

William Hogarth's 1735 A Rake's Progress depicts life inside the Bethlem Royal Hospital ("Bedlam") in London. Daniel M'Naghten was committed to Bedlam for twenty-one years after being found not guilty of murder by reason of insanity.

The Field Code

David Dudley Field (1805–1894)

It's all about the rules. That's what any lawyer worth his or her fee will tell you about the practice of law. Entry to the bar has rules. The trial court has rules. The appellate court has rules. The surrogate's court has rules. The family court has rules. Forget about possession; rules are nine-tenths of the law.

But the ubiquity of procedural regulations in courts wasn't always so. Until nearly the middle of the nineteenth century, most states maintained two types of courts: courts of equity for cases seeking nonmonetary relief and courts of law for cases seeking monetary damages. Forms of action dictated procedure in the one, and common-law pleading in the other. Then, in 1846, New York State eliminated courts of equity and created a single supreme court with jurisdiction over matters in both law and equity.

The next year, David Dudley Field, a successful trial lawyer who for years had advocated for legal reform, was appointed to a three-member commission charged with simplifying New York's law of pleading and procedure. Field's goal was simple: He sought the complete codification of the common law. In a biography of his brother, published in 1898, Henry Field noted that "above all professional or political ambitions was the Reform which he undertook in his early manhood, and which filled up the measure of his days till he breathed his last."

In 1848, the state adopted the commission's recommended Code of Civil Procedure, known almost immediately as the Field Code. Legal scholar and historian William LaPiana has described it as "one of the greatest changes wrought on the common law in the nineteenth century." Field sounded "a standard call of reformers in the nineteenth century common law world—a dispute that can be settled in the courts should be settled in one action, initiated by pleadings that told as simply as possible what happened, brought before a single court capable of giving all the relief appropriate." His Field Code became the foundation for most modern codes of practice, including the 1938 Federal Rules of Civil Procedure.

SEE ALSO The Law School Revolution (1870); The United States Code (1926); Rule 23 and Modern Class Action (1938).

David Dudley Field, c. 1870.

The Measure of Contract Damages

Hadley v. Baxendale

The foreseeability rule, a near-universal principle of contract law relating to the measure of damages, owes its existence to a broken crank in a steam engine belonging to Joseph and Jonah Hadley, brothers and owners of a flour mill in Gloucester, England.

On May 11, 1853, a fracture in the gear shaft crank caused the steam engine that ran the corn grinding machinery to break down. The Hadleys sent one of their employees with the broken crank to a local carrier company owned by Joseph Baxendale to be delivered to the London engineers who would supply a new part. The Hadley employee claimed that he told Baxendale's clerk that the mill would sit idle until a new crank was installed, so the broken crank needed to be sent immediately. That message of urgency apparently never made it to London, resulting in a lengthy delay.

The Hadleys sued Baxendale for £300 in lost profits. Baxendale argued that he couldn't have foreseen an idle mill and therefore wasn't liable for any related loss. The appellate court agreed and set forth what became one of the most famous rules of contract law:

> Where two parties have made a contract which one of them has broken, the damages the other party ought to receive in respect of such breach of contract should be such as may fairly and reasonably be considered either arising naturally, i.e., according to the usual course of things, from such breach of contract itself, or such as may reasonably be supposed to have been in the contemplation of both parties, at the time they made the contract, as the probable result of the breach of it.

In this case, the evidence at trial didn't show that Baxendale was made aware of a need for expediency in delivery. In the words of legal scholar Allan Hutchinson, the case "remains the fountainhead for all common law discussion about the test for the award of damages in contracts cases."

SEE ALSO Corporate Personhood and Liability (1897).

A dispute over the broken crankshaft of a steam engine resulted in the rule of foreseeability that is now used to determine the measure of damages from a breach of contract.

The *Dred Scott* Decision

Dred Scott (c. 1800–1858), **Harriet Robinson** (c. 1815–1876),
Irene Emerson (1815–1903), **Roger Taney** (1777–1864)

Dred Scott was born a slave to the family of Peter Blow, who sold him in 1833 to Johnson Emerson. Emerson and Scott settled at Fort Snelling, an area covered under the Missouri Compromise of 1820, which prohibited slavery in federal territories northwest of Missouri. There Scott married Harriet Robinson in a civil ceremony. After Emerson died, Scott attempted to purchase his family's freedom from Emerson's widow, Irene, but she refused. Scott filed suit seeking freedom for his family and himself.

In 1850, a jury found them to be free, reasoning that, because Scott and his wife had lived in free territory for several years, they had become free. On appeal, the Missouri Supreme Court overturned the decision. Scott then sought relief in the federal courts, arguing that slavery equated to wrongful imprisonment. Again Scott was unsuccessful, but Washington lawyer Montgomery Blair agreed to represent Scott in an appeal to the U.S. Supreme Court.

Scott's case was lost probably even before Blair argued it. Seven of the justices publicly supported slavery and wished to settle the issue in the new territories in favor of the "peculiar institution," as it was euphemistically known. Chief Justice Roger Taney wrote the majority opinion. Addressing whether the Court had jurisdiction to hear the case, he asserted that, while Scott might have been a citizen of Missouri, neither he nor any other black individual was a citizen of the United States of America.

The Court could have dismissed the case for lack of jurisdiction, but it ruled that Congress lacked the authority to prohibit slavery in the new territories and that, by denying citizens the right to own slaves, Congress was infringing on slave owners' Fifth Amendment rights.

Three months after the ruling, family friends purchased and freed Scott and his family, but the Supreme Court's decision remains one of the most contemptible rulings in American judicial history. It had an enormous impact, further dividing North and South, and the impending civil war that many long had feared soon became a reality.

SEE ALSO *The Amistad* (1839); The Emancipation Proclamation (1863); The Abolition of Slavery (1865).

Dred Scott, c. 1857.

The Government Printing Office

Joint Resolution No. 25, James Buchanan (1791–1868)

Documenting the labors of government represents a fundamental aspect of American legal history. Only by fixing words in tangible form—by printing them—can we openly chronicle the progression of legislative, executive, and judicial lawmaking.

Shortly after the First Congress in 1789, the Founding Fathers recognized the need for printing "laws and other proceedings." They hired local printers to publish the *House Journal* and acts of Congress, but they encountered frequent delays and inaccurate reporting. For forty years, Congress vacillated between a fixed-rate system whereby each chamber of Congress elected printers and set a fixed rate of payment, and a contract system in which printers bid on government printing opportunities. Because both systems eventually resulted in financial concern, the House and Senate passed a reform bill, Joint Resolution No. 25. President James Buchanan then signed it into law as the Printing Act of June 23, 1860, establishing a Government Printing Office (GPO).

The joint resolution provided for the "purchase of the necessary buildings, machinery, and materials" for the purpose of establishing a physical printing office. In December 1860, the government acquired a printing plant at the corner of North Capitol and H Streets, the same corner the GPO still occupies in Washington, D.C. The GPO soon achieved significant savings in printing costs, securing its own permanence as an indispensable part of government. Over the next century, the GPO printed some of the most important documents in American history, including the Emancipation Proclamation and constitutional amendments, as well as more mundane materials, such as Smokey the Bear flyers and cookbooks for military mess staff.

Celebrating the GPO's 150th anniversary, Public Printer Robert Tapella remarked, "There are vast differences in the way GPO carries out its work in this Digital Age, but our mission remains fundamentally the same: producing and distributing Government publications—*the documents of our democracy*—to keep America informed." Recognizing the GPO's embrace of an increasingly digital world, congressional legislation enacted in 2014 officially changed the agency's name to the Government *Publishing* Office.

SEE ALSO Law Reporting and Legal Publishing (1872); The United States Code (1926); The *Federal Register* (1936).

The Government Printing Office's typesetting room, c. 1910.

The Emancipation Proclamation

Historian Peter Kolchin aptly characterizes the nineteenth century as "the century of emancipation." In March 1856, Russian tsar Alexander II decreed an end to serfdom, Russia's own form of slavery, freeing approximately twenty-three million serfs, about one-third of the country's total population.

In America, hostilities over slavery had been growing. Weeks before Abraham Lincoln's 1861 inauguration, seven southern states—joined later by four more—seceded from the Union and formed the Confederate States of America. The next month, South Carolina troops attacked the federally controlled Fort Sumter and triggered the American Civil War.

Although Lincoln opposed slavery, he recognized its political importance and disavowed any intention of interfering with slavery in the states where it existed. But by the summer of 1862, with the Union Army experiencing disheartening losses, Lincoln came to believe that freeing the slaves was becoming a military necessity. Not only would emancipation deal a blow to the slave-labor engine that helped feed and clothe the Confederacy, but it could bolster the ranks of the Union Army.

On September 22, 1862, invoking his war powers as commander in chief, Lincoln issued a preliminary proclamation in which he declared that he would free all slaves in the rebelling states if the states didn't rejoin the Union by January 1, 1863. When none of the states complied, Lincoln signed the Emancipation Proclamation on January 1, 1863, remarking, "I never, in my life, felt more certain that I was doing right than I do in signing this paper."

The Proclamation announced that "all persons held as slaves within any State or designated part of a State, the people whereof shall then be in rebellion against the United States, shall be then, thenceforward, and forever free." Many argued that the Proclamation didn't immediately affect slaves in the Confederacy because its effectiveness depended entirely on the Union's victory.

Nevertheless, the Emancipation Proclamation had a significant impact. Thousands of slaves walked free, and many joined Union forces to aid the war effort. Equally important, it served as a bridge to the Thirteenth Amendment and the abolition of slavery altogether.

SEE ALSO The U.S. Constitution (1787); The *Dred Scott* Decision (1857); The Abolition of Slavery (1865); The Brazilian Slave Emancipation Act (1888).

An 1890 lithograph depicting the historic proclamation.

Emancipation Proclamation

WHEREAS on the Twenty-second day of September, in the year of our Lord one thousand eight hundred and sixty-two, a Proclamation was issued by the President of the United States, containing among other things the following, to-wit:

"That on the first day of January, in the year of our Lord one thousand eight hundred and sixty-three, all persons held as slaves within any State, or designated part of a State, the people whereof shall then be in rebellion against the United States, shall be then, thenceforward and forever free, and the executive government of the United States, including the military and naval authority thereof, will recognize and maintain the freedom of such persons, and will do no act or acts to repress such persons, or any of them, in any efforts they may make for their actual freedom.

"That the executive will, on the first day of January aforesaid, by proclamation, designate the States and parts of States, if any, in which the people thereof respectively shall then be in rebellion against the United States, and the fact that any State, or the people thereof, shall on that day be in good faith represented in the Congress of the United States by members chosen thereto at elections wherein a majority of the qualified voters of such State shall have participated, shall, in the absence of strong countervailing testimony, be deemed conclusive evidence that such State and the people thereof are not then in rebellion against the United States."

Now, therefore, I, ABRAHAM LINCOLN, President of the United States, by virtue of the power in me vested as Commander-in-Chief of the Army and Navy of the United States in time of actual armed rebellion against the authority and government of the United States, and as a fit and necessary war measure for suppressing said rebellion, do, on this first day of January, in the year of our Lord one thousand eight hundred and sixty-three, and in accordance with my purpose so to do, publicly proclaim for the full period of one hundred days from the day the first above mentioned order, and designate as the States and parts of States wherein the people thereof respectively are this day in rebellion against the United States, the following, to-wit:

ARKANSAS, TEXAS, LOUISIANA (except the parishes of St. Bernard, Plaquemines, Jefferson, St. John, St. Charles, St. James, Ascension, Assumption, Terre Bonne, Lafourche, St. Mary, St. Martin, and Orleans, including the city of New Orleans), MISSISSIPPI, ALABAMA, FLORIDA, GEORGIA, SOUTH CAROLINA, NORTH CAROLINA and VIRGINIA (except the forty-eight counties designated as West Virginia, and also the counties of Berkley, Accomac, Northampton, Elizabeth City, York, Princess Ann and Norfolk, including the cities of Norfolk and Portsmouth), and which excepted parts are, for the present, left precisely as if this Proclamation were not issued.

And by virtue of the power and for the purpose aforesaid, I do order and declare that all persons held as slaves within said designated States and parts of States are and henceforward shall be free; and that the executive government of the United States, including the military and naval authorities thereof, will recognize and maintain the freedom of said persons.

And I hereby enjoin upon the people so declared to be free, to abstain from all violence, unless in necessary self-defence, and I recommend to them that in all cases, when allowed, they labor faithfully for reasonable wages.

And I further declare and make known that such persons of suitable condition, will be received into the armed service of the United States to garrison forts, positions, stations and other places, and to man vessels of all sorts in said service.

And upon this act, sincerely believed to be an act of justice, warranted by the Constitution, upon military necessity, I invoke the considerate judgment of mankind, and the gracious favor of Almighty God.

In testimony whereof, I have hereunto set my name, and caused the seal of the United States to be affixed.

Done at the City of Washington, this first day of January, in the year of our Lord one thousand eight hundred and sixty-three, and of the Independence of the United States the eighty-seventh.

By the President:

William H. Seward
Secretary of State.

A. Lincoln

The Geneva Convention

Jean-Henri Dunant (1828–1910)

Just or not, there are no good wars. General William Tecumseh Sherman wrote: "You cannot qualify war in harsher terms than I will. War is cruelty, and you cannot refine it; and those who brought war into our country deserve all the curses and maledictions a people can pour out."

But paradoxically the unspeakable savagery of war sometimes leads to efforts to infuse an element of humanity into what is otherwise unmitigated horror. Jean-Henri Dunant, a thirty-year-old Swiss banker, traveled to Italy on business, arriving on June 24, 1859, as the Battle of Solferino was raging. He witnessed firsthand one of the war's bloodiest and most gruesome conflicts as the French army of Napoleon III and the Sardinian army of Victor Emmanuel II battled the Austrian army of Franz Joseph I. More than forty thousand dead and wounded lay abandoned on the field.

Shaken, Dunant set about aiding the wounded, most of whom died. Afterward, he wrote *A Memory of Solferino*, which Sanda Bossy, a member of the Secretariat of the League of Red Cross Societies, described as combining "one of the most vivid pieces of nineteenth-century war-reporting" with "a plea on behalf of the wounded in the field." More importantly, he devised a proposal for the creation of aid societies. With the help of a benevolent organization in Geneva, Dunant established what became the International Red Cross, described by the Nobel Committee as "the supreme humanitarian achievement of the nineteenth century" and for which Dunant shared the first Nobel Peace Prize in 1901.

In August 1864, Dunant convened a diplomatic conference to seek an international treaty addressing wartime military casualties. Twelve nations signed the first Geneva Convention for the Amelioration of the Condition of the Wounded and Sick in Armed Forces in the Field. Its central principles addressed relief to all wounded, regardless of affiliation, and the protection of medical personnel to be distinguished by a red cross on a white field. Subsequent Geneva Conventions added rules regulating wartime conduct, including providing protections for prisoners of war, civilians, and nonmilitary targets, and banning certain methods of warfare and weaponry, including chemical weapons.

SEE ALSO Peace of Westphalia (1648); The International Criminal Court (2002).

The bloody Battle of Solferino inspired Jean-Henri Dunant to establish what became the International Red Cross.

The Abolition of Slavery

Of the three constitutional amendments passed in the wake of the American Civil War, the first and arguably most important is the thirteenth, which permanently abolished slavery.

As originally introduced and passed by both houses of Congress in 1861, prior to the onset of the war, the Thirteenth Amendment actually guaranteed the future legality of slavery, not its abolition. But it failed to maintain national unity and avert combat. Once the war began, the amendment couldn't achieve ratification by three-quarters of the states.

On January 1, 1863, President Lincoln signed the Emancipation Proclamation, freeing thousands of Confederate slaves but not legally ending slavery. He recognized the limitations of his wartime order and understood that proper abolition of slavery could occur only by constitutional amendment.

Congressional proposals emerged in late 1863, and by the 1864 presidential election Lincoln endorsed an anti-slavery amendment. The Thirteenth Amendment became Lincoln's top priority after he won his second term. Although popular support for it was growing, Lincoln didn't have an easy time achieving the two-thirds majority required in both houses for a constitutional amendment. The Senate passed the amendment in April 1864 by a vote of 38–6, but opposition persisted among representatives from northern states, many of whom remained indifferent to slavery or owned slaves themselves. Lincoln and his cabinet lobbied exhaustively, and in January 1865 the House of Representatives voted in favor of passage, 119–56. By year's end, three-fourths of the states voted for ratification, and the Thirteenth Amendment took effect on December 18, 1865. Three days later the *New York Independent* opined that "a strange, grateful, and animated emotion beats in our veins at the thought of the United States government declaring with its official lips that American slavery is no more forever."

Legal scholar David S. Bogen has written that "some constitutional amendments have an impact beyond their terms: they transform the way people look at the world." The Thirteenth Amendment, he noted, "profoundly altered society . . . [and] pushed against the racial discrimination embedded in law," leading to the Civil Rights Act of 1866 and the Fourteenth Amendment.

SEE ALSO *The Amistad* (1839); The *Dred Scott* Decision (1857); The Emancipation Proclamation (1863); The Fourteenth Amendment (1868).

Building on the Emancipation Proclamation, the Thirteenth Amendment to the U.S. Constitution fully prohibited the institution of slavery.

FREEDOM FOR ALL, BOTH BLACK AND WHITE!

EDUCATION TO ALL CLASSES

PROCLAMATION OF EMANCIPATION

The Civil Rights Act of 1866

Lyman Trumbull (1813–1896), **Andrew Johnson** (1808–1875)

Although the Civil War ended in the spring of 1865, the country's black population still had battles to fight as the nation trudged through Reconstruction. The recently enacted Thirteenth Amendment had freed around four million slaves but fell short in conferring on them the same legal status enjoyed by whites.

After the war, many southern states enacted black codes, described by historian Eric Foner as "plans for getting things back as near to slavery as possible." The black codes permitted former slaves to own property and enter contracts but afforded them no civil or political rights and limited their employment options. But public disapproval in the North compelled Congress to act, which it did by passing the Civil Rights Act of 1866.

The bill originated with Senator Lyman Trumbull of Illinois and represented an attempt to give real meaning to the Thirteenth Amendment. Despite the bill's overwhelming congressional support, President Johnson vetoed it, which Eric Foner characterized as "a major blunder, the most disastrous miscalculation of his political career." Congress quickly overrode the veto, enacting the first major law over a presidential veto.

The Act speaks to citizenship and equality, proclaiming that "all persons born in the United States . . . are hereby declared to be citizens of the United States" and that "citizens of every race and color . . . shall have the same right[s]" and enjoy the "full and equal benefit of all laws . . . as is enjoyed by white citizens." Equally important was the Act's establishment of a mechanism to effectuate the specified rights. It created civil and criminal jurisdiction in the federal courts to hear claims alleging deprivation of rights and to impose penalties for violations. It also authorized federal officials to charge violators.

The Act had its deficiencies, however. A particularly glaring and ironic one bears mention: It stopped short of granting African Americans the right to vote, which had to wait for the ratification of the Fifteenth Amendment in 1870.

SEE ALSO The Emancipation Proclamation (1863); The Abolition of Slavery (1865); Prohibion of Racial Voter Discrimination (1869); The Civil Rights Cases (1883); *Plessy v. Ferguson*: Separate but Equal (1896); The Civil Rights Act of 1964.

South Carolinia congressman Robert B. Elliott delivering his famous speech in favor of the Civil Rights Act of 1875 in the House of Representatives on January 6, 1874.

Impeaching President Andrew Johnson

Andrew Johnson (1808–1875)

The constitutional power to remove an impeached president rests exclusively with the Senate, after a trial and a finding of guilt by a two-thirds majority: "The President . . . shall be removed from Office on Impeachment for, and Conviction of, Treason, Bribery or other high Crimes and Misdemeanors." Impeachment proceedings have touched only two Presidents: Andrew Johnson and William Clinton. (Both were impeached, but Senate trials acquitted each.)

When Vice President Johnson assumed the presidency in 1865 following Lincoln's assassination, the nation was suffering the throes of Reconstruction politics. Johnson, a Southern Democrat, demonstrated Confederate sympathies as president, alienating the Republican Congress, in particular its radical element bent on remaking, not restoring, the South. Among other unpopular stances, Johnson opposed the Fourteenth Amendment, and he denounced and vetoed both the Freedmen's Bureau Bill and the Civil Rights Bill. Congress subsequently enacted both over Johnson's veto.

Republican antipathy toward Johnson grew steadily. Fearful that he might cripple enforcement of the 1867 Reconstruction Act by removing Secretary of War Edwin Stanton, Congress passed the Tenure of Office Act, which required Senate consent before the president could vacate certain offices. In December 1867, Johnson suspended Secretary Stanton. When the Senate refused to consent, Johnson appointed an interim secretary of war. Republicans saw that move as a contravention of the Act. Within two months, the House passed eleven articles of impeachment against Johnson, the strongest of which charged violation of the Tenure of Office Act.

Johnson's trial was a spectacle; indeed, the galleries filled to capacity, and for the first time in the history of the Senate it required tickets for admission. After thirteen days of closing arguments, Johnson was acquitted by the margin of a single vote. Republican manipulation of the trial process, along with back-channel politicking on Johnson's behalf, prompted seven Senators to break with their party and vote for acquittal, finding that Johnson had violated no laws. None of the seven was reelected to office.

SEE ALSO The U.S. Constitution (1787); Presidential Subpoena Compliance (1974); Presidential Immunity (1997).

President Andrew Johnson as painted by Washington Bogart Cooper (1802–1888).

The Fourteenth Amendment

The end of the Civil War left many civil rights battles unfought, but a major victory came with the Thirteenth Amendment, which freed all remaining slaves, followed by the Civil Rights Act of 1866, which reinforced the Thirteenth Amendment by declaring all citizens "of every race and color" to have the same rights. But concerns remained about the vitality of that legislation, and uncertainty lingered about upcoming congressional elections and whether the Reconstruction Congress would retain its power. Some feared that a new Congress would repeal the Civil Rights Act. The solution was to embed its principles into the Constitution.

Historians and constitutional scholars describe the Fourteenth Amendment as the most important amendment since the adoption of the Bill of Rights in 1791. The Amendment's essence lies in its enforceable guarantee of legal equality to all citizens.

The profound importance of the Fourteenth Amendment flows from its first section. It not only establishes birthright citizenship—declaring all persons born in the United States of America to be citizens—but more significantly it prohibits states from abridging the privileges or immunities of citizens and forbids any state to "deprive any person of life, liberty, or property, without due process of law" or to deny any person "the equal protection of the laws." The word "equal" doesn't appear in the Constitution—except with regard to states having equal numbers of senators—but it finally appears in the Fourteenth Amendment.

The Bill of Rights restrained the federal government, but the Fourteenth Amendment enshrined legislation protecting individuals from violations of rights by states. Historian Eric Foner observes that "the Fourteenth Amendment makes the federal government . . . what the great abolitionist senator Charles Sumner called 'The Custodian of Freedom.'" Decades later it upheld the civil rights movement. As constitutional scholar Jethro Lieberman explains, the due process clause "became the basis for applying the Bill of Rights to the states," and the equal protection clause became "the basis for desegregating American society. These provisions have proved to be the most far-reaching of the amendments to the Constitution."

SEE ALSO The *Dred Scott* Decision (1857); The Emancipation Proclamation (1863); The Abolition of Slavery (1865); The Civil Rights Act of 1866; Prohibion of Racial Voter Discrimination (1869); The Civil Rights Cases (1883); *Plessy v. Ferguson*: Separate but Equal (1896); The Civil Rights Act of 1964.

Jacob M. Howard, the Michigan senator who authored the citizenship clause of the Fourteenth Amendment that reversed a portion of the U.S. Supreme Court's Dred Scott decision.

Prohibition of Racial Voter Discrimination

The Fifteenth Amendment prohibits states from denying individuals the right to vote based on "race, color, or condition of previous servitude." Although embedded in the Constitution for almost 150 years, that amendment certainly doesn't stand at the forefront of media attention, nor has it enjoyed the exposure of the First, Second, or Fifth Amendment. Indeed, according to political scholar D. Grier Stephenson Jr., "the Fifteenth Amendment is unique among all the statutory and constitutional extensions of the franchise because of its vacuity. . . . Never has so specific a constitutional directive been so plainly disregarded for so long." Yet no one can deny the profound importance of the fundamental right that it protects.

The Fifteenth Amendment was the last of the three Reconstruction Amendments that followed the end of the Civil War. The Thirteenth abolished slavery; the Fourteenth established U.S. citizenship as a birthright and prohibited states from denying citizens due process or equal protection of the law. But neither the Thirteenth nor the Fourteenth Amendment addressed the voting rights of the millions of former slaves who had become free citizens.

The amendment emerged from Congress in February 1869 and went to the states for ratification. In March 1870, the required three-quarters of the then thirty-seven states ratified it, and it became a part of the Constitution.

Despite this new constitutional protection, African Americans had only just begun to struggle for the right to vote. Both southern and northern states had developed effective approaches—legal and illegal—to disenfranchise them. Poll taxes and literacy tests emerged and were applied discriminatorily, and African Americans often faced intimidation and outright violence at the polls. An extraordinary number of judicial and legislative battles had to take place over the century that followed before the 1965 Voting Rights Act ended much—though not all—discrimination against African American voters.

SEE ALSO The Civil Rights Act of 1866; The Civil Rights Act of 1964; The Voting Rights Act of 1965.

This commemorative print celebrating the ratification of the Fifteenth Amendment shows a parade surrounded by images of African Americans enjoying their newly confirmed rights.

The Law School Revolution

William Blackstone (1723–1780), **Theodore Dwight** (1822–1892),
Christopher Columbus Langdell (1826–1906)

Legal education in early-eighteenth-century America followed the traditional English apprenticeship model but also incorporated study of classic legal texts, including Coke's *Institutes of the Laws of England* and later Blackstone's *Commentaries on the Laws of England*. Blackstone himself didn't much esteem apprenticeship: "If practice be the whole he is taught, practice must also be the whole he will ever know." Instead, he successfully lobbied to introduce law classes into the English university curriculum.

Following England's lead, the College of William & Mary in Virginia established the first American law professorship in 1779. Other institutions soon followed. Apprenticeship in law practice was still required of aspiring lawyers, but now they had to have formal university instruction on the subject. Early in the nineteenth century, some universities developed separate law schools, beginning with Harvard in 1817 and Yale in 1826.

In 1858, Theodore Dwight, whom scholar Robert Stevens describes as "the foremost legal educator" of the mid-nineteenth century, transformed Columbia College's newly formed School of Jurisprudence into the leading law school of the time. Dwight's lecture method became the dominant pedagogy at most of the twenty-one law schools in the country then.

Revolutionary changes to the lecture-based approach emerged soon after Christopher Columbus Langdell joined Harvard's law faculty in 1870. Langdell launched a new paradigm that became the standard for legal education for almost 150 years: the case method. Students read appellate opinions and then engaged with the instructor in a Socratic dialogue, answering questions designed to elicit legal principles from real cases. The case method's primary advantage lies in its focus on developing critical thinking skills. According to Professor Stevens, this new method "became the mark of the leading law schools."

Langdell also helped achieve many other lasting changes in legal education, including increasing the length of study from eighteen months to three years and insistence on a full-time faculty of scholars rather than one composed of part-time practitioners.

SEE ALSO The First Law School (c. 250); Blackstone's *Commentaries* (1765).

Harvard Law School's Langdell Hall is named after Christopher Columbus Langdell, one of the most influential figures in early legal education.

Law Reporting and Legal Publishing

John Briggs West (1852–1922)

Because a common-law system looks to precedent—previous decisions in factually similar cases—the availability of and access to records or reports of those prior decisions are essential. The recording of precedents most likely began in late-thirteenth-century England and was formalized by the mid-fourteenth century through handwritten annuals. These early records amounted to compilations of notes on proceedings. The advent of the printing press in the fifteenth century led to wider distribution, but the accounts of various "reporters"—here meaning distinguished lawyers—largely displaced the yearbooks during the sixteenth and seventeenth centuries.

Prior to the Revolutionary War, American lawyers relied on these English reporters but developed their own after independence. Beginning in the early nineteenth century, judges had to render written rather than oral decisions, leading to the appointment of official reporters and reports of courts' decisions. The volume of written decisions grew, but the volumes of decisions recording them kept a slow pace. It could take as long as a year before court clerks or reporters issued a new volume containing the most recent precedents. Lawyers found research increasingly difficult without ready access to current law. The problem became more acute as the number of reported decisions continued to expand, but a dramatic change was about to alter the very practice of law.

In 1872, John Briggs West—a salesman for a St. Paul, Minnesota, bookstore—started his own bookselling business (eventually West Publishing Co.) for lawyers, whose particular needs had become apparent as he traveled the Midwest. He soon revolutionized legal publishing itself. On October 21, 1876, West published the first issue of the *Syllabi*, the precursor to what's known today as an advance sheet. Every week, West published Minnesota court decisions and summaries of those decisions in issues of the *Syllabi*. Subscribers bound these pamphlets into more permanent volumes, so, taking their cue, West soon published its first reporter in book format, the *Northwestern Reporter*. The modern case reporter was born. Before long, West published case reporters covering court decisions in every state through a series still known as the National Reporter System.

SEE ALSO The Government Printing Office (1861); The United States Code (1926); The *Federal Register* (1936).

Law books—yearbooks, reporters, treatises, and more—form the backbone of legal practice.

1873

Obscenity and the Comstock Act

Anthony Comstock (1844–1915), **George Bernard Shaw** (1856–1950)

Born in Connecticut, Anthony Comstock fought in the Civil War and afterward settled in New York City. His strong religious background led him to work with the Young Men's Christian Association (YMCA), which in 1872 selected him to head their Committee for the Suppression of Vice, later the Society for the Prevention of Vice, which sought to outlaw corrupting or salacious materials.

Federal law at the time banned from the mail obscene materials—which by definition tended "to deprave and corrupt those whose minds are open to such immoral influences and into whose hands a publication of this sort may fall"—but the zealous Comstock found even that prohibition insufficient. In 1873, he persuaded Congress to enact stricter legislation with increased penalties and provisions for the seizure and destruction of covered material. That year Congress enacted a controversial law, An Act for the Suppression of Trade in, and Circulation of, Obscene Literature and Articles of Immoral Use. Popularly known as the Comstock Act, it reached beyond the purely obscene, barring the mailing of educational materials relating to birth control as well as legal contraceptive devices.

In the preface to his 1880 book, *Frauds Exposed; or, How the People Are Deceived and Robbed, and Youth Corrupted*, Comstock wrote: "My object is . . . to arouse a public sentiment against the vampires who are casting deadly poison into the fountain of moral purity in the children; and at the same time expose to public indignation the infidels and liberals who defend these moral cancer-planters." He boldly proclaimed: "It is a noted fact, that no sect nor class, as a sect or class, has ever publicly sided with the smut-dealer, and defended this nefarious business, except the Infidels, the Liberals, and the Free-Lovers."

By the early 1900s, a forward-looking society began to repudiate Comstock's extremist, exclusionary moralizing. Irish playwright George Bernard Shaw receives credit for coining the term "Comstockery" to refer to excessive prudery, a personal response to the removal of some of his works from a public library in 1905. A century after the Comstock Act passed, the Supreme Court transformed the definition of obscenity.

SEE ALSO The First Blue Laws (1629); Censorship and *Ulysses* (1933); The Limits on Obscenity (1957); The Body and the Right of Privacy (1965); A New Obscenity Standard (1973); The FCC and Filthy Words (1978).

The Comstock Act, named after moralist Anthony Comstock who is shown here, banned the circulation of educational materials related to legal birth control.

Admission of Women to the Bar

Bradwell v. Illinois, Myra Bradwell (1831–1894)

Women in the nineteenth century struggled to obtain equality in a host of areas, including the right to practice law. Myra Bradwell instrumentally helped to change cultural attitudes and overcome the legal and social barriers that barred women from the profession in which they now play a significant and ever-increasing role.

She began her career as a teacher, but after marrying an attorney and while raising their four children she went to work in her husband's law office, where she quietly studied to take the Illinois bar exam. In 1868, she founded the *Chicago Legal News*, which became the most widely circulated legal newspaper of the time. She also helped draft several key pieces of state legislation that gave women control of their own property and earnings.

In 1869, Bradwell passed the Illinois bar exam, but her admission was denied on the grounds that a married woman couldn't enter into contracts because of the common-law doctrine of coverture and also because of her gender; in the Illinois Supreme Court's view, women weren't entitled to practice law: "The natural and proper timidity and delicacy which belongs to the female sex evidently unfits it for many occupations of civil life. . . . The paramount destiny and mission of women are to fulfill the noble and benign office of wife and mother. This is the law of the Creator." Bradwell appealed unsuccessfully to the U.S. Supreme Court. In an 8–1 ruling, the Court affirmed the Illinois decision, holding that the Fourteenth Amendment didn't protect a right to practice law.

Soon after the decision, Bradwell wrote in the *Chicago Legal News*: "Although we have not succeeded in obtaining an opinion as we hoped . . . we are more than compensated for all our trouble in seeing, as a result of the agitation, statutes passed in several of the States, including our own, admitting women [to practice law] upon the same terms as men."

Bradwell continued working on the *Chicago Legal News* and advocating for women's rights. In 1890, the Illinois Supreme Court reconsidered her 1869 application and granted it *nunc pro tunc* (now for then), retroactively making her the first woman lawyer in Illinois.

SEE ALSO New Zealand Women's Suffrage (1893); Women's Right to Vote (1919); The Equal Rights Amendment (1972); Women's Admission to Private Clubs (1988).

Myra Bradwell, c. 1870.

Legal Aid Societies

Edward Salomon (1828–1909), **Arthur von Briesen** (1843–1920)

Reginald Heber Smith, author of *Justice and the Poor*, a comprehensive study of legal aid in America published by the Carnegie Foundation in 1919, assigned the honor of "the first true legal aid organization" to Chicago's Bureau of Justice, established in 1888. Smith described it as an organization that "undertook to supply legal services in all cases to all persons, regardless of nationality. . . . Leadership, control, and support were not derived from any particularly defined group, and income came from charitably disposed persons in the general public."

But the first organized effort to provide legal aid to the poor in New York City had appeared in 1876 under the auspices of the German Society of New York. Aided by Edward Salomon, a New York attorney and former governor of Wisconsin, the German Society incorporated the *Deutscher Rechts-Schutz Verein* (the German Legal Protection Society) and dedicated itself to rendering "legal aid and assistance gratuitously to those of German birth who may appear worthy thereof, but who from poverty are unable to procure it." Its purpose was "to protect German immigrants from the rapacity of runners, boarding-house keepers, and a miscellaneous coterie of sharpers who found that the trustful and bewildered newcomers offered an easy prey."

In 1890, under the leadership of Arthur von Briesen, the Deutscher Rechts-Schutz Verein opened its services to all, regardless of cultural heritage. Six years later, von Briesen formally changed the name of the organization to the Legal Aid Society.

Smith's study of legal philanthropy details that by 1910 "organized legal aid work was reasonably well established in all of the larger cities of the east. By 1913, there were twenty-eight Legal Aid organizations across the country. By 1917, the number had reached forty-one, with a presence in every major city." The Legal Aid Society's thousand lawyers in New York City annually handled more than three hundred thousand client matters, providing comprehensive legal services to those unable to afford private counsel and giving meaning to the Magna Carta's declaration "to no one will we sell, to no one will we refuse or delay, right or justice."

SEE ALSO The Star Chamber (c. 1350); The Right to Counsel in State Court (1963).

Edward Salomon, shown here c. 1870, helped provide legal aid to the poor in New York City.

The Berne Convention

Victor Hugo (1802–1885)

Early in the nineteenth century, a number of European countries entered into bilateral arrangements offering reciprocal protections for copyright holders. But according to Sam Ricketson, an international scholar of intellectual property law, "the unauthorized reproduction and use of foreign works were, for a long time, established features of European cultural and social life, and continued to be so for a considerable period after the adoption of national copyright laws by most countries."

Limitations of the bilateral approach, including a lack of uniformity, prompted a movement that began in France, seeking a universal law of copyright. In 1878, Victor Hugo and a group of artists and publishers formed the Association Littéraire et Artistique Internationale to pursue that cause. By 1882, the Association moved away from the idea of a universal law and sought instead the formation of an international copyright union. In 1883, a three-day conference of nations in Berne, Switzerland, yielded a treaty that, in 1886, became the Convention for the Protection of Literary and Artistic Works. In essence, the Berne Convention adopted a national treatment approach, entitling foreign authors who were nationals of signatory nations to the same protections as domestic authors.

In 1908, Berne Convention nations met in Berlin to consider revisions. Two important changes resulted from what became the Berlin Act. First, states no longer could insist on formalities—published notice, deposit, or registration with a copyright body—as a prerequisite to attaining copyright protection. Second, a minimum term of copyright protection obtained, measured then as fifty years after an author's death.

Ten initial countries signed the treaty. That number today stands at 167. Although the United States participated in the original proceedings and subsequent conferences, it elected not to become a Berne Convention member until March 1, 1989. One principal reason for that delay was differences between U.S. copyright laws and some of the key Berne provisions, in particular the latter's recognition of "moral rights," which allow an author or creator to object to "any distortion, mutilation or other modification of, or other derogatory action in relation to . . . the work."

SEE ALSO The Statute of Anne (1710); America's First Copyright Law (1790); Copyright in the Digital Age (1999); Expanded Copyrights (2001); Google Books and Fair Use (2010).

"The Pirate Publisher—An International Burlesque That Has the Longest Run on Record" satirizes the unjust practices that necessitated the Berne Convention.

The Insanity Defense

James Garfield (1831–1881), **Charles Guiteau** (1841–1882),
United States v. Guiteau

Throughout the nineteenth century, most American courts looked to Britain's M'Naghten Rule as the appropriate legal standard by which to judge criminal insanity. That rule, fashioned by a panel of jurists in 1843 in response to the perceived leniency of earlier approaches, instructed that a defendant be considered sane and therefore responsible for his actions if he was aware of the nature and consequences of his actions and understood them to be unlawful.

On March 4, 1881, James Garfield became the twentieth president of the United States. Four months later, Charles Guiteau—erstwhile theologian, lawyer, and bill collector—shot him at the Baltimore and Potomac Railroad Station in the District of Columbia. The nation reacted with outrage as the insanity defense took center stage in the prosecution of Guiteau.

Many observers might have considered Guiteau mad—after all, no sane person could have committed so heinous an act, they reasoned—but it proved impossible for him to avail himself of the defense so structured: He knew it was unlawful to shoot the president and that the likely consequences of firing his two shots would be the president's death. Historian Charles E. Rosenberg writes that observers recognized Guiteau as "perhaps not completely normal . . . [but] certainly 'sane enough to be responsible.'"

After a seven-week trial, the jury deliberated for just one hour. Found guilty, Guiteau was hanged to death on June 30, 1882. After publication of the autopsy results, many in the medical community who had staunchly resisted any suggestion of Guiteau's insanity came to agree that he genuinely had been deranged and, according to Rosenberg, "chronically and obviously so." Many "did not hesitate to call the trial a miscarriage of justice, disgraceful to the legal and medical professions alike."

When John Hinckley successfully invoked the same line of defense at his trial for the attempted assassination of President Ronald Reagan in 1981, an incensed public stirred Congress to pass the Insanity Defense Reform Act of 1984, which shifted the burden of proof to the defendant and made the defense more difficult to assert.

SEE ALSO The M'Naghten Rule (1843).

Puck *magazine commissioned this caricature of Guiteau for its July 13, 1881, cover.*

The Chinese Exclusion Act

Give me your tired, your poor,
Your huddled masses yearning to breathe free,
The wretched refuse of your teeming shore.
Send these, the homeless, tempest-tossed to me,
I lift my lamp beside the golden door!
— Emma Lazarus, "The New Colossus" (1883)

Large numbers of Chinese workers first started coming to America soon after the 1849 California gold rush. Entry into the United States became a simple matter after Congress ratified the Burlingame Treaty in 1868, which recognized "the inherent and inalienable right of man to change his home and allegiance, and also the mutual advantage of the free migration and emigration of . . . citizens and subjects."

Over time, however, various groups launched political efforts to restrict the entry of Chinese immigrants and to limit or hinder their ability to work in the country, beginning with state laws enacted in California. At the federal level, those efforts culminated in the passage of the Chinese Exclusion Act, which banned the immigration of Chinese laborers for ten years and barred existing Chinese residents from naturalization. Notably, the ban didn't apply to individuals engaged in certain trades or professions—merchants and teachers, for example.

As historian Erika Lee points out, the watershed act was "the country's first significant restrictive immigration law; it was also the first to restrict a group of immigrants based on their race, nationality, and class." Roger Daniels, a leading scholar on the history of immigration, described it as "the pivot point on which all American immigration policy turned, the hinge on which Emma Lazarus's 'Golden Door' began to swing toward a closed position."

The Chinese Exclusion Act was extended in 1892, and it wasn't repealed until 1943. By then, it already had catalyzed dramatic changes in the approach to immigration policy and spawned the creation of a federal bureaucracy, which eventually became the Immigration and Naturalization Service in 1933.

SEE ALSO The Alhambra Decree (1492); Equal Protection Rights (1886); The Emergency Quota Act (1921); The Displaced Persons Act (1948).

Suey Kee Lung (c. 1912) was one of many Chinese immigrants arrested for illegal entry into America.

Suey Kee Lung

The Civil Rights Cases

Decades after the Emancipation Proclamation, African Americans remained in a precarious state of "freedom." Although slavery had been abolished, restrictions on employment, transportation, housing, and nearly all other aspects of life prevented black Americans from enjoying the same freedoms as their white peers. To address these inequalities, Congress, relying on the Fourteenth Amendment, passed the Civil Rights Act of 1875, which granted "citizens of every race and color" equal access to "inns, public conveyances on land or water, theaters and other places of public amusement." Unfortunately, the act did little to mitigate racial tensions and soon faced challenges.

The Civil Rights Cases refer to five factually similar lawsuits consolidated before the Supreme Court for the purpose of determining whether the Civil Rights Act of 1875 was constitutional: *United States v. Stanley*; *United States v. Ryan*; *United States v. Nichols*; *United States v. Singleton*; and *Robinson and wife v. Memphis & Charleston R.R. Co.* In each case, hotels or other establishments had refused service to blacks based solely on their race, clearly defying the Civil Rights Act. To avoid penalties, the violators argued that Congress exceeded its constitutional power in forcing private establishments to serve blacks. Thus, the fates of the Civil Rights Act of 1875, Congress's interpretation of the Fourteenth Amendment, and the equality of African Americans all depended on this crucial Supreme Court decision.

In October 1883, the Court ruled the Civil Rights Act of 1875 unconstitutional, legitimizing the discriminatory treatment. The Court distinguished between governmental and private actions, stating that the Fourteenth Amendment granted Congress the power to combat racism in the former context but not in the latter. Salting the wound, the Court added that a time should come when a former slave "ceases to be the special favorite of the laws," showcasing its unwillingness to support additional anti-discrimination legislation.

The Civil Rights Cases landed a major blow to the early civil rights movement, and the decision ushered in an era of continued segregation and inequality, further validated by the Supreme Court's 1896 decision in *Plessy v. Ferguson*. Decades passed before Congress again concerned itself with civil rights legislation.

SEE ALSO The Civil Rights Act of 1866; Prohibition of Racial Voter Discrimination (1869); *Plessy v. Ferguson: Separate but Equal* (1896); The Civil Rights Act of 1964.

Even after ratification of the Fourteenth Amendment, racial discrimination remained entrenched in the American landscape.

Equal Protection Rights

Yick Wo v. Hopkins

After the discovery of gold in California in 1848, large numbers of Chinese immigrants came to America. In the early years, many worked in the mines or manufacturing or as laborers for the expanding railroad network. A good number of others opened laundry shops. Yick Wo arrived in San Francisco in 1861 and opened a laundry three years later, operating it successfully for more than two decades.

In 1880, responding to increasing hostility toward the Chinese, the city enacted an ordinance requiring all laundries not housed in brick or stone buildings—meaning wooden structures—to obtain a license from the Board of Supervisors. Of the 310 laundries within the bounds of San Francisco, 240 were Chinese-owned. All Caucasian owners who sought licenses received them, but Chinese owners didn't fare so well. Just *one* succeeded in obtaining the required license. Yick Wo refused to shut his laundry, despite lacking a license, and determined to challenge the discriminatory law. He was arrested and fined ten dollars, then jailed for ten days after refusing to pay the fine.

Yick Wo sought a writ of habeas corpus for unlawful imprisonment and pursued the case to the U.S. Supreme Court. In a unanimous decision, the Court vacated the conviction and established two groundbreaking precedents that paved the way for some of the civil rights battles that occupied American courts throughout the mid-twentieth century. Writing for the Court, Justice Stanley Matthews noted that Yick Wo had complied with all necessary health and safety regulations and that the Board of Supervisors could articulate no reason for its obvious discrimination between Caucasian and Chinese owners other than "hostility to the race and the nationality to which the petitioners belong, and which in the eye of the law is not justified."

The ultimate significance of the *Yick Wo* decision is two-fold. First, the Court established for the first time that a law that looked neutral might still be discriminatory if enforced differently between different classes or groups of citizens. Second, the Court established, also for the first time, that the Constitution's equal protection clause extended to all residents, not only citizens.

SEE ALSO The Habeas Corpus Act of 1679; The Fourteenth Amendment (1868); The Chinese Exclusion Act (1882).

In 1880, a San Francisco law specifically targeted Chinese laundries like this one, precipitating a landmark U.S. Supreme Court case that extended the Constitution's equal protection clause to all American residents.

1887

The Interstate Commerce Act

In the late nineteenth century, no industry proved so vital yet so publicly reviled as the railroads. At the time, trains provided the most efficient means of transporting goods and people across America, but the privately owned, unregulated, postwar railroad industry fostered deep public mistrust. One of the largest issues facing consumers was that railroad rates were inconsistent; companies changed rates when and as they saw fit. Some regions benefited from the services of multiple railroad companies, but many others didn't, resulting in monopolization. In the public eye, the railroads' unrestrained power served as a symbol of political corruption and manipulation.

In response to the outcry for intervention, Congress passed the Interstate Commerce Act in 1887, which encouraged competition among railroad companies. It required that rates be made public, outlawed unjust rate setting, and established the Interstate Commerce Commission (ICC) to oversee its enforcement. The establishment of the ICC itself was monumental because it was the first independent regulatory agency in the country. Unfortunately, the Act's language didn't establish clear guidelines in identifying discriminatory rates, and it proved far less effective than intended, a deficiency corrected with the Hepburn Act of 1906 and the Mann-Elkins Act of 1910.

Throughout the twentieth century, the scope of the Interstate Commerce Act and the power of the ICC fluctuated. Though created to regulate railways, the ICC eventually came to oversee other modes of transportation, including trucks and barges. Until the 1934 creation of the Federal Communications Commission (FCC), the ICC also regulated telegraph and cable communications. Courts even used the Act to further civil rights measures. Beginning in the 1940s, the Supreme Court invoked the commerce clause to strike down discriminatory railroad practices as violations of fundamental individual rights founded on the Act and deriving from congressional power to regulate commerce. In two cases decided in 1964, the Court upheld Congress's power under the commerce clause, rather than the Fourteenth Amendment's equal protection clause, to prohibit private discrimination based on race.

The Act technically remains in effect today, but, after the long wave of federal deregulation that began in the 1970s, the ICC ceased to exist in 1995.

SEE ALSO The Sherman Antitrust Act (1890); Busting the Trusts (1911); The Clayton Antitrust Act (1914); Congressional Regulation of Commerce (1824); The Microsoft Monopoly (2000).

Unfair and haphazard business practices by the railroad companies prompted Congress to enact the Interstate Commerce Act. Carleton Watkins (1829–1916) took this photo of a trestle on the Central Pacific Railroad in 1877.

The Brazilian Slave Emancipation Act

Isabel, Princess Imperial of Brazil (1846–1921)

The growth of slavery in Brazil largely mirrors the development of the sugarcane crop in the mid-sixteenth century. At the time, Portugal supplied most of Europe's sugar through plantations on its Atlantic islands of Madeira, São Tomé, and Principe. Concern that the French and English might establish settlements in its loosely controlled Brazilian colony, coupled with increasing worldwide demand for sugar, led Portugal to establish new sugar plantations in northeastern Brazil.

Increasing sugar output required a larger labor force, prompting Brazil to become one of the major buyers of African slaves. Demand for slave labor increased further after gold was discovered in Brazil, beginning in 1690, and again when coffee became a key economic crop. Professor Robin Blackburn, one of the U.K.'s preeminent slavery historians, notes that between 1500 and 1865 European traders purchased twelve million captives on the African coast, ten million of whom "survived to be sold into slavery in the New World." A little more than four million of them arrived in Brazil.

By 1865, Brazil still had one and a half million slaves, and formal emancipation lay nearly twenty-five years away. The importation of slaves from Africa was halted in 1850, but slavery continued unabated until 1871, when Brazil enacted the Rio Branco or Free Birth Law, granting freedom to the offspring of slaves when they turned twenty-one years old.

Abolitionist forces continued to chip away at the acceptability of slavery, and parts of the country granted slaves their freedom in the early 1880s. Then, on May 13, 1888, Princess Regent Isabel publicly approved the *Lei Áurea* (Golden Law), granting immediate emancipation. Ending more than three centuries of slavery, the law consisted of just two sentences, but they were profound: "From this date slavery is declared extinct in Brazil. All laws to the contrary are revoked."

That proclamation made Brazil the final nation to outlaw the brutal and deadly institution.

SEE ALSO The Black Code of Louis XIV (1685); The Emancipation Proclamation (1863); The Abolition of Slavery (1865).

Slaves on a coffee farm in Brazil, c. 1885, in a photograph by Marc Ferrez.

The Right to Privacy

Louis Brandeis (1856–1941), Samuel Warren (1852–1910)

Among the mountain of legal scholarship generated over the past century and a quarter, one article stands alone by virtue of its influence on the development of legal doctrine. In 1890, the *Harvard Law Review* published "The Right to Privacy," written by future Supreme Court justice Louis Brandeis and his then-colleague Samuel Warren. Roscoe Pound, a dean of Harvard Law School in the early twentieth century, summed up the magnitude of its impact best: Brandeis and Warren "did nothing less than add a chapter to our law."

The article's thesis holds that courts should recognize a right of individual privacy, or in its simplest form, "the right to be let alone." That principle derived from its authors' reactions to a zeitgeist of the times. In particular, they were reacting to an obtrusive and intrusive press—when yellow journalism was running rampant—along with the new technology of instantaneous photographs. Referring to "modern enterprise and invention," Brandeis and Warren wrote that "numerous mechanical devices threaten to make good the prediction that 'what is whispered in the closet shall be proclaimed from the house-tops.'"

The two men detailed the common law's evolution over time to accommodate political and economic changes in society; it did so, they argued, by expanding legal protections. For example, while the law originally protected only against physical injury and corporeal property, protections became necessary—and thus available—for threats of physical injury. Similarly, a cause of action for defamation developed to compensate for intangible damages suffered to reputation. Even intellectual property (trademarks, copyright, and the like) gained protection. The law needed to recognize assaults on another type of intangible property: personal privacy.

Some states, including New York, enacted legislation embodying this concept of a right to privacy; many others adopted a version of it as part of their common law. The American Law Institute notably codified a right of privacy in the Restatement of Torts in 1939, and scholars routinely credit the article by Brandeis and Warren as the seminal source of the right to privacy.

SEE ALSO Wiretaps (1928); The Body and the Right of Privacy (1965); *Roe v. Wade* (1973).

Associate Justice of the U.S. Supreme Court Louis Brandeis (c. 1916) had a major influence on law pertaining to the right to privacy.

The Sherman Antitrust Act

John Sherman (1823–1900)

The need for antitrust law arose after the Civil War as businesses grew larger and sometimes combined to avoid competition between and among themselves. These laws aim to ensure the viability of competition, which in turn promotes economic opportunity, fair prices, and market efficiency.

In 1888, the first antitrust law—named for Senator John Sherman of Ohio—was introduced, undergoing scrutiny, debate, and revision over the course of two congresses. The result was a law both broad and general that required a good deal of input from the courts called upon to interpret and apply it.

The Act's basic provisions remain the same today as when they first appeared. Section 1 prohibits contracts and combinations in restraint of interstate or foreign trade or commerce. (Given the requirement of a contract or combination, purely individual conduct is not covered.) Section 2 prohibits monopolization and attempts or conspiracies to monopolize interstate or foreign trade or commerce. Both sections allow the federal government to seek civil and criminal penalties. There's also provision for private remedies, which can include awards of treble damages paid to injured parties.

Courts interpreting Section 1 almost immediately came to hold that it proscribed only unreasonable restraints of trade, leading to the development of the "rule of reason." But courts also identified certain categories of illegal conduct deemed unreasonable per se and therefore unsalvageable. Those categories included price-fixing agreements, group boycotts, and agreements to divide markets.

The Sherman Antitrust Act found its first vigorous enforcement through the courts in 1911 with the government's separate suits against Standard Oil and American Tobacco, the former because of its power to control market prices and the latter because of predatory market conduct driving out competitors. In the twentieth century's largest antitrust case, the Department of Justice in 1974 forced telephone giant AT&T to divest itself of more than twenty local telephone companies in order to retain its long-distance and other operations.

SEE ALSO Congressional Regulation of Commerce (1824); The Interstate Commerce Act (1887); Busting the Trusts (1911); The Clayton Antitrust Act (1914); The Microsoft Monopoly (2000).

Senator John Sherman of Ohio, principal author of the Sherman Antitrust Act, c. 1870.

New Zealand Women's Suffrage

Mary Ann Müller (c. 1820–1901), **Kate Sheppard** (1847–1934),
David Boyle, 7th Earl of Glasgow (1833–1915)

In 1869, under the alias Femmina, Mary Ann Müller of Nelson, New Zealand, published and distributed pamphlets advocating for women's rights. Sixteen years later, in 1885, the Women's Christian Temperance Union (WCTU) of the United States founded fifteen branches in New Zealand and picked up the campaign where Müller had left off. Two years later, Kate Sheppard of Christchurch became the national franchise superintendent and the leader of the women-focused national body. Joined by household names from all over the country, Sheppard gained enormous support and recognition for the organization.

Despite growing support, the suffrage movement faced significant opposition along the way, with opponents' arguments ranging from the suggestion that changing gender roles threatened the very fabric of family bonds to the concerns of the liquor industry, which feared a financial crash from pro-temperance women voters.

From the inception of the group, the women of the WCTU sent annual petitions to Parliament. In 1891, they mustered nine thousand signatures; the following year, with support surging, they submitted twenty thousand; and in 1893 they sent nearly thirty-two thousand signatures to Parliament, a number representing one-quarter of New Zealand's population of adult women.

The message was becoming crystal clear, but it was still a close call in Parliament. On September 8, 1893, the Electoral Bill passed, 20–18. The governor-general, Lord Glasgow, signed the new Electoral Act into law. Women immediately rushed to register to vote for the quickly approaching November election. Nearly 110,000 registered—approximately 84 percent of those eligible—and slightly more than ninety thousand marched to the polls alongside men, vastly exceeding expectations. One of the Christchurch newspapers missed the point entirely and reported that "the pretty dresses of the ladies and their smiling faces lighted up the polling booths most wonderfully."

It had been a long march, but New Zealand became the first self-governing country to grant women the right to vote.

SEE ALSO Admission of Women to the Bar (1873); Women's Right to Vote (1919).

The inaugural meeting of the National Council of Women in Christchurch, New Zealand, in 1896.

Plessy v. Ferguson: Separate but Equal

Homer Plessy (1863–1925), **Henry Billings Brown** (1836–1913),
John Marshall Harlan (1833–1911)

In 1890, Louisiana passed the Separate Car Act, requiring blacks and whites to travel in different railway carriages. The Committee of Citizens, a Louisiana group, challenged the law in the hope of prevailing in the courts. On June 7, 1892, Homer Plessy, a shoemaker and member of the committee, purchased a first-class ticket and took his seat in a designated white car. When questioned about his race, the light-skinned Plessy stated that he was African American and was arrested when he refused to move. In a bench trial—in which Judge John Ferguson of the New Orleans Criminal District Court upheld the validity of the Separate Car Act—Plessy was convicted.

His appeal reached the U.S. Supreme Court in 1896 and became one of the most infamous cases in American history. In an opinion delivered by Justice Henry Billings Brown, the Court upheld the law as constitutional. Brown explained that states may enact racially based classifications if they are reasonable, with reasonableness dependent upon the "established usages, customs and traditions of the people, and with a view to the promotion of their comfort, and preservation of the public peace and good order." This law, he said, promoted racial peace. Nor did the Act place blacks in an inferior class; he concluded: "If this be so, it is not by reason of anything found in the act, but solely because the colored race chooses to put that construction upon it." The ruling gave legal sanction to the principle that states could segregate the races as long as they provided equal accommodations.

In one of the most influential dissents in Supreme Court history, Justice John Marshall Harlan wrote that states could not regulate conduct based on race. "In the eyes of the law, there is in this country no superior, dominant, ruling class of citizens. There is no caste here. Our constitution is color-blind, and neither knows nor tolerates classes among citizens. In respect of civil rights, all citizens are equal before the law." Those words provided inspiration for future advocates of desegregation, but almost sixty years passed before *Brown v. Board of Education* formally overturned *Plessy v. Ferguson*.

SEE ALSO The Civil Rights Cases (1883); Equal Protection Rights (1886); *Brown v. Board of Education* (1954); The Civil Rights Act of 1964; The Voting Rights Act (1965); Interracial Marriage (1967).

This memorial plaque is at the corner of Press and Royal Streets in New Orleans, Louisiana, where Homer Plessy was arrested.

PLESSY V. FERGUSON
PRESS STREET RAILROAD YARDS
Site of the Arrest of Homer Adolph Plessy

• • •

On June 7, 1892, Homer Adolph Plessy was removed from the East Louisiana Railroad train and arrested by Detective C.C. Cain at the corner of Royal and Press St. He was charged with violating the 1890 Louisiana Separate Car Act that separated railroad passengers by race.

Plessy's act of civil disobedience was a test case organized by the Comité des Citoyens (Citizens' Committee) whose aim was to overturn segregation laws that were being enacted across the South. The philosophy and strategies of the Comité des Citoyens foreshadowed Civil Rights movements of the 20th century. Although the Supreme Court ruled against Plessy on May 18, 1896, his case marked the first post-Reconstruction use of the 14th Amendment's "equal protection" provision in a legal challenge to segregation. In their final statement after the Supreme Court verdict, the Comité des Citoyens proclaimed, *"We as freemen still believe we were right and our cause is sacred...In defending the cause of liberty, we met with defeat but not with ignominy"*. Their position was vindicated when the Supreme Court upheld similar 14th Amendment arguments in the 1954 case of Brown v. Board of Education.
(Continued on other side)

CRESCENT CITY PEACE ALLIANCE

Corporate Personhood and Liability

Trustees of Dartmouth College v. Woodward, Salomon v. A. Salomon & Co., Hardinge Stanley Giffard, 1st Earl of Halsbury (1823–1921)

One of the law's many fictions is the juridical entity, a body that exists only by virtue of the law. For example, a corporation can contract, own property, sue, and be sued based solely on the statute that created it. (The Supreme Court affirmed that corporations have the same contract rights as natural persons in *Trustees of Dartmouth College v. Woodward* in 1819.) Before the corporate form, many businesses operated as partnerships. But joint and several liability presented a problem: Each partner was liable for the full debts and obligations of the partnership, and the partnership could be held liable for the private debts of a partner.

In Britain, only a royal charter or legislative action could grant corporate status. Then, in 1844, Parliament passed the Joint Stock Companies Act, permitting corporations through an act of registration. Corporate status still entailed individual shareholder liability, however. Recognizing that limited liability would promote investment and entrepreneurship, Parliament passed the 1855 Limited Liability Act and the 1862 Companies Act, granting limited liability to any properly registered company meeting certain financial thresholds. That approach held firm for the next century.

In 1892, Aron Salomon converted his leather-and-boot business to a corporation, taking twenty thousand shares of stock for himself and giving one share each to his wife and five children. When business declined and Salomon failed to pay his creditors, the company went into liquidation, and unsecured creditors sued Salomon personally.

The House of Lords unanimously found Salomon not personally liable for the corporation's debts. Lord Halsbury explained that the only question was whether the company had been constituted validly; the court had no right "to add to the requirements of the statute." Once legally incorporated, the corporation "must be treated like any other independent person with its rights and liabilities appropriate to itself."

The *Salomon* decision helped ensure the continued growth of the corporate form for closely held entities. Although the case continues to be cited, courts decline to do so when circumstances justify disregarding the corporate entity, as for example where it serves as an explicit and improper shield against liability.

SEE ALSO The Bubble Act (1720); Wall Street Regulation (1933); The Sarbanes-Oxley Act (2002).

The liquidation of a leather-and-boot business led to a landmark case in which the House of Lords ruled that individuals cannot be held personally answerable for the limited liability corporations that they form.

The German Civil Code

The 1871 Treaty of Versailles ended the Franco-Prussian War, but it resulted in a strengthened and unified German Empire. As historian Peter R. Senn observes, however, this new empire "included a wide variety of political forms: an imperial territory, kingdoms, free cities, grand-duchies, duchies, and principalities, each with its own territory, courts, and laws." Atop these systems lay three different legal codes: the Prussian Civil Code of 1794, the Napoleonic Code of 1804, and the Austrian Code of 1811.

A long-simmering desire for legal uniformity resulted in the appointment of a commission in 1874 to draft an appropriate code. After over a decade of effort, the commission submitted a draft for public consideration in 1888. The draft proved unacceptable, though, criticized for being "too Roman" and failing to incorporate enough Germanic tribal customary law. A new commission was appointed in 1890 to continue the effort, and a revised draft was completed in 1895. After further revisions, this version of the Bürgerliches Gesetzbuch passed into law on August 18, 1896, became effective as of January 1, 1900, and remains effective today.

"The legal status of man begins with his birth." Thus begins the imposing civil code, which originally contained 2,385 sections. Its five major divisions address general rules of law and personal rights, the law of obligations (contracts and torts), the law of real property, family law, and the law of succession. Walter Loewy wrote in the introduction to his 1905 translation of the document that its "tremendous political importance . . . lies in the fact that it completes German unity."

A long and deliberate effort preceded passage of the code, which helps explain its longevity. Modified over time, its basic structure and contents nevertheless have shown remarkable endurance, surviving multiple political revolutions, a Fascist regime, two world wars, two Allied occupations, and the 1990 reunification of West and East Germany. But it also had a significant influence on the development of other nations' legal systems, including those of Austria, Greece, Japan, Russia, the Scandinavian nations, and Switzerland.

SEE ALSO The Justinian Code (529); The Napoleonic Code (1804).

Taking effect at the turn of the twentieth century, the civil code of Germany, Bürgerliches Gesetzbuch, *satisfied a long-held desire for legal uniformity in the German Empire.*

Bürgerliches

Gesetzbuch

Textausgabe

mit alphabetischem Sachregister

Dritter Abdruck

München, C. H. Beck.

The Cuban Constitution of 1901

Christopher Columbus (c. 1451–1506), **María Cristina of Spain** (1858–1929), **William McKinley** (1843–1901), **Leonard Wood** (1860–1927), **Orville Platt** (1827–1905), **Domingo Méndez Capote** (1863–1934)

On Christopher Columbus's first voyage in October 1492, he first made landfall in what is now the Bahamas before proceeding and laying claim to what would become Cuba. Spain ruled Cuba until 1898, when the USS *Maine* suspiciously exploded and sank in Havana Harbor. Nearly three-quarters of the crew died. The incident drew America, under the leadership of President McKinley, and Spain, ruled by Queen Regent María Cristina, into the Spanish-American War, itself an outgrowth of the Cuban War for Independence, in which the U.S. had intervened on Cuba's behalf.

After Spain surrendered, American forces, under the command of Military Governor Leonard Wood, continued to occupy the island, helping to establish foundational infrastructure. Cuba's proximity to the United States, its position at the entrance of the Gulf of Mexico, and its status as the largest island in the Caribbean gave it important strategic value that America sought to protect. U.S. Senator Orville Platt of Connecticut introduced legislation that called for Cuba to recognize America's right to intervene in Cuban affairs and to "sell or lease to the United States lands necessary for coaling or naval stations." (This latter provision allowed for Cuba's perpetual lease of Guantánamo Bay to the U.S. government.)

President McKinley signed the Platt legislation into law, and the Constitutional Assembly in Cuba, headed by Domingo Méndez Capote, included the Platt Amendment as an appendix to the constitution it adopted in June 1901. That constitution bears many similarities to the U.S. Constitution: calling for a president, a bicameral legislature, an independent judiciary headed by a supreme court, and a bill of rights. But the Platt Amendment permitted America to dominate Cuban political affairs. That dominance laid the groundwork for hostilities and resentments that produced three more Cuban constitutions over the next seventy-five years and forever altered Cuba's relations with the U.S. and the rest of the world.

SEE ALSO The Alhambra Decree (1492); The Bubble Act (1720); *The Amistad* (1839).

This 1896 political propaganda cartoon published in Puck *magazine shows Uncle Sam nobly defending a supplicant Cuba from the evil wiles of Spain. The truth of the matter was rather more complicated.*

1908

Women in Factories

Muller v. Oregon

Sometimes courts reach decisions that yield immediately positive changes for society but at the same time enable unforeseen future evils. *Muller v. Oregon* offers a paradigmatic example. The same decision that upheld legislation designed to protect women laborers by limiting their work hours set the stage for future decades of gender discrimination.

In 1903, Oregon enacted legislation prohibiting women from working more than ten hours a day in factories or laundries. Two years later, an overseer at Grand Laundry in Portland required a female employee to work overtime. Curt Muller, the laundry's owner, was convicted in state court for violating the work law.

In an appeal to the U.S. Supreme Court, Muller argued that the law violated his and his workers' rights to freedom of contract under the equal protection clause of the Fourteenth Amendment. Attorneys for the state, backed by progressive reformers, argued that long work hours harmed women's health more than men's. Submitting data that detailed working women's hours, they claimed that overworking mothers directly impacted the welfare of the entire nation.

The Supreme Court unanimously upheld the Oregon law, agreeing with the state that "as healthy mothers are essential to vigorous offspring, the physical well-being of women becomes an object of public interest and care in order to preserve the strength and vigor of the race." The Court concluded that the physical differences between men and women justified "a difference in legislation."

That decision had a devastating impact on women's rights. It gave formal recognition to the legal principle that women could be treated differently than men. Several decades would pass before states abandoned their single-sex protection laws in favor of today's gender-neutral policies. Still, *Muller*'s legacy wasn't all bad. In 1917, the Supreme Court upheld an Oregon law setting maximum hours for male workers. The *Muller* decision also paved the way for important modern-day workplace regulations, such as the Fair Labor Standards Act, which established minimum wages and maximum work hours.

SEE ALSO Workers' Compensation Law (1910); The Child Labor Act of 1916; The National Labor Relations Act (1935); The Fair Labor Standards Act (1938).

This 1886 advertisement for a hosiery factory shows women demonstrating both handmade work and factory production.

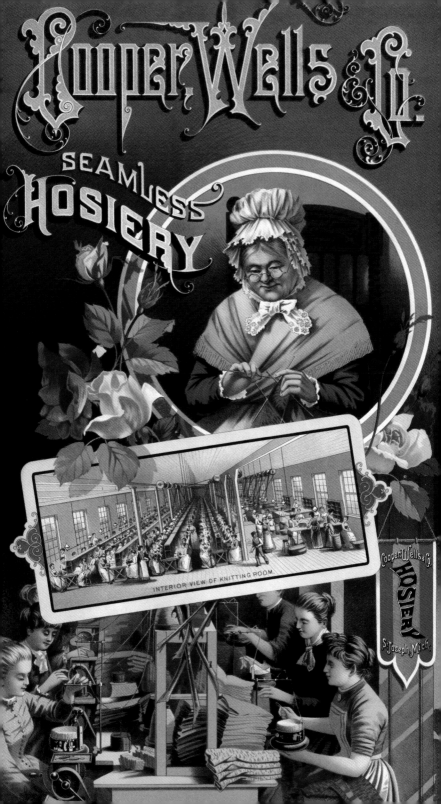

Congressional Power to Tax Income

William Howard Taft (1857–1930)

Income taxes existed in the distant past, although they were rare and primarily funded warfare. After Saladin conquered Jerusalem, King Henry II of England instituted the Saladin Tithe in 1188, collecting a tenth of his subjects' income and movable property to fund the Third Crusade. America's first income tax came in 1643 as a faculties and abilities tax established by several colonies. Prime Minister William Pitt the Younger introduced the Triple Assessment to Britain in 1798 to help fund the French Revolution. President Lincoln signed the Revenue Act of 1861 into law, which introduced an income tax to pay for Union expenditures in the Civil War, and a similar act the next year created the Bureau of Internal Revenue, but the act was repealed after the war.

The income tax made a brief return in 1894, when Congress established a 2 percent tax on annual incomes over $4,000 to address economic inequalities, but it proved short-lived. In *Pollock v. Farmers' Loan & Trust Co.*, the U.S. Supreme Court found that taxes on income from real or personal property were direct taxes and therefore unconstitutional in the absence of apportionment.

In the 1908 presidential election, Democrats supported an income tax, as did William Howard Taft, the Republican nominee. After winning the election, though, Taft didn't want to sign a personal income tax law that would face another constitutional challenge. His solution was a constitutional amendment that expressly permitted it. Taft's proposed amendment received unanimous approval in the Senate and passed overwhelmingly in the House of Representatives. State ratification proceeded slowly, but in February 1913 the last of the necessary ratifications took place to approve the Sixteenth Amendment: "The Congress shall have the power to lay and collect taxes on incomes, from whatever source derived, without apportionment among the several States, and without regard to any census or enumeration." Secretary of State Philander Knox certified adoption of the amendment, and later that year Congress passed the Revenue Act of 1913, which imposed a tax on net income at rates ranging from 1 to 6 percent, confirming that income taxes were here to stay.

SEE ALSO The Triple Assessment (Income Tax) (1798); Triple Assessment (Income Tax) (1798); The Supremacy of Federal Courts (1821); Celebrity Tax Prosecution (1989).

When ratified, the Sixteenth Amendment opened the door to a new branch of jurisprudence: tax law.

The White-Slave Traffic Act

James R. Mann (1856–1922), *Caminetti v. United States*

The suggestion that Congress or any legislative body can't legislate morality has become one of the great legal platitudes. But successful attempts to do just that remain an indelible part of legal history.

In June 1910, responding to a moral panic sweeping the country, Congress enacted the White-Slave Traffic Act. Better known by the name of the Congressman who sponsored the bill, James R. Mann of Chicago, Illinois, the Mann Act made it a felony to knowingly transport in interstate commerce "any woman or girl for the purpose of prostitution or debauchery, or for any other immoral purpose."

The Mann Act arose in an era of rapidly expanding immigration and urbanization and at a time when the nation "worried about prostitution with an intensity never before or after equaled," according to Professor David J. Langum. Despite the act's unambiguous aim, courts gave the Mann Act a more expansive reading, focusing on its catch-all reference to "any other immoral purpose."

In 1917, *Caminetti v. United States*—the first of three cases consolidated for argument before the U.S. Supreme Court—made clear that the purpose of the Mann Act was "to put a stop to a villainous interstate and international traffic in women and girls" and to "prevent panderers and procurers from compelling thousands of women and girls against their will and desire to enter and continue in a life of prostitution." But the Supreme Court held that the act proscribed not just white slavery and prostitution but consensual sexual encounters even in which no money changed hands.

As a result of that expansive interpretation, the Mann Act has been used to arrest and prosecute thousands of people over the years, including celebrities such as Jack Johnson, Frank Lloyd Wright, Charlie Chaplin, and Chuck Berry. Johnson, the first black heavyweight boxing champion, was convicted under the Mann Act in 1913 for paying one of his white girlfriends to travel from Pittsburgh to Chicago for "immoral purposes."

Although the Mann Act remains on the books, a 1986 amendment replaced the phrase "immoral purposes" with "any sexual activity for which any person can be charged with a criminal offense."

In the early 1940s, Charlie Chaplin had an affair with Joan Barry, an aspiring young actress. Skeptical of the actor's politics, the FBI indicted him for violating the Mann Act by buying a train ticket for her. This photo shows him right after his acquittal.

Workers' Compensation Law

Charles Evans Hughes (1862–1948)

As industrialization expanded in the late nineteenth century, so too did workplace dangers. People worked in trades that increasingly presented greater risks of accidental injury and death, particularly in coal mining and constructing the railroads. Labor economists Price V. Fishback and Shawn Everett Kantor write that "industrial accidents, along with the related financial hardship that they caused, were becoming a serious problem." Those and factors—such as growing restrictions on employers' defenses to accident claims and increased uncertainty as to the results of worker lawsuits, leading to increasing liability insurance rates—precipitated the rapid adoption of workers' compensation laws throughout the country.

Prior to the development of workers' compensation, injured workers' only remedy was lawsuits against their employers alleging negligence. Then they needed to prove that the employers' failure to exercise reasonable care proximately caused their injuries. Such claims proved problematic, however, because of the long-standing assumption of risk doctrine; it shielded many employers from liability on the theory that the worker, who well knew the workplace's inherent dangers, waived any right to sue.

Against this backdrop, two forces led to the creation and rapid proliferation of state workers' compensation statutes beginning in 1910. First, social reformers anxiously wanted to alleviate what they perceived as the asymmetrical economic burden that befell injured workers. Second, the legal climate was becoming less favorable to employers as courts began chipping away at legal defenses such as assumption of risk. This changing legal climate created uncertainty for employers, who faced a growing number of negligence lawsuits, and an attendant increase in the cost of liability insurance. Thus a compulsory workplace accident compensation system covering all employees became economically attractive to businesses.

In 1910, New York Governor Charles Evans Hughes signed the nation's first workers' compensation law. By the end of the decade, almost every other state had followed suit, creating what Fishback and Kantor refer to as "the first widespread social insurance program in the United States, paving the way for the later adoption of government programs for unemployment insurance, old-age pensions, and health insurance."

SEE ALSO The Social Security Act (1935); The Fair Labor Standards Act (1938); The Occupational Safety and Health Act (1970).

Charles Evans Hughes as governor of New York.

Busting the Trusts

United States v. E. C. Knight Co., Theodore Roosevelt (1858–1919),
Standard Oil Co. v. United States, Edward Douglass White (1845–1921)

When Congress enacted the Sherman Antitrust Act in 1890, it sought to address the growing power of corporations born of rapidly advancing industrialization. Its goal was protection of competition, lower prices, and greater options for consumers. Enforcement of the act in its first decade was relatively weak, however.

Assuming the presidency in 1901 after McKinley's death, Theodore Roosevelt mounted an aggressive campaign to bust the trusts, corporate entities that enabled large companies to evade the Sherman Act's strictures. In early 1902, Philander Knox, then U.S. attorney general, filed suit against the Northern Securities Company, a trust formed by the heads of two major railroads. The Supreme Court concluded that the trust represented an illegal combination that violated the Sherman Act. Roosevelt called the suit "one of the greatest achievements of my administration . . . for through it we emphasized . . . the fact that the most powerful men in this country were held to accountability before the law." The case also held enormous legal significance: It paved the way for the government's 1906 lawsuit against the Standard Oil Company of New Jersey and an even more consequential legal doctrine.

The government's suit against Standard Oil—which controlled more than 90 percent of the country's refining capacity—alleged a litany of anticompetitive activities. In a unanimous decision, the Supreme Court affirmed a finding of a Sherman Act violation and ordered that the company divest itself of its subsidiaries. For antitrust jurisprudence, the true import of the decision lies in the Court's adoption of the rule of reason. Chief Justice Edward White's opinion asserted that the Sherman Act was intended to proscribe only unreasonable restraints of trade. He found Standard Oil's conduct unreasonable because its intent and purpose was "to maintain dominancy over the oil industry, not as a result of normal methods . . . but by new means of combination . . . in order that greater power might be added than would otherwise have arisen."

SEE ALSO The Sherman Antitrust Act (1890); Busting the Trusts (1911); The Clayton Antitrust Act (1914); The Microsoft Monopoly (2000).

"The Infant Hercules and the Standard Oil Serpents," from the May 23, 1906, issue of Puck *magazine. President Theodore Roosevelt is grabbing the head of Senator Nelson Aldrich and the body of oil baron John D. Rockefeller.*

The Triangle Shirtwaist Fire

As history too often reminds us, sometimes tragedy offers the only impetus to necessary changes in the law. In New York City's history, there has never been a fire more deadly or more consequential than the one that consumed the Triangle shirtwaist factory in 1911. Occurring amid the country's growing labor movement, the catastrophe served as the catalyst for reversing generations of unsafe labor practices and protecting modern-day workers.

The Triangle Waist Company employed approximately five hundred women, mostly Jewish and Italian immigrants between the ages of thirteen and twenty-three. They worked on the top floors of a ten-story Manhattan building making shirtwaists, a kind of fashionable dress for well-to-do women. To keep employees at their cutting tables and sewing machines, company supervisors locked all doors to the workrooms from the outside. The fire began on the eighth floor and spread quickly. Those on the ninth floor couldn't open the locked exit doors. A rear fire escape collapsed. In fewer than fifteen minutes, 146 women died in the fire or jumped to their deaths. Damage from the intensity of the flames was so severe that authorities couldn't determine the fire's cause.

But if good can spring from tragedy, the Triangle fire provides a prime example. New York and other cities and states implemented important workplace safety regulations in the fire's aftermath. The fire also rallied support for workers across the nation and acted as the impetus for the International Ladies' Garment Workers' Union.

The Triangle owners were charged with manslaughter but were acquitted for lack of proof that they knew the exit doors were locked. But civil suits brought in 1914 resulted in payments of $75 to each of the twenty-three families who sued. For many survivors, the tragedy could never be forgotten. The fire's last survivor, Rose Freedman (née Rosenfeld), died in 2001 at the age of 107.

SEE ALSO Women in Factories (1908); Workers' Compensation Law (1910); The Child Labor Act of 1916; The National Labor Relations Act (1935); The Fair Labor Standards Act (1938); The Occupational Safety and Health Act (1970).

The New York Fire Department battles the great blaze at the Triangle shirtwaist factory in Greenwich Village on March 25, 1911.

The Federal Reserve Act

Alexander Hamilton (c. 1755–1804), **Woodrow Wilson** (1856–1924)

When asked why he robbed banks, Willie Sutton famously replied, "Because that's where the money is." However apocryphal his answer, it was right only because of the Federal Reserve System, which Congress created in 1913 with the Federal Reserve Act in response to financial panics and bank failures that had been plaguing the nation for decades. The central bank and the act that created it have played a foundational role both per se and in dozens of subsequent banking laws and regulations that have a daily impact on the world economy.

Alexander Hamilton had urged the formation of the federal First Bank of the United States, chartered in 1791, which later lapsed but influenced the creation of the Second Bank in 1816, which also later lapsed. What most spurred the creation of the Federal Reserve was the Bank Panic of 1907, which began when the National Bank of Commerce stopped clearing checks for the Knickerbocker Trust Company, leading to a run on the latter and a succession of additional bank failures. Congress responded in 1908 by creating the National Monetary Commission to study the problem and to recommend solutions. The commission studied banking systems across the world, produced thirty volumes of research, and identified seventeen defects in the nation's financial system. The most important related to the availability of cash reserves and various laws that prohibited their use when most needed.

Two widely diverging camps engaged in a lengthy battle in Congress over the appropriate legislation. One side sought to emulate the Bank of England by creating a single central bank owned by commercial banks and run by the bankers. The other side opposed a single central bank, viewing that approach as conferring a monopoly on an institution that operated for the benefit of the bankers. The compromise between the two resulted from a proposal by President Woodrow Wilson to combine private and public control: privately funded reserve banks overseen by a public board. The private banks would pool their gold reserves and make them available should a crisis require. Thus was born the Federal Reserve Board of Governors in Washington, D.C., its members appointed by the president, with twelve regional Federal Reserve Banks operated by bankers.

SEE ALSO The Coinage Act of 1792; Busting the Trusts (1911); Wall Street Regulation (1933); Wall Street Reform (2010).

The Federal Reserve System was created in response to a series of financial panics. It now oversees and regulates the nation's financial system, including the supply of money printed by the Treasury Department.

The Exclusionary Rule

Weeks v. United States, William R. Day (1849–1923)

The Fourth Amendment to the U.S. Constitution prescribes that "the right of the people to be secure in their persons, houses, papers, and effects, against unreasonable searches and seizures, shall not be violated." More than two centuries later, those words continue to generate controversy as courts construe and apply them. At the heart of the debate remains the question that Judge Benjamin Cardozo suggested in his 1926 New York Court of Appeals opinion in *People v. Defore*: Should the criminal go free because the constable has blundered? Generally speaking, the courts have answered yes, invoking the exclusionary rule, which bars evidence obtained unlawfully from criminal trials.

The U.S. Supreme Court formally articulated the exclusionary rule—described by political scientist William Lasser as "one of the most controversial rules ever laid down by the U.S. Supreme Court"—in *Weeks v. United States*, building on its previous decisions in *Boyd v. United States* and *Adams v. New York*. Freemont Weeks, charged with transporting lottery tickets through the mails in violation of federal gambling laws, was arrested at his workplace while state police simultaneously entered his home without a warrant and seized incriminating documents. A federal marshal subsequently went to Weeks's home to conduct his own search, seizing and retaining additional papers as evidence for trial.

Weeks petitioned for the return of his property, claiming it was taken unlawfully in violation of the Fourth and Fifth Amendments. The petition was denied, and Weeks was convicted at trial. On appeal, the Supreme Court ruled unanimously that the federal marshal's warrantless search and seizure at Weeks's home violated the Fourth Amendment and that the illegally seized evidence should have been excluded from the trial. (Evidence seized by the local police remained admissible, however, because the Fourth Amendment wasn't held applicable to state officials until 1961 in *Mapp v. Ohio*.)

The rationale for the exclusionary rule was simple: If materials could be seized and used as evidence of crimes against an accused person, the Fourth Amendment would be of no value and, in the words of Justice William Day, speaking for the Court in *Weeks*, "might as well be stricken from the Constitution."

SEE ALSO The Writs of Assistance Case (1761); States and the Exclusionary Rule (1961).

Justice Benjamin Cardozo famously got at the heart of the debate over the exclusionary rule: whether "the criminal is to go free because the constable has blundered." He found the rule inapplicable in the case he was deciding.

The Clayton Antitrust Act

Woodrow Wilson (1856–1924)

The Supreme Court's 1911 opinion that Standard Oil constituted an illegal monopoly under the Sherman Act remains a landmark in antitrust jurisprudence. Nonetheless, in its immediate aftermath, the ruling that the Sherman Act required application of a rule of reason left both sides unsettled in the larger battle over antitrust policy. Scholar Dow Votaw notes that the decision "brought both groups into convulsive action," explaining that "liberal forces were . . . alarmed because the . . . decision seemed to relax rather than increase the control over competition" as were "business forces" because they "saw their uncertain position becoming even more uncertain as a result of the ascendancy of judicial discretion."

Despite the success of the Sherman Act, Congress wanted new legislation that provided more certainty as to what constituted unlawful conduct. It had newfound concerns as well. One worry flowed from a realization that the Sherman Act had no mechanism for dealing with incipient monopolists; it spoke only to those who had done harm already. Another was the fear that a monopolist's predatory price discrimination could drive competitors out of business. There was also concern about mergers effected through purchases of a competing entity's stock as opposed to its assets.

In January 1914, President Woodrow Wilson addressed a joint session of Congress, urging legislation that would enhance or supplement the Sherman Act. Congress responded with the passage of two bills, the Federal Trade Commission Act, which created the Federal Trade Commission, and the Clayton Antitrust Act. The latter prohibited price discrimination, including predatory pricing, as well as product tying and exclusive dealing contracts. It also placed restrictions on certain types of corporate mergers. Earl Kintner, former chairman of the Federal Trade Commission and a preeminent antitrust authority, explains that the substantive sections of the Clayton Act "were all designed to reach in the incipiency acts or practices which might eventually lead to adverse competitive effects" and that unlike under the Sherman Act "illegality can be found in conduct which has the probable result of substantially lessening competition."

SEE ALSO The Sherman Antitrust Act (1890); Busting the Trusts (1911); The Microsoft Monopoly (2000).

This 1905 illustration shows John D. Rockefeller of Standard Oil prompting U.S. Senator Nelson Aldrich to play Congress like an organ.

The Prohibition of Illegal Narcotics

Francis Burton Harrison (1873–1957)

Throughout the nineteenth century, opium and its derivatives, including morphine, remained legally available in America. They found widespread therapeutic use both as painkillers and as components of patent medicines available without prescription.

By the late nineteenth century, however, opiate addiction had become a growing problem, due in part to large numbers of Civil War wounded treated with morphine — facilitated by the mid-century advent of the hypodermic syringe — as well as a burgeoning patent-medicine industry offering elixirs compounded with opium or its derivatives as purported cures for a panoply of ills.

At the turn of the century, the problems associated with widespread opium use were gaining international attention. In 1909, the United States spearheaded a meeting among twelve other nations, ultimately leading to a 1912 treaty requiring signatories to enact domestic legislation controlling the trade in opiates and limiting them to medical use. Although America already had enacted the Opium Exclusion Act of 1909, which prohibited the importation of nonmedical opium, it didn't address the problem of domestic production. The new international undertaking required more comprehensive legislation.

In 1913, Representative Francis Burton Harrison introduced a bill to address what he called "an almost shameless traffic in these drugs" and its "accompanying moral and economic degradation." The bill, enacted into law in 1914 and known as the Harrison Act, obliged those who imported, manufactured, sold, prescribed, or dispensed opiates to register with a federal agency and comply with record-keeping requirements. It also required payment of a special tax. Henceforth, opiates became lawful for medical purposes only and were subject to strict regulation and taxation from importation to dispensation. The constitutionality of the Harrison Act was upheld in a 1919 decision that deemed it unlawful for doctors to prescribe opiates for their addict patients. From that point forward, addicts no longer had any legal source of opiates, and a thriving market for illicit drugs followed.

SEE ALSO Prohibition (1918); The Repeal of Prohibition (1933); Legalization of Marijuana (1996).

At the turn of the century, widespread use of opiates such as heroin led to the Opium Exclusion Act of 1909, followed a few years later by the Harrison Act, which made opiates lawful only for medical purposes and subjected them to strict regulation and taxation.

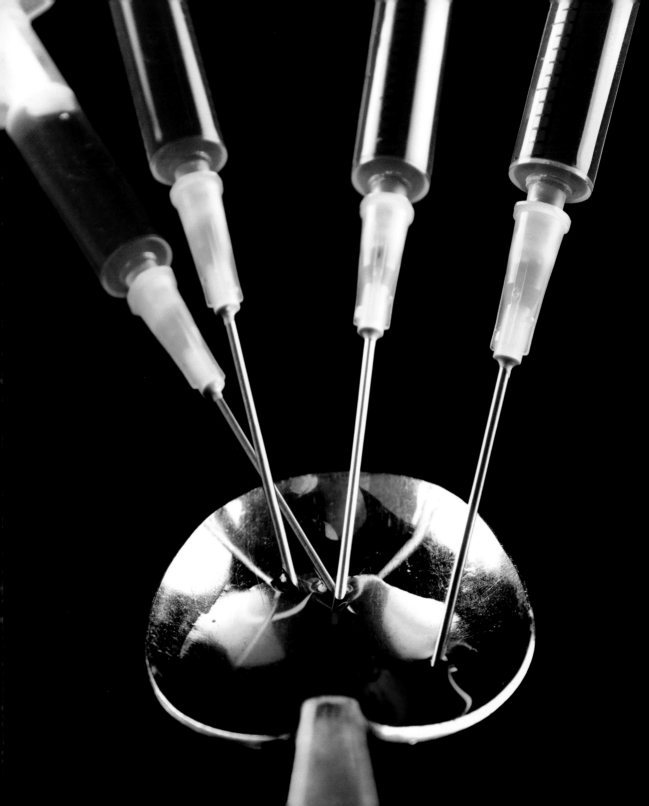

The Child Labor Act of 1916

Originating in England, the traditional use of child labor in colonial America was widely accepted. It continued as a standard practice well into the nineteenth century, becoming even more significant as industrialization increased. Indeed, labor historian Hugh Hindman writes that the labor of "women and children fueled the industrialization of America." But fuel is consumed in service to its purpose. Child laborers, not killed or maimed in their line of work, at the very least forfeited any educational opportunities for self-advancement.

In 1904, the National Child Labor Committee (NCLC) formed by consolidating the resources and missions of many existing state organizations working toward reform. In 1906, the NCLC endorsed the Beveridge Child Labor Bill, which banned goods produced by child labor from interstate commerce—but the bill died.

Continued efforts in Congress produced the Keating-Owen Act, which President Wilson signed into law in 1916. It became effective a year later and set a minimum work age of fourteen and maximum hour limits for children between the ages of fourteen and sixteen. The U.S. Supreme Court struck down the law in 1918, holding that the manufacture of goods fell outside Congress's power under the Constitution's commerce clause and that the law violated states' rights under the Tenth Amendment. Congress tried again in 1919, enacting the Child Labor Tax Act, which imposed a 10 percent excise tax on goods manufactured using child labor. The Supreme Court struck down that act as well, holding that it exceeded Congress's taxation powers.

These two legislative failures didn't spell the end for protective child labor laws, however. A number of states included the same age standards set out in the federal legislation in their own state labor laws, hoping to avoid future federal attempts at regulation. In 1924, the House and the Senate both passed an NCLC-sponsored constitutional amendment to authorize Congress to regulate child labor. Despite wide support, the amendment failed to receive ratification from the necessary number of states. Not until the 1938 enactment of the Fair Labor Standards Act did the country have its first lasting federal child labor law.

SEE ALSO The Triangle Shirtwaist Fire (1911); The Fair Labor Standards Act (1938).

A young boy at a mechanized loom in the North Pownal Mill in Vermont, August 1910.

The Expansion of Consumer Rights

MacPherson v. Buick Motor Co., Benjamin Cardozo (1870–1938)

On a summer day in 1911, Donald MacPherson was driving two friends to a hospital in a Buick Runabout, which he had purchased new the previous year from a local dealership. MacPherson's car ran off the road and struck a telephone pole, injuring him, while his two passengers escaped serious injury. MacPherson then sued Buick, claiming the accident resulted from a defective wheel.

When the case reached the New York Court of Appeals in late 1915, Buick invoked settled common-law principles dating back 150 years: A defendant's liability to a plaintiff suing for negligence requires privity of contract between the two parties, meaning a contractual relationship. Buick didn't sell directly to MacPherson—he had purchased the Runabout from a dealer—so Buick could bear no liability.

In the first of four landmark products-liability cases in the twentieth century, and certainly one that forever changed the economics of manufacturers' liability, Judge Benjamin Cardozo, writing for New York's highest court, upheld a jury verdict of $5,025 for MacPherson. Cardozo framed the question as "whether the defendant owed a duty of care and vigilance to any one but the immediate purchaser." The answer was yes:

> If the nature of a thing is such that it is reasonably certain to place life and limb in peril when negligently made, it is then a thing of danger. Its nature gives a warning of the consequences to be expected. If to the element of danger there is added knowledge that the thing will be used by persons other than the purchaser . . . then, irrespective of contract, the manufacturer of this thing of danger is under a duty to make it carefully.

It's worth noting the context for Cardozo's decision: The nascent auto industry was showing signs of explosive growth. Unit sales increased from 4,000 to 187,000 between 1900 and 1910. Six years later, sales had exploded to 1.6 million. Many scholars have read Cardozo's opinion as establishing public policy about who should shoulder the risks and costs associated with the industrialization of society.

SEE ALSO Strict Products Liability (1941); First Mandatory Seat-Belt Law (1984); The Hot Coffee Case (1994).

A car accident involving a Buick Runabout, like the one pictured here, expanded consumer rights by focusing legal attention on products liability.

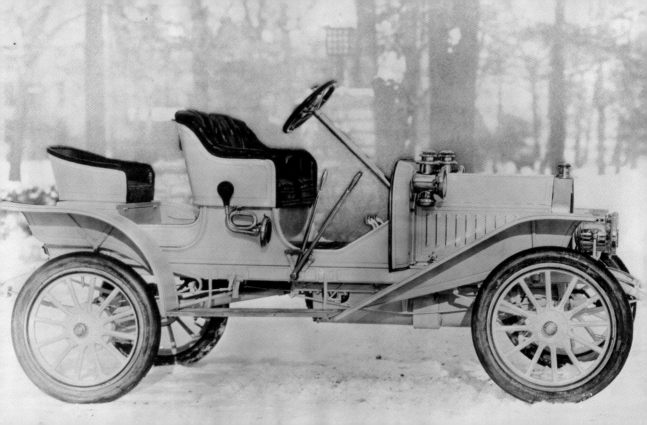

Prohibition

Andrew Volstead (1860–1947), Woodrow Wilson (1856–1924)

The sentiments of Prohibition trace back to well before the twentieth century, as we saw in the Blue Laws, but found their most effective expression beginning in 1895 with formation of the temperance movement's Anti-Saloon League. One of the League's early political successes, the 1913 Webb-Kenyon Act, prohibited the importation of liquor into states with laws that prohibited it. Although that Act was designed to prevent the ongoing circumvention of state liquor bans—achieved by mail-ordering liquor from out-of-state suppliers—the absence of any enforcement mechanism, coupled with meager Congressional funding, left it falling short.

Nonetheless, Webb-Kenyon's passage demonstrated compelling proof of the Anti-Saloon League's political power and spurred its next step. In early 1913, the league published an editorial advocating a prohibition amendment to the U.S. Constitution. Contemporaneous social historian Herbert Asbury called it "perhaps the most momentous in the history of the temperance movement."

By December 18, 1917, both houses of Congress had passed resolutions to submit a Constitutional amendment to the states. Just thirteen months later, on January 16, 1919, the secretary of state announced that the requisite three-quarters of the states had ratified the Eighteenth Amendment, which would go into effect one year from that date. Over the next three years, twelve more states ratified the amendment; only Rhode Island and Connecticut refused to ratify.

Constitutional amendments are not self-enforcing, though; they simply empower Congress to enact appropriate legislative measures. On May 19, 1919, Minnesota Representative Andrew Volstead, then chairman of the House Judiciary Committee, introduced the National Prohibition Act, popularly known as the Volstead Act, which outlawed the manufacture, sale, transportation, and possession of "intoxicating liquor." The bill readily passed in both the House and the Senate, but President Wilson vetoed it. Congress overrode the veto, and the law became effective on January 16, 1920, an epic moment in American history that ushered in the "great social experiment" of thirteen years of nationwide prohibition.

SEE ALSO The Prohibition of Illegal Narcotics (1915); The Repeal of Prohibition (1933).

New York City police officers watch as agents pour booze into a sewer after a raid, c. 1921.

Women's Right to Vote

Elizabeth Cady Stanton (1815–1902), **Lucretia Mott** (1793–1880), **Susan B. Anthony** (1820–1906), **Harry Thomas Burn** (1895–1977)

The formal fight began in 1848 in Seneca Falls, New York, at a convention where organizers Elizabeth Cady Stanton and Lucretia Mott presented their "Declaration of Rights and Sentiments," outlining a number of resolutions on the rights of women, including suffrage. In the years that followed, Stanton and suffragist Susan B. Anthony formed the National Woman Suffrage Association, later joining forces with the American Woman Suffrage Association to create the National American Woman Suffrage Association (NAWSA), which lobbied state by state for the right to vote.

Anthony appeared before every Congress between 1869 and 1906, the year she died, to seek a constitutional amendment. In 1913, Alice Paul and Lucy Burns—two members of NAWSA, then headed by Carrie Chapman Catt—formed the Congressional Union for Woman Suffrage and pushed for a federal constitutional amendment. They organized marches and rallies where they sometimes suffered assaults. During 1917 and 1918, members picketed the White House. Many suffragists were arrested, and after experiencing mistreatment in jail some turned to hunger strikes. President Wilson, concerned about publicity, issued pardons and slowly came to support a constitutional amendment. On June 4, 1919, Congress approved the amendment.

Another year of effort followed to achieve ratification. On August 18, 1920, Tennessee tipped the scales when Harry Thomas Burn of the Tennessee General Assembly changed his vote and approved the amendment after receiving a letter from his mother, who encouraged her son to "be a good boy and help Mrs. Catt put the 'rat' in ratification." The seventy-year fight that began at Seneca Falls had been won.

During this same time frame, the British Parliament enacted the Representation of the People Act in 1918, granting approximately 8.5 million women over the age of thirty (still less than half of all women) the right to vote. Between 1919 and 1928, eight bills were introduced in Parliament to make the women's franchise complete. The Representation of the People (Equal Franchise) Act became law on July 2, 1928, and lowered women's age of qualification to twenty-one, at last conferring on women the same voting rights as men.

SEE ALSO New Zealand Women's Suffrage (1893); The Voting Rights Act (1965); Enfranchising Eighteen-Year-Olds (1971); The Equal Rights Amendment (1972).

The cover of the program from a women's suffrage procession in Washington, D.C., on March 3, 1913.

Yelling "Fire!" in a Crowded Theater

Schenck v. United States, Oliver Wendell Holmes Jr. (1841–1935)

In August 1917, Charles Schenck, general secretary of the Socialist Party of America, oversaw the printing and mailing of more than fifteen thousand leaflets to potential World War I draftees. The leaflets criticized the draft and urged draftees to stand up for their Thirteenth Amendment rights (against involuntary servitude) and refuse submission for service. Schenck was convicted and sentenced to thirty years in prison for violating the Espionage Act of 1917, which made obstruction of the war effort a criminal offense. In an appeal to the U.S. Supreme Court, Schenck argued that the First Amendment protected the acts of speech that led to his conviction under the Espionage Act and that, to the extent the Espionage Act punished such conduct, that statute was unconstitutional.

The Court acknowledged that the Constitution forbids criminalizing protected speech, but it went on to explain the importance of the circumstances surrounding the speech at issue. In what has become one of the best-known legal sound bites, Justice Holmes wrote: "The most stringent protection of free speech would not protect a man in falsely shouting fire in a theatre and causing a panic." He then announced, for the first time, the now-famous necessary test: "The question in every case is whether the words used are used in such circumstances and are of such a nature as to create a clear and present danger that they will bring about the substantive evils that Congress has a right to prevent."

Because Schenck's leaflets were distributed during wartime, with the clear intention to impact the nation's war effort, the Court couldn't regard the content of the leaflets as constitutionally protected. A unanimous opinion upheld the constitutionality of the Espionage Act as well as Schenck's conviction.

The clear-and-present-danger test continued, with slight modifications, for the next fifty years until supplanted by a more speech-friendly approach requiring "imminent lawless action," as established in *Brandenburg v. Ohio*.

SEE ALSO Free Speech and Threats of Violence (1969).

Justice Oliver Wendell Holmes Jr., c. 1924, introduced the clear-and-present-danger test.

New York State Legalizes Boxing

James J. Walker (1881–1946)

Society's fascination with boxing dates back at least to the Ancient Greeks and almost certainly prior to that. "More than 500 movies have been made about sport," Kevin Mitchell, the chief sportswriter for the *Observer*, noted in 2005. "By far the most popular and successful genre is boxing, about which there have been at least 150 films."

Late-nineteenth-century New York City was a major boxing venue, even though the sport was legally banned. Historian Steven A. Riess refers to the city at that time as "the sporting capital of America" and, along with San Francisco, "the mecca of prizefighting." Aided by corrupt politicians and police, promoters staged fights in taverns and politician-owned arenas.

In 1896, Tammany Hall pressured the state legislature to pass the Horton Act, which allowed sparring matches in athletic-association facilities. Although the Act was repealed in 1900, boxing matches and prizefights continued in back rooms and private clubs. In 1911, renewed pressure from Tammany Hall produced the Frawley Act, which legalized some matches under the supervision of a state athletic commission. But that act was repealed in 1917, after the ring death of a fighter. Boxing was illegal in New York once again.

The sport's watershed moment came in 1920, when James J. Walker, the State Senate minority leader (and future New York City mayor) shepherded what became the Walker Act through the legislature. Significantly, the Act implemented rules that protected fighters. It limited matches to fifteen rounds, required the presence of a physician at all fights, and eliminated long-accepted aggressive tactics, including head-butting and hitting below the belt. Most importantly, it created a permanent regulatory body, the New York State Athletic Commission, to oversee the sport. New York's Walker Act immediately became the model for similar legislation across the country and helped make boxing a respectable sport. In testimony before the U.S. Senate in 1961, former heavyweight champion Gene Tunney reflected on the Walker Act and noted, "We had great days of prosperity for boxing and boxers under that law."

A zoopraxiscope, c. 1893, created by English motion-picture pioneer Eadweard Muybridge (1830–1904), shows two athletes boxing.

The Chicago "Black Sox" Trial

Charles Comiskey (1859–1931), **Joe Jackson** (1888–1951), **Kenesaw Mountain Landis** (1866–1944)

In the 1919 World Series, the Chicago White Sox were expected to clobber the Cincinnati Reds easily but lost. Widespread speculation that the showdown was fixed shocked the public and cast a cloud over the country's national pastime.

Before agents and multimillion-dollar salaries, the reserve clause granted teams exclusive bargaining rights for their players. If a player didn't accept his team's offer, he didn't play—for his team or any other. Feeling grossly underpaid by team owner Charles Comiskey, some of the White Sox bet on the game to make extra cash, receiving between $70,000 and $100,000.

Chicago had assembled some of the best players, forming what many baseball historians call the greatest team of all time. Yet they lost the World Series, five games to three. The following year, a Chicago grand jury expanded the scope of an ongoing investigation to include the 1919 World Series. Two White Sox players admitted their guilt and implicated six teammates on the advice of Comiskey's lawyer, whom they mistakenly believed to be representing them. The grand jury indicted the eight players for conspiracy to defraud various individuals and institutions. According to a report in the *Chicago Herald & Examiner*, as "Shoeless" Joe Jackson left the courthouse a young fan asked, "It ain't so, Joe, is it?" Jackson's reply: "Yes, kid, I'm afraid it is."

The indicted players stood trial the following summer. But just as the trial started the state attorney revealed that the confessions and waivers of immunity had disappeared from the grand jury's files. Rumor had it that professional gambler Arnold Rothstein orchestrated the theft to avoid being implicated. Without the documents, the state's case faltered. It suffered further when the judge charged the jury that the state had to prove that the defendants intended "to defraud the public and others and not merely to throw games." An acquittal arrived in fewer than three hours. Jubilation filled the courtroom, but it proved short-lived. The next day, Commissioner of Baseball, Judge Kenesaw Mountain Landis, banned all eight players from the game for life. None ever again wore a Major League uniform.

SEE ALSO Baseball's Reserve Clause (1970).

"Shoeless" Joe Jackson was one of the players from the 1919 Chicago White Sox banned from baseball for life.

Censorship and the Hays Office

Will H. Hays (1879–1954)

Sometimes, individuals in the private sector voluntarily adopt, abide by, and enforce courses of conduct they deem in the collective interest. Industry codes provide one example of this phenomenon of self-regulation or private law.

Sometimes, these codes arise from a desire to stave off impending government regulation, as was the case in Hollywood in 1922 when the major movie studios formed the Motion Picture Producers and Distributors of America (MPPDA), hiring Will H. Hays as its president. He took up his position just as the industry was struggling through the sensationalized criminal trial of silent movie star Fatty Arbuckle, who stood accused of raping and murdering a young actress at a wild party he had thrown in a San Francisco hotel.

The studios hoped that the MPPDA, later known as the Hays Office, and the Motion Picture Production Code it ultimately issued in 1930, would provide self-censorship sufficient to avert interference from numerous new state censorship boards. According to journalism and communications scholar Margaret A. Blanchard, 1921 saw the introduction of close to a hundred bills in thirty-seven state legislatures to regulate motion picture content.

Hays's efforts resulted in more than four decades of Hollywood censorship. According to author and self-described activist Jewelle Gomez, "Hays codified the xenophobia and erotophobia that lurked in the hearts of the descendants of the Puritan settlers." Under the Hays Code, which established standards on depictions of crime, sex, vulgarity, obscenity, profanity, and other objectionable or controversial subjects, producers had to submit scripts for pre-approval and then were told what to cut from a film in order to receive the office's seal of approval. Without that seal, films likely wouldn't play in any theater. Moreover, the Hays Office added moral turpitude clauses into many actors' contracts and developed a blacklist for anyone with a reputation for debauchery.

The Hays Code remained in place until 1967, when the MPPDA, now known as the Motion Picture Association of America (MPAA), created the film rating system that prevails today.

SEE ALSO Obscenity and the Comstock Act (1873); Censorship and *Ulysses* (1933); The Limits on Obscenity (1957); A New Obscenity Standard (1973); The FCC and Filthy Words (1978); The Communications Decency Act (1997).

Will H. Hayes (c. 1921), the postmaster general behind the crusade to save America from Hollywood.

The Emergency Quota Act

William P. Dillingham (1843–1923), **Warren Harding** (1865–1923)

Historian Roger Daniels cites the 1882 Chinese Exclusion Act as "the moment when the golden doorway of admission to the United States began to narrow." Following years of piecemeal immigration legislation, Congress enacted the Immigration Act of 1907, which created the United States Immigration Commission, popularly known as the Dillingham Commission for its chair, U.S. Senator William P. Dillingham of Vermont. The commission embarked on a three-year study, concluding that "economic, moral, and social conditions" required restrictions on immigrants from southern and eastern Europe. It also recommended a literacy test as a prerequisite to admission.

Those recommendations appeared in the Immigration Act of 1917, the first widely restrictive immigration law, which set the tone for more restrictive laws to follow. It imposed a literacy test on immigrants over age sixteen, increased the tax that immigrants paid upon arrival, and granted immigration officials wide exclusionary discretion. It also barred the immigration of most southern and southeastern Asians.

World War I helped increase American nationalism, which, along with the postwar Red Scare, provided an impetus for additional restrictions on immigration. (Communists earned the nickname *Reds* from their allegiance to the Soviet Union's predominantly red flag.) Renewed interest focused on the Dillingham Commission's earlier recommendation of using immigration quotas. As historian Robert Zeidel writes, "The setting of definitive limits on the number of alien arrivals . . . and for immigrants from the Western Hemisphere, offered a means for agitated Americans to defend their beleaguered society." In May 1921, President Warren Harding signed the Emergency Quota Act, the first U.S. law to impose a numerical cap on immigration.

The 1921 act was intended to serve as a one-year stopgap measure, but it was renewed for an additional two years and then made permanent by a series of laws beginning with the Immigration Act of 1924. Quotas initially were set at 2 percent of a particular immigrant group's population based on the 1890 census, and both quotas and literacy tests remained in place until the second half of the twentieth century.

SEE ALSO The Chinese Exclusion Act (1882); Equal Protection Rights (1886); The Displaced Persons Act (1948).

Joseph Keppler's 1882 cartoon "Uncle Sam's Lodging-House" depicts the tension America was facing as a result of an influx of immigrants from around the world. The nation's response took the form of restrictive immigration laws and, beginning in 1907, immigration quotas.

The Scopes "Monkey" Trial

John Scopes (1900–1970), **Clarence Darrow** (1857–1938), **William Jennings Bryan** (1860–1925)

The Roaring Twenties witnessed a burgeoning battle between faith and science. Thrice-unsuccessful Democratic nominee for president William Jennings Bryan had failed in politics but vowed to serve God by helping to draft laws forbidding the teaching of evolution in public schools. After the American Civil Liberties Union announced that it would defend anyone prosecuted under anti-evolution laws, John Scopes, a substitute biology teacher in Dayton, Tennessee, volunteered to be prosecuted.

Thousands swarmed to Dayton, creating a carnival atmosphere. Supporters for both sides, reporters from all over, and vendors hawking monkey paraphernalia filled the streets. Bryan jumped at the opportunity to serve on the prosecution's team, while renowned trial attorney Clarence Darrow led the defense.

The prosecution's case was simple: Scopes taught his students the theory of evolution in violation of Tennessee's Butler Act, which made it unlawful "to teach any theory that denies the story of the Divine Creation of man as taught in the Bible, and to teach instead that man has descended from a lower order of animals." The defense planned to rely on expert testimony about evolution, but the court wouldn't allow it. In a move as surprising as it was successful, the defense called Bryan himself to the stand. Darrow had little trouble exposing the fallacies of biblical literalism, a tenet of Christian fundamentalism. Bryan became increasingly tangled in contradictions, unable to make sense of the Bible's literal words. One journalist observed: "Bryan was broken, if ever a man was broken. Darrow never spared him. It was masterly, but it was pitiful."

But Darrow's brilliance couldn't forestall the inevitable: Scopes was convicted and fined $100. On appeal, the Tennessee Supreme Court upheld the constitutionality of the Butler Act but reversed the trial court's judgment on a technicality. To prevent further appeals, the state attorney general dismissed the indictment, officially ending the case.

Tennessee never again enforced the Butler Act, which was repealed in 1967. The next year, the U.S. Supreme Court ended further debate, holding Arkansas's anti-evolution statute unconstitutional for violating the First Amendment's separation of church and state.

SEE ALSO Compulsory Education Laws (1616).

John Scopes was fined $100 for violating Tennessee's Butler Act, which forbade teaching evolution in schools.

The United States Code

Although the United States of America is a common-law jurisdiction, where legal principles derive from judicial decisions as opposed to a civil code, statutory law remains a vital component of the legal system. At the federal level, legislative enactments exist in two basic formats: the United States Statutes at Large and the United States Code (U.S.C.). The Statutes at Large began publication in 1845 (but includes laws enacted by the first Congress in 1789), while the U.S.C. arrived much later, in 1926.

The significance of the U.S.C. lies in an understanding of the process of lawmaking and the publication of enacted laws. Once both the House and Senate approve a piece of legislation, which the president then signs into law, the Government Printing Office prints an exact copy in the form of a slip law. Each slip law appears in order of passage in the United States Statutes at Large. As a rule, the Statutes at Large constitute the official source of all federally enacted legislation, but the chronological arrangement affords no systematic way to locate laws by subject matter. Moreover, that order doesn't allow for a determination of the currency or validity of a law later amended or repealed.

Recognizing these problems, in 1919, the House Committee on the Revision of Laws undertook to codify the entirety of United States laws to create a code that arranged all laws by subject matter and reflected all current and past amendments. It took until 1926 for the House and Senate to reach agreement on the appropriate legislative solution, the Act of June 30, 1926, chapter 712. That act created the fifty titles—each covering different subject matter from agriculture to war—comprising the U.S.C., which was "intended to embrace the laws of the United States, general and permanent in their nature, in force on the 7th Day of December, 1925." Today's Code of fifty-four titles contains hundreds of thousands of provisions and tens of millions of words.

SEE ALSO The Field Code (1848); The Government Printing Office (1861); Law Reporting and Legal Publishing (1872); The *Federal Register* (1936).

Good Legislation *by painter and poet Elihu Vedder (1836–1923) appears in the Library of Congress. The Library's Office of the Law Revision Counsel incorporates enacted congressional legislation into the United States Code.*

GOOD ADMINISTRATION

The Danger Zone in Tort Law

Palsgraf v. Long Island Railroad Co.

On August 25, 1924, New York City's major newspapers reported an explosion that had taken place the preceding day at a Brooklyn train station. Headlines ranged from "Fireworks Blast Rocks Picnickers" to "Bomb Blast Injures 13 in Station Crowd." Coverage of the incident faded quickly, but one ensuing lawsuit garnered a unique place in legal history.

On the platform of the Long Island Railroad's East New York station in Brooklyn, Helen Palsgraf was waiting with her two daughters for the Sunday train to the beach. A man carrying a package raced to catch a departing train. A conductor extended a hand to help the man aboard, and another pushed him from the platform. As the man boarded, his package fell. The train struck the package, causing its contents—fireworks—to explode. The force toppled a large penny scale, which hit Mrs. Palsgraf. She brought suit against the railroad, alleging negligence by the conductors in causing the package to drop and setting the dangerous events in motion.

Mrs. Palsgraf prevailed at trial, but the New York Court of Appeals vacated the award and dismissed the suit. The decision was authored by then Chief Judge (later Supreme Court justice) Benjamin Cardozo, who concluded that the conductors weren't negligent toward Mrs. Palsgraf even if they were negligent as to the man with the package. Therefore the railroad didn't owe her any duty as to an unseen peril carried by a passenger more than thirty feet away. In oft-quoted language, Cardozo wrote: "The risk reasonably to be perceived defines the duty to be obeyed, and risk imports relation; it is the risk to another or to others within the range of apprehension." As for Mrs. Palsgraf, "Nothing in the situation gave notice that the falling package had in it the potency of peril to persons thus removed. Negligence is not actionable unless it involves the invasion of a legally protected interest, the violation of a right. Proof of negligence in the air, so to speak, will not do."

SEE ALSO The Expansion of Consumer Rights (1916); Strict Products Liability (1941); The Hot Coffee Case (1994); Limits on Punitive Damages (1996).

The toppling of a penny scale, similar to the one shown here, prompted a ruling that introduced the concept of foreseeability into tort law, limiting liability to reasonably foreseeable consequences of a negligent act.

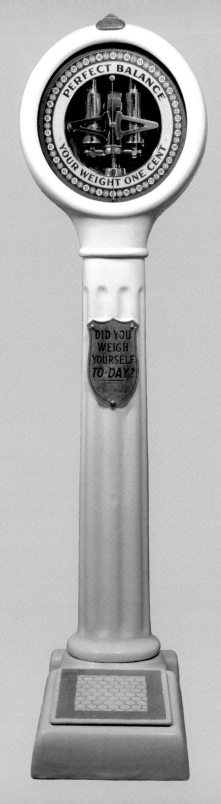

Wiretaps

Roy Olmstead (1886–1966), *Olmstead v. United States*, **William Howard Taft** (1857–1930), **Louis Brandeis** (1856–1941)

During Prohibition bootlegging ran rampant. In their ongoing efforts to find and eliminate the responsible criminal enterprises, law enforcement authorities developed new investigatory methods and tools for gathering evidence needed for prosecution. Foremost among these was the use of wiretaps on the phone lines of suspected bootleggers.

On November 26, 1924, Roy Olmstead was arrested for violating the National Prohibition Act. Much of the evidence against him had been obtained through wiretaps placed on his home and office phone lines. Olmstead was indicted on federal charges in January 1925. After his conviction at trial, he was sentenced to eight years in prison and fined $8,000.

On appeal to the U.S. Supreme Court, Olmstead argued that the wiretap evidence was inadmissible on the grounds that it had been obtained in violation of his rights under the Constitution's Fourth Amendment, which protects citizens against unreasonable searches and seizures. The Supreme Court employed a narrow, literalist reading of the Fourth Amendment and upheld Olmstead's conviction. The Court reasoned that the agents who placed the wiretaps did not enter any residence and therefore never effected a "search." Moreover, a conversation couldn't be "seized." In the words of Chief Justice William Howard Taft, "There was no searching. There was no seizure. The evidence was secured by the use and sense of hearing and that only."

In a now-famous dissent, Justice Louis Brandeis urged analysis of the rationale underlying the Fourth Amendment, asserting that the Constitution needed to remain adaptable to protect American citizens from this very sort of privacy invasion. Although the majority's endorsement of wiretapping helped establish it as a standard tool of law enforcement, Brandeis's dissent laid the groundwork for a changing constitutional jurisprudence in the area of individual privacy. Safeguarding that right has become the basis for much modern-day constitutional analysis, and in 1967 the ruling in *Katz v. United States* expressly repudiated the rationale of the *Olmstead* decision.

SEE ALSO The Right to Privacy (1890); Prohibition (1918); The The Repeal of Prohibition (1933); States and the Exclusionary Rule (1961).

William Howard Taft answers a call from President Theodore Roosevelt to learn that he has secured the Republican nomination for president in the 1908 election. Taft upheld the use of wiretaps when he later served as chief justice of the Supreme Court.

Hitler's Rise to Power

Paul von Hindenburg (1847–1934), Adolf Hitler (1889–1945)

The 1919 Treaty of Versailles that concluded World War I didn't sit well with Germany, particularly the "war guilt clause" and the obligation to make reparations. The onerous terms of the peace fostered deep resentment among Germans, leading some historians to view it as paving the way for Adolf Hitler's rise to power. By the summer of 1932, Hitler's National Socialist Party had become the largest political party in the German Parliament (the Reichstag), although it still lacked a parliamentary majority. In January 1933, amid a roiling political climate, Paul von Hindenburg, the Weimar Republic's eighty-four-year-old president, reluctantly named Hitler chancellor of Germany, asking him to form a coalition government. Unable to do so, Hitler convinced von Hindenburg to dissolve the Reichstag and schedule a new election, set for March 5.

One week before the election, a fire destroyed the Reichstag building. Hitler seized the opportunity and painted the disaster as part of a "Bolshevist plot," hoping to weaken support for the opposition, the Communist Party, before the election. He then persuaded von Hindenburg to suspend certain constitutional rights, including those of speech and assembly, and continued a campaign of coercion.

With opposition diminished, Hitler's National Socialist Party won the election, ensuring Hitler's tightening control of the government. On March 24, the Reichstag passed the Enabling Act—officially the "Law to Remove the Danger to the People and the Reich"—to solidify Hitler's power further and effectively creating his totalitarian regime. As explained by Matthew Lippman, a leading legal authority on the Shoah, the act "authorized the Reich cabinet to promulgate laws and treaties without parliamentary approval for a period of four years . . . [and] was empowered to deviate from the requirements of the constitution." Following it came laws that abolished unions and collective bargaining and even more significantly the Law against the Establishment of Parties, "which established the National Socialist German Workers' Party as the 'only political party in Germany.'" In short, the Enabling Act effectively eliminated German democracy and enabled Hitler's assumption of dictatorial powers.

SEE ALSO The German Civil Code (1900); The Nuremberg Laws (1935); The Nuremberg Trials (1945).

Adolf Hitler, 1934.

Wall Street Regulation

Ferdinand Pecora (1882–1971), **Charles Mitchell** (1877–1955), **Franklin Delano Roosevelt** (1882–1945)

In 1933, as America struggled through the Great Depression, Congress enacted a flurry of financial-sector laws aimed at protecting investors. Among them were the Glass-Steagall Banking Act of 1933, which created federal deposit insurance, and the Securities Act of 1933, which mandated the disclosure of material information relevant to the issuance of securities. The Securities Exchange Act followed in 1934.

The immediate need for such protections became all too apparent during congressional hearings conducted in early 1933 by the Pecora Commission, named for Ferdinand Pecora, chief counsel to the Senate's Committee on Banking and Currency. He led the hearings, investigating the causes of the 1929 stock market crash. A former assistant district attorney in Manhattan with a reputation as an honest, talented prosecutor, Pecora soon become known as the "hellhound of Wall Street."

He joined the committee's investigation as it was winding down, and no one expected much from him. But he needed only ten days to expose the abusive and manipulative practices of the largest financial institutions of the time, including National City Bank of New York (known today as Citibank), and its then respected president and chairman, Charles Mitchell, a man of "unimpeachable integrity" and "almost mythical business genius and foresight."

Pecora painstakingly exposed years of Wall Street's unsavory conduct, triggering the enactment of significant financial regulations. Wall Street's bankers—dubbed "banksters" by the media—were shamed and ridiculed when Pecora revealed that National City knowingly offered unsound securities to the public and failed to disclose information relevant to investors' decisions. His performance created the political climate necessary for the Roosevelt administration to enact federal legislation regulating the banks.

Pecora's conduct of the commission's hearings and the results he achieved had a profound and lasting impact on the regulation of Wall Street and government protection of investors. It resonates still in Washington's efforts over the ensuing decades and into the twenty-first century to oversee and police the conduct of the financial services industry.

SEE ALSO The Securities Exchange Act (1934); Wall Street Reform (2010).

A crowd gathered outside the New York Stock Exchange after the market crashed on Black Tuesday, October 29, 1929.

Censorship and *Ulysses*

James Joyce (1882–1941), **Margaret Anderson** (1886–1973), **John M. Woolsey** (1877–1945)

Published serially from 1918 to 1920 in the *Little Review* and then as a single volume in Paris in 1922, James Joyce's *Ulysses* stands as a hallmark of Modernist literature. Even in 1934 a *New Yorker* critic classified it "among the dozen or so greatest literary works of all time." The novel also helped lay the groundwork for changes in the way the First Amendment protects artistic expression.

Joyce's stream-of-consciousness narrative includes graphic imagery, most notoriously a scene of masturbation. Three times between 1918 and 1920, U.S. postal authorities confiscated and burned issues of the *Little Review*. After a fourth run-in, New York's district attorney charged Joyce's publishers, Margaret Anderson and Jane Heap, with printing and distributing "indecent matter." The court found *Ulysses* obscene by the test of whether the work would "deprave and corrupt," fined the publishers $50 each, and banned *Ulysses* from entry into the United States.

Joyce continued to urge that, as a whole, the work wasn't capable of corrupting minds—but no one wanted to risk publishing an American edition. By 1932, however, Random House offered to publish *Ulysses* in New York and fight the certain legal battle that would follow. Copies were mailed to New York, and Customs officers duly seized them. Random House and Joyce contested the seizure at a trial before Judge John M. Woolsey in Manhattan federal court in 1933.

Joyce's attorneys argued that community standards change with time, that a decade had passed since the original serialized publication, and that *Ulysses* as a whole could no longer be viewed as obscene. Judge Woolsey agreed, and, in a much-lauded opinion, he wrote:

> *Ulysses* is a sincere and honest book. . . . [M]y considered opinion, after long reflection, is that whilst in many places the effect of *Ulysses* on the reader undoubtedly is somewhat emetic, nowhere does it tend to be an aphrodisiac. *Ulysses* may, therefore, be admitted into the United States.

The Second Circuit Court of Appeals later affirmed Woolsey's decision. The government didn't appeal.

SEE ALSO Obscenity and the Comstock Act (1873); The Limits on Obscenity (1957); A New Obscenity Standard (1973); The FCC and Filthy Words (1978); The Communications Decency Act (1997).

A newly discovered manuscript draft of the "Circe" chapter of Ulysses, nearly banned from the United States when first published in 1932.

The Repeal of Prohibition

The U.S. Constitution has been amended twenty-seven times in its history, but only one amendment has ever been repealed. Historians have offered many explanations for the early failure of what President Herbert Hoover described in his 1928 presidential campaign as "a great social and economic experiment, noble in motive and far-reaching in purpose." Regardless of the causes, Prohibition clearly demonstrates the place of law in society and why it does not and cannot stand still.

Contemporaneous social historian Herbert Asbury wrote that Congress believed the nation would greet the Eighteenth Amendment with "joy and thanksgiving" and was "sublimely confident that the existing judicial machinery would easily be able to handle the few prosecutions that might be necessary." As such, the Department of Justice made no plans for dealing with violations. No increase in the number of prosecutors took place, nor any effort to increase jail capacity. Within a few months, the federal courts and jails where overwhelmed. Many have pointed to the lack of enforcement as a significant factor leading to repeal.

But other issues influenced the reversal. A few states began to succumb to changing mores, repealing their own enforcement laws in what social historian Norman H. Clark called the "shifting moral and spiritual values which overwhelmed Americans during the first quarter of the twentieth century." Advances in technology, urbanization, and industrialization, along with their by-products—cars, telephones, radios, movies— occasioned some of this change. As Clark concluded, "Prohibition was simply inappropriate to the circumstances of life in the new society."

The Wall Street crash of 1929 and the ensuing Great Depression added a new dimension to Prohibition's problems: economics. With the nation's focus shifting from liquor to lucre, repeal held out hope of stimulating the economy through employment and sorely needed tax revenue.

As the 1932 presidential campaign approached, leaders of the growing repeal movement drafted a proposed Twenty-First Amendment, which Congress approved in February 1932. To prevent defeat of a ratification vote in state legislatures, Congress called for ratifying conventions of delegates in each state. By December 5, 1933, the amendment was ratified and Prohibition came to an end.

SEE ALSO Prohibition (1918); Legalization of Marijuana (1996).

The front page of French newspaper L'Illustré du Petit Journal *from 1933 shows Americans celebrating the end of Prohibition by drinking beer in a bar.*

The Federal Communications Act

Radios operate on a spectrum of frequencies. When multiple stations attempt to transmit content on the same frequency, the signals scramble together. If you've listened to broadcast radio and heard interference, that's what's happening. Because the radio spectrum is finite, there's a limit on the number of stations that can use it before they begin to interfere with one another. This interference quandary drove the initial federal regulation of the communications industry.

Developed in the late nineteenth century, radio technology grew rapidly in the early twentieth. In 1910, radio communication was used almost exclusively for military and maritime safety purposes, but by the end of World War I entrepreneurs had come to recognize its potential for commercial applications. Within a few years, hundreds of commercial radio stations were crowding the airwaves, and the Department of Commerce—the original government agency that managed spectrum usage—was encountering difficulty enforcing effective remedies. As a result, Congress passed the Radio Act of 1927, which established a new government agency, the Federal Radio Commission, to manage the spectrum.

Radio was the most popular form of mass communication at the time, but it wasn't the only one. The telegraph system, born in the 1830s, and telephony were also expanding and similarly needed government oversight. Seven years after passage of the Radio Act, Congress enacted the Communications Act of 1934, which combined much of the previous radio legislation with wire communications regulations. Most importantly, the Communications Act established the Federal Communications Commission (FCC) for "regulating interstate and foreign commerce in communication by wire and radio so as to make available . . . a rapid, efficient, nationwide, and world-wide wire and radio communication service."

As amended and updated by the Communications Act of 1996, the Communications Act of 1934 and the FCC remain at the head of federal communications regulation today. With the advent of television and the Internet, their importance and scope have only increased. Without them, America's and the world's mass communication and media systems wouldn't have the structure they do today.

SEE ALSO The Fairness Doctrine (1969); The FCC and Filthy Words (1978); The Communications Decency Act (1997).

An RCA ad promotes the regular broadcasting of television from the NBC studios to the New York metropolitan area on April 30, 1939, for "an hour at a time, twice a week."

The Radio Corporation of America Tells
What TELEVISION will mean to you!

The NBC-RCA Television Antenna on the Empire State Building, New York.

On April 30th RCA television was introduced in the New York metropolitan area. Television programs, broadcast from the lofty NBC mast at the top of the Empire State Building, cover an area approximately fifty miles in all directions from that building. Programs from NBC television studios are sent out initially for an hour at a time, twice a week. In addition, there will be pick-ups of news events, sporting events, interviews with visiting celebrities and other programs of wide interest.

How Television will be received!

To provide for the reception of television programs, RCA Laboratories have developed several receiving sets which are now ready for sale. These instruments, built by RCA Victor, include three models for reception of television pictures and sound, as well as regular radio programs. There is also an attachment for present radio sets. This latter provides for seeing television pictures, while the sound is heard through the radio itself. The pictures seen on these various models will differ only in size.

Television—A new opportunity for dealers and service men

RCA believes that as television grows it will offer dealers and service men an ever expanding opportunity for profits. Those, who are in a position to cash in on its present development, will find that television goes hand in hand with the radio business of today.

In Radio and Television—It's RCA All the Way

Radio Corporation of America
RADIO CITY, NEW YORK

RCA MFG. CO., INC. • RADIOMARINE CORP. OF AMERICA • NATIONAL BROADCASTING CO. • R.C.A. COMMUNICATIONS, INC. • RCA INSTITUTES, INC.

The Securities Exchange Act

To rectify the havoc caused by the 1929 stock market crash, Congress passed various securities and banking regulations in the early 1930s. Yet despite the 1933 enactment of both the Securities and Glass-Steagall banking acts, much remained to be done to restore faith in America's financial institutions. Congress responded by passing the Securities Exchange Act of 1934, expanding the federal government's right to regulate the sale of securities and, most significantly, creating the Securities and Exchange Commission (SEC) to enforce the nation's new securities laws.

Reiterating the foundational principles of the Securities Act of 1933, the Securities Exchange Act emphasized disclosure above all and expanded disclosure obligations. In the 1933 act, only issuers had to provide pertinent information to investors regarding the security being sold and the offering company. The 1934 act extended this disclosure requirement to brokers and traders—even when unrelated to the primary issuers—involved in the trading of stocks after their initial sale. It therefore became "unlawful for any person . . . to use or employ, in connection with the purchase or sale of any security . . . any manipulative or deceptive device or contrivance in contravention of such rules and regulations as the [Securities and Exchange] Commission may prescribe." This sweeping language assured investors that they would always have a remedy against any party who deceived them in the sale of securities.

Initially, the SEC "prohibited the buying of stock without adequate funds to pay for it, provided for the registration and supervision of securities markets and stockbrokers, established rules for solicitation of proxies, and prevented unfair use of nonpublic information in stock trading." Legislative amendments to the act have expanded these powers. Critics have challenged the SEC's authority, accusing the government of too much interference with the financial markets, but it remains to others an important guardian of the integrity of the American economy by virtue of uncovering and prosecuting insider trading, curbing deceitful securities practices, and preventing another catastrophic stock market crash.

SEE ALSO Wall Street Regulation (1933); The Sarbanes-Oxley Act (2002); Wall Street Reform (2010).

Shown here are traders on the floor of the New York Stock Exchange in the early 1930s. The Securities Exchange Act created the Securities and Exchange Commission (SEC) and expanded the federal government's regulatory powers.

The National Labor Relations Act

Robert F. Wagner (1877–1953), **Franklin Delano Roosevelt** (1882–1945), **William Green** (1873–1952)

Despite significant membership growth through the early twentieth century, unions found themselves repeatedly embroiled in disputes with employers, including violent strikes, between 1920 and the mid-1930s. Spearheaded through the National Industrial Recovery Act (NIRA), President Roosevelt's New Deal programs incorporated protective labor provisions, including the creation of the National Labor Relations Board (NLRB) in 1934, but the lack of an enforcement mechanism ensured their ineffectualness. In the six months following the enactment of NIRA, more than a million workers engaged in work stoppages, protesting employers' violations of the applicable codes of conduct. Against this "rising tide of industrial discontent," Senator Robert F. Wagner of New York drafted what became the National Labor Relations Act (NLRA) or simply the Wagner Act.

The heart of the Wagner Act, section 7, grants employees "the right to self-organization, to form, join, or assist labor organizations, to bargain collectively through representatives of their own choosing, and to engage in other concerted activities for the purpose of collective bargaining or other mutual aid or protection." For the first time in history, the federal government was safeguarding workers' rights to join unions and to bargain collectively. Section 8 of the Act protected these rights by barring "unfair labor practices," including discrimination or retaliation on account of union membership or activity or anything else that interfered with section 7 rights. Importantly, the Act also reconstituted the NLRB, empowering it to hear and rule on charges of unfair labor practices and providing enforcement mechanisms.

Despite vehement opposition from the National Association of Manufacturers, the Wagner Act had overwhelming support in the Senate and passed in the House with little difficulty. William Green, head of the American Federation of Labor, described the Wagner Act as the Magna Carta of the labor movement.

SEE ALSO Recognition of Labor Unions (1842); FDR and the Court-Packing Plan (1937); The Fair Labor Standards Act (1938).

This 1904 illustration satirizes perceptions of the labor movement, depicting John Mitchell (United Mine Workers) and Samuel Gompers (American Federation of Labor) as witches stirring a cauldron.

The Nuremberg Laws

Adolf Hitler (1889–1945)

Founded in the mid-eleventh century, the Bavarian city of Nuremberg is best known as the site of the postwar Nuremberg trials, where the highest echelons of Nazi leadership stood trial for the war crimes they had committed. But the city's legal significance dates back to 1935, when Adolf Hitler convened Germany's Reichstag there to enact what became known as the Nuremberg Laws.

The Nuremberg Laws essentially codified the racist dogma on which Hitler predicated his rise to power and his subsequent conscience-shocking reign of terror. The Reich Citizenship Law declared that only those of German blood could be citizens of the Reich and stripped German Jews of their political rights. The Law for the Protection of German Blood and Honor (the "Blood Law") outlawed marriage and extramarital intercourse between Jews and Germans, among other points.

Both laws, but particularly the Blood Law, extended Hitler's obsession with ensuring the "racial purity of the German people," an important part of the political ideology he first espoused in *Mein Kampf*, published in two volumes in 1925 and 1926. Discussions about the need for such laws had been taking place for several years between the ministries of Justice and the Interior, but leading members of the Nazi Party were growing impatient and demanding legislative action. Ingo Müller, a former law professor and author of *Hitler's Justice*, details a December 1934 telegram to the minister of the Interior "demanding immediate passage of a law with draconic penalties 'to prevent all further Jewish racial poisoning and contamination of German blood.'"

The German courts quickly applied the Blood Law. According to Müller, they "consistently and repeatedly referred to the Law for the Protection of German Blood in terms such as a 'fundamental law' or 'one of the most important laws of the National Socialist state.'" Müller notes that "one of the most passionate commentators on the law reminded the courts that 'dishonoring the race is a crime almost as abominable as the other great crimes against society—treason and high treason.'"

SEE ALSO Hitler's Rise to Power (1933); The Nuremberg Trials (1945); The International Criminal Court (2002).

According to the Nuremberg Laws, only people with four German grandparents (white circles, left) were of "German blood." Jews descend from three or four Jewish grandparents (black circles, right). In the middle are people of "mixed blood." The chart also includes a list of allowed and forbidden marriages.

Die Nürnberger Gesetze

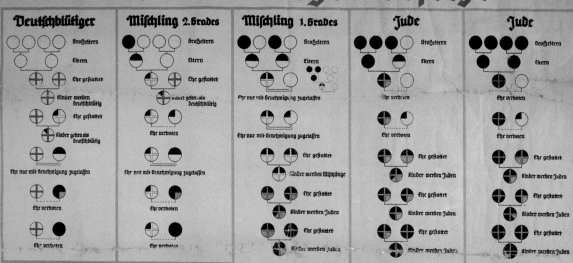

The Social Security Act

Franklin Delano Roosevelt (1882–1945)

In 1934, the nation lay mired in the Great Depression. A quarter of the workforce was unemployed. Many of the elderly and those who couldn't work or seek work lacked a steady income for survival. Voices for reform implored the federal government to provide the leadership that individual states could not. President Roosevelt answered the call with an executive order establishing the Committee on Economic Security, which was directed to formulate an appropriate program of social insurance.

In August 1935, a modified version of the proposal that Roosevelt's team had submitted to Congress became law as the Social Security Act. It had four major elements: (i) a federal-state unemployment insurance system to be administered by the states and funded by a uniform nationwide tax on employers; (ii) federal grants for state welfare payments to needy populations; (iii) federal grants to states for a variety of public health programs; and (iv) "old-age insurance" to be funded by employers and workers through a payroll tax. Welfare policy scholar Andrew W. Dobelstein calls it "America's premier social welfare policy document, providing the legislative authority for the administration of over one hundred social welfare programs in America, and dispensing over 60 percent of the federal budget to fund them."

The Social Security Act wasn't universally popular, however, particularly among business interests, and it became a focal point in the 1936 presidential election. Three cases made their way to the Supreme Court to challenge the constitutionality of the Act, but in the spring of 1937, the Supreme Court upheld the act, finding that it fell comfortably within Congress's constitutional powers to tax and spend.

In 1940, Mrs. Ida May Fuller of Ludlow, Vermont, became the first recipient of a monthly Social Security retirement check in the amount of $22.54. By the time she died in 1975, she had received a total of $22,888.92. For the year 2012, 56.8 million Americans received monthly Social Security benefits totaling $775 billion. Policymakers today face challenges to ensure the program's continued viability due to demographic changes that are increasing the number of Social Security beneficiaries while also reducing the number of workers contributing to the benefits fund.

SEE ALSO An Act for the Relief of the Poor (1601).

Post offices issued the first Social Security cards in November 1936, but many people needed to be reminded of the cards' importance—a message promoted in this poster, c. 1941.

The *Federal Register*

Franklin Delano Roosevelt (1882–1945)

The validity of the old adage that "ignorance of the law is no excuse" requires the opportunity to know of the law. One important means through which the federal government enables knowledge of the law is the *Federal Register*, published by the National Archives and Records Administration's Office of the Federal Register. Appearing on March 14, 1936, the first issue of the *Federal Register* contained just sixteen pages, but despite those modest beginnings, the publication marked a revolutionary change in lawmaking.

President Roosevelt's New Deal had begun with the Emergency Banking Act of 1933, signed into law just five days after he took office. The New Deal instituted a sweeping series of social and economic programs designed to move the country out of the Great Depression, spawning a host of new legislation and presidential executive orders and an unparalleled expansion of federal regulation. Surprisingly, though, no centralized record-keeping system existed to organize or maintain these crucial documents.

A critical impetus for the *Federal Register* arose during the 1934 oral arguments of what are known as the "Hot Oil" cases, the first legal challenges to the constitutionality of Roosevelt's National Industrial Recovery Act, the centerpiece of the New Deal. What preoccupied the justices was that the government had predicated its position on the "false assumption" that a particular executive order had remained wholly in effect. The absence of a centralized, up-to-date publication source had obscured the simple fact that a subsequent executive order had eliminated the relevant language.

The *Federal Register* serves as a daily journal of the business of the executive branch agencies of the U.S. government. It stands as the official source of notices, proposed regulations, and final regulations for all administrative agencies as well as all presidential executive orders. In recent years, it has averaged more than eighty thousand pages annually, and through it, citizens are deemed to have received notice of all published final regulations, which thereby have the full force of law. Although it continues to be printed on a daily basis, it is also now published in a variety of online formats.

SEE ALSO The Government Printing Office (1861); Law Reporting and Legal Publishing (1872); The United States Code (1926); The Freedom of Information Act (1966); The *Pentagon Papers* (1971); Administrative Agency Determinations (1984).

Construction of the National Archives and Records Administration building in Washington, D.C., nears completion in September 1934. Two years later, NARA began daily printing of the Federal Register.

THE ARCHIVES BUILDING
BEING CONSTRUCTED BY
U.S. TREASURY DEPARTMENT
OFFICE OF SUPERVISING ARCHITECT
... JOHN RUSSELL POPE ARCHITECT

GEORGE A. FULLER
COMPANY
BUILDING CONSTRUCTION

FDR and the Court-Packing Plan

Franklin Delano Roosevelt (1882–1945), *National Labor Relations Board v. Jones & Laughlin Steel Corp.*

In July 1935, just days after President Roosevelt signed the National Labor Relations Act into law, the Jones & Laughlin Steel Corporation fired ten union leaders at one of its plants. After an administrative hearing in April 1936, the NLRB concluded that Jones & Laughlin had terminated the workers because of their union involvement, and it ordered them reinstated with back pay. An appeal to the U.S. Supreme Court followed later that year.

President Roosevelt's relationship with the Supreme Court during this period proved stormy. The conservative court had stifled many of his New Deal laws by ruling them unconstitutional. Political scientist Richard Cortner notes that the two opposing forces "precipitated the gravest constitutional crisis witnessed by the nation since the Civil War." Roosevelt sent Congress proposed legislation devised to overcome the Court's conservative majority. Known as the "court-packing plan," Roosevelt's proposal would have allowed him to appoint up to six additional justices, affording him more power against future legal challenges to his policies.

When the Supreme Court issued its *Jones & Laughlin* decision in April 1937, it became clear that Roosevelt's political gambit had worked. By a 5–4 majority, including at least one of the conservatives whom Roosevelt seemed to be targeting, the Court upheld the constitutionality of the Wagner Act finding that the phrase "interstate commerce" in the Constitution's commerce clause was to be defined expansively and might include even wholly intrastate activities. The decision landed a significant victory for organized labor, and, as legal journalist Tony Mauro notes, "it marked the end of an era in the life of the Supreme Court." From this point forward, the Court came to take "a much bolder view of the role the government could take in monitoring and regulating the economy."

SEE ALSO Recognition of Labor Unions (1842); The National Labor Relations Act (1935); The Fair Labor Standards Act (1938).

The official portrait of President Franklin Delano Roosevelt, 1947.

Cameras in the Courts

New Jersey v. Bruno Richard Hauptmann, Estes v. Texas, Chandler v. Florida

> *It is not merely of some importance but is of fundamental importance that justice should not only be done, but should manifestly and undoubtedly be seen to be done.*
> —Gordon Hewart, 1st Viscount Hewart, 1924

Cameras first appeared in an American courtroom during the 1935 trial of Bruno Richard Hauptmann, charged with the kidnapping and murder of American hero Charles Lindbergh's twenty-month-old son. Estimates put the press coverage at seven hundred reporters and cameramen in daily attendance. The organized bar found the excessive coverage and incessant barrage of flashbulbs unseemly.

In 1937, the American Bar Association adopted Judicial Canon 35, barring photographic and broadcast coverage of state court proceedings. In 1944, Congress implemented a similar ban in federal criminal cases. Until 1965, Texas allowed television cameras in the courtroom. But in *Estes v. Texas*, the Supreme Court ruled that televising a criminal trial violated a defendant's right to a fair trial. Nonetheless, a handful of states thereafter experimented with rules permitting limited television coverage.

In 1981, the Supreme Court heard a defendant's challenge to his conviction based on the courtroom presence of television cameras, which Florida rules permitted at the discretion of the presiding judge. Advances in camera technology and the rapidly increasing cultural importance of television convinced the court in *Chandler v. Florida* to modify the rule announced in *Estes* and to allow states to permit television cameras in courtrooms absent evidence of actual prejudice to a defendant.

By 2012, all states (but not the District of Columbia) permitted cameras in certain courts at least conditionally and with varying levels of restrictiveness. Federal courts have begun pilot programs allowing television access in civil cases where the parties and witnesses consent. The U.S. Supreme Court has never permitted cameras in its courtroom and continues to reject the prospect of televised coverage of its proceedings, notwithstanding sustained congressional efforts to require it.

SEE ALSO The Trial of Charles Manson (1970); The Child Molestation Case (1983); The O.J. Simpson Murder Trial (1995).

Photographers captured attorney Edward J. Reilly and his client Bruno Hauptmann, the defendant in the Lindbergh baby kidnapping case, looking over their program for the day at the Hunterdon County Court in Flemington, New Jersey.

Rule 23 and Modern Class Action

The concept of collective litigation pursued by delegates dates at least to the early twelfth century according to some scholars. Stephen Yeazell, an authority on class action litigation, cites an 1125 writ of King Henry I to the archbishop of Canterbury: "according to our law and custom . . . villages and communities . . . ought to be able to prosecute their pleas and complaints in our courts . . . through three or four of their number."

Class actions originated in courts of equity, which applied a "compulsory joinder" rule requiring all parties with a material interest be joined in order to be bound by a court's decree. Exceptions occurred when the number of plaintiffs became unwieldy, and courts permitted representative plaintiffs to proceed on behalf of all possible plaintiffs, each bound by the final decision. This approach found formal expression in the federal courts in 1842, appearing first as Federal Equity Rule 48 and becoming Equity Rule 38 in 1912. It also appeared in New York's 1848 Field Code.

In 1938, with the adoption of the Federal Rules of Civil Procedure and the merger of law and equity into one form of action, Rule 23 formally introduced the class action, largely replicating Equity Rule 38. In 1960, a newly constituted advisory committee on the Federal Rules of Civil Procedure began to rewrite that rule, adopting a revised version that became effective in 1966. The essence of that rule hasn't changed significantly since enactment, though class action litigation itself has. The rule sets out the elements required to maintain a class action: that there are so many plaintiffs that joining them all would be impracticable; that they share common questions of law or fact; that the class representative's claims are typical of those of other class members; and that he or she will adequately represent them. It also establishes many procedural safeguards, including strict judicial control over the process of certifying a class and equally strict oversight on issues of settlement and awards of attorney fees to class counsel. Many states have adopted their own versions of Rule 23 as well.

SEE ALSO The Field Code (1848); Attorneys' Fee Awards (1975); Limits on Punitive Damages (1996); Google Books and Fair Use (2010).

Modern class action litigation in the United States can be traced back to the 1966 revision of Rule 23 that permitted representative plaintiffs to proceed on behalf of all possible plaintiffs.

The Food, Drug, and Cosmetic Act

1938

Medieval kings often employed food tasters—called "sewers," from the Anglo-French *asseour* meaning to cause to sit, as at a dining table—to ensure their meals contained no poison. From 1902 to 1907, twelve men known as the Poison Squad played a similar role. They worked for Harvey Wiley, chief chemist for the U.S. Department of Agriculture's Bureau of Chemistry, predecessor to the Food and Drug Administration (FDA). The volunteers agreed to eat foods treated with chemical preservatives to assess their health effects. Through his work, Wiley persuaded President Roosevelt and Congress to enact the Pure Food and Drug Act in 1906. As FDA historian Wallace Janssen observes, "No single event has had greater significance in the history of consumer protection laws or the industries they regulate."

Concerns over food adulteration and the federal government's new focus on protecting consumers from the consequent health dangers primarily spurred the 1906 act. Upton Sinclair's *The Jungle* had just been published, and its powerful descriptions of squalid slaughterhouses helped focus attention on the need for oversight. It also reflected growing anxiety about drug purity and labeling and helped pave the way for later legislation that authorized regulators to seize adulterated or misbranded drugs and to remove unsafe drugs from the market.

By 1931, the Bureau of Chemistry had become the FDA, but the 1906 statute was proving inadequate. As Janssen notes, "the onrush of technological change would soon make it outmoded." The Food, Drug, and Cosmetic Act arrived in 1938 partly in response to the deaths of more than a hundred people from Elixir Sulfanilamide, a new antibiotic that the Massengill Company brought to market without sufficient testing.

Among other points, the 1938 act required manufacturers to submit a "new drug application" and prove the drug's safety before selling it. The act also authorized the FDA to remove unsafe drugs from the market and marked the beginning of specific labeling requirements. Health and science author Philip J. Hilts describes the law as "a landmark in civil governance, not just for the United States, as it turned out, but for the democratic governments around the world." Every developed nation came to adopt the act's principles, requiring scientific evidence to support drug approvals.

SEE ALSO The Expansion of Consumer Rights (1916); Strict Products Liability (1941); The Hot Coffee Case (1994).

This 1909 ad for Malt Rainier, a malt tonic produced by the Seattle Brewing & Malting Company, misleadingly claimed to provide "new vigor and strength in every drop."

The Fair Labor Standards Act

Franklin Delano Roosevelt (1882–1945)

Several battles took place between President Roosevelt and Congress before the country achieved its first uniform federal minimum-wage law. Some states had enacted minimum-wage legislation for women—Massachusetts, first, in 1912—but none except Oklahoma provided minimum-wage protection for men.

In 1933, as part of the New Deal, President Roosevelt signed the National Industrial Recovery Act (NIRA). One of the act's first accomplishments was the president's Reemployment Agreement, which asked employers to agree to a thirty-five to forty hour workweek and a weekly minimum wage of $12 to $15. The employers of more than sixteen million employees signed on, but, in 1935, the Supreme Court found NIRA unconstitutional and struck down state minimum-wage laws.

In May 1937, Roosevelt sent Congress a fair labor standards bill providing for minimum wages and including a child-labor provision—a popular cause in Congress. He insisted that "a self-supporting and self-respecting democracy can plead no . . . economic reason for chiseling workers' wages or stretching workers' hours." The Senate passed a watered-down version of the bill, but conservatives in the House tied it up in the Rules Committee. Political wrangling continued for another year, particularly between northern and southern representatives struggling over preserving the vitality of the southern economy. After seventy-two proposed amendments, a compromise bill emerged that lowered the initial minimum wage from 40 cents per hour to 25 and weakened the Labor Department's authority. President Roosevelt signed the Federal Labor Standards Act (FLSA) into law on June 13, 1938.

In 1941, the Supreme Court upheld Congress's constitutional authority to enact the FLSA. In addition to providing for incremental minimum-wage increases, amendments to the FLSA have extended the act to include most federal and state government employees and to address gender-based pay discrimination via the Equal Pay Act and age-related discrimination in the Age Discrimination in Employment Act. More recently, unpaid interns have brought suits under the FLSA alleging entitlement to compensation as employees. That area of law remains unsettled.

SEE ALSO Women in Factories (1908); The Child Labor Act of 1916; The National Labor Relations Act (1935); The Occupational Safety and Health Act (1970).

Labor-strike picketers in New York City, December 1937.

YORKVILLE RADIO
SHOES
BATHING
PLEASE HELP US WIN!
WE ARE MEMBERS OF
C.I.O.

Militias and the Right to Bear Arms

United States v. Miller

Many arguments flow from differing interpretations of the Second Amendment to the U.S. Constitution: "A well regulated Militia, being necessary to the security of a free State, the right of the people to keep and bear Arms, shall not be infringed." But the U.S. Supreme Court didn't consider a direct challenge to it for almost a century and a half.

In *United States v. Miller*, Jack Miller and Frank Layton, two former Oklahoma bank robbers, had been indicted under the National Firearms Act of 1934 for possessing a sawed-off shotgun. The trial judge dismissed the indictment after finding that the act violated the Second Amendment. The press speculated that the indictment was brought as a test case, with the government attempting to procure a Supreme Court decision upholding the constitutionality of federal gun control. The Supreme Court reinstated the indictment based on its view that the Second Amendment protected gun ownership only in relation to a "well regulated militia." The Court wrote that, since it couldn't discern any relationship between the sawed-off shotgun and a well-regulated militia, "we cannot say that the Second Amendment guarantees the right to keep and bear such an instrument." Although the government prevailed, the Court's opinion did not per se uphold the constitutionality of federal gun control.

Scholars questioned the correctness of *Miller* once lower courts began relying on it as limiting the Second Amendment to protecting a collective right. The collective right allowed for the bearing of arms as a member of the militia rather than an individual's independent right to possess a gun. Legal scholars Robert Levy and William Mellor have noted that the Second Amendment refers specifically to "the right of the people" and that it appears within the Bill of Rights, which "deals exclusively with the rights of individuals." Other scholars agree that the Second Amendment confirms an individual right, but as Levy and Mellor explain, "that right is not absolute; it is subject to regulation." The acceptable scope of regulation remained an open question until the Supreme Court's more recent decisions in *District of Columbia v. Heller* (2008) and *McDonald v. Chicago* (2010).

SEE ALSO The U.S. Constitution (1787); The Bill of Rights (1791); The Legality of Gun Control (2008).

A 1939 Supreme Court decision reinstated the indictment of two former Oklahoma bank robbers for possession of a firearm, sparking part of the debate on the constitutionality of federal gun control that continues today.

RESOLVED
ARTICLES in addition to, and amend
original Constitution
article of the Constitution
Congress: that there shall be no
two hundred, after which
persons.
and Representat
or prohibiting
time of peace
to be secure in their
by Oath or affirmation
to answer for a capital, or otherwise
crime
service in time of War or public danger; nor shall a
witness against himself, nor be deprived of life, liberty
cutions, the accused shall enjoy the right to a speedy a
previously ascertained by law, and to be informed of
in his favor, and to have the Assistance of
where the value in controversy shall exceed twenty
States, than according to the rules of the common

The Alien Registration Act

Howard W. Smith (1883–1976), **Franklin Delano Roosevelt** (1882–1945),
Zechariah Chafee Jr. (1885–1957), **Harry S. Truman** (1884–1972)

America's antipathy toward Communism began with the Bolshevik Revolution of 1917 and grew as Communism crept across Europe following World War I. By the late 1930s, the threat of domestic Communism infiltrated deeper into the American consciousness after a number of highly publicized espionage cases. The resulting anxiety helped give rise to the House Un-American Activities Committee (HUAC) in 1938.

In 1798, Congress enacted four statutes known collectively as the Alien and Sedition Acts, stemming from fears of subversive conduct by French citizens living in America. All four acts expired before the Supreme Court could hear any challenge to their constitutionality under the First Amendment. Nearly a century and a half later, on June 29, 1940, President Roosevelt signed the Alien Registration Act into law. Known as the Smith Act, after Howard W. Smith, the Virginia representative whose amendment broadened the law's reach, it prohibited any citizen or foreigner from advocating the violent overthrow of the government or being a member or affiliate of any group that so advocated.

Zechariah Chafee Jr., a leading First Amendment scholar, called the statute "a loaded revolver" and noted the misleading nature of its title; much of the law had nothing to do with registering aliens, and its prohibitions applied to foreigners and citizens alike. He also highlighted that the membership clause imputed guilt based on association, not conduct, and therefore couldn't withstand a First Amendment challenge.

The Smith Act saw little use once America entered World War II and counted the Soviet Union an ally. But when the war ended, Soviet relations crumbled. In July 1948, responding to Republican charges that the Truman administration was ignoring the threat of homegrown Communism, the Justice Department pursued Smith Act indictments of eleven New York City Communist Party leaders. All eleven were tried and convicted, setting the stage for the Supreme Court's consideration of the Smith Act's constitutionality in *Dennis v. United States* (1951).

SEE ALSO Yelling "Fire!" in a Crowded Theater (1919); The Hollywood Ten (1948); Rejection of the Alien Registration Act (1951); The Rosenberg Trial (1951); The Communist Control Act (1954).

This French poster for the film Resurrection *(1927) features Mexican actress Dolores del Rio, accused of promoting Communism in 1934 after attending a screening for a film with socialist overtones.*

Strict Products Liability

Gladys Escola (1912–2006), *Escola v. Coca-Cola Bottling Co.*,
Roger Traynor (1900–1983)

Accidents happen all the time. Sometimes no one is immediately at fault, yet someone sustains serious injury. Who then, if anyone, is responsible for compensating the victim?

During an evening dinner shift, Gladys Escola, a waitress at a California Waffle Shop, sustained a severely lacerated finger when a glass bottle of Coca-Cola that she was handling exploded. Escola filed suit, alleging negligence against the local Coca-Cola bottler and distributor that had filled and recently delivered the case containing the exploding bottle. The jury awarded Escola $2,900 in compensatory damages, relying on the common-law doctrine of *res ipsa loquitur*, first developed in the U.K. in 1863. Meaning "the matter speaks for itself" in Latin, the doctrine is invoked when a plaintiff sustains an injury from something within the defendant's exclusive control and the injury is of a type that wouldn't ordinarily occur had the defendant exercised proper care.

The case reached the California Supreme Court in 1943, which upheld the jury's verdict for Escola. The importance of that court's decision lay not in its confirmation of the lower ruling but in the concurring opinion of Justice Roger Traynor. He wrote that, as a matter of public policy, a manufacturer should incur "an absolute liability when an article that he has placed on the market, knowing that it is to be used without inspection, proves to have a defect that causes injury to human beings."

An essential part of Traynor's opinion derived from the earlier landmark case of *MacPherson v. Buick Motor Co.*, which he cited as "paving the way for a standard of liability that would make the manufacturer guarantee the safety of his product even where there is no negligence." But it took two decades and another landmark case (*Greenman v. Yuba Power Products*) for the California Supreme Court to adopt Traynor's opinion as the rule of law. Other states followed suit in short order, and by 1976 more than forty states had adopted the theory of strict liability for defective products.

SEE ALSO The Expansion of Consumer Rights (1916); The Danger Zone in Tort Law (1928); The Hot Coffee Case (1994).

An exploding bottle of Coca-Cola resulted in a landmark ruling in products liability law.

California's Anti-Okie Statute

Edwards v. California

During the mid-1930s, widespread natural disaster compounded the devastation of the Great Depression. Severe drought hit the Southwest and the Great Plains, producing the infamous Dust Bowl, in which dust storms and wind erosion ravaged arid land. California's fertile soils and temperate weather seemed particularly attractive, so more than one million Dust Bowl refugees headed west in search of opportunity.

But the migration of these Okies and Arkies, as they came to be called, didn't sit well with many Californians. In 1937, California enacted legislation to address the situation. Section 2615 of its Welfare and Institutions Code made it a misdemeanor, punishable by six months' imprisonment, for anyone to bring or assist in bringing "into the State any indigent person who is not a resident of the State, knowing him to be an indigent person." Connecticut, New York, Vermont, Michigan, New Hampshire, and Ohio all had enacted similar anti-migrant laws.

In 1939, California resident Fred Edwards drove Frank Duncan, his unemployed brother-in-law, from Texas to California to stay with him and his wife and to find work. Tried and convicted under section 2615, Edwards appealed his conviction and the constitutionality of the California statute. The U.S. Supreme Court overturned the conviction, finding that section 2615 violated the Constitution's commerce clause because the transportation of people unquestionably constituted "commerce" and states could not regulate citizens' freedom to travel within the country.

The Court's unanimous decision recognized the social and economic problems that states like California were attempting to address but found flatly unacceptable a legislative solution through which one state attempted "to isolate itself from difficulties common to all of them by restraining the transportation of persons and property across its borders." The Court turned to Justice Cardozo's timeless observation that the Constitution "was framed upon the theory that the peoples of the several states must sink or swim together, and that in the long run prosperity and salvation are in union and not division." For the first time, the Supreme Court had recognized the rights of citizens to travel freely between the states, even though the Constitution didn't expressly delineate that right.

SEE ALSO The Emergency Quota Act (1921); Congressional Regulation of Commerce (1824); Administering Native Peoples (1824); Internment of Japanese Americans (1942); The Displaced Persons Act (1948).

Rear view of an "Okie" car passing through Amarillo, Texas, on its way west in 1941.

Internment of Japanese Americans

Franklin Delano Roosevelt (1882–1945), **Fred Korematsu** (1919–2005),
Hugo Black (1886–1971)

After the bombing of Pearl Harbor on December 7, 1941, American animosity toward the Japanese rapidly intensified, particularly in California. Rumors of sabotage and attacks on military properties stoked local citizens' fears. Several months later, President Roosevelt issued two executive orders authorizing military commanders to designate zones of military significance from which anyone could be excluded and then to relocate Japanese Americans from those zones. A month later, the Western Defense Command designated a large swath of the West Coast as an exclusion area. U.S. Attorney General Francis Biddle opposed the relocation, but Assistant Secretary of War John J. McCloy notoriously replied, "If it is a question of the safety of the country . . . why, the Constitution is just a scrap of paper to me." More than 120,000 Japanese Americans, including 70,000 U.S. citizens, were relocated to internment camps over the next two years.

Fred Korematsu, an American citizen who had lived his entire life in Northern California, was arrested for failing to leave the area as required. Convicted and sentenced to five years in prison, he was immediately paroled and then processed to an internment camp. Korematsu challenged the constitutionality of his treatment, claiming that the exclusion of all Japanese Americans from selected areas violated the due process clause of the Fifth Amendment.

The Supreme Court upheld Korematsu's conviction despite the famously ironic statement in Justice Black's majority opinion that "all legal restrictions which curtail the civil rights of a single racial group are 'immediately suspect' and should be given 'the most rigid scrutiny.'" Black nonetheless gave obeisance to the "military imperative," thereby condoning Roosevelt's deplorable disregard of basic civil liberties.

In 1984, U.S. District Judge Marilyn Hall Patel vacated Korematsu's conviction after a published discovery that the Army had lied to the Supreme Court about the military justifications. Four years later, Korematsu and others received an official apology from Congress and a congressionally authorized reparations check in the amount of $20,000. President Clinton awarded Korematsu the Presidential Medal of Freedom in 1998.

SEE ALSO *Plessy v. Ferguson*: Separate but Equal (1896); California's Anti-Okie Statute (1941).

Fred Korematsu with President Clinton after receiving the Presidential Medal of Freedom in 1998 for his legal challenges against the forced relocation of Japanese Americans.

The G.I. Bill

America has a long history of expressing gratitude for the service of its soldiers. Congress has always sought to provide appropriate benefits to military veterans returning from wars and to the families of those who didn't return. Legislative measures followed the Revolutionary War, the War of 1812, the American Civil War, the Spanish-American and Philippine-American Wars, and World War I. But the G.I. Bill of Rights, enacted in 1944 in anticipation of the end of World War II, has had an unprecedented impact on millions of veterans and the nation itself.

The Servicemen's Readjustment Act of 1944, the G.I. Bill's proper name, was enacted on June 22, 1944, more than a year before the end of the war in the Pacific. It provided returning veterans with unemployment compensation, low-cost home loans, and generous educational and training assistance. All of these benefits went beyond those afforded to World War I veterans, and in part the G.I. Bill reflected an effort to avoid the resentment and unrest resulting from that earlier program. Equally important was the Roosevelt administration's goal of avoiding that economic and political instability that might follow the latter war as twelve million veterans deactivated.

The educational and training benefits proved among the most important. For each year of service, up to a total of four, veterans could receive all educational fees, tuition, books, and supplies (to a maximum of $500 per year) in addition to subsistence allowances of $50 or $75 per month, depending on marital status. Average private annual college tuition in the early 1940s was $273. By the end of the G.I. Bill in 1951, 37 percent of returning veterans took advantage of the education and training benefits, with more than two million going to college. Political scientist Dennis Johnson writes that the bill "has been hailed by educators, social scientists, and historians as one of the most important pieces of legislation in the twentieth century."

SEE ALSO Compulsory Education Laws (1616).

President Roosevelt signs the Servicemen's Readjustment Act of 1944 into law.

The Nuremberg Trials

After World War II, the Allies sought to bring to justice the leaders of the Nazi war machine that had ravaged Europe. Representatives from America, Britain, France, and the Soviet Union drafted the London Charter, which created the International Military Tribunal and set forth the protocols for a trial. The Charter included two legal principles that later became accepted tenets of international law: First, the defendants could be charged with waging offensive war; second, they couldn't raise as a defense that they were following orders.

The trial took place in the Palace of Justice in Nuremberg, the symbolic home of the Nazi Party that had given its name to the anti-Semitic laws that helped launch Hitler's death machine. The twenty-one defendants stood trial for crimes against peace, war crimes, crimes against humanity, and conspiracy.

More than four thousand documents were introduced into evidence, many containing damning admissions of guilt written by the defendants themselves. The reality of the Nazi horrors also came from a film revealing the gruesome sights that the Allies encountered at Dachau, Buchenwald, and Bergen-Belsen. "The wrongs which we seek to condemn and punish have been so calculated, so malignant, and so devastating that civilization cannot tolerate their being ignored, because it cannot tolerate their being repeated," observed Justice Robert Jackson, the lead prosecutor. Few of the defendants who testified showed any remorse. But Hans Frank, when asked whether he had participated in the annihilation of Jews, replied, "My conscience does not allow me to throw the responsibility solely on these minor people. . . . A thousand years will pass and still this guilt of Germany will not have been erased."

On October 1, 1946, the four Allied judges delivered a unanimous verdict of conviction for eighteen of the defendants, eleven sentenced to death by hanging. Hermann Göring escaped the hangman by committing suicide the night before the executions. Author Gerald Dickler has written that "the trial justified itself magnificently. No future generation will challenge the crystal-clear record on the bestiality of Nazism, the corruptibility of the Prussian officer class, or the primary responsibility for World War II."

SEE ALSO The Geneva Convention (1864); Hitler's Rise to Power (1933); The Nuremberg Laws (1935); The International Criminal Court (2002).

Reichsmarschall and Luftwaffe Commander Hermann Göring at trial in Nuremberg, 1946.

Rent Control

Franklin Delano Roosevelt (1882–1945)

Landmark legislation can result from long-standing, systemic problems requiring social change or from the needs of a point in time when events call for government intervention. In the latter case, the legislation often outlasts the exigency, becoming a permanent part of the legal and sometimes economic landscape. Its perseverance arises not necessarily from need or wisdom but rather from acculturated expectations. Such was the case with federal rent-control laws enacted as an emergency measure in 1942 after America entered World War II.

Rent control first appeared in the United States during World War I when the U.S. Federal Bureau of Industrial Housing and Transportation helped form localized fair-rent committees in cities across the country. The committees had no true legal power, but, through arbitration and publicity, they sought to oppose profiteering landlords. Despite some modest success, the committees disappeared once the war ended. At the local level, however, a number of cities, most notably New York and the District of Columbia, had implemented temporary rent-control legislation to address the housing shortage, and some of those measures survived the war's end.

In July 1941, President Roosevelt asked Congress to draft price and rent-control legislation. Not until after Pearl Harbor did Congress respond, passing the Emergency Price Control Act in January 1942. It took another six months before federal rent regulations took force, but those controls spread rapidly. In October, the entire country was designated for potential control. Of cities with a population larger than one hundred thousand, only Scranton, Pennsylvania, wasn't subject to federal rent controls by January 1945.

Legal scholar John W. Willis writes, "If the history of rent control teaches any lesson, it is that once such controls have been imposed they are difficult to remove." New York has retained rent-control regulation unto the present, and other cities throughout the country have acceded to the demands of tenant movements and restored some form of rent regulation. To date, the Supreme Court has rejected the claim that rent-control legislation constitutes an unconstitutional taking of private property.

SEE ALSO Public Purpose and Eminent Domain (2005).

This World War II–era poster admonishes tenants to take care of their rental properties in order to prevent the U.S. government from having to repeal rent controls.

TENANTS' WARTIME PLEDGE

I will take the best possible care of the place I rent just as if I owned it . . .

I will keep my landlord's repair bill as low as possible . . .

Because this is the least I can do in return for the special wartime protection Uncle Sam is giving me . . .

Because I want to help conserve scarce materials and labor . . .

Because this is the only home I can be sure of until after the war . . .

UNCLE SAM
keeps your rent down
YOU MUST
keep your home up!

FOR DETAILS OF THE RENT REGULATIONS FOR THIS AREA CONSULT

The Protection of Trademarks

Fritz Garland Lanham (1880–1965), **Harry S. Truman** (1884–1972)

According to the U.S. Patent and Trademark Office, a trademark is "a word, phrase, symbol, or design, or a combination thereof, that identifies and distinguishes the source of the goods of one party from those of others." Experts point to wall paintings of Ancient Egyptian field workers branding animals as one of humanity's first ownership signs and to stonecutters' marks in Egyptian structures dating back more than six thousand years as a means for a stoneworker to identify his work.

In America, trademark law emerged in the mid-1800s, serving the dual purpose of protecting the property and reputation of a mark-holder as well as protecting the public from deception. Dissatisfaction with the Federal Trademark Act of 1905 led to efforts at legislative overhaul. In 1938, Congressman Fritz Garland Lanham of Texas introduced the bill that ultimately bore his name. But opposition from the Justice Department, which considered trademarks monopolistic, as well as the intervening war years, delayed its passage. President Truman finally signed the bill into law on July 5, 1946, and it became effective one year later.

One of the Lanham Act's major advances was its creation of a central federal registry for trademarks, but registration isn't a requirement for trademark protection. (Registration does provide advantages, however, including constructive public notice of the mark and a legal, though rebuttable, presumption of validity.) Equally important, the Lanham Act created for the first time a substantive federal right in trademarks, essentially codifying years of common-law doctrine, including the touchstone issue at the center of disputes relating to trademark infringement: whether a party's use of a mark that is identical or similar to that of the trademark owner is likely to cause confusion to consumers.

The commercial world has undergone enormous changes since 1946, and Congress has sought to address some of that change in various amendments to the Lanham Act, including those designed to combat trademark counterfeiting and cybersquatting (whereby a person or entity preemptively purchases rights to an Internet domain name likely to be sought by an existing business, intending to sell it at a high profit to that business).

SEE ALSO The Berne Convention (1878); The Copyright Act of 1976; Expanded Copyrights (2001).

Registered trademarks cover the LED screens of Times Square in New York City.

Colonialism and Postwar Independence

Franklin Delano Roosevelt (1882–1945), **Winston Churchill** (1874–1965), **Mohandas Gandhi** (1869–1948), **Clement Attlee** (1883–1967)

Six years after Columbus's first transatlantic voyage, Portuguese explorer Vasco de Gama sailed around the Cape of Good Hope, discovering the sea route from Europe to the East. England, France, and Spain soon began colonizing lands rich in desired resources. In 1600, Queen Elizabeth chartered the East India Company, the first of its kind, which traded in spices, silks, ivory, and precious stones. The British government slowly took control of the company's affairs and appointed a governor general to India in 1786.

Britain colonized much of Africa and many islands in the Indian and Pacific Oceans; France took hold of Northern Africa and Indochina; and Spain dominated the Americas. Colonization often brought with it the legal systems of the colonizing powers. Historian and anthropologist Nicholas Dirks noted that in India the British introduced a system whereby "the Indians and the new colonial government would be regulated according to law and new forms of property." Similarly, after Spain ceded the Philippines to America in 1898, Congress passed the Philippine Organic Act, which functioned as a constitution and called for an American-style system of governance.

In August 1941, President Franklin Roosevelt and Prime Minister Winston Churchill issued the Atlantic Charter, which included a declaration that the parties "respect the right of all people to choose the form of government under which they will live" and a desire to see "sovereign rights and self-government restored to those who have been forcibly deprived of them." Whether intended or not, the message contained an expression of anti-colonialism, feeding a growing hunger in the colonies for independence. By the end of World War II—in which many colonial soldiers had fought—the decolonization movement was under way, spurred by mutual mistrust and a growing nationalism that demanded self-rule.

Mohandas Gandhi had been pressing India's case for independence throughout the 1930s and '40s, and on July 4, 1947, Prime Minister Clement Attlee presented the bill that granted independence to India five weeks later. On November 26, 1949, India adopted a new constitution, which historian Granville Austin described as "perhaps the greatest political venture since that originated in Philadelphia in 1787."

SEE ALSO Peace of Westphalia (1648); No Man's Land (1959); Creation of the European Union (1993).

Belvedere House in Kolkata (formerly Calcutta), India, once served as the official residence of the viceroys of India. Today it houses the National Library of India.

General Agreement on Tariffs and Trade

The years following World War II posed enormous challenges for restoring financial stability to the global community. Recognizing the importance of economic cooperation in achieving those goals, the leadership of the Allied nations turned first to monetary issues, establishing the International Monetary Fund and the World Bank in 1944 in Bretton Woods, New Hampshire. Three years later, their focus turned to trade.

The concept for the International Trade Organization (ITO) was advanced formally at the inaugural session of the United Nations in 1947. Four international conferences later convened to address creating such an entity. In Geneva, Switzerland, work toward an ITO continued during the third conference, but twenty-three attending nations also began discussions about reducing tariffs. The result was the first multilateral trade agreement lowering tariffs and largely eliminating import quotas. It was finalized as the General Agreement on Tariffs and Trade (GATT), effective January 1, 1948. GATT was intended as an interim measure, pending formation of the ITO, but the ITO was stillborn, leaving GATT as the operative mechanism.

The most important principles underlying GATT—designed to lower existing trade barriers and preclude new ones—were remarkably simple. First was an overall reduction in the level of tariffs among the contracting nations. Participating governments negotiated a lowering of their tariffs in exchange for reductions by others, ultimately resulting in lists of controlling tariff rates. Second, each nation agreed not to interpose other nontariff barriers that would inhibit or discourage importation. Finally, GATT imposed a principle of nondiscrimination through a Most Favored Nation rule, which required (subject to certain exceptions) members to extend to all nations, including non-GATT nations, the same trade advantages made available to others.

In 1995, GATT was replaced by the World Trade Organization, which international trade scholar Susan Ariel Aaronson describes as providing "a permanent arena for member governments to address international trade issues" and which "oversees the implementation of the trade agreements negotiated in the Uruguay Round of trade talks," the last of the GATT rounds.

SEE ALSO Congressional Regulation of Commerce (1824); The Interstate Commerce Act (1887).

A container ship, like this one in Asia, would be impossible without the GATT.

The U.N. Convention on Genocide

Raphael Lemkin (1900–1959)

Mass killing isn't a modern phenomenon. Thucydides wrote of the Spartans' brutal destruction of their enemies throughout the fifth century BCE The Roman Republic annihilated Carthage by 146 BCE, and Julius Caesar massacred at least three German tribes a century later. The obliteration of entire peoples continued throughout the centuries, but it wasn't until 1943 that lawyer and author Raphael Lemkin coined the term *genocide* in his book *Axis Rule in Occupied Europe*, combining the Greek word *genos*, meaning race or tribe, and the Latin suffix *-cide*, meaning killing. Lemkin's definition of genocide included the attempted destruction of ethnic, religious, and political groups as well as the systematic destruction of cultures.

Lemkin's work quickly took hold in the international community, and the notion of genocide served as a basis for the Nuremberg Trials in 1945. The term appeared in the indictments that underlaid the prosecutions, though not in the final judgments. One year later, the U.N. General Assembly unanimously adopted Resolution 96(I), which declared genocide a crime under international law.

In 1948, the General Assembly unanimously adopted the Convention on the Prevention and Punishment of the Crime of Genocide, which came into effect in January 1951 and which has become a principle of customary international law. The convention's preamble confirms that "genocide is a crime under international law, contrary to the spirit and aims of the United Nations and condemned by the civilized world." It defines genocide as certain acts, such as killing or seriously harming, directed at "a national, ethnical, racial, or religious group, as such" committed with the "intent to destroy, in whole or in part," such a group.

The preamble to the convention expressed the conviction that international cooperation was required "to liberate mankind from such an odious scourge," but international law scholar Yuval Shany notes that "the international mechanism put in place for curbing genocide was under-effective and could not, realistically speaking, have eradicated genocidal practices." The strongest criticisms of the convention focus on its inadequate measures to address acts of genocide as they occur, as opposed to after the fact.

SEE ALSO The Nuremberg Trials (1945); The Eichmann Trial (1961); The International Criminal Court (2002).

*The main gate to the Auschwitz concentration camp, where approximately one million Jewish prisoners were killed, reads "*ARBEIT MACHT FREI*" (Work shall set you free).*

The Hollywood Ten

J. Parnell Thomas (1895–1970), **John Howard Lawson** (1894–1977),
Bertolt Brecht (1898–1956), **Ring Lardner Jr.** (1915–2000)

After World War II, America fell victim to a second Red Scare. The House Un-American Activities Committee (HUAC), formed in 1938 to expose Communist infiltration of the government, was already on the prowl. Hollywood offered a natural target because of the number of writers belonging to the Communist Party and the resulting publicity.

HUAC scheduled hearings for October 1947. Among those subpoenaed to testify were objectivist author Ayn Rand and Ronald Reagan, then president of the Screen Actors Guild. They and others spoke about Communist efforts to subvert motion pictures. During the hearings, twenty-two witnesses identified more than one hundred individuals as Communist Party members.

The committee next called eleven individuals suspected as Communists. The first, screenwriter John Howard Lawson, was prevented from reading a statement. Committee Chairman J. Parnell Thomas famously asked him, "Are you now, or have you ever been a member of the Communist Party of the United States?" Lawson challenged the question, which resulted in a citation for contempt and his removal from the hearing room. Ten others followed. Nine received the same treatment and contempt citations. The tenth, playwright Bertolt Brecht, stated that he had never been a member of any Communist Party. Excused, he promptly returned to East Germany.

After the hearings, the major Hollywood studios fired the group, now known as the Hollywood Ten, and announced that they wouldn't knowingly employ Communists. The infamous Hollywood blacklist followed, which prevented any known or suspected members of the Communist Party from working in Hollywood.

In 1948, Lawson and another were tried for contempt of Congress. Both were convicted, and their one-year jail sentences were suspended pending appeal. The remaining eight agreed to stand on the records of the first two trials. After the Supreme Court refused to hear their appeals, they served their sentences. Before the decade ended, though, Thomas was tried for fraud and salary kickbacks. He, too, refused to answer questions and was convicted and sentenced to jail time, which he served in the same prison as Ring Lardner Jr.

SEE ALSO The Alien Registration Act (1940); Rejection of the Alien Registration Act (1951); The Rosenberg Trial (1951); The Communist Control Act (1954).

Ring Lardner Jr. (left) and Lester Cole (right), two of the Hollywood Ten, arriving at court in 1950.

Universal Declaration of Human Rights

Eleanor Roosevelt (1884–1962)

The United Nations' 1948 Universal Declaration of Human Rights was born into a world emerging from the atrocities and horrors of global war. It represented the commitment of participating states to address and thereafter prevent such depravations.

Conceptually the declaration originated at the U.N. General Assembly's first session in 1946 as a draft titled *Declaration on Fundamental Human Rights and Freedoms.* That document was referred to the eighteen-member Commission on Human Rights, chaired by Eleanor Roosevelt. At its first meeting in 1947, the commission undertook a preliminary draft of an International Bill of Human Rights. Roosevelt later described the completed declaration as "humanity's Magna Carta." The commission's final draft was circulated among all U.N. member governments in 1948, and it underwent rounds of revisions. Hernán Santa Cruz, Chilean ambassador to the U.N., called it "a truly significant historic event in which a consensus had been reached as to the supreme value of the human person. . . . In the Great Hall . . . there was an atmosphere of genuine solidarity and brotherhood among men and women from all latitudes."

The General Assembly's final deliberations began in September 1948, and the declaration was adopted unanimously (with eight abstentions) in December 1948. Political scientist George J. Andreopoulos highlights its core tenets as "a commitment to the inherent dignity of every human being and a commitment to nondiscrimination," and identifies some of its key civil and political rights—freedom from torture, to have an effective remedy for human rights violations, and to take part in government—as well as key economic, social, and cultural rights—a right to work, to form and to join trade unions, and to participate in "the cultural life of the community."

The nonbinding nature of the declaration has led to criticism concerning its effectiveness, but as Andreopoulos notes, most commentators view it as having achieved the authority of customary international law. He concludes: "More than any other instrument, the UDHR is responsible for making the notion of human rights nearly universally accepted."

SEE ALSO The Declaration of the Rights of Man (1789); The Bill of Rights (1791); The European Court of Human Rights (1959).

Eleanor Roosevelt holds a Spanish-language version of the Declaration in November 1949.

The Displaced Persons Act

Harry S. Truman (1884–1972)

The end of World War I, writes historian Richard S. Kim, "ushered in a period of conservatism, nativism, xenophobia, and isolationism within the United States," while the close of World War II presented a refugee crisis of epic proportions: approximately eight million displaced persons in Europe alone.

Throughout World War II, most Americans showed indifference to the plight of European Jews seeking entry to the United States. Legislation to increase allowable quotas from European countries never gained sufficient support in Congress or the White House. Nonetheless, in December 1945 President Truman issued a directive on immigration allocating half the quotas for European countries to the category of "displaced persons." His directive also altered the interpretation of the "likely to become a public charge" clause. In place of affidavits of support from financially capable sponsors, social service agencies now could issue guarantees for large numbers of refugees.

In late 1946, the American Jewish Committee and the American Committee for Judaism established the Citizens Committee on Displaced Persons to lobby for legislation allowing displaced persons to immigrate to the United States. The committee succeeded in having a bill introduced in Congress in April 1947 that authorized the immigration of one hundred thousand displaced persons above the quota numbers for the European countries in each of four years. The bill allowed current quotas to be "mortgaged" against future quotas, but most significantly it continued the policy initiated by President Truman that allowed voluntary social service agencies to issue blanket guarantees holding that immigrants wouldn't become public charges. Congress had never before sanctioned a role for private agencies in immigration matters. This was the first significant piece of legislation in U.S. history to address refugees and the first time in the twentieth century that the United States eased its restrictive immigration policies.

In November 1947, the United Nations adopted Resolution 181, partitioning Palestine into separate Jewish and Arab states effective in May 1948 when the British Mandate was scheduled to end. On May 14, 1948, the United States and the Soviet Union both recognized the creation of the state of Israel.

SEE ALSO The Chinese Exclusion Act (1882); The Emergency Quota Act (1921); The Nuremberg Laws (1935).

Many refugees grudgingly admitted to America under the Displaced Persons Act ironically came face-to-face with Bartholdi's Statue of Liberty rising above New York Harbor.

Rejection of the Alien Registration Act

Howard Smith (1883–1976), **Francis Waldron** (1905–1961),
Learned Hand (1872–1961)

The Alien Registration Act, frequently called the Smith Act after one of its sponsors, Representative Howard Smith of Virginia, was enacted in 1940 but saw little use until after World War II when the Soviet Union was no longer an ally. The law made it illegal to "advocate, abet, advise, or teach the duty, necessity, desirability, or propriety of overthrowing or destroying any government in the United States by force or violence." It also outlawed membership in any group seeking to accomplish those aims.

In 1948, the Justice Department obtained indictments against eleven leaders of the Communist Party of America—including Francis Waldron, the party's general secretary, better known by his pseudonym, Eugene Dennis—for violations of the Smith Act. They were charged with conspiring to organize groups that advocated the violent overthrow of the government. Commentators have described the highly publicized nine-month trial that followed as raucous and a bitter affair.

Experts have questioned the strength of the evidence offered against the defendants, but the jury returned guilty verdicts against each. Professor Michael Belknap writes that what "convicted the Communist leaders was not the strength of the government's case but the intensity of public hostility toward Communism."

On appeal, Judge Learned Hand upheld the constitutionality of the Smith Act and affirmed the convictions using a modified version of the clear-and-present-danger test articulated by Oliver Wendell Holmes Jr. in 1919. Since no evidence proved that the defendants' conduct posed any immediate danger, Judge Hand explained that the court "must ask whether the gravity of the 'evil' discounted by its improbability, justifies such invasion of free speech as is necessary to avoid the danger." The element of time was no longer a part of the test. A plurality of the Supreme Court agreed with Judge Hand and upheld the convictions. That decision spurred additional indictments in succeeding years and helped stoke the remaining flames of McCarthyism, as articulated in a 1951 *Los Angeles Times* editorial: "We are fighting Communism with blood and money on both sides of the world; now the Supreme Court permits us to fight it at home."

SEE ALSO The Alien Registration Act (1940); The Hollywood Ten (1948); The Rosenberg Trial (1951); The Communist Control Act (1954).

Smith Act defendants Robert G. Thompson and Benjamin J. Davis Jr., members of the Communist Party of America, leave the federal courthouse in New York City in 1949.

The Rosenberg Trial

Julius Rosenberg (1918–1953), **Ethel Rosenberg** (1915–1953),
Morton Sobell (b. 1917), **Irving Saypol** (1905–1977)

In 1950, a nuclear physicist who had worked on the Manhattan Project—America's effort to develop the atomic bomb—was arrested in England. He admitted to providing atomic secrets to the Soviet Union between 1941 and 1949 and implicated others, including David Greenglass, who also had worked on the Manhattan Project. When questioned by the FBI, Greenglass implicated his brother-in-law and sister, Julius and Ethel Rosenberg. Both Rosenbergs had belonged to Communist groups previously.

Julius was arrested on July 17, 1950; Ethel three weeks later. They, along with Julius's friend Morton Sobell, were charged under the Espionage Act of 1917 for conspiracy to commit wartime espionage. A month-long trial that gripped the nation began on March 6, 1951. U.S. Attorney Irving Saypol led the prosecution, assisted by Roy Cohn, who later served as counsel to Senator Joseph McCarthy during the infamous McCarthy hearings. At its end, the Hearst newspapers editorialized about the trial: "Its findings disclosed in shuddering detail the Red cancer which the government is now forced to obliterate in self-defense. The sentences indicate the scalpel which prosecutors can be expected to use in that operation."

Julius and Ethel were convicted and sentenced to death. Sobell was sentenced to thirty years' imprisonment. The Second Circuit Court of Appeals upheld the convictions, and the U.S. Supreme Court declined to hear a further appeal. Repeated clemency requests were made to President Eisenhower, including two from Pope Pius XII, but in June 1953, Julius and Ethel were electrocuted to death at Sing Sing prison.

Their convictions validated the existence of a Communist threat and helped sustain McCarthy's notorious witch hunts. Debates about the couple's guilt continued for decades, but in 1997 a former KGB officer revealed that he had recruited Julius, who had transmitted secrets to the Soviets. Then in 2008, Morton Sobell admitted his and Julius's spying activities to the *New York Times*.

SEE ALSO The Hollywood Ten (1948); The Communist Control Act (1954).

Julius and Ethel Rosenberg were convicted and sentenced to death for violating the Espionage Act of 1917.

The E.U. and the Treaty of Paris

Today's European Union traces its roots to the Treaty of Paris signed in 1951. It created the European Coal and Steel Community (ECSC), the first organization to tie together certain economic interests among six European nations (France, Germany, Italy, Belgium, the Netherlands, and Luxembourg), and it provided what became the blueprint for the future of Europe—a European union.

France and Germany had been at war three times in the preceding century, so the creation of the ECSC helped resolve economic and political issues between them. A Franco-German partnership based on the two countries' important coal and steel sectors was, as the French foreign minister Robert Schuman emphasized in his declaration, "indispensable for the preservation of peace" after World War II.

While the ECSC focused on a relatively narrow sector of the economy, it laid the foundations for the European Union as the first organization to act supranationally. It had power over individual member states by virtue of each state's participation in the community. Most other organizations act intergovernmentally; that is, power exists between governments so that certain laws have effect only when an individual state consents to them. Here, the ECSC's High Authority, composed of representatives from the national governments, created and enforced directives independent of their home states' interests to foster the development of a common European market for coal and steel. States had to enforce High Authority directives within their own jurisdictions even if a particular directive wasn't in that state's interest.

After witnessing the success of the ECSC, Europe began to consider an alliance on a larger scale. The Treaty of Rome, signed in 1957, created the European Community, or EC (formerly the European Economic Community), as well as the European Atomic Energy Community, both of which have perpetual duration. The EC brought the coal and steel industries under its jurisdiction in 2002 on the fifty-year expiration of the 1951 treaty. Subsequent treaties continued the integration of Europe, culminating with the 1993 Maastricht Treaty, which formally created the European Union.

SEE ALSO The European Court of Human Rights (1959); Creation of the European Union (1993); The International Criminal Court (2002).

The European Union owes its existence to the 1951 Treaty of Paris, which united the economic interests of six European nations. As of mid-2015, the EU consists of the twenty-eight countries shown on this map.

Brown v. Board of Education

Linda Brown (b. 1942), **George Wallace** (1919–1998), **Orval Faubus** (1910–1994)

In rare instances, the legal system abandons long-established precedent to right previously unrecognized injustices and foster social progress. *Brown v. Board of Education of Topeka* marked the beginning of the end for racial segregation in America.

In early 1951, the National Association for the Advancement of Colored People (NAACP) sued the Topeka, Kansas, school board on behalf of Linda Brown, who was forced to attend a distant, segregated black school. When she attempted to enroll at an all-white school near her home, she was turned away. Joining with other plaintiffs, Brown's suit alleged that blacks were being denied equal protection under the law in violation of the Fourteenth Amendment.

The panel of three federal judges before whom the case was first heard acknowledged that segregation was detrimental to black children. Nonetheless, the panel held in favor of the board of education based on the "separate but equal" doctrine, an 1896 precedent that the Supreme Court had established in *Plessy v. Ferguson*. Because the schools were substantially equal, there was no basis for relief.

On appeal, a unanimous Supreme Court now rejected *Plessy*: "in the field of public education, the doctrine of 'separate but equal' has no place. Separate educational facilities are inherently unequal." After hearing additional argument on the practical question of how to accomplish desegregation, the Court issued a second decision, directing all schools to desegregate "with all deliberate speed."

Heralded via front-page headlines in major newspapers across the country, the ruling was met with jubilation in some quarters and outcry in others. Southern backlash continued for years to come. In response to *Brown's* mandate, a number of states organized campaigns to close public schools rather than desegregate. Governor George Wallace famously blocked the door to black students at the University of Alabama, and Governor Orval Faubus of Arkansas called in the National Guard to prevent black students from entering Little Rock Central High School.

SEE ALSO The Civil Rights Act of 1866; The Fourteenth Amendment (1868); *Plessy v. Fergusson*: Separate but Equal (1896); The Civil Rights Act of 1964; Court-Ordered School Busing (1971).

(Clockwise from top left): Harry Briggs Jr., Spottswood Bolling Jr., Ethel Louise Belton Brown, and Linda Brown Smith—four of the five plaintiffs in Brown v. Board of Education—at a press conference on the tenth anniversary of the Supreme Court's landmark decision.

The Communist Control Act

Joseph McCarthy (1908–1957), Hubert Humphrey (1911–1978)

Following World War II, anti-communist propaganda as well as Senator Joseph McCarthy's accusations of Communist subversion in the government and the entertainment industry fueled the hysteria, but Americans had legitimate reasons to fear Communist power. In 1949, the Soviet Union successfully tested a nuclear bomb, and Mao Zedong led a military revolution that transformed China into a Communist state. The following year marked the onset of the Korean War, in which hundreds of thousands of American soldiers fought against Communist-backed North Korean forces.

But by 1954, Senate opposition to McCarthy's witch hunt was growing. He was censured that December, yet the nation remained hostile to the threat of Communism. Legal writer Robert M. Lichtman describes a 1954 Ford Foundation study as confirming "politicians' judgment that public opinion would support virtually any sanction imposed on Communists." So it perhaps wasn't surprising that Senator Hubert Humphrey, after announcing he was "tired of reading headlines about being 'soft' toward Communism," introduced the Communist Control Act of 1954.

The Act was controversial for many reasons, including its lack of clarity. It declared: "The Communist Party of the United States, though purportedly a political party, is in fact an instrumentality of a conspiracy to overthrow the Government of the United States." With this pronouncement, the act terminated the "rights, privileges, and immunities" of the party. At the same time, however, the Act disavowed any intention to amend the Internal Security Act of 1950, which expressly held that mere membership in the Communist Party couldn't result in arrest or penalties. So, while the Communist Control Act purported to outlaw the Communist Party, it had no such effect.

"What does this bill really entail? Nobody really knows," said Representative Emanuel Celler. As Lichtman notes, "the act was opposed by the Eisenhower administration and afterward was not utilized by the executive branch." The Communist Control Act's ultimate significance remains steeped in irony: It embodied a national antipathy toward Communism that coincided with a total rejection of McCarthyism.

SEE ALSO The Hollywood Ten (1948); The Rosenberg Trial (1951).

In this 1883 political cartoon, "A Destructive Worm," a caterpillar labeled "Communism" sets its sights on the fruits of society that a grape leaf labeled "Capital" is protecting.

The Interstate Highway Act

Dwight Eisenhower (1890–1969)

As early as 1776, Adam Smith observed in *The Wealth of Nations* that "good roads . . . put the remote parts of the country more nearly upon the level with those in the neighborhood of the town. They are upon that account the greatest of improvements." The federal government recognized that wisdom and enacted legislation in 1806 to build a national turnpike from Maryland to Ohio. Subsequent efforts, however, were retarded by the rise of the railroads and financial resistance from states that already enjoyed the benefits of infrastructure and saw such roads as paving the way for future competition.

In the 1890s, the Good Roads Movement developed, spurred by bicyclists as well as farmers seeking alternatives to the railroads. The advent of the automobile and the industries that followed, however, marked the true turning point. By 1910, the nation had just under half a million automobiles; that number soared to nearly eight million in 1920—one for every four families. But support for the construction of roads to accommodate them proved sporadic at best.

The champion of the law that eventually modernized and unified the country's highway system was President Eisenhower, who, in 1954, declared the existing system obsolete and called for a $50 billion, ten-year highway program. In 1956, Congress overwhelmingly passed the Interstate Highway Act, formally the Federal-Aid Highway Act, calling for $31 billion in funds over thirteen years.

Few laws enacted by Congress literally touch the entire nation, from coast to coast, border to border, state to state—but the Interstate Highway Act did just that. Although the interstate highway system today comprises just 1 percent of the nation's total highways, it carries nearly 25 percent of the motor vehicle traffic. It reduced travel times between major cities by at least 20 percent and is estimated to have saved almost two hundred thousand lives during its first forty years of operation through inherently safer travel. According to political scientist Dennis Johnson, the highway system it created "is the critical infrastructure supporting America's dominant automobile culture and has helped transform how and where Americans drive, live, shop, and conduct their business."

SEE ALSO The Interstate Commerce Act (1887).

The Interstate Highway Act created a vast infrastructure of roadways that forever changed the way Americans move around the country.

The Limits on Obscenity

Samuel Roth (1893–1974), *Roth v. United States*, **William J. Brennan Jr.** (1906–1997)

The jurisprudence relating to obscenity and the laws that address it is plentiful but not always clear. Prior to the 1934 decision in *United States v. One Book Entitled* Ulysses *by James Joyce*, the test of whether a work was obscene asked whether it had a tendency "to deprave or corrupt those whose minds are open to such immoral influences." But the Supreme Court had never squarely addressed whether any criminal laws relating to obscenity withstood constitutional scrutiny. The first such constitutional challenge arose in the 1957 case of *Roth v. United States*.

Samuel Roth, a New York City publisher and seller of erotic books and magazines, was convicted of mailing obscene material in violation of a federal obscenity statute. On appeal to the U.S. Supreme Court, Roth challenged the statute as a violation of his rights under the First Amendment.

Justice Brennan's opinion for the 5–4 majority first made clear that obscenity lay beyond the protection of the First Amendment because historically it had been regarded as "utterly without redeeming social importance." He then defined the appropriate standard as "whether to the average person, applying contemporary community standards, the dominant theme of the material taken as a whole appeals to the prurient interest." Measured against that standard, the Court upheld Roth's conviction. The changes in the interpretation of obscenity law were twofold: First, the test looked to the effect of the material on the average person as opposed to a specific class of individuals. Second, a court needed to evaluate a work as a whole and couldn't simply look at a particular excerpt.

But the *Roth* decision left a number of questions unanswered. For example, it provided no guidance as to what it means to "appeal to the prurient interest." Nor was it clear what the appropriate contemporary community standard would be in any given case. Answers to those questions would need to await future cases, which were neither long in coming nor in short supply thereafter.

SEE ALSO Obscenity and the Comstock Act (1873); Censorship and the Hays Office (1921); Censorship and *Ulysses* (1933); A New Obscenity Standard (1973); The FCC and Filthy Words (1978); The Communications Decency Act (1997).

Henry Miller's Tropic of Cancer, *originally published in France in 1934, was banned in America and involved in later obscenity trials.*

TROPIC OF CANCER

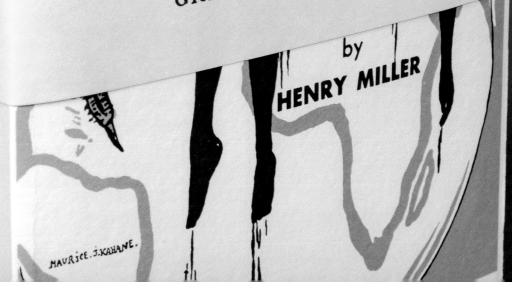

FOR SUBSCRIPTION.

MUST NOT BE TAKEN INTO
GREAT BRITAIN OR U. S. A.

by
HENRY MILLER

MAURICE. J. KAHANE.

The Wolfenden Report and Gay Rights

David Maxwell Fyfe, 1st Earl of Kilmuir (1900–1967), **Baron John Wolfenden** (1906–1985)

In the mid-1950s, an individual charged with committing a homosexual act in the U.K. could face jail time ranging from ten years to life imprisonment. According to British scholar Jeffrey Weeks, Britain then was "widely regarded as having one of the most conservative sexual cultures in the world, with one of the most draconian penal codes." In August 1954—five months after Lord Montagu of Beaulieu was convicted of conspiracy to commit "serious offenses with male persons" and two months after Alan Turing's suicide—Home Secretary David Maxwell Fyfe appointed Sir John Wolfenden to head a thirteen-member committee to evaluate those laws as well as those relating to prostitution.

Following three years of hearings, interviews, and study, the long-awaited "Report of the Committee on Homosexual Offences and Prostitution" was published in September 1957. According to Weeks, the committee's report "made a crucial distinction between private actions and public order" and "proposed that it should not be the function of the law to regulate private behavior that did not harm anyone else.

The committee rejected the arguments commonly used as justification for criminalizing homosexuality and offered the groundbreaking recommendation that homosexual relations between consenting adults above the age of majority, twenty-one at the time, be decriminalized. The committee's recommendation on prostitution was less radical: increase the maximum fine, and add a short jail sentence for three-time offenders. The committee expressed misgivings about homosexuality in general, but only one member, James Adair, disagreed with its findings, arguing that decriminalization would encourage the practice.

During this same time, the Mattachine Society, an early gay rights organization, had formed in America. It aimed to educate and enlighten the public about homosexuality and eliminate misconceptions and stereotyping. Both the society and report marked a modest turning point in societal attitudes toward homosexuality. The report generated widespread attention and public debate, although another decade passed before its recommendations achieved legal status with the 1967 Sexual Offences Act, which decriminalized private sexual relations between men.

SEE ALSO The First Ban on Gay Marriage (1973); The First Gay Marriage Laws (1989); The Legal Fight for Gay Marriage (2004).

The 1954 conviction of Lord Montagu of Beaulieu, shown here, spurred the creation of the Wolfenden Committee.

The European Court of Human Rights

The atrocities of World War II elicited a need among European nations for a mechanism to protect human rights. On the heels of the 1948 United Nations Universal Declaration of Human Rights, the Council of Europe, which today consists of forty-seven member states, established the European Convention on Human Rights, an international treaty entered into force in 1953 that enumerated the civil and political rights believed necessary for the preservation of peace and democracy. The convention also provided for the creation of the European Court of Human Rights to adjudicate claims by individuals alleging rights violations against member states. Constituted in 1959 in Strasbourg, France, the court was the first to enable citizens to sue their government in an international forum.

In 2011, Michael O'Boyle, the court's deputy registrar, noted that "the jurisprudence that the Court has established . . . is generally accepted to constitute the major achievement of the European system of human rights protection." In the eyes of the Council of Europe "the Court is today the guarantor of human rights in Europe—the very conscience of Europe." During its first fifty years, the court issued more than twelve thousand judgments most commonly relating to violations of the right to a fair and speedy trial but also to the right to be free from torture, the right to liberty and security, the right to privacy and family life, and the rights to freedom of expression, assembly, association, and religion.

The court hasn't lacked its share of problems or critics. Some scholars have pointed to its overwhelming—perhaps stifling—caseload and a steady stream of hostile criticism targeting the decisions it does issue. Others have cited the daunting volume of cases as proof that the court is a victim of its own success, and efforts are under way to address the issue. A more intractable problem, however, is the view of the political leadership in some European countries that an "international" court shouldn't dictate legal policies to individual nations.

SEE ALSO The Declaration of the Rights of Man (1789); The Bill of Rights (1791); Universal Declaration of Human Rights (1948).

The European Court of Human Rights, located in Strasbourg, France.

No Man's Land

Law usually applies to people living in a particular place governed by a sovereign who enacts and enforces applicable rules. But law also can play a role in uninhabited, uncontrolled places. First discovered in 1820, Antarctica surrounds the South Pole. The British Antarctic Survey, a leading environmental research center, describes it as a place "where there has never been a war, where the environment is fully protected, and where scientific research has priority." That status results directly from the Antarctic Treaty System (ATS), a family of treaties that began in 1959 with an agreement among twelve nations: America, Argentina, Australia, Belgium, Britain, Chile, France, Japan, New Zealand, Norway, South Africa, and the Soviet Union. The original treaty barred military maneuvers, installations, or weapons testing and prohibited the disposal of radioactive waste, while promoting scientific research, cooperation, and exchange. The ATS has proven remarkably effective and stands as one of the most successful international agreements.

In October 1967, the U.N. Treaty on Principles Governing the Activities of States in the Exploration and Use of Outer Space, Including the Moon and Other Celestial Bodies (known as the Outer Space Treaty) came into force. Although the U.N. didn't effectuate the ATS, many of the Outer Space provisions derived from its framework. The Treaty bars the use of nuclear weapons in outer space, in orbit around the Earth, or on any celestial bodies. It also stipulates that celestial bodies be used for peaceful purposes and prohibits military use or weapons testing on them. Finally, the Treaty makes nations responsible for their own activities in space as well as for those of private enterprises, entities, and individuals—an important consideration in light of efforts under way to commercialize space travel.

The U.N. subsequently implemented four additional international treaties relating to outer space: the Agreement on the Rescue of Astronauts, the Return of Astronauts, and the Return of Objects Launched into Outer Space (1968); the Convention on International Liability for Damage Caused by Space Objects (1972); the Convention on Registration of Objects Launched into Outer Space (1976); and the Agreement Governing the Activities of States on the Moon and Other Celestial Bodies (1984).

SEE ALSO Peace of Westphalia (1648); The Geneva Convention (1864); The Endangered Species Act (1973); The Rio Conference (1992).

This computer-generated image of Antarctica is based on NASA satellite data.

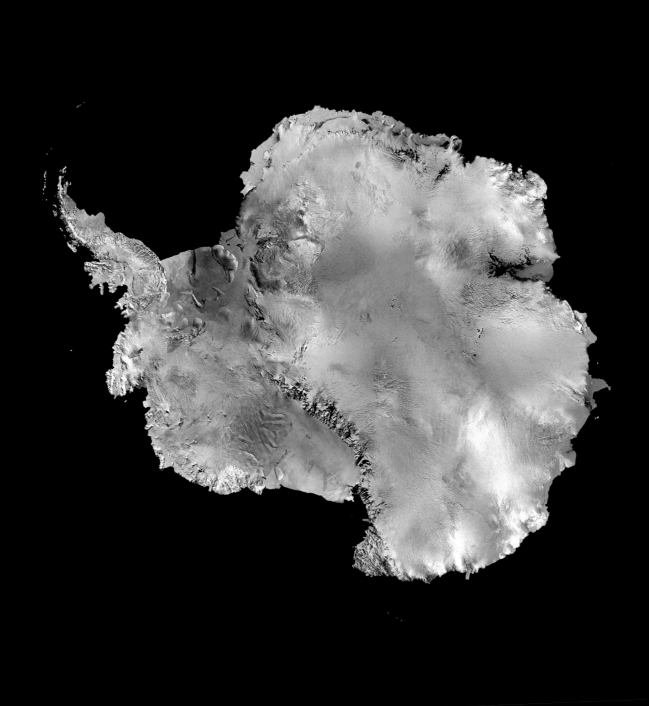

States and the Exclusionary Rule

Wolf v. Colorado, Dollree Mapp (1923–2014), *Mapp v. Ohio*

By 1961, the exclusionary rule announced in *United States v. Weeks* was well established for federal criminal prosecutions. At trial, federal prosecutors couldn't introduce evidence obtained unlawfully. In state prosecutions, however, *Weeks* had made clear that the Fourth Amendment didn't address misconduct by state officials and therefore application of the exclusionary rule wasn't required under the Constitution, which the Court emphatically reiterated in *Wolf v. Colorado* in 1949.

In May 1957, Cleveland police officers, acting on a tip about the location of a suspect in a local bombing, sought entry at the home of Dollree Mapp, falsely claiming to have a valid warrant. Once inside, the police arrested Mapp after finding books and photos the officers believed to be obscene. Mapp was indicted for felony possession of obscene materials and convicted at trial. In appeals through the state courts, Mapp unsuccessfully challenged the legality of the search and the constitutionality of Ohio's obscenity statute. Although four of the seven judges of Ohio's highest court found the obscenity law unconstitutional, a state constitutional provision required a supermajority—six of the seven sitting judges—to declare a state law unconstitutional.

Against long odds, Mapp's lawyers convinced the U.S. Supreme Court to hear the case. The Ohio chapter of the ACLU filed an amicus curiae (Latin for "friend of the court") brief also challenging the obscenity statute.

From all appearances, the case was positioned for—and the parties were expecting—a decision addressing the statute's constitutionality. Indeed, according to archival research by political scientist Carolyn N. Long, all nine justices had voted during their post-argument conference to invalidate the Ohio statute. It was more than a little surprising, therefore, that in its decision overturning Mapp's conviction, the Court passed over that issue and instead announced that the exclusionary rule be applied thenceforth in state criminal proceedings, reversing its previous decision in *Wolf*.

As Professor Long notes, "The breadth of *Mapp v. Ohio* was extraordinary. In one fell swoop, the Supreme Court imposed the exclusionary rule on half the states in the union," making it potentially applicable to hundreds of thousands of cases each year.

SEE ALSO The Fourteenth Amendment (1868); The Exclusionary Rule (1914); The Limits on Obscenity (1957).

Dollree Mapp was arrested for felony possession of obscene materials after police entered her home and falsely claimed they had a search warrant.

THIS
WAY
OUT

The Eichmann Trial

Adolf Eichmann (1906–1962)

One of the most momentous trials the world has ever witnessed took place in 1961 in Jerusalem as Israel prosecuted Adolf Eichmann for crimes against the Jewish people and humanity during World War II. Author Bernard Ryan Jr. describes Eichmann as "the most despicable of all Nazi officials in the German high command" except Hitler. Eichmann had eluded capture after the war, eventually making his way to Argentina. In May 1960, Israeli agents arrested him near Buenos Aires and spirited him out of the country. He was brought to Israel to stand trial under Israel's 1950 Nazis and Nazi Collaborators (Punishment) Act.

Eichmann's eight-month trial offered Israel an opportunity to document the horrors of the Holocaust—in particular, the Nazis' "Final Solution to the Jewish Problem"—and provide an indelible lesson for generations to come. In the words of Prime Minister David Ben-Gurion, "the trial is to show . . . people here and . . . throughout the world the danger of authoritarian society."

Controversy immediately arose over whether Israel had a right to prosecute Eichmann, whose forcible abduction was said to have violated international law. Challenges were also raised to Israel's jurisdiction to try Eichmann for crimes committed in Europe at a time when Israel didn't yet exist and on the basis of a statute enacted years afterward, the classic example of an ex post facto law.

The Supreme Court of Israel upheld Eichmann's conviction and death sentence, relying on long-standing tenets of international law that afford all nations universal jurisdiction to try an individual for crimes against humanity. The court pointed to legal precedents dating back to the Middle Ages and preeminent authorities, including Hugo Grotius, who established the principle that any nation could try and punish an individual on the grounds that he was *hostis humani generis*, an enemy of the human race. Indeed, it held that nations had a moral duty to punish those who "violated in extreme form the law of nature or the law of nations." Adolf Eichmann was executed by hanging.

SEE ALSO *On the Law of War and Peace* (1625); The Nuremberg Laws (1935); The Nuremberg Trials (1945); The International Criminal Court (2002).

Holocaust architect Adolf Eichmann on trial in Jerusalem in 1961. He was convicted and executed by hanging on May 31, 1962.

The Trial of Nelson Mandela

Nelson Mandela (1918–2013)

Nelson Mandela will be remembered best for his heroic opposition to and help in ending South African apartheid. Living under a stringent system of racial segregation, Mandela joined the African National Congress (ANC) in 1944, eventually leading its militant wing. That role ultimately gave rise to his conviction in the infamous Rivonia Trial, named for the town outside Johannesburg that served as a hideout for ANC militants.

In July 1963, seven ANC members were arrested under South Africa's Sabotage Act of 1963 for an ongoing campaign to attack government posts. Several documents linked Mandela, who already was serving a prison sentence for inciting a strike, to the group. He and nine other men were eventually charged with sabotage.

At his previous trial a year earlier, Mandela had refused to testify; instead, he remonstrated from the dock against the authority of the all-white court. His counsel for the Rivonia Trial worried that by testifying now Mandela would appear hypocritical and unprincipled. The defense decided that Mandela again wouldn't testify but would address the court in a statement. Speaking for nearly five hours, he told of the injustices blacks faced and spoke of the ideal society he envisioned, in which people lived together peacefully. He concluded with a powerful and daring statement: "It is an ideal which I hope to live for and to achieve. But if needs be, it is an ideal for which I am prepared to die."

The Rivonia arrests and trial garnered worldwide attention. The United Nations General Assembly voted 106 to 1 to condemn apartheid, "abandon the arbitrary trial," and release all those imprisoned for having opposed apartheid. South Africa cast the one dissenting vote, and the U.N. condemnation went unheeded.

The verdict was announced in June 1964. Only one defendant was acquitted. Mandela and the remaining eight defendants were spared the death penalty, but they were sentenced to life imprisonment. Mandela remained imprisoned for twenty-seven years until his release in 1990.

Mandela's bravery inspired many others to continue the fight against apartheid, but its last vestiges weren't eliminated until 1994. In the free elections of 1994, the ANC won 62 percent of the vote, and Mandela became South Africa's first black president.

SEE ALSO The End of Apartheid (1990); South Africa's Constitution (1996).

Nelson Mandela and his wife Winnie walk together after his release from prison in Cape Town, South Africa, in February 1990.

The Right to Counsel in State Court

Clarence Earl Gideon (1910–1972), *Gideon v. Wainwright,*
Abe Fortas (1910–1982)

The Sixth Amendment provides that "in all criminal prosecutions, the accused shall enjoy the right to . . . have the Assistance of Counsel for his defence." It remains silent, however, as to cases in which the defendant is financially unable to retain an attorney.

The jurisprudence surrounding the provision of counsel to criminal defendants has evolved over the years. In 1932, the Supreme Court established that in cases subject to the death penalty, the Fourteenth Amendment's due process clause required states to provide indigent defendants with defense counsel. Six years later, the Court held that the Sixth Amendment required appointment of counsel in all federal felony prosecutions. In 1942, it declined to extend that holding, ruling in *Betts v. Brady* that the Sixth Amendment didn't require states to provide appointed counsel to defendants in non-capital cases, absent "special circumstances." More than two decades passed before the court formally overruled *Betts* in *Gideon v. Wainwright,* which law professor James Tomkovicz has called "one of the most significant and well known of the decisions that collectively brought about a revolution in constitutional criminal procedure."

Clarence Earl Gideon, "not one of God's nobler creatures," according to political science professor Tinsley Yarbrough, was convicted in Florida of breaking and entering with intent to commit larceny. Although this was Gideon's fifth felony conviction, none of his crimes involved violence. His pretrial request for a court-appointed lawyer had been denied. When the Florida Supreme Court denied him relief, Gideon composed a handwritten, five-page petition for a writ of certiorari to the U.S. Supreme Court, seeking review.

Gideon composed the petition without the assistance of counsel, so there's a measure of irony in the Court's decision to grant it. The Court's rules required counsel for all parties, so the court appointed Abe Fortas, later a Supreme Court justice, to represent Gideon on his appeal. On March 18, 1963, the Court unanimously overturned Gideon's conviction, holding that the Sixth Amendment required states to provide counsel to all felony defendants. Less than a decade later, the Court expanded its ruling to cover misdemeanor defendants as well.

SEE ALSO The Fourteenth Amendment (1868); Miranda Warnings (1966).

Page one of Gideon's petition to the Supreme Court, which appointed counsel to represent Gideon on the appeal.

DIVISION OF CORRECTIONS

CORRESPONDENCE REGULATIONS

MAIL WILL NOT BE DELIVERED WHICH DOES NOT CONFORM WITH THESE RULES

No. 1 -- Only 2 letters each week, not to exceed 2 sheets letter-size 8 1/2 x 11" and written *on one side only*, and if ruled paper, do not write between lines. *Your complete name* must be signed at the close of your letter. *Clippings, stamps, letters* from other people, *stationery* or *cash must not be enclosed* in your letters.

No. 2 -- All *letters* must be addressed in the *complete prison name* of the inmate. *Cell number*, where applicable, and *prison number* must be placed in lower left corner of envelope, with your complete name and address in the upper left corner.

No. 3 -- *Do not send any packages without a Package Permit.* Unauthorized *packages* will be destroyed.

No. 4 -- *Letters* must be written in English only.

No. 5 -- *Books, magazines, pamphlets,* and *newspapers* of reputable character will be delivered *only if* mailed direct from the publisher.

No. 6 -- *Money* must be sent in the form of *Postal Money Orders* only, in the inmate's complete prison name and prison number.

INSTITUTION ____________ CELL NUMBER ____________

NAME ____________ NUMBER ____________

In The Supreme Court of The United States
Washington D.C.

clarence Earl Gideon
Petitioner
vs.
H. G. Cochran, Jr, as director, Divisions of corrections State of Florida

Petition for a Writ of Certiorari Directed to The Supreme Court State of Florida.

No. 890 Misc.
OCT. TERM 1961
U. S. Supreme Court

To: The Honorable Earl Warren, Chief Justice of the United States

Comes now the petitioner, Clarence Earl Gideon, a citizen of The United states of America, in proper person, and appearing as his own counsel. Who petitions this Honorable Court for a Writ of Certiorari directed to The Supreme Court of The State of Florida. To review the order and Judgement of the court below denying The petitioner a writ of Habeus Corpus.

Petitioner submits That The Supreme Court of The United States has The authority and jurisdiction to review The final Judgement of The Supreme Court of The State of Florida the highest court of The State Under sec. 344(B) Title 28 U.S.C.A. and Because The "Due process clause" of the

Limits on Libel Laws

Martin Luther King Jr. (1929–1968), Lester Bruce Sullivan (1921–1977), *New York Times v. Sullivan*

For many publishers, the content they make public always risks offending someone. In cases where a published statement sullies a reputation, the legal remedy is an action for defamation: libel when the statement is printed and slander when spoken. No case has defined this area of law more than *New York Times v. Sullivan*, which legal journalist Tony Mauro has called "the touchstone for modern press freedom in the United States."

On March 29, 1960, the *New York Times* ran "Heed Their Rising Voices," a full-page ad soliciting donations for Martin Luther King Jr.'s defense fund. In describing race riots in Montgomery, Alabama, and the involvement of the Montgomery Police Department, the ad misstated some minor facts. After word of the ad reached Alabama, Lester Bruce Sullivan, the Montgomery public safety commissioner, sued the *Times* for libel.

Sullivan initially succeeded in state court, and the Alabama Supreme Court affirmed the jury verdict of $500,000 against the *Times*. But a unanimous U.S. Supreme Court decision overturned that result, finding that Alabama's libel law—which considered a publication "libelous per se" if the words tended to injure a person's reputation or subject him to "public contempt"—violated the First Amendment. The Court viewed the case "against the background of a profound national commitment to the principle that debate on public issues should be uninhibited, robust, and wide-open, and that it may well include vehement, caustic, and sometimes unpleasantly sharp attacks on government and public officials."

The Court then announced a new standard in defamation cases that became a bedrock principle of modern First Amendment jurisprudence. Concluding that the *Times* hadn't libeled Sullivan, the Court noted that constitutional guarantees required "a federal rule that prohibits a public official from recovering damages for a defamatory falsehood relating to his official conduct unless he proves that the statement was made with 'actual malice'—that is, with knowledge that it was false or with reckless disregard of whether it is false or not." Sullivan's case couldn't satisfy that standard.

Thus was born the now widely accepted "actual malice" standard, which later was extended to cases involving public "figures" as well as public officials.

SEE ALSO The Trial of John Peter Zenger (1735); Free Speech and Threats of Violence (1969); Parody and the First Amendment (1984).

Martin Luther King Jr. at a press conference in 1964.

The Civil Rights Act of 1964

John F. Kennedy (1917–1963), **Lyndon Johnson** (1908–1973)

Civil protest and violence marred the path leading to enactment of one of the most consequential pieces of legislation in America's history. It emerged toward the latter part of the Civil Rights Movement, which sought to combat the extreme segregation and discrimination endemic throughout the southern states.

Cases such as *Brown v. Board of Education*, which ended school segregation, had become major victories for the movement. Under pressure from many prominent civil rights leaders to end segregation once and for all, President Kennedy sent a proposed act to Congress in June 1963. Shortly after Kennedy's assassination in November 1963, President Johnson urged Congress to pass the legislation as a legacy to the country's slain leader. Through political acumen and influence, Johnson steered the bill through both the House and the Senate and signed it into law on July 2, 1964, noting that "its purpose is to promote a more abiding commitment to freedom, a more constant pursuit of justice, and a deeper respect for human dignity."

At its core, the Civil Rights Act prohibits discrimination on account of race, color, sex, religion, and national origin in (i) public accommodations, (ii) federally assisted programs, (iii) employment, (iv) schools, and (v) voting. The act also creates procedures and agencies (for example, the Equal Employment Opportunity Commission) to effectuate its underlying purposes.

The act remains a true landmark. Constitutional law scholar Henry L. Chambers Jr. described it as having had "the greatest transformative effect on American society of any single law . . . with profound effects on almost every facet of American life." With the sole purpose of ending discrimination, it has played a critically important role in the pursuit of equality for all. Equally important, the act has served as the model for subsequent legislation designed to protect additional classes of individuals in areas not specifically covered by the Civil Rights Act itself. Two principal examples are the 1967 Age Discrimination in Employment Act and the 1990 Americans with Disabilities Act.

SEE ALSO The Civil Rights Act of 1866; The Civil Rights Cases (1883); *Plessy v. Ferguson*: Separate but Equal (1896); *Brown v. Board of Education* (1954); The Voting Rights Act (1965); The Equal Rights Amendment (1972); Affirmative Action (1978); The Americans with Disabilities Act (1990).

President Lyndon Johnson signs the Civil Rights Act into law.

The Voting Rights Act

Lyndon Johnson (1908–1973)

At his final presidential press conference, Lyndon Johnson recounted his happiest moment and greatest accomplishment as president: signing the Voting Rights Act of 1965. Even though the Fifteenth Amendment prohibits denial or abridgement of a citizen's right to vote "on account of race, color, or previous condition of servitude," blacks continued to experience significant barriers to voting for decades after 1870.

On March 15, 1965, soon after the violence of the Selma, Alabama, civil rights march, President Johnson addressed a joint session of Congress and delivered what biographer Robert Dallek described as his "greatest speech and one of the most moving and memorable presidential addresses in the country's history." Two days later, Johnson sent Congress proposed voting rights legislation and a demand for action. It passed with overwhelming support in both the House and the Senate.

The Voting Rights Act enforced the Fifteenth Amendment by granting the executive branch the necessary authority and eliminating the need for case-by-case adjudication of every challenge. In the main, it proscribed states' or subdivisions' use of voting prerequisites, including literacy or other qualifying tests, to deny citizens the right to vote on account of race or color. A key part of the act, which required Congressional renewal every five years, imposed Justice Department review and monitoring of voting in states that historically had used discriminatory procedures and had a voter registration rate of less than 50 percent of voting-age residents.

Political scientist and voting rights scholar Chandler Davidson writes that the act "overwhelmed the major bulwarks of the disenfranchising system," and refers to a Justice Department estimate that "in the five years after passage, almost as many blacks registered in Alabama, Mississippi, Georgia, Louisiana, North Carolina, and South Carolina as in the entire century before 1965." The act has proven enormously effective; indeed, the Supreme Court's 2013 decision in *Shelby County v. Holder* cutting back some provisions of the act, which the Court deemed unnecessary in light of changed times, has led some to question whether the act has become a victim of its own success.

SEE ALSO Prohibition of Racial Voter Discrimination (1869); Women's Right to Vote (1919); The Civil Rights Act of 1964; Enfranchising Eighteen-Year-Olds (1971).

President Lyndon Johnson and Martin Luther King Jr. shake hands before the former signed the Voting Rights Act in August 1965.

Conscientious Objection

Daniel Seeger (b. 1934), *United States v. Seeger*

Even through the Revolutionary War, many of the colonies accorded legal protection for those who objected to war on religious grounds or were "conscientiously scrupulous of bearing arms." Religious exemptions applied to the Militia Act of 1862 and Enrollment Act of 1863, and the Draft Act of 1917, as expanded by presidential executive order, included an exemption for those from "a well-recognized religious sect . . . whose principles forbade participation in war" and those with "personal scruples against war."

With the Draft Act of 1940 and the Selective Service Act of 1948, Congress modified its approach, tying the exemption to opposition based on "religious training and belief"—rather than sect membership—defined as "an individual's belief in a Supreme Being involving duties superior to those arising from any human relation." Importantly, no exemption obtained for political or philosophical views or an individual's moral code.

The draft form that Daniel Seeger received in 1959 asked if he believed in a Supreme Being and provided two boxes in which to mark an answer, yes or no. Seeger drew a third box, marking it "See attached pages." Those pages explained that Seeger conscientiously opposed participation in war by reason of his "belief in and devotion to goodness and virtue for their own sakes, and a religious faith in a purely ethical creed," adding that he preferred to leave open the question as to a belief in a supreme being. Seeger was convicted at trial for refusing to submit to induction.

In 1965, the Supreme Court unanimously overturned the conviction but avoided addressing the constitutionality of the "belief in a Supreme Being" requirement. It held the relevant statutory test to be "whether a given belief that is sincere and meaningful occupies a place in the life of its possessor parallel to that filled by the orthodox belief in God of one who clearly qualifies for the exemption." Seeger's belief was found to qualify.

As a result, many young men hoping to avoid being drafted during the Vietnam War invoked the objector exemption, among them heavyweight boxing champion Muhammad Ali, who had recently converted to Islam. His refusal to be drafted also met with a conviction, which the Supreme Court overturned in 1970.

SEE ALSO The Vietnam-Era Draft Laws (1967).

The armed forces used the image of Uncle Sam to recruit soldiers for World Wars I and II.

The Body and the Right of Privacy

Estelle Griswold (1900–1981), *Griswold v. Connecticut*

The concept of a right of privacy is simple enough, yet the law has often struggled to identify its provenance or precise contours. *Griswold v. Connecticut* provides an important milestone in the development and articulation of the right of privacy and its range of applicability. Indeed, it paved the way for commonly understood privacy principles to extend to controversial areas of life, namely the regulation of access to birth control and contraception and eventually to abortion.

In November 1961, Estelle Griswold, executive director of Connecticut's Planned Parenthood League, helped launch a Planned Parenthood birth control clinic in New Haven. Less than ten days after the clinic opened, local police arrested Griswold under an 1879 state law that made the use of any contraceptive device, even by married couples, a criminal offense. Griswold was convicted at trial and fined $100. After unsuccessful appeals in the Connecticut courts, Planned Parenthood convinced the U.S. Supreme Court to hear Griswold's appeal.

In June 1965, the Supreme Court struck down the Connecticut statute and vacated Griswold's conviction. In essence, the Court found an implied right of privacy that "emanated" from the Bill of Rights. This holding reflected a drastic shift in perceptions about and interpretations of the right of privacy. As the two *Griswold* dissenters then and many others later pointed out, the Constitution doesn't expressly provide or even address the issue of privacy. Nonetheless, *Griswold* made clear the Court's willingness to look beyond the four corners of the Constitution to protect what it viewed as fundamental rights.

Griswold's most important legacy is the precedent it set, serving as the critical underpinning for the Supreme Court's 1973 decision in *Roe v. Wade*, where Justice Harry Blackmun wrote: "the Court has recognized that a right of personal privacy, or a guarantee of certain areas or zones of privacy, does exist under the Constitution."

SEE ALSO The Bill of Rights (1791); The Right to Privacy (1890); *Roe v. Wade* (1973); The Legal Fight for Gay Marriage (2004).

The Griswold *ruling articulated a complex concept of privacy through its analysis of the scope and legality of legislation that governs a woman's right to contraception.*

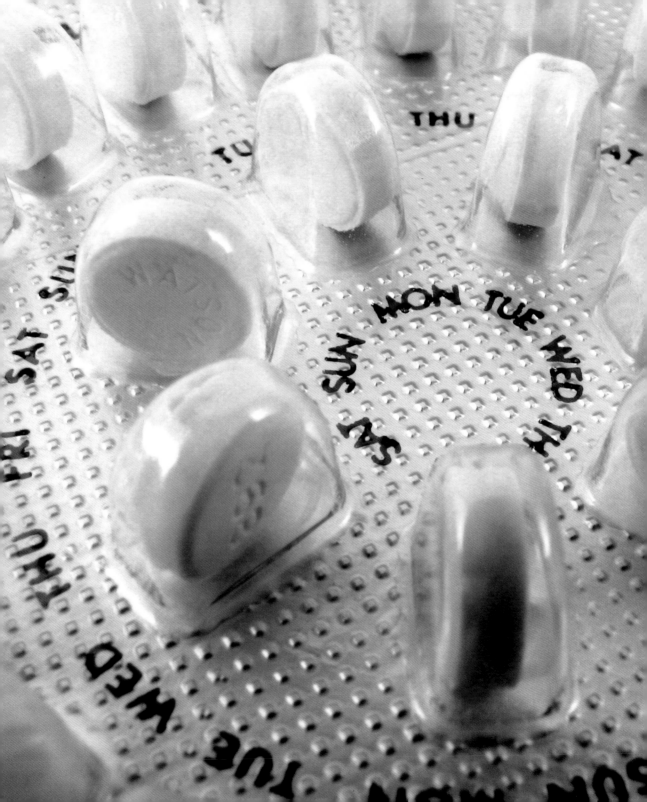

The Freedom of Information Act

John E. Moss (1915–1997), **Lyndon Johnson** (1908–1973)

In his 1953 book, *The People's Right to Know*, attorney and author Harold L. Cross noted in bewilderment "that in the absence of a general or specific act of Congress creating a clear right to inspect—and such acts are not numerous—there is no enforceable legal right in public or press to inspect any federal non-judicial record." As a result, much of the government's work remained a mystery to the people. Even those who tried to access government records could be turned away rightfully because they had no legally recognized ability to do so.

This atmosphere of secrecy and lack of accountability motivated Congressman John E. Moss of California to incite change. In 1955, Moss initiated hearings on excessive governmental secrecy, thereby formulating the basis for a "freedom of information" bill. The idea of granting the people the right to inspect the government's work troubled many politicians. Even President Johnson privately expressed his disdain. According to Moss, Johnson, on learning of the bill, said, "What is Moss trying to do, screw me? I thought he was one of our boys." But with the persistent backing of the media, the president signed the Freedom of Information Act (FOIA) into law in 1966.

The FOIA provides that "any person has a right, enforceable in court, to obtain access to federal agency records, except to the extent that such records (or portions of them) are protected from public disclosure" by certain exclusions. These exclusions touch on topics such as national security, protection of agency personnel privacy, and interference with law enforcement.

Since 1966, the FOIA has undergone several revisions. Following the Watergate scandal, Congress passed the Privacy Act Amendments, which strengthened the FOIA and individuals' rights to access governmental information. In 1996, the Act was amended to require federal agencies to maintain websites where individuals could make FOIA information requests electronically. As a result, the federal government now handles over four million FOIA requests annually. Among the most significant disclosures made under the FOIA was the FBI's release of thousands of documents concerning the 1960s surveillance and investigation of Martin Luther King Jr.

SEE ALSO The *Pentagon Papers* (1971).

The FOIA allows anyone to obtain access to federal agency records—except those pertaining to national security or agency personnel or those that would interfere with law enforcement agencies.

Miranda Warnings

Ernesto Miranda (1941–1976), **Earl Warren** (1891–1974)

If you've regularly watched a TV crime show, you can probably recite the Miranda rights from memory: "You have the right to remain silent. Anything you say can and will be used against you. . . . You have the right to an attorney," and so on. But who was Miranda, and why have the rights named for him marked our consciousness so indelibly?

In 1963, while investigating a series of sexual assaults, police in Phoenix, Arizona, took Ernesto Miranda into custody, where he was identified in a station-house lineup. When asked if he wanted to make a statement, Miranda hand-wrote and signed a confession, which was used at trial to convict him of kidnapping and rape.

In 1966, the U.S. Supreme Court overturned Miranda's conviction. A *New York Times* headline proclaimed: "High Court Puts New Curb on Powers of the Police to Interrogate Suspects." Chief Justice Earl Warren's majority opinion announced a new rule, prohibiting the in-court use of a defendant's custodial statements without the safeguards now known as Miranda warnings. In the Court's view, custodial interrogations seethed with the potential for intimidation and coercion and therefore required these measures. "The very fact of custodial interrogation exacts a heavy toll of individual liberty and trades on the weakness of individuals," Warren wrote. Police now had to "mirandize" every person taken into custody.

But Miranda's victory in the Supreme Court proved pyrrhic. At a retrial that excluded his confession, Miranda was convicted again. Less than four years after his 1972 parole, he was stabbed to death in a Phoenix bar fight. In a bitter twist of fate, police read his accused assailant his Miranda warnings upon arrest.

At the time, *Miranda's* critics warned that the new requirements would cripple law enforcement, but those expectations proved unwarranted. Post-*Miranda* research has shown no negative impact on conviction rates. Indeed, Miranda himself had been convicted upon retrial despite exclusion of his confession.

SEE ALSO The Bill of Rights (1791); The Fourteenth Amendment (1868); States and the Exclusionary Rule (1961); The Right to Counsel in State Court (1963).

Ernesto Miranda (right) appears in court with his attorney, John J. Flynn (left), on February 15, 1967.

Interracial Marriage

Richard Loving (1933–1975), **Mildred Jeter Loving** (1939–2008),
Loving v. Virginia

Regrettably the law isn't always fair. In response to evolving societal values and mores, however, it can and does change, and the groundbreaking *Loving v. Virginia* case provides a good example.

For many years, a number of states maintained anti-miscegenation laws prohibiting interracial marriages. In 1958, Virginia and sixteen other states had such a law, in this case the Racial Integrity Act of 1924, the violation of which was a felony. Two Virginia residents, Richard Loving (white) and Mildred Jeter (black) wanted to marry but knew they couldn't in their home state. They traveled to Washington, D.C., where they legally married in a civil ceremony, and returned home. A few weeks later, they were arrested for violating the Racial Integrity Act. The Lovings pleaded guilty and were sentenced to one year in prison. In lieu of the prison sentence, the Lovings accepted a twenty-five-year exile from Virginia and moved to the District of Columbia.

In 1963, the Lovings sought to overturn their convictions, arguing that the statutes under which they were charged violated the equal protection and due process clauses of the Fourteenth Amendment. After two lower courts upheld the constitutionality of the statutes, the Lovings appealed to the Supreme Court.

In its ruling, the Supreme Court unanimously struck down the Virginia law and the miscegenation laws of all other states. Chief Justice Earl Warren wrote: "The Fourteenth Amendment requires that the freedom of choice to marry not be restricted by invidious racial discrimination. Under our Constitution, the freedom to marry, or not marry, a person of another race resides with the individual and cannot be infringed by the State." On June 13, 1967, one day later, President Johnson nominated Thurgood Marshall to the Court. The Senate confirmed him on August 30, 1967, and he became the Court's first black Justice.

The Court's decision marked another victory in the Civil Rights Movement. Using data from the U.S. Census Bureau, researchers studying marriage reported in 2012 that more than 35 percent of Americans identified themselves as having at least one immediate family member or close relative who is married to someone of a different race.

SEE ALSO The Fourteenth Amendment (1868); The Civil Rights Act of 1964; The First Ban on Gay Marriage (1973); The First Gay Marriage Laws (1989); The Legal Fight for Gay Marriage (2004).

This photograph of Mildred and Richard Loving was taken the day after the Supreme Court ruled in their favor.

The Vietnam-Era Draft Laws

Lyndon Johnson (1908–1973), **Richard Nixon** (1913–1994)

The history of conscription dates back at least to the time of Ancient Greece and the Roman Republic. In America, conscription first appeared during the Civil War, returning again when the U.S. entered World War I in 1917. But laws often need to change in accordance with the will of the people. Such changes aren't typically or best accomplished through the courts but rather through the legislative and executive branches of government, which in theory are charged with being responsive to the electorate. But popular changes in the law do occur. The Vietnam-era draft laws and their eventual elimination exemplify this paradigm.

With the outbreak of the Korean War in 1950, Congress reauthorized the draft through the Universal Military Training and Service Act, requiring all males between the ages of eighteen and twenty-six to register. Congress had reauthorized the draft in 1959 and again in 1963 without any significant public resistance. But American involvement in what soon became the Vietnam War had begun, and hostilities in Vietnam escalated beginning in 1964. As historian George Q. Flynn put it, "Fires lit in Southeast Asia soon became a conflagration that engulfed the nation."

The Selective Service System, long a part of the nation's social and political fabric, faced harsh criticism amid allegations of unfairness and class bias in draft deferments. Those attacks, coupled with increasing antiwar protests, led President Johnson to create the Marshall Commission to study and recommend improvements to the draft system. By the spring of 1967, the commission's report prompted passage of the Military Selective Service Act. Nonetheless, public opposition to the draft and to the war itself continued to grow. Facing mounting pressures, President Johnson withdrew from the 1968 presidential race. Richard Nixon, who pledged late in his campaign to support an all-volunteer army, was elected president in 1968. He continued the draft with some modifications during his first term, but in August 1972, less than three months before the next presidential election, he announced the draft would end in July 1973. He was elected to a second term, and since that time America has relied on armed services composed entirely of volunteers.

SEE ALSO Conscientious Objection (1965); The Court-Martial of William Calley Jr. (1970); Enfranchising Eighteen-Year-Olds (1971).

A few members of Company "A," 3rd Battalion, 22nd Infantry (Mechanized), 25th Infantry Division, gather around a guitar to sing a few songs in January 1968.

No-Fault Divorce

Poet William Blake wrote that "love to faults is always blind," but until the twentieth century the same couldn't be said of divorce laws.

Legal historian Lawrence Friedman notes that until the early nineteenth century judicial divorce "was basically unavailable in England" or America. Unhappy spouses could seek relief only by petitioning the relevant legislature for a private bill of divorce. By the turn of the twentieth century, every state except South Carolina permitted judicial divorce actions, though the grounds and procedures varied widely. The grounds typically included adultery, desertion, or other "cruel and inhuman treatment."

Marriage can be difficult, but divorce certainly was, too, by virtue of various state statutes, which legislators resisted liberalizing for political reasons. Yet demand for divorces continued to rise over the nineteenth and twentieth centuries. Divorcing spouses and their lawyers discovered that working together—if not in marriage at least in ending it—could expedite the process. Collusion soon became the law's best-known secret. According to Friedman, "After 1870, as far as we can tell, most divorces were collusive; there was no real courtroom dispute." He quotes a Massachusetts judge who, after spending thirty-five years overseeing divorce cases, claimed: "There is probably no tribunal in the country in which perjury is more rife than in the Divorce Court."

All of this began to change when California enacted the Family Law Act of 1969, the nation's first no-fault divorce law. All that the state required for a party to obtain a "dissolution of marriage"—note the new phrase—was "irreconcilable differences" causing the "irremediable breakdown of the marriage." Other states quickly followed, and by 1989 forty-nine states and the District of Columbia had adopted no-fault divorce legislation. The one hold-out, New York, finally adopted it in 2010.

The liberalization of American divorce law was called "the silent revolution" because little public discourse took place. In contrast, during the mid-1980s and mid-1990s, Irish lawmakers, the Church, and the citizenry debated fervently prior to a successful 1995 referendum on a constitutional amendment that legalized divorce in Ireland; then the 1996 Family (Divorce) Act allowed for no-fault divorce.

SEE ALSO Palimony (1976).

The Family Law Act of 1969 allowed marriages to be dissolved on the basis of "irreconcilable differences."

Free Speech and Threats of Violence

Brandenburg v. Ohio

In 2012, the polling company Rasmussen Reports released the results of a survey in which participants answered questions about the importance of certain constitutional rights. Freedom of speech led the poll with 85 percent of participants classifying the right as "Very Important." Despite that clear importance, the exercise of free speech nonetheless can generate substantial controversy, particularly in cases involving speech considered abhorrent or advocating the use of force or violence. The latter issue came before the U.S. Supreme Court in *Brandenburg v. Ohio*.

Clarence Brandenburg, a Ku Klux Klan leader, was convicted under a state syndicalism law for advocating violence as a means of political reform. He had been identified in a video of a Klan rally calling for "revengeance" against the government if it continued to "suppress the white, Caucasian race." Brandenburg fought his conviction under the theory that his recorded words constituted protected speech.

In a decision described by legal journalist Tony Mauro as "one of the most expansive interpretations of the First Amendment ever announced," a unanimous Supreme Court held that "the constitutional guarantees of free speech . . . do not permit a State to forbid or proscribe advocacy of the use of force . . . except where such advocacy is directed to inciting or producing imminent lawless action and is likely to incite or produce such action." The decision represented a stronger, more protective version of the clear-and-present-danger test that Justice Holmes had announced half a century earlier in *Schenck v. United States*. Brandenburg's words, no matter how ugly or hateful in their advocacy of violence, didn't produce the "imminent lawless action" against which the Court had warned. On the contrary, it found Brandenburg's words constituted "mere advocacy" and therefore couldn't constitutionally support a conviction.

Brandenburg remains a vital part of contemporary free speech jurisprudence. First Amendment scholar Donald Downs calls it "the lynchpin of the modern doctrine of free speech, which seeks to give special protection to politically relevant speech and to distinguish speech from action."

SEE ALSO Yelling "Fire!" in a Crowded Theater (1919); Limits on Libel Laws (1964); The Son of Sam Law (1978).

Purported Ku Klux Klan members support U.S. Senator Barry Goldwater's campaign for the presidential nomination at the Republican National Convention in San Francisco, July 1964.

The Fairness Doctrine

1969

Red Lion Broadcasting Co. v. FCC

Broadcast radio stations operate through use of the radio spectrum, which consists of a finite number of frequencies, owned and controlled by the government, that can transmit media content across the airwaves. The FCC, a federal agency established in 1934, regulates use of the spectrum by licensing frequencies to individual stations. In exchange for their licenses, radio stations must agree to abide by FCC rules, one of which requires stations to promote "free and fair competition of opposing views."

As time went on, this rule was interpreted to mean that broadcasters, after airing one perspective on a matter of public concern, had to provide equal airtime to opposing perspectives so as to promote well-rounded public discussion. This requirement came to be known as the Fairness Doctrine, and the FCC sanctioned stations that refused to comply. In 1964, however, two radio stations fought back, arguing that a regulation that required them to air certain content violated broadcasters' First Amendment freedoms of speech and press. Five years later, their case found its way to the Supreme Court in *Red Lion Broadcasting Co. v. FCC*.

In a unanimous decision, the Court upheld the Fairness Doctrine, stating that the "scarce" number of radio frequencies available along the spectrum meant there could be no constitutional right to hold and monopolize use of a broadcast license. Government regulations requiring a station to share its frequency for the purpose of presenting opposing viewpoints couldn't be considered a constitutional violation. "It is the right of the viewers and listeners, not the right of the broadcasters, which is paramount," wrote Justice Byron White.

Although the bulk of the doctrine was repealed in 1987, *Red Lion*, in the words of legal journalist Tony Mauro, "established, in the clearest terms yet, the constitutional framework for assessing the First Amendment right of broadcasters." In later cases involving broadcast media, the *Red Lion* decision provided judges with the justification to uphold a variety of regulations imposed on broadcasters that would otherwise suggest an unconstitutional violation of the First Amendment freedoms of speech and press.

SEE ALSO The Bill of Rights (1791); The Federal Communications Act (1934); A New Obscenity Standard (1973); The FCC and Filthy Words (1978); The Communications Decency Act (1997).

The Fairness Doctrine established that, because of the scarcity of radio frequencies, government regulations requiring a station to share its frequency for the presentation of opposing viewpoints couldn't be considered a constitutional violation.

The National Environmental Policy Act

Richard Nixon (1913–1994)

After public outcry over the 1969 Santa Barbara oil spill, former California governor and then-president Richard Nixon signed the National Environmental Policy Act (NEPA) into law on January 1, 1970, proclaiming the 1970s the "Decade of the Environment."

It wasn't the first major piece of environmental legislation—President Johnson had signed the Clean Air Act into law in 1963—but Senator Henry "Scoop" Jackson of Washington called NEPA "the most important and far-reaching environmental and conservation measure ever enacted." More than a hundred countries and at least fifteen states have adopted similar legislation.

In addition to establishing sweeping policy regarding environmental protection, NEPA required all federal agencies to provide an "environmental impact statement" with every recommendation or report on proposals for legislation and "other major Federal actions significantly affecting the quality of the human environment." In preparing those statements, agencies must consult with and solicit comments from other agencies with jurisdiction or expertise and, significantly, make all comments available to the public, thereby also affording a right of public comment.

April 22, 1970, marked the first celebration of Earth Day, a nationwide expression of environmental concern that included rallies, protests, and teach-ins that drew more than twenty million participants. So many senators and representatives headed to their home states to participate in local festivities that Congress scheduled no business for the day, which thereafter became an annual event. Nixon capped the year by creating the Environmental Protection Agency.

Although different constituencies hold diverging views on NEPA's success, there's no dispute that by mandating consideration of environmental issues and ensuring that decision makers and the public had access to information about potential environmental consequences, the statute squarely focused government attention where it hadn't previously been.

SEE ALSO The Endangered Species Act (1973); Attorneys' Fee Awards (1975); Administrative Agency Determinations (1984); The Rio Conference (1992).

NEPA has been called "the most important and far-reaching environmental and conservation measure ever enacted."

The Court-Martial of William Calley Jr.

William Calley Jr. (b. 1943), **Seymour Hersh** (b. 1937), **Ronald Haeberle** (b. 1940)

On March 16, 1968, a U.S. Army platoon entered the Vietnamese hamlet of Sơn Mỹ (better known inaccurately as My Lai). American soldiers rounded up villagers—mostly women, children, and the elderly—and summarily executed nearly five hundred of them. Uncertainty still clouds much of that day, but history has recorded the highly publicized court-martial and conviction of Second Lieutenant William Calley Jr. for the murder of twenty-two Vietnamese civilians.

The platoon's mission followed a briefing in which Calley's superiors portrayed Sơn Mỹ as a Viet Cong stronghold to be destroyed. Despite the absence of resistance, the soldiers engaged the villagers accordingly. Ronald Haeberle, an Army photographer who eventually sold his graphic photos to *Life* and *Time* magazines, captured the carnage, and an Army investigation led to charges against Calley and others. The inquiry garnered little attention, however, until journalist Seymour Hersh wrote a November 1969 news story about a suspected cover-up of the massacre that Dispatch News Service syndicated to more than thirty newspapers.

The three-month trial began in November 1970. Calley admitted to ordering and participating in the killings but maintained that he was following orders to kill everyone in Sơn Mỹ. But after Nuremberg, that defense wasn't valid. In March 1971, the six-officer jury found Calley guilty, and he was sentenced to life in prison. Public opinion overwhelmingly opposed the verdict, though, and public support for Calley prompted President Nixon to intervene. That summer, Calley's sentence was reduced to twenty years; three years later, it dropped to ten.

Calley sought relief in the federal courts. The district court ordered the conviction quashed, finding that Calley had been denied a fair trial, in particular because of prejudicial pretrial publicity. Calley was paroled in August 1974, and Nixon granted him a presidential pardon, but his military conviction ultimately was reinstated.

SEE ALSO The Geneva Convention (1864); The Nuremberg Trials (1945); The Eichmann Trial (1961); The Trial of Manuel Noriega (1991); The International Criminal Court (2002).

A sculpture in the garden of the Sơn Mỹ Memorial in Tịnh Khê, Vietnam.

Public Health and Cigarettes

James Bonsack (1859–1924), **Luther Terry** (1911–1985)

James Bonsack's 1880 automatic rolling machine made cigarettes more widely available at lower prices. As smoking increased, some states sought to curb it as a public nuisance. By the late 1920s, though, efforts to regulate tobacco had dissipated. States discovered the revenue available through taxing cigarettes. Soldiers returning from World War I had become inveterate smokers. Prohibition was in full swing, and the country couldn't brook another moral proscription. Most importantly, the nascent advertising industry had joined forces with the tobacco companies.

Not until the 1960s did the anti-smoking movement began to stir. In 1964, U.S. Surgeon General Luther Terry issued his "Report on Smoking and Health," concluding: "Cigarette smoking is a health hazard of sufficient importance in the United States to warrant appropriate remedial action." Congress responded with the 1965 Federal Cigarette Labeling and Advertising Act, requiring for the first time that manufacturers include warning labels: "Caution: Cigarette smoking may be hazardous to your health." Two years later, the Federal Trade Commission reported "virtually no evidence that the warning statement on cigarette packages has had any significant effect."

But as evidence of the hazards mounted, Congress considered additional legislation. With acquiescence from the cigarette industry, Congress passed the Public Health Cigarette Smoking Act of 1970, which strengthened the package warning and made it unlawful "to advertise cigarettes on any medium of electronic communications subject to the jurisdiction of the Federal Communications Commission." This legislation marked the first time that Congress regulated cigarette advertising. The industry agreed to the ban because the FCC's recently developed Fairness Doctrine required broadcasters to provide equal airtime to warnings about the dangers of smoking, and those anti-smoking messages concerned the tobacco industry.

SEE ALSO The Prohibition of Illegal Narcotics (1915); Prohibition (1918); The Fairness Doctrine (1969); Smoking Litigation (1992); Legalization of Marijuana (1996).

In this 1950s anti-smoking poster, a doctor wearing a stethoscope rejects the offer of a cigarette because of smoking's potential to cause disease.

The RICO Act

G. Robert Blakey (b. 1936)

Law professor Robert Blakey, former chief counsel of the Senate Subcommittee on Criminal Laws and Procedures and one of the chief architects of the Racketeer Influenced and Corrupt Organizations (RICO) Act, describes that act "as the end product of a long process of legislative effort to develop new legal remedies to deal with an old problem: 'organized crime.'" Earlier, that problem had attracted public and congressional attention through the televised 1951 organized-crime hearings of the Kefauver Committee, which found, among other points, that "criminals and racketeers are using the profits of organized crime to buy up and operate legitimate enterprises."

Two decades passed before Congress enacted RICO as part of the Organized Crime Control Act of 1970. The broadly written statute identifies and makes unlawful four activities: using income from a "pattern of racketeering activity" to acquire an interest in an enterprise, acquiring or maintaining an interest in such enterprise through such pattern, conducting the affairs of such enterprise through such pattern, and conspiring to do any of the first three. A "pattern of racketeering activity" is defined as at least two instances of certain specified offenses, including bribery, extortion, mail or wire fraud, money laundering, prostitution, and narcotics trafficking, among others.

Although targeted at organized crime's infiltration or manipulation of legitimate businesses, RICO has both a criminal and a civil component. The attorney general as well as private citizens injured in their business or property can bring RICO suits.

Commentators have recognized the impact that RICO has had on both criminal and civil law. From the prosecutorial perspective, RICO has been a success. Not only has it significantly reduced the prevalence and impact of organized crime, but prosecutors have capitalized on RICO's extraordinary breadth, invoking it even against individuals not involved in traditional organized-crime activities, including cases of political corruption and securities fraud. In its civil application, RICO has stirred controversy as a result. Because it allows a successful plaintiff to recover treble damages as well as attorneys' fees, RICO has become an attractive alternate path by which to pursue run-of-the-mill commercial fraud cases.

SEE ALSO The White-Slave Traffic Act (1910); The Clayton Antitrust Act (1914); The Prohibition of Illegal Narcotics (1915); The Repeal of Prohibition (1933); The Securities Exchange Act (1934); Attorneys' Fee Awards (1975); The Trial of Manuel Noriega (1991).

Luciano crime family boss Frank Costello testifies before the Kefauver Committee, which investigated organized crime, in 1951. Some of its findings led to enactment of the RICO statute twenty years later.

Baseball's Reserve Clause

Curtis Flood (1938–1997), **Bowie Kuhn** (1926–2007), *Flood v. Kuhn*

Among 2013's thirty Major League Baseball teams, the average player earned $3.6 million. But in 1920, the mean salary was $5,000, and Babe Ruth, the highest paid player, earned the princely sum of $20,000, a fraction of today's average salary even in current dollars. So what caused the dramatic escalation?

Curt Flood—a seven-time Gold Glove–winning, all-star center fielder—spent most of his Major League career with the St. Louis Cardinals. When the Cardinals traded him to the Philadelphia Phillies in 1969, Flood didn't pack his bags. Instead, he brought suit the next year against Commissioner of Baseball Bowie Kuhn and the twenty-four Major League teams, alleging that the reserve clause—a part of all players' contracts that effectively gave teams perpetual rights to a player—violated antitrust laws as an illegal restraint of trade. The reserve clause confined a player exclusively to the team that had him under contract; the team could freely assign that contract and had the unilateral right to renew it annually, subject to a stated minimum salary. Flood argued that the system impinged on his freedom and violated the involuntary servitude provisions of the Thirteenth Amendment. For Flood, the issue was less about money than autonomy.

Two lower courts ruled against Flood, invoking a 1922 Supreme Court precedent that professional baseball stood exempt from antitrust law because it didn't involve interstate commerce. In 1972, the Supreme Court upheld those rulings, suggesting that any change in the law had to come from Congress.

Although he lost his legal battle, Flood led others to take harder stands against the clause and to an increasingly stronger Major League Baseball Players Association. That, in turn, led to a collective bargaining agreement with team owners that included neutral grievance arbitration. In 1975, an arbitrator rejected the reserve clause and declared two players to be free agents, granting them the right to choose the team for which they would play. Flood had paved the way for free agency.

Flood died twenty-five years after his defeat in the Supreme Court and just one day before Senator Orrin Hatch introduced the Curt Flood Act, which expressly subjected Major League Baseball to the antitrust laws.

SEE ALSO The Chicago "Black Sox" Trial (1921).

Curt Flood, one of baseball's greatest center fielders, spent most of his career playing for the St. Louis Cardinals. The team's attempt to trade him to the Philadelphia Phillies in 1969 forever changed the national pastime.

The Occupational Safety and Health Act

In 1969 congressional hearings, former Secretary of Labor George P. Shultz estimated that annual industrial accidents killed 14,500 workers and injured or disabled an additional 2.2 million, causing losses of more than $8 billion in gross national product. The federal government needed to regulate health and safety in the workplace, which it did the next year with the Occupational Safety and Health Act, described by Senator Harrison A. Williams Jr. as "a landmark achievement in safeguarding the health and lives of America's working men and women" and a "safety bill of rights for close to sixty million workers."

Prior to the act, state legislatures decided issues of worker health and safety, but the states were neither uniform nor always effective in handling such matters. Moreover, according to Congressman Lloyd Meeds, who took part in drafting the federal law, worker health and safety conditions were exacerbated by "the spiraling introduction of new substances and technologies into industries—technologies and substances whose effects on workers had not even been studied."

Central to the new legislation was the delegation of authority to the U.S. Department of Labor to establish and enforce standards and the creation of an oversight commission. Thus was born the Occupational Safety and Health Administration (OSHA). OSHA's principal responsibilities included ensuring compliance with safety standards through workplace inspections, receiving employee complaints about violations, and sanctioning employers who violated standards. OSHA oversaw the extensive record keeping requirement imposed on businesses and also provided education and training for both employers and employees.

OSHA's early years met with mixed success, and within two years of enactment, legislators introduced more than eighty proposed amendments to the act. Through subsequent amendments and accommodation by OSHA, the regulatory scheme— along with earplugs, protective eyewear, hard hats, vehicle back-up alarms, and other measures—has become part of the modern workplace for the more than 130 million workers employed at more than 8 million worksites around the nation.

SEE ALSO Women in Factories (1908); The Triangle Shirtwaist Fire (1911); The Child Labor Act of 1916; The National Labor Relations Act (1935); The Fair Labor Standards Act (1938).

Many safety measures have become mandatory as a result of the Occupational Health and Safety Act.

CONSTRUCTION SITE

No unauthorized personnel allowed on site

All workers must have a Safe Pass Card

Hard Hats must be worn

Visitors & deliveries must report to Site Office

Foot Protection must be worn

Ear Protection must be worn

Accidents must be reported

Caution heavy vehicles in use

The Trial of Charles Manson

Charles Manson (1934–), **Sharon Tate** (1943–1969), **Richard Nixon** (1913–1994), **Vincent Bugliosi** (1934–2015)

The turbulent 1960s ended with unthinkable slaughter in the Hollywood Hills, where Charles Manson orchestrated the brutal slaying of eight people in what became known as the Tate-LaBianca murders. Manson had spent most of his life in trouble with the law. Following release from prison in 1967, he attracted a cult-like following of misfits who considered themselves members of his "family." They worshipped him, and he controlled them completely. Manson believed a racial war was imminent and that at its conclusion he would lead the survivors. He called for a series of brutal, high-profile murders to spark that war. On August 9, 1969, members of the Manson Family butchered pregnant actress Sharon Tate, wife of director Roman Polanski; three houseguests; and another individual. The next night, they did the same to Leno and Rosemary LaBianca.

When opening statements in the trial against Manson and three co-defendants began, Manson appeared in the courtroom with an X carved into his forehead (said to symbolize having "X'd" himself from the world). Shortly after opening statements, the already sensational press coverage exploded. At a conference of law enforcement officials, President Nixon remarked that Manson "was guilty, directly or indirectly, of eight murders." A front-page *Los Angeles Times* headline screamed: MANSON GUILTY, NIXON DECLARES. The defense moved for a mistrial, which was denied because the jury had been sequestered since being impaneled.

Prosecutor Vincent Bugliosi called "Manson's mission . . . perhaps the most inhuman, nightmarish, horror-filled hour of savage murder and human slaughter in the recorded annals of crime." When the nine-month trial ended, it had been the longest in U.S. history. The jurors had been sequestered for 225 days, the longest period to that date. All four defendants were sentenced to death. But, in 1972, the California Supreme Court struck down the state's death penalty as unconstitutional. (The U.S. Supreme Court followed suit several months later.) The defendants' sentences were commuted to life in prison. In 2012, the California Board of Parole Hearings denied Manson's twelfth request for parole. His next hearing is set for 2027; he will be ninety-two years old.

SEE ALSO Banning the Death Penalty (1972); The Son of Sam Law (1978).

Charles Manson "Helter Skelter" *by Ze Carrion.*

Enfranchising Eighteen-Year-Olds

Franklin Delano Roosevelt (1882–1945), **Jennings Randolph** (1902–1998), **Richard Nixon** (1913–1994)

When President Roosevelt lowered the draft age to eighteen during World War II, he set in motion three decades of effort to lower the constitutionally imposed twenty-one-year-old voting age. In October 1942, Congressman Jennings Randolph of West Virginia introduced a resolution to amend the Constitution to lower the voting age to eighteen. A 1971 Senate report indicates that "since that time, more than 150 similar proposals have been introduced, at least one in each subsequent Congress." None found success.

By the late 1960s, campus unrest over the already unpopular Vietnam War was growing. Protesters revived a slogan that had first appeared during World War II: "Old enough to fight, old enough to vote." In 1970, as part of legislation extending parts of the Voting Rights Act of 1965 for an additional five years, Congress included a provision lowering the voting age to eighteen in all federal and state elections. President Nixon signed the bill into law despite his view that lowering the voting age through legislation rather than the constitutional amendment process violated the Constitution.

A challenge to the legislation came almost immediately in *Oregon v. Mitchell*. On December 20, 1970, a splintered Supreme Court held that, while Congress had the authority to lower the federal voting age, it had no such authority when it came to state elections. The implications of that decision—different voting ages for different elections—threatened chaos. Looking ahead to the 1972 elections, Congress took note of popular support for granting the right to eighteen-year-olds and acted quickly.

On January 25, 1971, now Senator Jennings Randolph introduced a joint resolution proposing a constitutional amendment to lower the voting age to eighteen. This resolution marked his eleventh such proposal over the preceding thirty years. In under two months, the amendment received near unanimous support in both the House and the Senate, and it was immediately submitted to the states for ratification. The National Archives and Records Administration notes that the "26th Amendment was ratified in 100 days, faster than any other amendment."

SEE ALSO Women's Right to Vote (1919); The Voting Rights Act (1965).

The Twenty-Sixth Amendment to the Constitution lowered the federal voting age to eighteen.

The *Pentagon Papers*

Robert McNamara (1916–2009), **Daniel Ellsberg** (1931–), *New York Times Co. v. United States*, **Hugo Black** (1886–1971)

Freedom of the press has long stood as a core American principle. Sometimes, however, courts confront challenges to that freedom in the name of national security. One of the most notable arose in 1971, involving the Vietnam War and efforts to end it.

In 1967, Defense Secretary Robert McNamara commissioned a comprehensive history of American relations with Vietnam. The forty-seven-volume work, known as the *Pentagon Papers*, was completed in 1969 and classified top secret. Daniel Ellsberg, a former Pentagon employee who opposed the war, surreptitiously photocopied all seven thousand pages, intending to make them public. He eventually provided all but the last four volumes to the *New York Times*, which printed the first of a series of articles, along with excerpted documents, on June 13, 1971. Two more articles followed, revealing that the government had misrepresented its aims in Vietnam—helping South Vietnam remain independent—when its actual purpose was containing China. Documents also revealed President Johnson's intention to escalate American involvement, contrary to public statements, and unreported bombings of Cambodia and Laos.

On June 15, the Justice Department obtained an unprecedented restraining order forbidding further publication, pending a June 18 court hearing. On June 19, the court ruled in favor of the *Times*. By now, Ellsberg had also provided copies of the *Pentagon Papers* to the *Washington Post*, also sued after publication.

On June 30, after expedited appeals, the Supreme Court ruled in favor of both newspapers, concluding that the government had failed to carry its burden of showing justification for a prior restraint on publication, for which there was "a heavy presumption against . . . constitutional validity." Justice Black noted that "the press must be left free to publish news, whatever the source, without censorship, injunctions, or prior restraints." But three of the six majority justices left open the possibility that a prior restraint might be justified if the government could prove, in Justice Stewart's words, "direct, immediate, and irreparable damage" from publication. It was a resounding victory for the press, particularly given the government's remonstrations about national security.

SEE ALSO The Government Printing Office (1861); The Freedom of Information Act (1966); Free Speech and Threats of Violence (1969).

Three years after the New York Times *brought the* Pentagon Papers *to the public's attention, it reported that President Nixon had resigned.*

"All the News
That's Fit to Print"

The New York Times

VOL.CXXIII....No.42,566

© 1974 The New York Times Company

LATE CITY EDITION

Weather: Partly cloudy today; cool
tonight. Fair, pleasant tomorrow.
Temp. range: today 65-78; Thursday
64-85. Highest Temp.-Hum. Index
yesterday: 75. Details on Page 66.

NEW YORK, FRIDAY, AUGUST 9, 1974

20c beyond 50-mile radius of New York City
except Long Island. Higher in air delivery cities

15 CENTS

NIXON RESIGNS

HE URGES A TIME OF 'HEALING'; FORD WILL TAKE OFFICE TODAY

'Sacrifice' Is Praised; Kissinger to Remain

By ANTHONY RIPLEY
Special to The New York Times

WASHINGTON, Aug. 8—
Vice President Ford praised
President Nixon tonight for
"one of the greatest personal
sacrifices for the country and
one of the finest personal decisions on behalf of all of us as
Americans."

Mr. Ford, who will take office as the 38th President at
noon tomorrow, vowed to continue Mr. Nixon's foreign policy
and announced that Secretary
of State Kissinger had agreed
to stay on in the new Administration.

"I pledge to you tonight, as

I will pledge to you tomorrow
and in the future, my best efforts in cooperation, leadership
and dedication to what's good
for America and good for the
world," he said.

The Vice President, who
never sought the nation's highest office and disclaimed any
intention of seeking it after Mr.
Nixon's term, will be sworn in
a private ceremony at the White
House.

Thus will he become the first
man to serve as President without being chosen by the American people in an election. Tomorrow night he will address
the nation on radio and television. It is expected that he
will speak at 6 P.M.

All day today the signs of
the historic change were in the
air, sensed by the crowds that
gathered along Pennsylvania

Text of Mr. Ford's remarks
appears on Page 3.

SPECULATION RIFE ON VICE PRESIDENT

Some Ford Associates Say
Selecting a Successor

The 37th President Is First to Quit Post

By JOHN HERBERS
Special to The New York Times

WASHINGTON, Aug. 8—Richard Milhous Nixon, the 37th
President of the United States, announced tonight that he
had given up his long and arduous fight to remain in office
and would resign, effective at noon tomorrow.

Gerald Rudolph Ford, whom Mr. Nixon nominated for
Vice President last Oct. 12, will be sworn in tomorrow at
the same hour as the 38th President, to serve out the 895
days remaining in Mr. Nixon's second term.

Less that two years after his landslide re-election
victory, Mr. Nixon, in a conciliatory address on national

Text of the address will be found on Page 2.

television, said that he was leaving not with a sense
bitterness but with a hope that his departure would star
"process of healing that is so desperately needed in Americ

He spoke of regret for any "injuries" done "in the cou
of the events that led to this decision." He acknowled
that some of his judgments had been wrong.

The 61-year-old Mr. Nixon, appearing calm and resi
to his fate as a victim of the Watergate scandal, becam
first President in the history of the Republic to resign
office. Only 10 months earlier A...ro Vice President,
T. Agnew, became the first man to ... the Vice Presi

Vice President Ford meeting with newsmen last night

President Nixon on TV as he announced his resignation

POLITICAL SCENE
SHARPLY ALTERED

Rise and Fall

Appraisal of Nixon Career

JAWORSKI ASSERTS
NO DEAL WAS MADE

1971

Employment Discrimination

Griggs v. Duke Power Co.

Title VII of the Civil Rights Act of 1964 prohibits employment discrimination, but after Congress enacted the law, workplace discrimination didn't disappear; it merely changed forms. Instead of overtly rejecting black applicants or segregating black employees, many businesses implemented policies that appeared neutral but had a discriminatory impact. Such was the case at Duke Power Company in Draper, North Carolina.

Prior to the enactment of Title VII, Duke consigned its black employees to the labor department, where the highest wage earned fell substantially below the lowest wage earned in departments staffed by white employees. After Title VII made such discrimination unlawful, Duke implemented a new requirement for non-labor-department jobs: a high school diploma or a score above an established minimum on a standardized IQ test. But this requirement had no bearing on an employee's ability to perform work outside the labor department; it operated only to disqualify black employees from higher-paying departments.

When thirteen black employees brought suit challenging the new policy, their claims were rejected in both the trial court and the court of appeals. Both courts viewed Duke's policy as permissible, absent a showing of discriminatory intent. The Supreme Court agreed to hear the appeal to address whether an employer's intent should be considered in assessing whether a particular employment policy was discriminatory.

In a unanimous decision, the Court held that the Civil Rights Act "proscribes not only overt discrimination, but also practices that are fair in form, but discriminatory in operation. . . . If an employment practice which operates to exclude Negroes cannot be shown to be related to job performance, the practice is prohibited." The impact of *Griggs* was curtailed briefly by another Supreme Court case decided in 1989, but the Civil Rights Act of 1991 undid the holding of that case and restored the burden-of-proof rule set forth in *Griggs*, which continues to stand as a major milestone in the development of employment discrimination law.

SEE ALSO The Civil Rights Act of 1866; The Civil Rights Cases (1883); Equal Protection Rights (1886); *Plessy v. Ferguson*: Separate but Equal (1896); The Civil Rights Act of 1964; Affirmative Action (1978).

Warren E. Burger on June 23, 1969, after taking the oath to become the fifteenth chief justice of the U.S. Supreme Court. Burger authored the majority opinion in Griggs v. Duke Power Co., *holding that the utility was discriminating against African American employees.*

Court-Ordered School Busing

Swann v. Charlotte-Mecklenburg Board of Education

Despite the Supreme Court's landmark ruling in *Brown v. Board of Education*, many school districts refused to implement proactive desegregation strategies. One such district, North Carolina's Mecklenburg County, served approximately 84,500 students in the late 1960s, 29 percent of whom were black. Though the district no longer enforced an official policy of segregation, the pervasiveness of de facto segregation was undeniable. During the 1969–1970 school year, "two-thirds of the Charlotte-Mecklenburg district's 24,700 black students remained confined to twenty-five schools where more than ninety-eight percent of the students were black," according to historian Thomas J. Davis. The turning point came when six-year-old James Swann, one of Charlotte-Mecklenburg's black students, was denied admission to a predominantly white school in his neighborhood. His parents sued the district, and their case—backed by statistics demonstrating the district's indirect segregationist policies—went on to become another milestone in the history of desegregation.

In a unanimous decision, the U.S. Supreme Court fully supported a controversial desegregation plan that involved redrawing district lines and implementing an expansive busing scheme to achieve racial integration. The plan would cost more than $1 million to implement and require busing thirteen thousand more students than in previous school years. In response to arguments that these costs far outweighed any benefits, the Court observed: "The remedy for such segregation may be administratively awkward, inconvenient, and even bizarre in some situations and may impose burdens on some; but all awkwardness and inconvenience cannot be avoided in the interim period when remedial adjustments are being made to eliminate the dual school systems."

Legal journalist Tony Mauro writes that *Swann* sent "a firm message to public schools that strong and sometimes controversial measures . . . had to be used to end school segregation once and for all." But while the case represented a momentous step forward in the battle for school desegregation, the progress was short-lived. A newly conservative Supreme Court subsequently issued a string of decisions rejecting other similar proactive busing plans.

SEE ALSO *Plessy v. Ferguson*: Separate but Equal (1896); *Brown v. Board of Education* (1954).

An integrated school bus in 1971.

Banning the Death Penalty

William Henry Furman (b. 1941), *Furman v. Georgia*

Capital punishment has existed in America since colonial times. Support for its abolition has waxed and waned over time, but it wasn't until the latter half of the twentieth century that continued imposition of the death penalty gave impetus to serious questions. By some accounts, the movement to overturn capital punishment began with a 1963 memorandum orchestrated by Supreme Court Justice Arthur Goldberg and his law clerk, Alan Dershowitz, which suggested that the death penalty as it then existed constituted "cruel and unusual punishment," prohibited by the Eighth Amendment. The memo revitalized the abolition movement, but the Supreme Court didn't address the issue until *Furman v. Georgia*.

On August 11, 1967, William Micke Jr., a white father of five, awoke to discover an armed black man, William Henry Furman, in his Savannah home. Furman fled but accidentally shot Micke in the chest, killing him instantly. Because Furman was committing a felony when the shooting happened, he was charged with murder, and, after a one-day trial, a jury found him guilty and sentenced him to death. An appeal to the Georgia Supreme Court upheld both conviction and sentence. The U.S. Supreme Court heard the next appeal, combined with two other death-penalty cases.

The Supreme Court's unsigned per curiam opinion held that "the imposition and carrying out of the death penalty in these cases constitute cruel and unusual punishment in violation of the Eighth and Fourteenth Amendments." The five majority justices each wrote concurring opinions explaining their rationales, but the conclusions were the same: All existing death penalty statutes were unconstitutional because they provided no guidelines or limits for a jury's exercise of discretion.

The decision didn't prohibit capital punishment outright, leaving room for legislative action, but thereafter no death sentence could be imposed or enforced until existing statutes changed, which in effect saved the lives of hundreds of death-row prisoners. Furman's lead lawyer, Anthony Amsterdam, called it "the biggest step forward that criminal justice has taken in 1,000 years."

That progress, however, proved short-lived.

SEE ALSO The Death Penalty Returns (1976).

The electric chair in the death chamber of the Red Hat Cell Block at the Louisiana State Penitentiary, also known as Angola. The U.S. Supreme Court's decision in Furman v. Georgia *put the chair out of commission for a time.*

The Equal Employment Opportunity Act

In the early 1960s, various minorities were fighting for equality in education, voting rights, and employment. Televised marches, protests, and violence resulted in President Kennedy's push for civil-rights legislation, proclaiming that "race has no place in American life or law." After Kennedy's assassination, President Lyndon Johnson continued fighting for comprehensive civil-rights legislation, eventually signing into law the landmark Civil Rights Act of 1964.

Title VII of that act outlawed employment discrimination based on race, color, religion, sex, or national origin, and created the Equal Employment Opportunity Commission (EEOC), which began operations on July 2, 1965. In its early years, the EEOC lacked enforcement powers and often was called "a toothless tiger."

Recognizing the failings, Congress amended Title VII with the Equal Employment Opportunity Act of 1972, expanding the EEOC's jurisdiction and endowing it with the ability to sue private employers engaged in discriminatory conduct. Celebrating its thirty-fifth anniversary in 2000, the EEOC described the 1972 act as having "inaugurated a new era of enforcement" with "significant progress in the development of employment law . . . legal protections extended to millions of persons, and the elimination of many discriminatory practices."

Employment-law experts Barbara Lindemann and Paul Grossman write that Title VII "has generated a body of decisional law unprecedented in scope, volume, and depth among the federal statutory causes of action." A prerequisite to the initiation of all such lawsuits is the filing of a charge of discrimination with the EEOC, which is required to review all claims prior to litigation. The EEOC may recommend mediation, issue a Notice of Right to Sue, or bring its own lawsuit if it is unable to settle the claim. For fiscal year 2014, the EEOC reports that it received more than 63,500 charges of alleged discrimination under Title VII, which by virtue of additional amendments, now also covers age and disability discrimination.

SEE ALSO The Civil Rights Act of 1964; Employment Discrimination (1971); Affirmative Action (1978).

The Equal Employment Opportunity Act permitted the EEOC to sue private employers who engaged in discriminatory conduct, helping to increase workplace participation by women and minorities. Here, a female pediatrician examines a child in 1974.

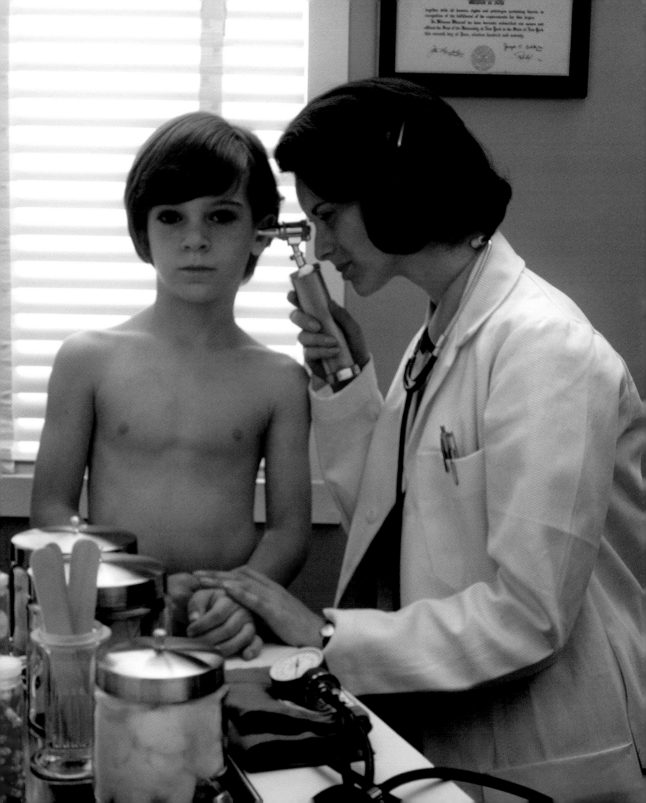

The Equal Rights Amendment

Alice Paul (1885–1977), **Phyllis Schlafly** (b. 1924)

Although the law is always evolving, certain changes can be hard to make. A proposed amendment to the Constitution first must garner a two-thirds majority in both houses of Congress; then three-quarters of the states in the union must ratify it. Despite an amendment's passing both houses, state ratification sometimes proves unattainable, as happened with the Equal Rights Amendment (ERA), which would have explicitly extended the equal protection provisions of the Fourteenth Amendment to women.

Congress considered an early version of the ERA in 1923. Written by Alice Paul, a leading voice for women's suffrage, it provided the foundation for the version that emerged in the late 1960s. In 1944, the ERA received a vote of confidence from the Democratic Party, which included the amendment in campaign platforms, but it wasn't until 1958 that the proposed amendment received presidential support. Despite President Eisenhower's endorsement, opposition to the ERA remained staunch, particularly from influential, male-dominated labor unions. For many legislators, a "yes" vote risked a loss of support from labor; a "no" vote risked losing the support of women.

As congressional and public support expanded, however, opponents of the amendment, led by political activist Phyllis Schlafly, grew more vocal. Schlafly was outspoken in her criticism, arguing that the bill would remove many gender-specific privileges that women enjoyed, including "dependent wife" benefits under Social Security and exemption from Selective Service registration. Nonetheless, the ERA gained sufficient congressional support and finally passed both the Senate and the House of Representatives in 1972.

But even as the U.K. Parliament passed the Sex Discrimination Act in December 1975—prohibiting gender discrimination in housing, education, and the workplace— the American amendment was stalling. It failed to achieve the requisite number of state ratifications by the 1979 legislative deadline, although popular support for the ERA continued. Its success in Congress has served as a galvanizing, symbolic victory for women's rights activists and given rise to the emergence of important feminist groups, including the National Organization for Women and the National Women's Political Caucus.

SEE ALSO The Fourteenth Amendment (1868); Admission of Women to the Bar (1873); Women's Right to Vote (1919).

Phyllis Schlafly, one of the most vocal opponents of the Equal Rights Amendment, wears a "Stop ERA" button while demonstrating outside the White House.

The Trail of Broken Treaties

Nervous about a Lakota gathering in response to the seizure of their lands and breached treaties, the U.S. 7th Cavalry Regiment surrounded their camp near Wounded Knee Creek in South Dakota in December 1890. The ensuing violence resulted in the deaths of more than two hundred tribe members and made Wounded Knee a rallying point for later Native activism.

Since the Treaty of Fort Pitt with the Lenape in 1778, the U.S. has ratified more than 370 treaties with various tribes, but countless disputes have arisen over treaty rights. In the late 1950s, different tribes began coordinating their efforts, asserting treaty rights on behalf of all tribes. Political scientist Jeffrey Dudas notes that Native activists—united across diverse tribes and willing to act politically—learned from the Black Power movement of the 1960s to pursue not only grassroots efforts but also lobbying strategies to address the intolerable living conditions and the abiding neglect of treaty rights.

During the 1960s and 1970s, organizations such as the National Congress of American Indians and the American Indian Movement (AIM) emerged. The most radical, AIM participated in occupying Alcatraz, the former federal penitentiary on the eponymous island in San Francisco Bay, for nearly two years, citing the 1868 Treaty of Fort Laramie, which promised the return of unused federal land to the Sioux. The Alcatraz occupation achieved national attention but accomplished little else.

In 1972, AIM participated in the Trail of Broken Treaties, a march on Washington, D.C., to spotlight Natives' plight and reassert demands for enforcement of treaty obligations. The march led to the week-long occupation and near destruction of the Bureau of Indian Affairs' offices. The next year, AIM members joined with two hundred Sioux activists and seized control of the Wounded Knee site. The ten-week occupation failed to generate tangible federal concessions, although media attention generated national sympathy.

In 2000, during a ceremony marking the 175th anniversary of the Bureau of Indian Affairs, Kevin Gover, assistant secretary of Indian Affairs, apologized on behalf of the agency, which, he said, had "profoundly harmed the communities it was meant to serve."

SEE ALSO Administering Native Peoples (1824); Colonialism and Postwar Independence (1947).

American Indian Movement members take part in "The Longest Walk," a 1978 protest in Washington, D.C., against anti-Native legislation.

The Endangered Species Act

"And of every living thing of all flesh, two of every sort shalt thou bring into the ark, to keep them alive with thee." Thus was Noah commanded according to Genesis 6:19. By the early 1900s, a new kind of conservationist movement had developed. New organizations, including the National Audubon Society and the New York Zoological Society, had been founded, and Congress enacted the country's first federal wildlife-protection law, the Lacey Act, in 1900. But it wasn't until Congress passed the Endangered Species Conservation Act of 1969 that endangered species began to enjoy protection from eradication. For the first time, the law covered invertebrates as well as species outside America. That act also gave rise to the eighty-nation Convention on International Trade in Endangered Species of Wild Fauna and Flora (CITES).

The 1973 CITES helped catalyze further conservationist action, resulting in Congress's passage of the Endangered Species Act of 1973. Holly Doremus, an expert on endangered species and biodiversity protection, observes that it "was, and remains, a landmark, the strongest mandate for protection of the biota on the globe." The act protected the habitats and ecosystems of endangered wildlife against incursions by commercial development. It required the secretary of the Interior to publish and maintain a list of all species "in danger of extinction throughout all or a significant portion of its range" as well as those likely to become endangered within the foreseeable future. The act prohibited hunting, capturing, or in any way harming any endangered species and banned their import and export. Importantly, through administrative regulations, it also proscribed the adverse modification or degradation of species' habitats. Substantial civil and criminal penalties serve as a means of enforcement.

Critics point to significant economic and societal costs occasioned by limitations it has imposed on development, but the Act has been a great success. A 2012 study by the Center for Biological Diversity noted that 110 species "have seen tremendous recovery while protected under the Act," and only 10 of the 1,400 species protected by the Act have been declared extinct (8 of them likely extinct before protection). Scientists estimate that at least 227 species would have gone extinct in the Act's absence.

SEE ALSO The National Environmental Policy Act (1970); The Rio Conference (1992).

The official symbol of America, the bald eagle teetered on the verge of extinction until being listed as endangered (through 1995) and then threatened (through 2007). As a result of the Endangered Species Act, it is now flourishing.

The First Ban on Gay Marriage

Richard John Baker (b. 1942), **James Michael McConnell** (b. 1942), *Baker v. Nelson*

The uphill battle for the legalization of gay marriage began in 1970 when Gerald Nelson, a Hennepin County clerk, declined to issue a marriage license to Jack Baker and Mike McConnell, even though Minnesota law didn't expressly forbid gay marriage. The Hennepin County District Court was unsympathetic to Baker and McConnell's arguments. So was the Minnesota Supreme Court, which rejected *Loving v. Virginia* and *Griswold v. Connecticut* as precedents in the matter. In October 1972, the U.S. Supreme Court refused to hear the appeal, leaving the lower court's holding intact as an established precedent. Courts in Washington and Kentucky, two other states with laws that didn't expressly prohibit gay marriage, rejected similar claims of other gay couples whose applications for marriage licenses had also been denied.

In January 1973, perhaps seeking to avoid a similar challenge, the Maryland General Assembly enacted what became section 2-201 of its Family Law Code, providing that "only a marriage between a man and a woman is valid in this State." Maryland thus became the first state to erect a formal legal barrier to gay marriage.

Maryland's law remained on the books for more than a quarter of a century and survived a 2007 judicial challenge before the Maryland Court of Appeals, the state's highest court. But a changing tide of public support for gay marriage that was building across the country—leading legislatures and courts in states including Massachusetts, California, Connecticut, Iowa, and Vermont to allow it—swept into Maryland in 2011. In March 2012, the Old Line State enacted the Civil Marriage Protection Act, becoming the eighth state to legalize gay marriage. Maryland's voters approved the legislation in a November 2012 ballot initiative, and it took effect the following January.

The final chapter on same-sex marriage remains unwritten, although the U.S. Supreme Court is expected to issue another pronouncement prior to July 2015.

SEE ALSO The Wolfenden Report and Gay Rights (1957); The First Gay Marriage Laws (1989); The Legal Fight for Gay Marriage (2004).

By enacting section 2-201 of the Family Law Code in 1973, Maryland became the first state to ban gay marriage.

A New Obscenity Standard

Potter Stewart (1915–1985), *Miller v. California*, **Warren Burger** (1907–1995)

The effort to devise a clear and objective standard for defining obscenity has proved to be an extraordinarily difficult task for the U.S. Supreme Court. In one of the Court's most quoted statements from a concurring opinion, Justice Potter Stewart famously wrote with confidence in the 1964 case of *Jacobellis v. Ohio*: "I know it when I see it." But the difficulty of applying that statement in judicial matters reappeared in *Miller v. California*, in which a more conservative court announced a new test.

Marvin Miller was convicted of violating California's anti-obscenity law by mass-mailing catalogs for adult books that contained sexually explicit photographs. The Court affirmed Miller's conviction in a 5–4 decision authored by Chief Justice Warren Burger. The Court's opinion clearly reaffirmed the already established principle that obscene materials didn't fall within the protections afforded by the First Amendment. The stumbling block, however, was arriving at a definition of "obscene."

Chief Justice Burger's opinion set forth a three-part standard that became the new test of obscenity, modifying the previous test established in *Roth*. Under this new approach, a work could be considered obscene only if (1) "the average person, applying contemporary community standards, would find that the work, taken as a whole, appeals to the prurient interest"; (2) the work "depicts or describes, in a patently offensive way, sexual conduct specifically defined by the applicable state law"; and (3) taken as a whole, the work "lacks serious literary, artistic, political, or scientific value." Significantly, the Court eliminated the prosecution's previous burden to prove that a work lacked "redeeming social value." Instead, a defendant now needed to show that the challenged work had serious literary, artistic, political, or scientific value. Equally important was the adoption of a community-standards test as the gauge for assessing appeal to prurient interest and patent offensiveness.

Despite the seeming clarity of this new test, the Supreme Court hadn't seen the last of what Justice John Marshall Harlan called "the intractable obscenity problem."

SEE ALSO Censorship and *Ulysses* (1933); Obscenity and the Comstock Act (1873); The Limits on Obscenity (1957); The FCC and Filthy Words (1978); The Communications Decency Act (1997).

A mural, c. 1895, by George R. Barse Jr. in the Library of Congress personifies erotica.

EROTICA

COPYRIGHT BY
BARSE-JR.
1896.

Roe v. Wade

Norma McCorvey (b. 1947), **Henry Wade** (1914–2001)

One of the Supreme Court's most widely known and controversial cases began in 1970 when, under the alias Jane Roe, Norma McCorvey brought suit against the district attorney of Dallas County, Henry Wade, challenging a Texas statute that made abortion illegal except "for the purpose of saving the life of the mother."

At the time, McCorvey, twenty-one years old and separated from her husband, was pregnant with her third child. Unable to obtain a legal abortion, McCorvey elected to continue her pregnancy. By the time her suit reached the Supreme Court, McCorvey had given birth to a baby girl who was adopted anonymously.

The fundamental issue for the Court was trying to reconcile a mother's right to control her own body and an unborn child's right to life. In a controversial 5–4 decision, the Court concluded that during the first trimester of pregnancy a woman's right of choice outweighed any state interest and therefore states couldn't prohibit abortion during the first trimester. During the second trimester, states would be permitted to regulate abortions but only to ensure the health of the woman. In the third trimester, when the fetus was believed to be viable—defined as "capable of meaningful life outside the mother's womb"—the state's interest in protecting life became compelling and the state would be allowed to prohibit abortions except in cases where necessary to protect a woman's life or health.

The ruling struck down the Texas statute and paved the way for legal abortions across the country. In the 1990s, Norma McCorvey converted to Catholicism and ironically became a staunch anti-abortion advocate. The issue remains contentious more than forty years after this landmark decision. Although *Roe* hasn't been overruled, commentators have noted some erosion in its vitality. The fulcrum for much of the continuing debate centers on the question of when life begins and which branch of government should answer that question, the courts or state legislatures.

SEE ALSO The Body and the Right of Privacy (1965).

Pro-choice campaigners demonstrate in New York in July 1973.

The War Powers Act of 1973

Richard Nixon (1913–1994)

The Constitution designates the president as commander in chief of the army and navy, but it doesn't grant him the power to declare war. The Founding Fathers purposely delegated that power to Congress. Despite this deliberate bifurcation, presidents have interpreted their powers more broadly over time, asserting a right to use armed forces in various circumstances. They have sent troops into conflicts not declared "wars" and have sanctioned covert operations involving engagements with opposing military forces. Presidents have deployed military personnel outside the U.S. hundreds of times, yet none has sought a congressional declaration of war since President Roosevelt in 1941.

But after the advent of the atomic bomb, the nature of warfare changed. Direct hostilities between nuclear powers would result in what physicist and game theorist John von Neumann called mutually assured destruction: All-out war between two such powers would lead to joint annihilation and global devastation. From that knowledge arose the Cold War. The Soviet Union and the United States tested those new waters in the Korean War (1950–1952).

The long-simmering battle over presidential war powers boiled over with the Vietnam War, which Congress had authorized through the 1964 Gulf of Tonkin Resolution. It repealed the resolution in 1971 after learning it had been misled about the basis for it. Troubled that the balance of power had swung too far to the executive branch and by President Nixon's continued war efforts, Congress passed the War Powers Act—over Nixon's veto—in November 1973. According to historian Richard F. Grimmett, "Every President since . . . has taken the position that it is an unconstitutional infringement on the President's authority as Commander-in-Chief."

Designed to allow flexibility in cases of emergencies, attacks, or sudden hostilities, the War Powers Act authorizes the president to use armed forces for up to ninety days without congressional approval. It requires the president to report any use of U.S. forces and encourages him to consult with Congress "in every possible instance" prior to committing forces. The act mandates that, after ninety days, any use of armed force must terminate unless authorized by Congress.

SEE ALSO The *Pentagon Papers* (1971); Presidential Subpoena Compliance (1974).

U.S. troops patrol amid a napalm strike in Vietnam. Congress passed the War Powers Act largely as a result of President Nixon's continued war efforts in Vietnam.

Presidential Subpoena Compliance

Richard Nixon (1913–1994), **John Sirica** (1904–1992), **Leon Jaworski** (1905–1982)

President Theodore Roosevelt famously declared, "No man is above the law." Some seventy years later, the Supreme Court applied that dictum directly to a sitting president. The 1972 burglary of the Democratic Party's Watergate offices led to the appointment of a special prosecutor to investigate. When President Nixon refused to turn over tapes of conversations recorded in his White House office, a new special prosecutor, Leon Jaworski, obtained a subpoena ordering him to do so. U.S. District Judge John Sirica denied Nixon's motion to quash the subpoena, rejecting his claim of executive privilege. After Nixon went to the Court of Appeals for the District of Columbia, Jaworski took the unusual step of seeking immediate Supreme Court review.

Given the importance of the issue and a need for speedy resolution, the Supreme Court agreed to hear the appeal without the benefit of an intermediate appellate decision. Less than three weeks after arguments in the case, the Court unanimously affirmed Judge Sirica's decision. (Justice William Rehnquist—formerly a high-ranking member of the Nixon Justice Department and who had involvement with the special prosecutor—recused himself.)

The Court rejected the president's argument that his claim of executive privilege was not reviewable by the judiciary, citing *Marbury v. Madison*'s famous pronouncement that "it is emphatically the province and duty of the judicial department to say what the law is." Reaching the merits of the case, the Court found, for the first time, "constitutional underpinnings" for a claim of executive privilege but refused to define that privilege as absolute. Unless the president can identify specific dangers that can arise from disclosure of information claimed to be subject to the privilege, a prosecutor's particularized showing of need will overcome the privilege. As a result, Nixon was ordered to provide the tapes for the District Court's private inspection.

Nixon turned over the disputed tapes shortly after the Court's July 24, 1974, decision. Transcripts were made public on August 5. Three days later, President Nixon became the only sitting U.S. president to resign from office.

SEE ALSO The Power of Judicial Review (1803); Presidential Immunity (1997).

President Richard M. Nixon on July 8, 1971, three years before he announced his resignation from office to avoid impeachment over the Watergate scandal.

Attorneys' Fee Awards

Alyeska Pipeline Service Co. v. Wilderness Society

In litigation, a prevailing party may be entitled to a wide range of remedies. A judge can award damages (a money judgment), an injunction (a court order preventing further harm), and in some cases attorneys' fees. With respect to the last of these, there are two views regarding when a successful party can recover its attorneys' fees from its opponent. The English rule, followed in most of the world, allows successful litigants to recover attorneys' fees from losing parties as a matter of course. The American rule, applied almost exclusively in the United States, mandates that each party pay its own attorneys' fees, regardless of outcome. Some exceptions to the American rule do exist, however, and in *Alyeska Pipeline Service Co. v. Wilderness Society* the Supreme Court was asked to support the creation of a new one.

In *Alyeska*, three environmental groups had successfully sued to prevent the construction of a trans-Alaska oil pipeline. The suit constituted public interest litigation in that a single party sought to protect public rights. Public interest litigation is notoriously underfunded, and so many public rights go unrepresented in court. Consequently, the attorneys in *Alyeska* argued that an exception to the American rule was not only appropriate but necessary. The exception would permit environmental groups to recover attorneys' fees from those who sought to build the pipeline so that the money could be used to fund future public interest litigation.

But in a devastating blow to public interest litigation, the Supreme Court refused to support what it termed a "far-reaching" exception to the American rule. In the Court's view, "the circumstances under which attorneys' fees are to be awarded and the range of discretion of the courts in making those awards are matters for Congress to determine." This loss was short-lived, however. The widely criticized ruling prompted action. The following year, Congress passed the Civil Rights Attorneys Fees Award Act of 1976, which granted the recovery of attorneys' fees in certain types of public interest litigation.

SEE ALSO Rule 23 and Modern Class Action (1938); The Civil Rights Act of 1964; Attorney Advertising (1977).

A photo of the trans-Alaska pipeline (near Pump Station 4), maintained by the Alyeska Pipeline Service Company.

Restrictions on Involuntary Commitment

Kenneth Donaldson (1908–1995), *O'Connor v. Donaldson*

The legal system still struggles with the conflicts that arise when certain approaches to mental-health treatment prove inconsistent with modern notions of individual liberty. In 1957, the father of Kenneth Donaldson, who believed his adult son was suffering from delusions, instituted proceedings to have him committed to a Florida state mental hospital. After a hearing, Kenneth was diagnosed as suffering from paranoid schizophrenia and committed for "care, maintenance, and treatment." He received no treatment in the hospital and posed no danger to himself or others, yet he remained hospitalized for the next fifteen years, despite numerous requests for release.

Donaldson brought suit against the hospital superintendent in 1971, alleging deprivation of his constitutional right to liberty. A jury found in Donaldson's favor, awarding him compensatory and punitive damages. The Fifth Circuit Court of Appeals affirmed the award and held that an involuntarily committed individual had a constitutional right to treatment.

The Supreme Court unanimously confirmed that Donaldson was entitled to release, holding "a State cannot constitutionally confine, without more, a non-dangerous individual who is capable of surviving safely in freedom by himself or with the help of willing and responsible family members or friends." Notably, however, the Supreme Court didn't address the constitutional right to treatment. Nonetheless, *O'Connor* changed the constitutional landscape in civil commitment proceedings. By the end of the decade, every state had reworked their relevant statutes to include a dangerousness requirement. Doctors Megan Testa and Sara G. West noted in 2010 that the "number of psychiatric inpatients declined precipitously from a high of more than 550,000 in 1950 to 30,000 by the 1990s." Other factors contributed to the decline prior to 1975, but the standard set forth in *O'Connor* played a significant role.

After his unconditional release, Donaldson wrote a memoir, *Insanity Inside Out*, published in 1976. He died in Sierra Vista, Arizona, at the age of eighty-seven.

SEE ALSO The M'Naghten Rule (1843); The Insanity Defense (1881); Health Care and the Duty to Warn (1976).

The outcome of O'Connor v. Donaldson *made it illegal for states to commit people whom were not deemed dangerous to themselves or others, which helped decrease the number psychiatric inpatients.*

Racism and U.N. Resolution 3379

Daniel Patrick Moynihan (1927–2003)

The road to Resolution 3379—which stated that "Zionism is a form of racism and racial discrimination"—began in 1963 with the adoption of another resolution censuring all forms of racial discrimination. A decade later, the U.N. condemned "the unholy alliance between South African racism and Zionism." Then, in 1975, in response to a proposal for the U.N. to denounce anti-Semitism, the Soviet Union offered a counter-proposal that condemned "Zionism, Nazism, neo-Nazism and all other forms of the policy and ideology of colonialism, national and race hatred and exclusiveness." Neither proposal was accepted, but the Soviet Union's political efforts—which entailed uniting the Communist Bloc with the Arab and sub-Saharan African nations—bore fruit in the passage of 3379 on November 10, 1975.

After the vote, Daniel Patrick Moynihan, American ambassador to the U.N., rose to speak: "The United States rises to declare before the General Assembly of the United Nations and before the world that it does not acknowledge, it will never abide by, it will never acquiesce in this infamous act." Historian Gil Troy notes that Moynihan's audience was larger than the General Assembly; he was addressing "the American people, the world media, and indeed the bar of history." Moynihan called the perceived anti-Semitism of 3379 "a great evil . . . loosed upon the world."

Troy describes 3379 as "a consciousness-raising moment for many Americans, heralding a changing world." The *New York Times* later called it the U.N.'s "nadir" that "pushed many Americans toward full-scale disillusionment with that world body."

In 1988, the Palestinian National Council issued the Palestinian Declaration of Independence from Israel. Three years later, Israel made revocation of Resolution 3379 a requirement for attending the Madrid Peace Conference that year for talks among Israel, the Palestinians, and surrounding countries. In U.N. history, only one resolution—the one that had denied fascist Spain entry to the world body—had ever been reversed. But on December 16, 1991, it happened again, and Resolution 46/86 revoked 3379. In 2012, the U.N. passed Resolution 67/19 recognizing Palestine as a nonmember observer state.

SEE ALSO The Geneva Convention (1864); The U.N. Convention on Genocide (1948); The Nuremberg Trials (1945).

This map of Palestine shows the boundaries recommended by the 1947 U.N. General Assembly Resolution 181 for a Jewish State (purple) and an Arab State (yellow).

PALESTINE
NORTH SHEET

SCALE 1:250,000

REFERENCE

Compiled drawn & printed by Survey of Palestine, Aug. 1944

MEDITERRANEAN SEA

The Right to Die

Karen Quinlan (1954–1985)

Among the many milestone decisions that courts have made over the years, few are more important than those addressing matters of life and death. Not surprisingly, such cases rank among the most controversial and widely publicized of their times. One such case, *In re Quinlan*, presented a court, for the first time, with the challenging task of determining whether individuals possess a right to die.

In April 1975, twenty-one-year-old Karen Quinlan arrived at a hospital emergency room, comatose and unable to breathe on her own, and was placed on a respirator. After several months of grim prognoses, her family and doctors had given up hope of recovery. Her parents requested that the hospital remove the respirator, but her primary physician refused on the grounds that accepted standards of medical practice and ethics didn't allow it. Her father then sought a court order appointing him his daughter's guardian and authorizing "discontinuance of all extraordinary means of sustaining" her life.

The trial court refused to permit removal of the respirator. In March 1976, the New Jersey Supreme Court unanimously reversed that decision, however, holding that the family could withdraw life support if the doctors had concluded there was no "reasonable possibility of Karen's ever emerging from her present comatose condition to a cognitive, sapient state." Importantly, the court specified that the withdrawal of life support would involve no civil or criminal liability.

The court found the rationale for its decision in the constitutional right to privacy enunciated in *Griswold v. Connecticut* and extended in *Roe v. Wade*, a right the court found "broad enough to encompass a patient's decision to decline medical treatment under certain circumstances." Quinlan's condition precluded her ability to make that decision, so the court determined that her guardian father could assert it for her. For the first time, a court recognized a constitutional right to die.

Quinlan's respirator was removed in May 1976, but to everyone's surprise she continued to breathe on her own for nine more years. She died from complications of pneumonia without ever emerging from her original coma.

SEE ALSO The Body and the Right of Privacy (1965); *Roe v. Wade* (1973); Physician-Assisted Suicide (1997).

Julia Quinlan, mother of Karen Quinlan responds to an interview question at her home in Wantage, New Jersey, in 2005, while holding a copy of her memoir, My Joy, My Sorrow.

KAREN ANN'S MOTHER REMEMBERS

MY JOY,
MY SORROW

Health Care and the Duty to Warn

Tarasoff v. Regents of the University of California

Landmark legal decisions often arise from cases involving mutually conflicting interests. One interest ultimately must be sacrificed to preserve the other. That was the result of the California Supreme Court's decision in *Tarasoff v. Regents of the University of California*.

In 1968, Prosenjit Poddar, a U.C. Berkeley graduate student, met and befriended Tatiana Tarasoff, a college student who didn't requite his romantic interest in her. Spiraling into severe mental illness, Poddar sought psychological counseling, during which he threatened to harm Tarasoff. Dr. Lawrence Moore, the treating therapist, urged campus police to commit him as a danger to the welfare of others. Poddar was detained briefly but released after exhibiting no abnormal behavior. No one informed Tarasoff about Poddar's threats. In October 1969, he stabbed her to death.

At Poddar's criminal trial, the Tarasoff family learned for the first time of the involvement of mental health professionals prior to their daughter's murder. They sued the university and those involved in Poddar's treatment. Although the trial court dismissed the complaint, the California Supreme Court reinstated it, positing a duty on mental health care providers to warn a third party if they reasonably should have determined that a patient might be violent.

According to legal experts Peter Schuck and Daniel Givelber, that decision "unleashed a firestorm of protest in the mental health establishment," members of which asked the court to rehear the case. The rehearing slightly modified the standard, replacing the duty to warn a third party with a duty to exercise reasonable care to protect a third party if the professional knows or should have known, according to professional standards, that a patient poses a serious danger of violence to that third party. The court rejected the mental health care community's argument that such a rule would harm patient confidentiality and lead providers to refuse to treat potentially violent patients.

The rule that *Tarasoff* announced has continued to evolve, but as Schuck and Givelber note, the case "has been woven into clinical practice and has become a professional standard of practice among providers."

SEE ALSO The M'Naghten Rule (1843); The Insanity Defense (1881); Restrictions on Involuntary Commitment (1975).

Sather Tower rises above the campus of the University of California at Berkeley at sunset. Prosenjit Poddar, a student from Bengal, India, was living in the nearby International House when he met Tatiana Tarasoff.

The Copyright Act of 1976

In 1905, President Theodore Roosevelt called on Congress to overhaul existing copyright laws, which resulted in the Copyright Act of 1909—a significant improvement but far from perfect. Its shortcomings were amplified by the rapid technological developments of the changing times. The advent of motion pictures, the phonograph, radio, and television added new challenges for the courts and rights holders alike.

In 1955, Congress commissioned the U.S. Copyright Office to study existing laws and recommend proposed revisions. The Copyright Office issued a detailed report in 1961, leading to legislative proposals, extensive hearings, and cycles of revisions. President Gerald Ford signed into law the Copyright Act of 1976 in October of that year.

The new law became effective on January 1, 1978, and embodied a number of significant revisions. Among the most important were the extension of the term of copyright from two twenty-eight-year terms to a single term measured by the life of the author, plus fifty years after his or her death, and codification of the "fair use" defense, a common-law concept that courts were already applying, sometimes inconsistently. Along with enumerated fair-use criteria, the act provided limited safe harbors for nonprofit, library, educational, and public-broadcast users, insulating them from liability for specified uses of copyrighted materials. The act established the Copyright Royalty Tribunal, charged with overseeing compulsory license programs, under which specific uses of copyrighted works are permitted on payment of royalties and compliance with statutory conditions (typically for musical compositions).

At the most general level, copyright under the 1976 act grants creators of "original works"—including literary, dramatic, musical, artistic, and certain other intellectual works—the exclusive right to reproduce, distribute, perform, and display their work publicly. Protection of the work is immediate upon its creation in a fixed form. There is no longer a requirement for an author to register a work with the Copyright Office, nor, since 1989, is there a requirement to display a copyright notice (©) on the work itself, although doing both has its legal advantages.

SEE ALSO America's First Copyright Law (1790); The Berne Convention (1878); Time-Shifting and Fair Use (1984); Expanded Copyrights (2001).

The Copyright Act of 1976 expanded and clarified many copyright protections.

OPY-PROTECTED

by the software no

tected to prevent

Those who succe

COPYRIGHT

and authors exc

may so publish

The Death Penalty Returns

Gregg v. Georgia, Gary Gilmore (1940–1977)

Almost immediately after the U.S. Supreme Court's decision in *Furman v. Georgia*—which effectively invalidated all then-active death-penalty statutes—a tidal wave of backlash swept the country. Polls showed that Americans not only disapproved of the Court's decision but also supported the death penalty more than ever. Within just four years, thirty-five states enacted new, more discerning capital punishment schemes to comport with the standard announced in *Furman*.

Because of *Furman*'s five divergent opinions, however, state legislatures had little guidance on how to reinstate the death penalty in accordance with constitutional principles. Some states made the death penalty mandatory for certain crimes, thereby removing the arbitrariness with which the punishment once had been applied. Others required a bifurcated trial in which two hearings were held, one to determine guilt and a second to determine the sentence. Seeking to give coherence to these and other approaches, the Supreme Court agreed to reconsider the constitutionality of the death penalty in *Gregg v. Georgia*, which consolidated four other similar cases.

In a 7–2 decision, the Court held that "the punishment of death does not invariably violate the Constitution" and ruled that Georgia's amended capital punishment legislation embodied one example of a constitutional death-penalty scheme. In doing so, the Court suggested two constitutionally required baselines for evaluation of future death-penalty statutes: First, a jury's discretion to impose death "must be suitably directed and limited so as to minimize the risk of wholly arbitrary and capricious action." Second, before a sentence of death may be imposed, "the circumstances of the offense, together with the character and propensities of the offender," must be taken into account. A death-penalty scheme meeting these two guidelines generally could withstand constitutional scrutiny.

In January 1977, the death penalty's four-year hiatus ended when a Utah firing squad executed Gary Gilmore for two murders, making him the first person executed in more than a decade. Since that time, over 1,300 individuals have been executed; thousands more await the same fate.

SEE ALSO The U.S. Constitution (1787); The Bill of Rights (1791); Banning the Death Penalty (1972).

The gas chamber at the Missouri State Penitentiary in Jefferson City, Missouri.

Palimony

Lee Marvin (1924–1987), **Michelle Marvin** (née Triola) (1932–2009),
Marvin v. Marvin

Supreme Court Justice Joseph Story famously said that the law "is a jealous mistress, and requires a long and constant courtship." The law wasn't the jealous mistress of Oscar-winning actor Lee Marvin, but his seven years of unmarried cohabitation with Michelle Triola were long and constant enough to forge new law that thereafter permitted unmarried partners to sue for financial support.

When a married couple obtains a divorce or legal separation, the court granting the decree may order a spouse to pay a reasonable amount deemed necessary for the support of the other spouse. As a general rule the court determines the amount and the payment period based on the standard of living established during the marriage, taking into consideration a variety of circumstances. Those support payments are known as alimony. But if the parties never married, neither would have a legal basis for an award of alimony or other support—at least that was the case until 1976.

After Marvin ended their relationship, Triola—who legally had changed her surname to Marvin—brought suit seeking to enforce what she claimed was a contract with Marvin under which she alleged she was entitled to half of Marvin's property as well as future support payments based on promises he had made to her. The California Supreme Court upheld Triola's right to seek compensation noting that both express and implied contracts, if proved, would be enforced. It returned the case to the Superior Court for trial, which resulted in a $104,000 judgment in Triola's favor.

The judgment was overturned on appeal in 1981, but the case nonetheless had a significant impact. Other states followed California's lead and allowed suits for support between unmarried couples. The case did something else, too: It led to the neologism *palimony* (pal + alimony). Coined by a member of the media, the word never appeared in the court's opinion, and it was also a misnomer: Triola's short-lived $104,000 victory didn't represent alimony but damages for Marvin's breach of their agreement.

Triola died in 2009 at the home of her partner, Dick Van Dyke, with whom she had lived for thirty years. The two never married.

SEE ALSO The Measure of Contract Damages (1854); No-Fault Divorce (1969).

At the 1966 Academy Awards, Lee Marvin holds the Oscar for Best Actor, which he won for his role in the film Cat Ballou. *Michelle Triola stands beside him.*

Attorney Advertising

Bates v. State Bar of Arizona

Worldwide spending on advertising reached nearly half a trillion dollars in 2012, with the United States as the largest market at $152.3 billion. Lawyer and law-firm advertisements account for only a small fraction of those expenditures, but they wouldn't exist at all if not for the Supreme Court's decision in *Bates v. State Bar of Arizona*.

Inheriting both the ethos and the traditions of the English bar, American lawyers of the eighteenth and nineteenth centuries typically were ill-disposed to promoting either themselves or their services through advertising. The Canons of Professional Ethics adopted by the American Bar Association (ABA) in 1908 noted that "the most worthy and effective advertisement possible . . . is the establishment of a well-merited reputation for professional capacity and fidelity to trust." In the twentieth century, the ABA's 1969 Code of Professional Responsibility, which governed the conduct of lawyers in most states, prohibited advertising beyond listing specified information on business cards, stationery, office signs, and approved law directories.

In 1976, John Bates and Van O'Steen placed an advertisement in a Phoenix newspaper for their legal clinic. The advertisement announced: "LEGAL SERVICES AT VERY REASONABLE FEES" and set out specific prices for particular services, such as uncontested divorces, adoptions, bankruptcy filings, and change of name. The State Bar of Arizona suspended them from practice for violating a disciplinary rule applicable to Arizona lawyers that prohibited advertising.

Reiterating holdings that commercial speech fell under the protection of the First Amendment, the U.S. Supreme Court struck down the Arizona ethics-code provision barring lawyer advertising. It found that advertising that communicates truthful and valuable information to consumers serves both individual and societal interests and therefore could "not be subjected to blanket suppression." Importantly, the Court carefully limited its ruling, not commenting on advertising that relates to the quality of legal services offered and leaving states free to regulate attorney advertising (including false, deceptive, or misleading claims) through "reasonable restrictions on the time, place, and manner."

SEE ALSO Legal Aid Societies (1876); Attorneys' Fee Awards (1975); Administrative Agency Determinations (1984).

Prior to the U.S. Supreme Court's decision in Bates v. Arizona, *lawyers couldn't advertise their services beyond listing specific information on business cards, stationery, and office signs.*

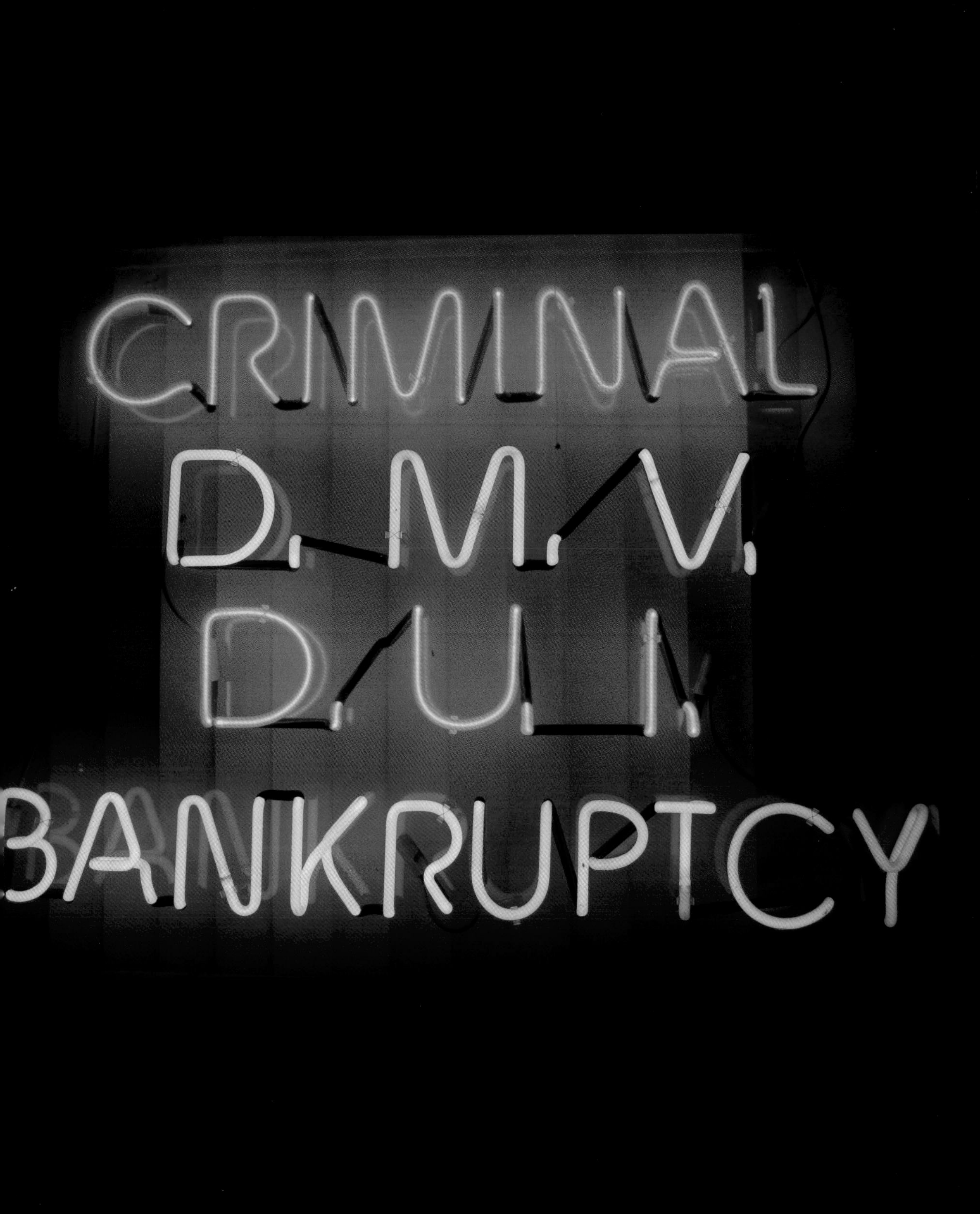
CRIMINAL
D.M.V.
D.U.I.
BANKRUPTCY

Affirmative Action

Regents of the University of California v. Bakke

In 1943, Supreme Court Justice Harlan Stone wrote in *Hirabayashi v. United States*, "Distinctions between citizens solely because of their ancestry are by their very nature odious to a free people whose institutions are founded upon the doctrine of equality." Some argue that minority preferences help offset the effects of centuries of discrimination; others assert that such preferences themselves constitute discrimination. As with other divisive issues, questions about affirmative action and its legitimacy eventually found their way to the Supreme Court.

In 1970, the University of California at Davis Medical School began setting aside sixteen of its one hundred admission slots for qualified minorities. The scores and grades of those selected for the sixteen slots tended to rank substantially lower than those of applicants chosen through the regular admissions process.

Two years later, Allan Bakke, a white applicant with scores considerably higher than some admitted minority applicants, was denied admission. After a second rejection in 1974, he filed suit, claiming that the school's admissions policy violated the Fourteenth Amendment's guarantee of equal protection as well as Title VI of the Civil Rights Act of 1964, which forbids racial preferences in federally funded programs.

The trial court ruled in favor of Bakke but didn't require the university to admit him. Bakke appealed to the California Supreme Court, which affirmed the trial court's ruling but ordered U.C. Davis to grant him admission. The school appealed to the U.S. Supreme Court, which addressed the issue of affirmative action for the first time.

In June 1978, the Supreme Court held the special admissions program unlawful and upheld Bakke's admission, describing the university's policy as an illegal quota. However, the Court declined to hold that a university's consideration of race as part of a competitive admissions process was impermissible. Rather, a school would be free to consider race as one among many factors in the admissions decision process.

The debate surrounding affirmative action didn't end with *Bakke*, but the basic principles announced in that case were reaffirmed in 2003 in *Gratz v. Bollinger* and *Grutter v. Bollinger*.

SEE ALSO The Fourteenth Amendment (1868); The Civil Rights Cases (1883); The Civil Rights Act of 1964; Employment Discrimination (1971).

Allan Bakke, shown here in 1977, successfully challenged his denial of admission to the Medical School at the University of California at Davis as "reverse discrimination."

The FCC and Filthy Words

George Carlin (1937–2008), *FCC v. Pacifica Foundation*

In 1972, comedian George Carlin shocked audiences with his monologue "Seven Words You Can Never Say on Television." Unsurprisingly, the monologue teemed with taboo expletives, making it wholly unsuitable for children. For his next comedy album, he recorded a new version of the piece, "Filthy Words," which radio station WBAI in New York City aired one afternoon. A young boy riding in the car with his father briefly heard the broadcast. This inadvertent exposure led to FCC sanctions for the radio station as well as the landmark case *FCC v. Pacifica Foundation*, which required balancing broadcasters' First Amendment freedoms of speech against the FCC's authority to regulate indecent content.

The First Amendment prohibits laws "abridging the freedom of speech," but over time certain restrictions have been applied. For example, courts had established that obscene speech—patently offensive speech that appeals to the prurient interest and lacks serious value—wasn't worthy of First Amendment protection. Carlin's monologue, though shocking to some, didn't sink to the level of obscenity. Thus, the Supreme Court used *Pacifica* to shed light on a new category of lesser-protected speech: indecency.

In *Pacifica*, the Court upheld the FCC's authority to regulate indecent speech—speech that's not obscene but still unsuitable for children—on broadcast radio even though the regulation undermines broadcasters' freedom of speech. The Court explicitly ruled that broadcasted speech was worthy of only the "most limited of First Amendment protections" due to radio and television's accessibility to children and "pervasive" nature.

Pacifica didn't eliminate a broadcaster's right to air indecent material but did subject that airing to certain rules. Broadcast radio stations could include indecent material in their programming but only late at night when children are presumed to be sleeping and not listening. This indecency regulation remains in effect today, having been upheld by the Supreme Court in its 2012 decision in *FCC v. Fox Television Stations, Inc.*

SEE ALSO The Bill of Rights (1791); The Limits on Obscenity (1957); The Fairness Doctrine (1969); A New Obscenity Standard (1973); The Communications Decency Act (1997).

George Carlin performing onstage in 1981. His "seven dirty words" routine made NPR's list of the one hundred best lists.

The Son of Sam Law

David Berkowitz (b.1953), Henry Hill (1943–2012)

First known as the .44 Caliber Killer, David Berkowitz achieved notoriety as the Son of Sam, a name he had given himself in a bizarre crime scene letter. His notoriety grew so great that his crimes and the events surrounding them led to enactment of eponymous legislation designed to foreclose a criminal's right to profit through commercial exploitation of his story.

In 1978, Berkowitz pleaded guilty to six cold-blooded murders committed across three New York City boroughs between October 1976 and August 1977, making him one of the most terrifying serial killers that New York City had ever confronted. Anticipating that Berkowitz would receive lucrative offers from publishers in exchange for the story of his gruesome crimes—which had enthralled as much as terrorized New Yorkers—Albany enacted N.Y. Executive Law § 632-a, known as the Son of Sam law. It required that any entity contracting for rights to a criminal's or accused criminal's story deposit the contract and any income derived from the contract with the New York Crime Victims Compensation Board. The board would then deposit the funds in an escrow account to satisfy possible later judgments against the criminal in suits brought by victims or their families.

Simon & Schuster sued after its 1985 book, *Wiseguy: Life in a Mafia Family*, was found subject to the law because it told the story of Henry Hill, a convicted member of the Mafia. The publishers had paid Hill and writer Nicholas Pileggi nearly $100,000, which the New York Crime Victims Board ruled had violated the statute. In 1991, Simon & Schuster challenged the law on First Amendment grounds before the U.S. Supreme Court.

The Supreme Court unanimously found the law unconstitutional because it imposed a content-based financial penalty on only one type of speech and because it was overly broad. Within months of the ruling, New York crafted a more narrowly tailored law that remains in effect today and has served as a model for other states' laws.

SEE ALSO The Trial of John Peter Zenger (1735); Censorship and *Ulysses* (1933).

David Berkowitz "Son of Sam" *by Ze Carrion.*

The Entrapment Defense

The history of the entrapment defense is an ancient one: "First interposed in Paradise: 'The serpent beguiled me and I did eat.'" So wrote New York Supreme Court Justice William Johnson Bacon in 1864, quoting Genesis 3:13, noting that Eve's defense "was overruled by the great Lawgiver . . . and has never since availed to shield crime or give indemnity to the culprit." As news reports over the years have reminded us, law enforcement's use of undercover sting operations continues to yield defendants claiming to have been beguiled by a government serpent and seeking refuge in what constitutional scholar Jethro Lieberman describes as a "'yes-but' defense: 'Yes, I did it, but I should be acquitted because I am not a criminal type and the police suckered me into it.'"

Can the government lure someone into committing a crime and then charge that person with that crime, which wouldn't have occurred but for the government's conduct? It depends. Through a series of cases decided over the years, the United States Supreme Court has delineated the boundaries of the entrapment defense carefully. The 1932 case of *Sorrells v. United States* enunciated the two elements of this affirmative defense: government inducement of the crime and a lack of predisposition on the part of the defendant to engage in the criminal conduct.

In most cases, the only real issue is predisposition, which focuses on whether the defendant was an "unwary innocent" or an "unwary criminal" who readily availed himself of the opportunity to commit the crime. The most famous—though unsuccessful—assertions of the defense arose as a result of the government's Abscam (from Abdul Enterprises + scam) sting operation in 1978, which resulted in the trials and convictions of Congressman Michael Myers and five other congressmen, Senator Harrison A. Williams Jr., three Philadelphia City Council members, a New Jersey state senator, and a number of others. Those defendants accepted payments from undercover agents acting as representatives of fictitious Arab sheiks in exchange for political influence and favors relating to, among other matters, immigration issues, government contract awards, and casino licenses.

SEE ALSO Miranda Warnings (1966); The First Evidentiary Use of DNA (1986).

Jurors watching secretly recorded tapes of Senator Harrison A. Williams Jr. accepting a bribe from an undercover agent.

The McMartin Molestation Case

Virginia McMartin (1907–1995), Peggy McMartin Buckey (1926–2001)

History offers many reminders that the law can be misused. After all, it ultimately depends on people both to create it and to invoke it. When used improperly and left unchecked, injustice often results, as when an innocent person is wrongfully convicted. But sometimes equal injustice arises in cases of accusations and trials.

Virginia McMartin and her daughter, Peggy Buckey, owned and ran the well-regarded McMartin Preschool in Manhattan Beach, California. In August 1983, Judy Johnson complained that her two-and-a-half-year-old son had been molested by twenty-five-year-old Raymond Buckey, a part-time aide at the school and Peggy Buckey's son. The police arrested Raymond but, finding no evidence to support a charge, released him. Nonetheless, Police Chief Harry Kuhlmeyer Jr. thereafter communicated with scores of parents, identified Raymond Buckey as a child-molesting suspect, alluded to the commission of particular criminal acts, and suggested specific, insinuating questions for parents to ask their children.

A media frenzy soon developed, followed by what sociologist Mary de Young described as a cultural response with "all of the characteristics of . . . a moral panic: it was widespread, volatile, hostile, and overreactive." The unsupported allegations of Judy Johnson—an alcoholic with a history of mental illness, whose bizarre charges included claims of satanic rituals at the school—spawned a witchhunt abetted by a sensationalizing press and an obliging legal system. According to de Young, by the end of 1984, "McMartin had become a household word, synonymous with evil." Despite the absence of any credible evidence, indictments charged Raymond and Peggy with multiple counts of child sexual abuse.

After a twenty-eight-month trial and two months of deliberations, the jury acquitted Peggy on all counts and Raymond on all but thirteen, on which they were deadlocked. Following a second trial against just Raymond—who been held without bail for five years—the jury again was deadlocked. The prosecutor chose not to pursue a third trial and dismissed all charges. Seven years had elapsed since charges first were filed, and the case cost $15 million, making it the longest and most expensive criminal trial in U.S. history.

SEE ALSO The Salem Witchcraft Trials (1692); The Hollywood Ten (1948).

Peggy McMartin Buckey wipes away a tear in January 1990 after she and her son, Raymond Buckey, were acquitted.

First Mandatory Seat-Belt Law

As America moved into the twentieth century, the automobile played an increasingly prominent role in people's lives and unfortunately in their deaths. By 1916, domestic automobile production reached 1.6 million, with 3.3 million registered. By 1929, the production number had reached almost 5 million, with 23 million registered. More cars led to better roads and higher speeds but also more accidents and fatalities.

In 1966, Congress enacted the National Traffic and Motor Vehicles Safety Act, which called for the development and implementation of vehicle safety standards. When President Lyndon Johnson signed the act into law, he remarked that more than 1.5 million Americans had died on streets and highways already, nearly three times as many Americans as had been lost in all the country's wars. Among other points, the act required that all new cars include seat belts.

Although manufacturers had to make seat belts standard equipment in all cars beginning in 1968, traffic injuries and fatalities remained high. As automakers had predicted in opposing the legislation (in broader opposition to industry regulation), most Americans weren't inclined to use seat belts. Meanwhile, a number of countries around the world had begun to enact mandatory usage laws.

In 1984, New York passed the nation's first mandatory seat-belt law making it illegal for drivers and front-seat passengers to ride without wearing one. Adults are subject to fines for themselves as well as for any passengers under age sixteen not wearing seat belts. The law was challenged almost immediately, but a 1985 New York Supreme Court decision upheld it as a valid constitutional exercise of legislative power. It remains in effect today.

Every state other than New Hampshire has followed New York's lead and enacted mandatory seat-belt laws. In 1994, the seat-belt usage rate was just 58 percent, but the U.S. Department of Transportation's National Highway Safety Administration reports that nationwide seat-belt use reached 86 percent in 2012. Statistics from the same agency show that seat belts dramatically reduce the risk of both death and serious injury among drivers and front seat passengers by 45 percent and 50 percent respectively.

SEE ALSO The Expansion of Consumer Rights (1916); The Interstate Highway Act (1956); The Occupational Safety and Health Act (1970).

Less than thirty years after New York passed the first mandatory seat-belt law, nationwide seat-belt usage reached 86 percent.

Administrative Agency Determinations

Chevron U.S.A. v. Natural Resources Defense Council, Inc.

Federal administrative agencies have come to play an increasingly important role in the law over the past century. By definition, such an agency is an "official governmental body empowered . . . to direct and supervise the implementation of particular legislative acts." This power, however, doesn't go unchecked. Much as the judiciary can determine the constitutionality of laws passed by Congress, so too can it review administrative agency decisions. But how closely can or should courts examine these decisions? The Supreme Court's decision in *Chevron U.S.A. v. Natural Resources Defense Council, Inc.* set out what remains the governing standard.

In its 1977 amendment of the Clean Air Act, Congress introduced vague language into the statute. In response, the Environmental Protection Agency, charged with the law's implementation, announced an interpretation of the amendment that displeased environmental groups. These groups in turn asked the courts to review the determination, ultimately setting the stage for the Supreme Court to decide how much interpretational leeway to afford agency decision-makers in implementing the laws for which they were responsible.

The Supreme Court's unanimous decision set out a singular guiding principle that eventually attained talismanic status: deference to administrative agencies. The Court held: "If the statute is silent or ambiguous with respect to the specific issue, the question for the court is whether the agency's answer is based on a permissible construction of the statute." In essence, the Court decided that an administrative agency's decision merely has to be acceptable in light of a statute's language. It doesn't have to be the best or even a good interpretation of that language.

The *Chevron* framework dramatically expanded agency power. In the words of law scholar E. Donald Elliott, "Prior to *Chevron*, the lower federal courts primarily held the power to determine 'what the law is' when a statute was unclear. Post-*Chevron*, a substantial portion of that power shifted from the judiciary" to administrative agencies.

SEE ALSO The Supremacy of the Supreme Court (1803); The FCC and Filthy Words (1978).

In 1984, the Supreme Court unanimously determined that courts must defer to administrative agencies, such as the EPA, on questions of statutory compliance, e.g., whether smokestack emissions comply with the Clean Air Act.

Parody and the First Amendment

Jerry Falwell (1933–2007), **Larry Flynt** (b. 1942), *Hustler Magazine Inc. v. Falwell*, William Rehnquist (1924–2005)

In November 1983, *Hustler*, the notorious adult magazine published by Larry Flynt, featured a spoof of a Campari liqueur advertisement. Playing on sexual undertones, the original ad showcased celebrities recalling their first time trying the aperitif. The *Hustler* spoof showed Reverend Jerry Falwell, cofounder of the Moral Majority organization and an outspoken critic of the magazine, describing a sexual encounter with his mother in an outhouse. At the bottom of the page, a brief disclaimer identified the ad as a parody. Falwell sued *Hustler* and Flynt for libel as well as intentional infliction of emotional distress.

During his testimony at the 1984 trial, Falwell denied every action and statement attributed to him in the parody. Flynt then testified that, in light of the reverend's standing as a paragon of propriety, the idea of Falwell having an incestuous relationship with his mother was patently absurd and could be construed only as parody—and therefore wasn't actionable in libel. Flynt added that if he had intended to defame Falwell, he would have written something believable. At the conclusion of the trial, the judge instructed the jury that, to succeed on a claim of intentional infliction of emotional distress, Falwell needed to show only that Flynt intended to inflict distress and that the conduct at issue was "outside the accepted bounds of decency."

In its verdict, the jury rejected the claim for libel, finding that the spoof didn't purport to make factual allegations. However, the jury found in favor of Falwell on the claim for intentional infliction of emotional distress and awarded damages. Flynt appealed, eventually to the Supreme Court, which unanimously reversed the ruling, holding that the First Amendment protected Flynt's parody, which therefore couldn't serve as the basis for a claim of intentional infliction of emotional distress. Chief Justice Rehnquist explained that the price of entering the public forum included opening oneself to criticism. *Hustler*'s parody of a public figure was entitled to no less protection under the First Amendment than that accorded to political cartoonists.

SEE ALSO Yelling "Fire!" in a Crowded Theater (1919); Limits on Libel Laws (1964); Free Speech and Threats of Violence (1969); The FCC and Filthy Words (1978); The Communications Decency Act (1997).

Larry Flynt sits on the shoulders of bodyguard Roger "Ollie" Brooke in front of The Hustler club on Gay Street in Columbus, Ohio, on its 1971 grand opening. His brother and business partner, Jimmy Flynt, stands on the left.

The Hustler
COCKTAILS....
The Hustler TM
COCKTAILS....
The Hustler
Yes
OPEN

Time-Shifting and Fair Use

1984

Sony v. Universal City Studios, Inc., Gerald Ford (1913–2006), *Harper & Row, Publishers, Inc. v. Nation Enterprises*

For many, a great joy of contemporary video technology is the ability to record programs for later viewing or to record one show while watching another. Today's DVR makes both possible. That ability is called "time-shifting," a phrase that became a pivotal part of a key fair-use decision.

In 1976, Sony released the Betamax, which became the first successful home VCR. It weighed forty pounds, cost $1,295, and Sony sold thirty thousand of them that year. But the Betamax didn't just record; it enabled prescheduled recording. Sony marketed it with ads proclaiming: "Watch Whatever Whenever" and "With Sony's Betamax, You Won't Miss a Thing." Universal quickly sued for copyright infringement in California court. In the 1984 appeal, the Supreme Court sided with Sony, concluding that time-shifting constituted fair use, which copyright laws specifically exempt from liability.

Sony's Supreme Court victory—characterized by some as the Magna Carta of the electronic age—paved the way for the nascent prerecorded videocassette business to grow into an industry with annual revenues of more than $20 billion.

The next year, the Supreme Court rejected a fair-use defense in a more traditional copyright lawsuit involving President Gerald Ford's memoirs, *A Time to Heal*. Harper & Row had contracted with *Time* magazine for the latter to publish prepublication excerpts of the book in an article highlighting the details of Ford's pardon of President Nixon. Prior to that publication, however, the *Nation* magazine surreptitiously obtained a copy of Ford's manuscript and published an article, of which approximately three hundred words came from the Ford manuscript. The Supreme Court found that the *Nation* article exceeded the scope of fair use even though there was strong public interest in the subject matter. It reasoned that, despite the appropriation of only an "infinitesimal" amount of content, the importance of the content outweighed the size of the taking and that Harper & Row had been deprived of the full value of its contractual right of first publication through *Time* magazine.

SEE ALSO America's First Copyright Law (1790); The Berne Convention (1878); The Copyright Act of 1976; Expanded Copyrights (2001); Google Books and Fair Use (2010).

Sony's Betamax cassette tapes weren't compatible with the VHS format used by VCR machines, and they offered only half the recording time.

Peremptory Challenges to Jury Selection

Swain v. Alabama, Batson v. Kentucky

The right to trial by jury dates back to twelfth-century England, but for the right to have meaning, the composition of the jury pool—the venire—as well as the panel selected to serve must be derived fairly. Peremptory challenges—objections to the seating of a particular juror for which counsel need not offer any reason or explanation—have played a part in the selection process since colonial times. They ensure a defendant's ability to stand trial before an unbiased jury. Over time, however, both sides were allotted peremptory challenges, and that approach holds today.

In 1879, the Supreme Court held for the first time that the systematic exclusion of racial minorities from the venire violated a criminal defendant's equal protection rights under the Fourteenth Amendment. It soon became apparent, however, that prosecutors were using peremptory challenges to exclude blacks from criminal juries. As late as 1965, in *Swain v. Alabama*, the Supreme Court sanctioned the use of peremptory challenges to remove all black jurors during the impaneling process. But only the systematic and repeated exclusion of blacks qualified as a constitutional violation.

Because *Swain* erected an almost insuperable obstacle to a successful challenge, it attracted much criticism. U.S. Court of Appeals Judge Theodore McMillian described *Swain* as "one of the most criticized Supreme Court decisions" over the two ensuing decades. In the wake of that criticism, the Supreme Court revisited the use of peremptory challenges in *Batson v. Kentucky*, in which it essentially reversed *Swain* and set a new standard for equal protection challenges to the process of jury selection.

Batson set out a three-part test to determine whether peremptory challenges were being used discriminatorily. After a defendant makes a prima facie (Latin for "at first appearance") showing of challenges based on race, the prosecution bears the burden of showing a race-neutral basis for striking the juror in question. The trial court then determines whether purposeful discrimination has taken place. The Supreme Court has consistently expanded the *Batson* holding to include other protected groups (gender and ethnicity) and to govern the defense as well as the prosecution and all parties in civil cases.

SEE ALSO The Right to Counsel in State Court (1963); Miranda Warnings (1966).

Lawyers must balance their responsibility to seat people who will undertake jural duties conscientiously with their obligation not to use peremptory challenges to strike jurors in a discriminatory manner.

The First Evidentiary Use of DNA

Alec Jeffreys (b. 1950)

In a 1991 paper on the use of population genetics in forensic DNA typing, genetics experts Richard Lewontin and Daniel Hartl write that "appropriately carried out and correctly interpreted, DNA typing is possibly the most powerful innovation in forensics since the development of fingerprinting in the last part of the 19th Century."

Scientists had been examining DNA since its accurate discovery in the 1950s, but its first successful application in the field of law came in 1986. British geneticist Sir Alec Jeffreys had discovered the previous year that each organism possesses a unique DNA sequence. In his own words, he "accidentally solved another major problem in human genetics, namely the issue of biological identification and the establishment of family relationships in forensic and legal medicine." After developing what he called the first "DNA fingerprint," he applied the technique to resolve a paternity dispute and then to what he called "our first forensic investigation in 1986 in the Enderby murder case," which "triggered the application . . . to criminal investigations worldwide."

DNA first appeared in an American appellate court in 1988, when the Florida District Court of Appeal upheld the admissibility of genetic evidence used to convict a defendant of sexual battery. Congress's Office of Technology Assessment reported in July 1990 that forensic DNA testing and analysis, first introduced into U.S. criminal proceedings in 1986, has since been admitted into evidence in at least 185 cases by 38 states and the military. By 1997, it had been deemed admissible in every state as well as in all federal circuits.

DNA's introduction to the criminal justice system provided a dual benefit. First, it gave prosecutors the ability to definitively identify and exclude suspects with compelling scientific evidence for convictions. Second, it offered the potential to vindicate the wrongfully convicted. The Innocence Project, an organization dedicated to that purpose, reported a total of 325 postconviction DNA exonerations in the United States through December 2014. Those 325 individuals had served a total of more than 4,150 years in prison.

SEE ALSO Miranda Warnings (1966); Stem Cell and Cloning Legislation (1995).

Edna Ardales, a researcher from the International Rice Research Institute, reviews DNA profiles using UV light.

Pregnancy Discrimination

California Federal Savings & Loan Association v. Guerra

When Lillian Garland, a receptionist for California Federal Savings & Loan Association, became pregnant, she began training the person she believed to be her temporary replacement because she intended to return to work once she gave birth. After eight weeks of unpaid leave, Garland informed the bank that she wished to return. California Federal told Garland that they had filled her position and that no other similar jobs were available.

Garland filed a complaint with the California Department of Fair Employment and Housing, charging California Federal with violating the state's Fair Employment and Housing Act. That law prohibited discrimination based on pregnancy and required reinstatement of an employee at the end of pregnancy leave.

California Federal countered with a federal lawsuit against Mark Guerra, the director of the state's Department of Fair Employment and Housing. The bank asserted that Title VII of the Civil Rights Act of 1964 (as amended by the 1978 Pregnancy Discrimination Act, which made it unlawful to discriminate against employees based on pregnancy) "preempted" the state law because the latter conflicted with the former; mandatory reinstatement of female employees after maternity leave would violate Title VII by discriminating against male employees returning from other forms of medical or disability leave, who were not required to be reinstated.

Agreeing with California Federal, the district court held that under the Constitution's supremacy clause, federal law preempted and therefore voided the conflicting state law. But the Supreme Court rejected that reasoning. It found no conflict between the California statute and Title VII, noting that both laws "share a common goal . . . 'to achieve equality of employment opportunities and remove barriers that have operated in the past to favor an identifiable group of . . . employees over other employees.'"

In upholding the viability of California's law, the Supreme Court helped ensure that no woman would have to choose between her family and her job. The decision also demonstrated for the first time how the protections of the Pregnancy Discrimination Act could be used as a sword rather than a shield.

SEE ALSO Civil Rights Act of 1964; Employment Discrimination (1971); The Equal Employment Opportunity Act (1972); The Equal Rights Amendment (1972); The Americans with Disabilities Act (1990).

The Supreme Court's decision in California Federal Savings & Loan Association v. Guerra *freed working women from fear of adverse employment consequences as a result of becoming pregnant.*

Robert Bork's Supreme Court Nomination

Lewis F. Powell Jr. (1907–1998), **Ronald Reagan** (1911–2004), **Robert Bork** (1927–2012)

Between 1789 and 1986, the Senate confirmed 109 presidential appointments to the Supreme Court, rejecting eleven nominees. (Fifteen nominations were either withdrawn or not acted upon.) But the tenor of the process changed forever when the Senate rejected President Ronald Reagan's nomination of Robert Bork.

In August 1981, President Reagan nominated Sandra Day O'Connor, who became the first female justice to serve on the Supreme Court—a historic appointment that helped diversify the Court. Five years later, the Senate unanimously confirmed Bork to the U.S. Court of Appeals. But when Justice Lewis F. Powell Jr., a moderate, announced his retirement in June 1987, President Reagan faced what the *New York Times* called "a historic opportunity to shape the future of the court." The future he envisioned included Bork, former U.S. solicitor general, a Yale Law School professor, and an acknowledged conservative intellectual.

"Many qualified observers of judicial personnel considered Bork to be the most meritorious nominee to the high bench since FDR's selection of Felix Frankfurter in 1939," writes Supreme Court scholar Henry J. Abraham, but intellect wasn't the paramount consideration. Instead, the process devolved into partisan politics less than an hour after starting. Bork's record both offended and frightened liberal interest groups; they in turn undertook a smear campaign the likes of which had never before been seen.

Writing in 1992, U.S. Court of Appeals Judge Roger J. Miner described Bork as perhaps "the last of the straight shooters. He answered honestly, directly, without guile and with some intellect, all the questions put to him." As a result, his nomination failed by a vote of 58–42. As Judge Miner noted, Bork "accurately predicted that direct answers would never again be the norm." No one wanted to be "borked," a neologism meaning to defame or vilify, particularly in the media, to prevent an appointment to public office. Bork's *New York Times* obituary described that repudiation as "a historic political battle whose impact is still being felt."

SEE ALSO The Judiciary Act of 1789; The Power of Judicial Review (1803); Confirming Clarence Thomas (1991).

Robert Bork speaks to the press in the White House briefing room during his fight for Senate confirmation.

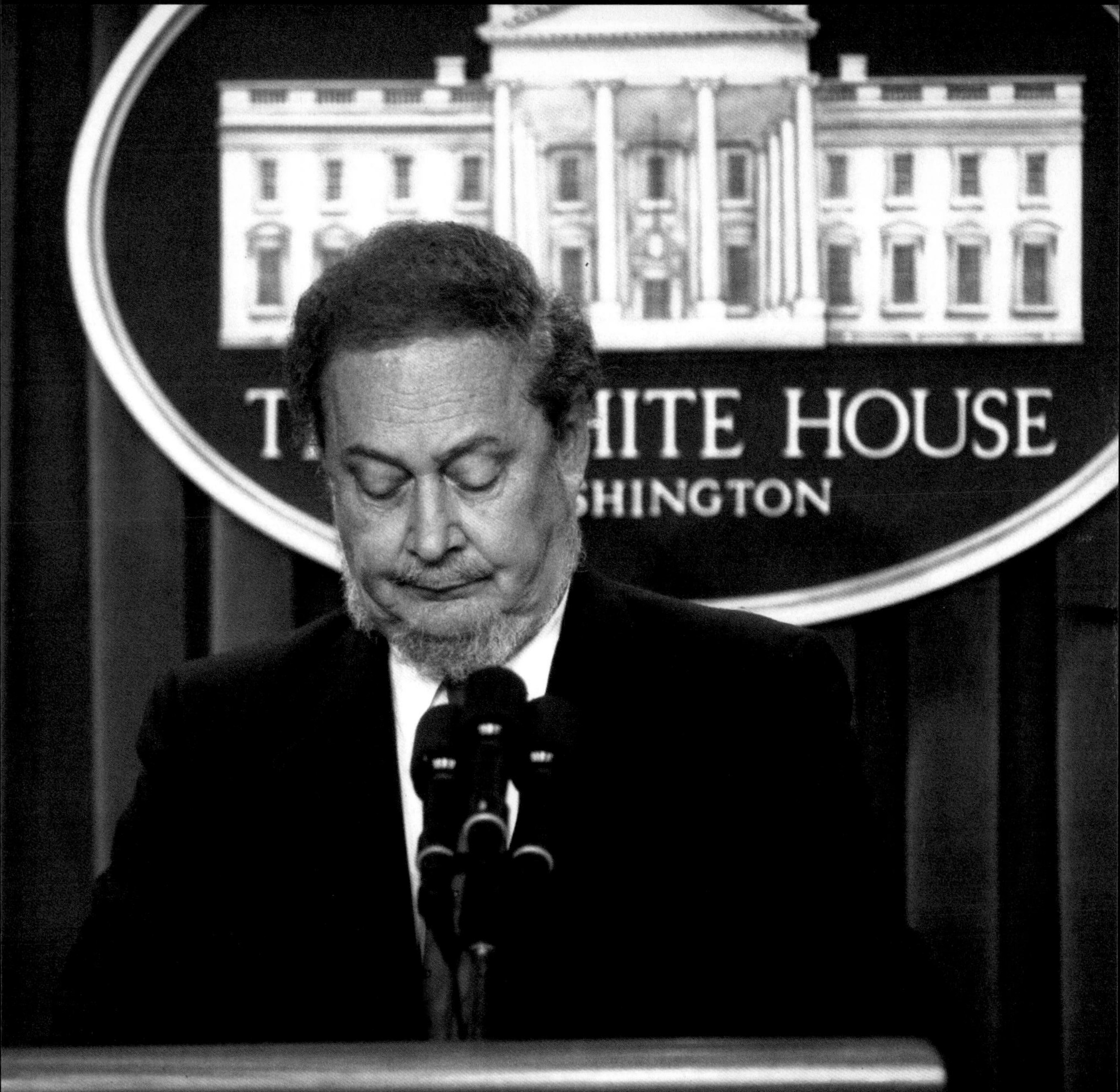
HITE HOUSE
SHINGTON

Surrogate Motherhood

In the Matter of Baby M

Starting in 1986, headlines reported an unusual custody battle taking place between a married couple and the woman who had agreed to conceive and carry a baby for them. The case arose during the nascency of surrogate motherhood and resulted in the first significant appellate decision addressing surrogacy.

William and Elizabeth Stern, a married couple in their forties, wanted to start a family but feared that a pregnancy might have repercussions on Elizabeth's health. Discouraged by the lengthy adoption process, they decided to use a surrogate. Through the Infertility Center of New York, the Sterns met Mary Beth Whitehead, who in exchange for $10,000 agreed to become pregnant through artificial insemination using William's sperm. The agreement stipulated that she carry the child to term, deliver the child to the Sterns, and then take the necessary steps to terminate her maternal rights.

After giving birth, Whitehead refused to relinquish custody. The Sterns sued to enforce the surrogacy contract, and the trial judge awarded them custody, reasoning that Whitehead had surrendered her rights as a biological mother by entering into the contract. The judge terminated her parental rights and allowed Mrs. Stern to adopt the baby immediately.

The New Jersey Supreme Court reversed that decision, however, holding that the contract was unenforceable because it contravened the state's established laws on adoption. The court ruled that a natural mother may not irrevocably agree to surrender her child prior to birth and deemed illegal any payment made to a mother for such purpose. Nonetheless, it named Mr. Stern and Mrs. Whitehead as the legal parents and awarded full custody to Mr. Stern with visitation rights to Ms. Whitehead.

In declaring all surrogacy contracts involving an exchange of money as void, the court established a standard for deciding similar future cases: Custody was to be based on the best interests of the child. *In Re Baby M* settled some questions, but everexpanding developments in reproductive technologies and approaches have reshaped the laws governing reproduction and surrogacy today from state to state as society continues to confront and reevaluate the definition of family and the laws that govern it.

SEE ALSO *Roe v. Wade* (1973); Pregnancy Discrimination (1987).

In 1988, the New Jersey Supreme Court ruled that a natural mother may not irrevocably agree to surrender her child prior to birth and that any payment made to a mother for that purpose is illegal.

1986

Women's Admission to Private Clubs

New York State Club Association v. City of New York, **Byron White**
(1917–2002)

Once considered unsuited for working outside the home or pursuing higher education, women have indisputably demonstrated otherwise. Yet, notwithstanding years of progress, women continue to encounter barriers in male-dominated spheres.

In 1965, New York City adopted the Human Rights Law, which prohibited discrimination in places of public accommodation but exempted institutions deemed "distinctly private," such as private men's clubs. The New York City Council amended that law in 1984 after concluding that admission to such clubs would prove essential to women's career opportunities. Local Law 63 extended the prohibitions of the Human Rights Law to clubs with more than four hundred members that provided regular meal service and regularly received money from nonmembers who used the club or its facilities "for furtherance of trade or business." Any club meeting those criteria wasn't considered "distinctly private" and therefore couldn't claim the exemption. Some found irony in that approach: The more exclusive the club, the more distinctly private it is, thereby entitling it to immunity from this antidiscrimination law.

The New York State Club Association immediately filed suit in state court challenging Local Law 63 as violating their First Amendment rights to freedom of association. The trial court and New York's two appellate courts upheld the law, concluding that the law's elimination or prevention of discrimination outweighed any individual's associational rights.

In a unanimous opinion, the Supreme Court affirmed those rulings and upheld the constitutionality of Local Law 63. Reasoning that the law didn't violate the association's rights to expressive association, Justice Byron White's majority opinion explained that "the law merely prevents an association from using race, sex, and the other specified characteristics as shorthand measures in place of . . . more legitimate criteria for determining membership." The Supreme Court's decision had enshrined the elimination of yet another barrier for women.

SEE ALSO The Fourteenth Amendment (1868); Admission of Women to the Bar (1873); Women's Right to Vote (1919); The Civil Rights Act of 1964; The Equal Rights Amendment (1972).

New York City has a large number of private clubs that traditionally limited their membership to men, such as the Yale Club, pictured here.

The Fatwa against *The Satanic Verses*

Salman Rushdie (b. 1947), Ruhollah Khomeini (1902–1989)

An Indian-born Muslim educated in England, Salman Rushdie satirized Islam and the Prophet Muhammad in his fourth novel, *The Satanic Verses*. Published in 1988, it became a Booker Prize finalist in the U.K. but was banned almost immediately in India, Pakistan, Saudi Arabia, Egypt, and elsewhere. Riots ensued in many Islamic countries, protests in Pakistan resulted in five deaths, and a riot in Mumbai killed twelve.

On February 14, 1989, Iran's Ayatollah Khomeini declared Rushdie guilty of apostasy and blasphemy and delivered a fatwa—a legally binding opinion—condemning Rushdie and urging his execution. (Author Christopher Hitchens cheekily called it "the single worst review any novelist has ever had.") The fatwa extended to all involved in the book's publication. U.S. booksellers pulled the books from shelves amid safety concerns, which had merit: London bookstores had been firebombed, the Japanese translator was killed, and attempts were made on the lives of two other translators. British police took Rushdie into protective custody, and he remained in hiding with a bounty on his head for almost three years. The fatwa continued even after Khomeini's death.

On Christmas Eve 1990, Rushdie announced that he wouldn't seek to have the novel published in paperback and stated his disagreement with characters in his novel who insulted Muhammad or cast "aspersions upon Islam." The new ayatollah remained unmoved. But according to Raj Bhala, author of a widely used text on Islamic law, the Quran doesn't designate blasphemy a crime nor proscribe punishment for it. Nor does the Quran prohibit desecration of Islam or its symbols. Disrespectful depictions of Muhammad may be insulting but don't constitute blasphemy, Bhala suggests, because Mohammad was human rather than divine.

If Khomeini meant to suppress the book, he failed spectacularly. The ideological battle that played out across the world, among radical and conservative Muslims on the one hand and ardent supporters of free speech on the other, virtually guaranteed the book's commercial success. It became an international bestseller. Although a bounty no longer hangs over Rushdie's head, the fatwa formally remains in place. He continues to lead his life in the company of armed guards.

SEE ALSO The Quran (652).

Iranian security agents silhouetted in front of a colossal portrait of Ayatollah Ruhollah Khomeini during an official Friday prayer held in Tehran, Iran, in 2003.

Celebrity Tax Prosecution

Leona Helmsley (1920–2007), *United States v. Helmsley*

Prosecutors enjoy wide discretion in deciding which cases or defendants to prosecute. The limits on that discretion come into play only when a decision is based on race, religion, or other arbitrary classification or when the prosecutor acts vindictively. But the prosecutor can freely pursue some violators of a law while choosing not to prosecute others. We don't know exactly why both federal and state prosecutors pursued tax evasion charges against Harry and Leona Helmsley in April 1988, but pursue them they did, and to great effect.

Leona had garnered celebrity status as head of the twenty-six hotels that formed a part of her husband's real-estate empire. She was virtually a household name in New York City, where her image appeared in television and print ads promoting the hotels. She made quite a mark through that extensive advertising, but she also earned a less-than-favorable personal reputation. Her arrogance and ill-treatment of others gave rise to the nickname the "Queen of Mean."

Prosecutors charged her with allocating expenses attributable to her Connecticut estate to her business enterprises. From 1983 to 1986, she failed to pay $1.7 million in taxes, a mere fraction of the $270 million in taxes that she had paid in that same period.

Her husband was found incompetent to stand trial, but in August 1989, after a six-week trial splashed across the New York media, Leona Helmsley was convicted on thirty-three counts. One of the most memorable pieces of evidence from the trial came from witness testimony that attributed to Helmsley the statement that "only the little people pay taxes." She was sentenced to four years in prison and fined more than $7 million. At sentencing, the trial judge remarked, "I trust that the sentence today will make it very clear that no person, no matter how wealthy or prominent, stands above the law." The conviction was affirmed on appeal, and she began her sentence in 1992 on April 15 — Tax Day.

SEE ALSO Congressional Power to Tax Income (1909); The O.J. Simpson Murder Trial (1995).

Tax-evading Leona Helmsley, the "Queen of Mean," leaves the New York federal courthouse on August 28, 1989.

The First Gay Marriage Laws

The institution of marriage as a civil union between two parties is universal, occurring throughout the world in widely varying cultures and legal systems. Of an ancient heritage, it has existed in all previous societies known to humankind. But equally universal has been the controversy about whether the institution properly may include gay couples.

In 1984, the Danish government commissioned a study and report on eliminating discrimination against gays and lesbians. As enacted by the Danish parliament, the law held that, on registering their relationship with an official registry, gays and lesbians were to have the same rights as their heterosexual counterparts. However, it expressly prevented those registered partners from adopting children or conducting wedding ceremonies in the Church of Denmark.

One of the most important steps on the way to recognition of gay marriage, Denmark's groundbreaking Registered Partnership Act followed in 1989 and became a worldwide media event. It also served as a model for the many nations that subsequently enacted similar legislation. The remaining Nordic nations—Norway, Sweden, Iceland, and Finland—each enacted parallel registered partnership laws, as did other European countries: the Netherlands in 1998, France in 1999, and Germany in 2001.

In 1999, Denmark eliminated its prohibition on gay adoption. The following year, the Netherlands became the world's first country to permit gay couples to marry, as opposed to registering a domestic partnership, starting the following April. Just after midnight on April 1, 2001, Amsterdam's then-mayor, Job Cohen, married four gay couples at city hall: Helene Faasen and Anne-Marie Thus, Dolf Pasker and Gert Kasteel, Ton Jansen and Louis Rogmans, and Frank Wittebrood and Peter Lemke. Two years later, Belgium passed similar legislation. Spain, Canada, and South Africa followed suit in 2005, as did Norway in 2008 and Sweden in 2009.

None of these enactments happened overnight, however. Each resulted from many years of effort and incremental progress in recognizing the rights of gays and lesbians. Despite almost three decades of enormous progress, gay marriage hasn't yet achieved universality because of the complicated relationship between the law and religion.

SEE ALSO Interracial Marriage (1967); The First Ban on Gay Marriage (1973); The Legal Fight for Gay Marriage (2004).

Protester signs in support of gay marriage during London's 2012 Gay Pride parade. An estimated twenty-five thousand people took part in the march.

SOM
PEOPLE
ARE GAY.
GET
OVER
IT!
Stonewall
SAY I DO
TO EQUAL
MARRIAGE

The Americans with Disabilities Act

America as a nation takes root in beliefs of liberty, equality, and inclusivity. Those values lie at the heart of the Declaration of Independence—"all men are created equal"— and conclude the Pledge of Allegiance—"with liberty and justice for all." Many of the nation's landmark laws ultimately derive from these core principles. One such law is the Americans with Disabilities Act (ADA), hailed by Arlene Mayerson of the Disability Rights Education and Defense Fund as "the most comprehensive piece of disability civil rights legislation ever enacted, and the most important piece of civil rights legislation since the 1964 Civil Rights Act."

In general terms, the ADA extends to the disabled the same protections afforded by the Civil Rights Act of 1964, which made it illegal to discriminate based on race, color, gender, religion, or national origin. The ADA similarly prohibits discrimination in public accommodations—meaning physical or architectural barriers in hotels, restaurants, stores, schools, offices, and the like—and in employment.

One of the challenging issues of complying with the ADA can be understanding precisely whom it covers. Definitions under the statute are specific, but judicial interpretations have generated significant confusion. To start, protection is available only to an "otherwise qualified individual with a disability." Broadly, a disability is defined as an actual or perceived physical or mental impairment that substantially limits one or more major life activities, such as hearing, seeing, standing, walking, or communicating. In the employment context, an otherwise qualified individual is someone who can perform the essential functions of the job with or without reasonable accommodation— modifications in policies, practices, or procedures; removal of barriers; auxiliary aids and services—unless doing so would require an undue hardship. Employers generally are obligated to make reasonable accommodation.

No one denies the laudable purposes of the ADA or the positive impact it has had on thousands of lives, but it remains a controversial statute and a significant source of litigation. In 2008, Congress amended the ADA to overturn a number of Supreme Court decisions that it viewed as erroneous due to the Court's narrow interpretation of what constituted a disability.

SEE ALSO Equal Protection Rights (1886); The Civil Rights Act of 1964; Golf Carts on the PGA Tour (2001).

President George H. W. Bush signs the Americans with Disabilities Act into law on the South Lawn of the White House on July 26, 1990.

The End of Apartheid

F. W. de Klerk (b. 1936), **Nelson Mandela** (1918–2013)

The Dutch established the first European colony in what became South Africa when Jan van Riebeeck founded a naval rest and refreshment station for the Dutch East India Company in what is now Cape Town in 1652. Since then, South Africa has been a loosely segregated society. But by the mid-1940s, Afrikaners (white South Africans of Dutch descent) began to use the ideology of apartheid—meaning separateness—to denote and reinforce the segregation of blacks and whites.

In 1948, the Afrikaner-dominated National Party came to power after a close election and quickly enacted legislation that formalized apartheid into racial laws that soon shaped all aspects of South African life. The 1950 Group Areas Act established separate residential and business sections for each race, and the Land Acts of 1954 and 1955 set aside more than 80 percent of the nation's land for the white minority. The National Party also strengthened existing "pass" laws, which required blacks to carry travel documents in racially restricted areas.

During the 1970s and 1980s, the international community condemned apartheid and the National Party's brutal attempts to enforce its dictates. In 1984 and 1985, scores of American companies withdrew, and loans to the government dried up. The U.S. implemented economic sanctions in 1986 that included investment and import bans. Growing domestic resistance to apartheid led to President P. W. Botha's resignation in 1989.

F. W. de Klerk, a cabinet member in Botha's administration who had become critical of apartheid, took his place, and in February 1990 de Klerk stunned the world by rescinding the laws that had banned the African National Congress and other opposition parties. One week later he ordered Nelson Mandela's release after twenty-seven years of political imprisonment. Within a few years, de Klerk eliminated the last de jure vestiges of apartheid. By 1994, the country had universal suffrage, electing a black majority government and Nelson Mandela as president.

SEE ALSO *Brown v. Board of Education* (1954); The Trial of Nelson Mandela (1963); Court-Ordered School Busing (1971); South Africa's Constitution (1996).

These jubilant residents of Soweto, South Africa, are waiting to hear a recently freed Nelson Mandela speak at a African National Congress rally in February 1990.

Confirming Clarence Thomas

Clarence Thomas (b. 1948), **Anita Hill** (b. 1956)

Between 1987 and 1991, the U.S. Senate Judiciary Committee conducted confirmation hearings on the nominations of five Supreme Court nominees: Robert Bork, Douglas Ginsburg, Anthony Kennedy, David Souter, and Clarence Thomas. The Senate rejected the Bork nomination. Ginsburg withdrew from consideration after acknowledging that he had smoked marijuana as a law student and professor. After largely uneventful hearings, Kennedy and Souter each were confirmed. Thomas was confirmed as well, but his hearings were anything but uneventful.

After nine days of testimony, just two days prior to the Senate vote, news broke that Anita Hill, a law professor and one of Thomas's former colleagues while he headed the Equal Employment Opportunity Commission, had come forward with allegations of sexual harassment. The Judiciary Committee held three additional days of hearings—"a circus sideshow" according to law professor Kim A. Taylor—that were likely the most watched Supreme Court confirmation hearings ever held. Communications expert Dianne Rucinski estimates that they were aired on cable and network TV as well as radio to as many as twenty-seven million homes.

Partisan politicking peppered three days of he-said-she-said testimony that Thomas himself characterized as "a national disgrace. From my standpoint as a black American, it is a high-tech lynching for uppity blacks who in any way deign to think for themselves, to do for themselves." The Senate confirmed Thomas by the closest vote of the century: 52–48.

Increased national consciousness made a lightning rod of the issue of sexual harassment, galvanizing action. Supreme Court scholar Henry J. Abraham observes: "many women made the Judiciary's supposedly callous treatment of Anita Hill a major campaign issue in the 1992 elections. . . . When the political dust had cleared, four more women had joined" the Senate. Political communication expert Dianne Bystrom also points to record-breaking numbers of sexual harassment inquiries made to and charges filed with the EEOC in the years immediately following.

SEE ALSO The Judiciary Act of 1789; Robert Bork's Supreme Court Nomination (1987).

Associate Justice of the U.S. Supreme Court Clarence Thomas in his official portrait, taken on September 24, 2007.

The Trial of Manuel Noriega

Manuel Noriega (b. 1934)

Manuel Noriega's rise to power began with his participation in the coup that installed Omar Torrijos as Panama's leader in 1968. Noriega became commander of the Panamanian National Guard in 1981, transforming it into the Panamanian Defense Forces and appointing himself general. After Torrijos died in a plane crash, Noriega ruled the country himself. Throughout the 1980s, America worked closely with Noriega to stem the flow of Colombian cocaine into the U.S., but by 1989 Noriega was suspected of laundering Colombian cartel money.

On December 20, 1989, after a federal grand jury indicted Noriega on charges of racketeering, drug smuggling, and money laundering, twenty-five thousand U.S. troops invaded Panama in what has been called the costliest and deadliest arrest in history. Less than two weeks later, Noriega surrendered—technically as a prisoner of war—and was taken to Miami to face the charges.

The government presented more than twenty witnesses—all convicted of drug offenses and many offering testimony in exchange for leniency—who supplied overwhelming evidence of Noriega's involvement with the Colombian cocaine cartel. The trial ended in April 1992. It was the first time that the U.S. had criminally prosecuted a former head of state in an American court. The jury found Noriega guilty on eight of the ten counts. He was sentenced to forty years, imprisonment.

In 1997, Peter Eisner, a journalist and editor who had covered Latin America for many years, collaborated with the deposed general to write *America's Prisoner: The Memoirs of Manuel Noriega*. The first line of Eisner's introduction reads: "Rarely has a figure in this century been so universally vilified as Manuel Antonio Noriega."

After a sentence reduction, the former Panamanian leader was released in September 2007—only to be extradited to France where he had been convicted in absentia on money laundering charges. France then agreed to extradite Noriega to Panama, where he had been convicted (also in absentia) for the murder of a political opponent. In December 2011, he traveled from France back to Panama, where he continues to serve the balance of three twenty-year prison sentences.

SEE ALSO The Geneva Convention (1864); The Nuremberg Trials (1945); The RICO Act (1970); The International Criminal Court (2002).

Two U.S. Drug Enforcement Agents escort Noriega onto a U.S. Air Force plane after his surrender in Panama on January 3, 1990.

Smoking Litigation

Cipollone v. Liggett Group, Inc.

In 1866, the *United States Tobacco Journal* called cigarette smoking "one of the vilest and most suicidal habits of the present day." Starting in the mid-1950s, unsuccessful lawsuits began against tobacco companies. The plaintiffs knew of cigarettes' dangers, yet they chose to smoke. "Everyone" knew of the health consequences, so how could anyone but the smoker be responsible for his or her injuries?

The legal landscape began to change in 1984, when a New Jersey federal court refused to dismiss Rose Cipollone's lawsuit against Liggett Group, Inc., maker of Chesterfields and L&M cigarettes. Cipollone's physician had recently diagnosed her with lung cancer, attributed to nearly forty years of smoking. Liggett sought dismissal based on compliance with the federal warning requirements imposed under the 1965 Federal Cigarette Labeling and Advertising Act and the 1969 Public Health Cigarette Smoking Act, which Liggett argued preempted state-law claims for smoking-related injuries. Cipollone died in 1984, but four years later a jury found for her family based on the company's failure to warn smokers prior to 1966. The jury assessed Liggett's responsibility at 20 percent and awarded damages in the amount of $400,000, making it the first time a plaintiff had ever sued a tobacco company successfully for smoking-related injuries.

The Third Circuit Court of Appeals set aside the verdict and remanded for a new trial, but the U.S. Supreme Court then agreed to hear the case. In 1992, it held that the Public Health Cigarette Smoking Act did preempt some state-law claims — those predicated on a failure to warn — but the Court also ruled that the federal statutes did not preempt other state-law claims, including breach of warranty, fraudulent misrepresentation, and fraudulent concealment of health-related facts.

The Court's decision was a mixed blessing for the Cipollones. Although they retained valid claims against Liggett, they needed to be retried. But after almost ten years of litigation, the family had had enough. They dropped the case rather than suffer another grueling ordeal.

SEE ALSO The Prohibition of Illegal Narcotics (1915); Prohibition (1918); Public Health and Cigarettes (1970); Legalization of Marijuana (1996).

Up in $moke *by Senior Airman Nathan Lipscomb. The Department of Defense estimates that it spends about* $875 *million per year on health care for smoking-related illnesses and lost productivity.*

The Rio Conference

The first global environmental summit, the U.N. Conference on the Human Environment, met in Stockholm in 1972 and marked the beginning of political awareness of global environmental issues. Environmental law scholar Daniel Bodansky describes Stockholm as "perhaps *the* major catalyst . . . in the emergence of international environmental law."

Twenty years later, an unprecedented 35,000 participants, including emissaries from 172 governments and 2,400 representatives of nongovernmental organizations, gathered in Rio de Janeiro, Brazil, to continue where Stockholm ended. This U.N. Conference on Environment and Development (the "Earth Summit" or "Rio Conference") assembled the largest gathering of national leaders to date. It produced the Rio Declaration on Environment and Development; the Authoritative Statement of Principles for a Global Consensus on the Management, Conservation, and Sustainable Development of All Types of Forests; and Agenda 21, a detailed action plan for implementation of the conference's objectives.

Those three documents emerging from Rio are considered soft law because they have no binding force, but many nations committed themselves, at least symbolically, to accommodating environmental concerns in their pursuit of economic development. Two binding treaties also emerged from Rio: the Convention on Biological Diversity, which principally addressed endangered species; and the Framework Convention on Climate Change, which required nations to reduce greenhouse gas emissions. Rio also opened a dialogue between industrialized and developing nations. The latter resisted restrictive environmental measures that might hamstring their economic growth, and to some extent they remain resistant.

One year after Rio, Daniel C. Esty, then an international affairs fellow at the Council on Foreign Relations, wrote that Rio would be "much less remembered for the agreements produced and much more remembered for the symbolic emergence of the environment as a global issue of first-order importance." Five years after Rio, participating countries drafted the Kyoto Protocol, an international treaty to reduce greenhouse gasses. So far the U.S. has declined to ratify the protocol.

SEE ALSO The National Environmental Policy Act (1970); The Endangered Species Act (1973).

At the 1992 Earth Summit in Rio de Janeiro, a small boy holds hands with planet Earth—a symbol of hope for humanity's future.

Creation of the European Union

In the last weeks of 1991, the Belavezha Accords sounded the death knell of the Soviet Union. Two years later, the nations of Europe—once caught uneasily between the two superpowers of the Cold War—officially formed the European Union (E.U.) with the Maastricht Treaty, establishing a long-sought united Europe and much-wanted stability through economic and political interdependence.

Like the U.K., a kingdom of countries, the E.U. is a supranational entity described conceptually as three pillars supporting a common institutional framework. One of the pillars represents the European Community; a second signifies a common foreign and security policy; the third stands for cooperation in domestic affairs and justice, which includes issues relating to the movement of citizens within the E.U.'s borders. In one of the most important changes, the E.U. established the euro as a common currency for financial markets and businesses—although the E.U. and the Eurozone remain separate areas because not all E.U. nations adopted the euro.

Article I of the Maastricht Treaty specifies one of the overarching principles that bind together the twenty-eight sovereign nations sharing common economic and social policies in the form of the E.U.: "This Treaty marks a new stage in the process of creating an ever closer union among the peoples of Europe, in which decisions are taken as closely as possible to the citizen." Those decisions happen by means of different institutional arms that perform a variety of functions similar to those of the American executive, legislative, and judicial branches of government.

The European Council, composed of the heads of state of the member states, sets the general policy directions for the E.U., although it doesn't engage in legislative activity. The European Commission, which represents the interests of the E.U. as a whole, proposes legislation, which is then considered and voted upon by the European Parliament (members elected directly by citizens of the E.U.) and the Council (or Council of Ministers), which represents and provides a voice to the governments of the member states. Finally, the Court of Justice oversees the consistent interpretation and application of E.U. laws across the member states.

SEE ALSO Peace of Westphalia (1648); Colonialism and Postwar Independence (1947); The E.U. and the Treaty of Paris (1951); The European Court of Human Rights (1959).

The European Commission building in Brussels, Belgium, which serves as the capital of the union of nations.

The Hot Coffee Case

Stella Liebeck (1913–2004), *Liebeck v. McDonald's Restaurants*

If it bleeds, it leads. The press often follows calamity and misfortune. But even well-intentioned, impartial reporting can present an incomplete or inaccurate account of events. The infamous case involving a spilled cup of McDonald's coffee illustrates how media coverage can dictate public perception and distort attitudes.

When seventy-nine-year-old Stella Liebeck purchased a cup of coffee from an Albuquerque McDonald's one morning in 1992, she never imagined what lay in store. Sitting in her grandson's parked car, she placed the coffee between her knees. As she removed the lid, scalding coffee spilled over her lower body, causing third-degree burns.

After a week in the hospital, Liebeck underwent painful skin grafts and reconstructive surgery. She asked McDonald's for reimbursement of her medical expenses, estimated at nearly $20,000. When McDonald's offered just $800, Liebeck sued, alleging that McDonald's coffee was dangerously "defective" because it was served at more than 180 degrees Fahrenheit, well above industry standards.

The trial revealed that McDonald's had previously received more than seven hundred reports of injuries caused by its coffee. The jury awarded Liebeck $160,000 in compensatory damages and $2.7 million in punitive damages. The trial judge reduced the latter amount to $480,000, and the parties ultimately reached a confidential settlement.

But the press had a field day, recasting the case as a frivolous lawsuit by an elderly woman looking for a payday. A *San Diego Tribune* editorial opined, "When Stella Liebeck fumbled her coffee cup . . . she might as well have bought a winning lottery ticket. . . . This absurd result is a stunning illustration of what is wrong with America's civil justice system." Media reporting created a poster child for tort reform, and polls indicated public outrage at the size of the verdict. Yet anyone familiar with the record on which the jury based its verdict would be shocked by those reactions, not by Liebeck's justified victory. Despite the press coverage, the case provided a major impetus for change in how McDonald's and others prepare and label their products, thereby reaffirming the importance of tort remedies.

SEE ALSO The Expansion of Consumer Rights (1916); The Danger Zone in Tort Law (1928); Strict Products Liability (1941); Limits on Punitive Damages (1996).

A spilled cup of McDonald's coffee occasioned a famous lawsuit—erroneously viewed by many as frivolous—that forced companies to reexamine how they prepare and label their products.

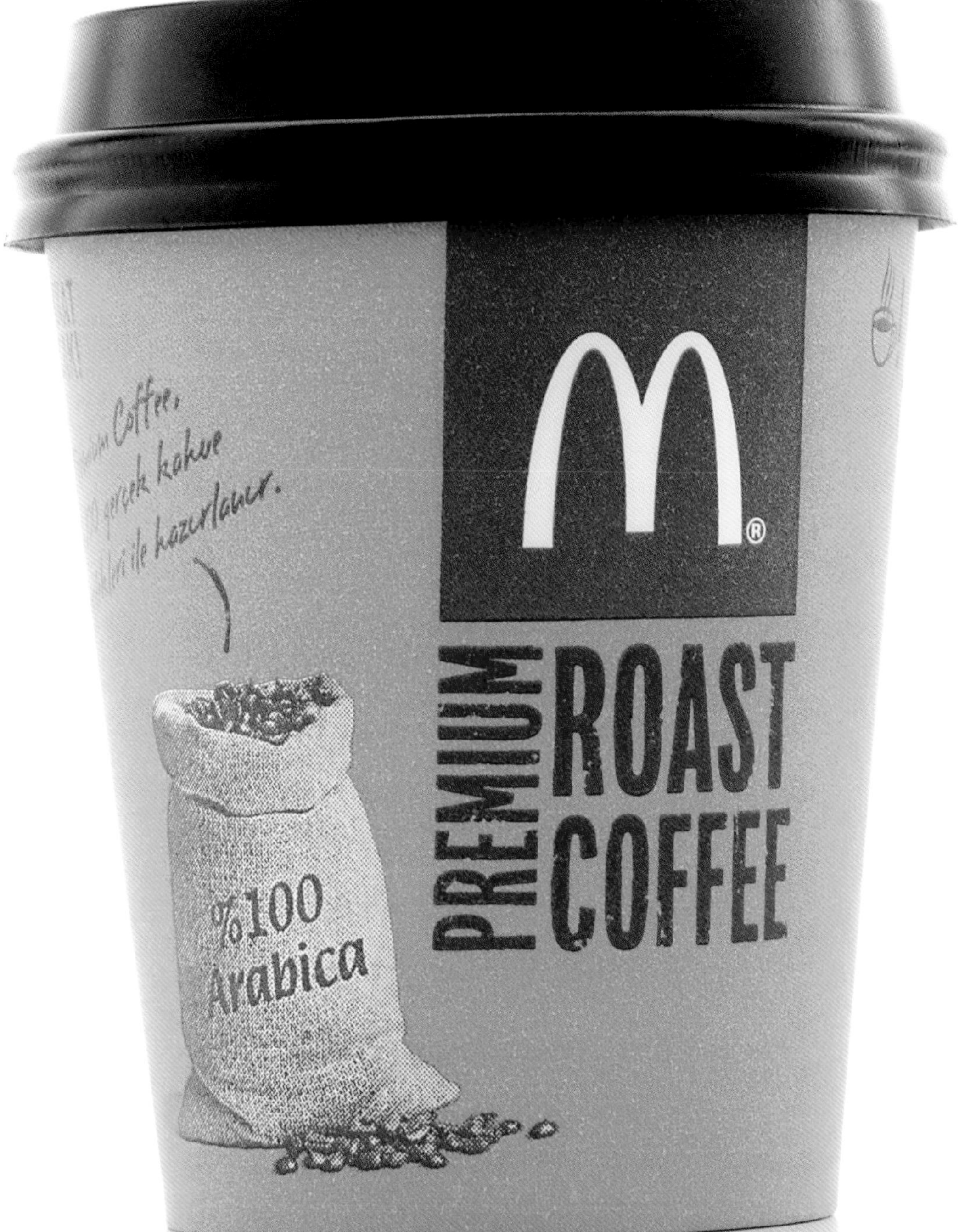
%100
Arabica
PREMIUM
ROAST
COFFEE

Stem Cell and Cloning Legislation

Embryonic stem cells in mammals have much scientific value for treating cancer, diabetes, and other medical conditions; engineering tissue; and cloning. Research involving this type of stem cell, however, continues to draw ire from the religious and anti-abortion communities because embryonic stem cells are harvested from four- to five-day-old embryos, which means they are coming from embryos that are being destroyed.

In 1995, the National Institutes of Health Human Embryo Research Panel appealed to President Bill Clinton to permit federal funding for research on embryos left over from in vitro fertility treatments as well as embryos created solely for research purposes. The Clinton administration declined to support the latter but agreed to fund research on the leftover embryos. Congress intervened and passed the Dickey-Wicker Amendment, which banned the use of federal funds for the destruction of any embryo, regardless of source. In 1998, private researchers isolated the first human embryonic stem cell. In 2001, the Bush administration limited the number of stem cell lines that researchers could use, a policy overturned by President Obama in 2009. Current U.S. law still prohibits federal funding for the creation of new stem cell lines but permits funding for research on lines created by public and private funds.

Many European countries severely restrict or prohibit the use of embryonic stem cells, but the U.K. has taken the lead in this area, successfully cloning the world's first animal, Dolly the sheep (1996–2003), and permitting research on human-animal hybrid embryos, known as chimeras. Singapore, Asia's stem cell center, has more than forty stem cell research groups, part of a strategic effort to enhance the country's role in biomedical research. Permitting the use of embryos for therapeutic purposes has proven an attractive inducement. Other nations that have permitted stem cell research for therapeutic but not reproductive purposes include Belgium, China, India, Israel, Japan, Saudi Arabia, South Africa, South Korea, and Sweden.

No federal law bans human cloning, but at least fifteen states have enacted bans on reproductive cloning. The United Nations addressed the issue in March 2005, when the General Assembly adopted the United Nations Declaration on Human Cloning, which called on member states to prohibit all forms of human cloning.

SEE ALSO The Body and the Right of Privacy (1965); *Roe v. Wade* (1973); The Affordable Health Act (2012).

A colony of embryonic stem cells from the H9 cell line.

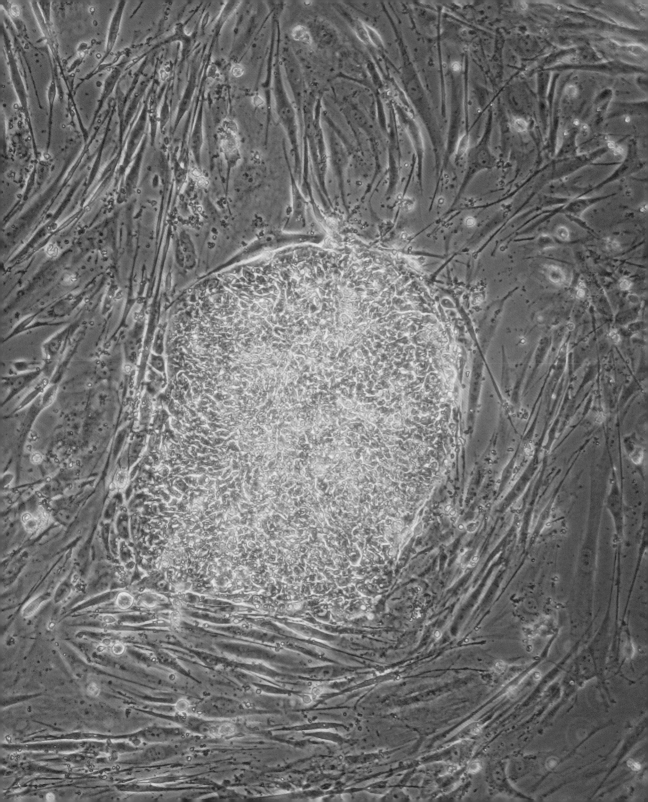

The O. J. Simpson Murder Trial

Nicole Brown Simpson (1959–1994), **Ronald Goldman** (1968–1994),
O. J. Simpson (b. 1947)

A black man, a Southern California car chase, a media circus, and a controversial verdict that outraged and enthralled the nation—in 1991 it was Rodney King, severely beaten by four Los Angeles police officers. The verdict that acquitted them triggered the deadliest American riots since the 1860s and primed the country for courtroom drama. Four years later, it was O. J. Simpson. Media scrutiny began with news of the murders of Nicole Brown Simpson and her friend Ronald Goldman. But even before the Simpson trial began, the case attracted unimaginable attention. On June 17, 1994, Simpson refused to surrender to authorities as agreed, leading to a surreal, low-speed police chase down a Los Angeles highway in a white Ford Bronco toward Mexico. Footage of the chase aired live nationally, interrupting the NBA Finals, seen by an estimated ninety-five million viewers. After hours of pursuit, Simpson finally surrendered to police in the driveway of his Brentwood home.

Then his trial played out on the media stage. News cameras broadcast each day's testimony, arguments, and rulings. Anyone with a television could follow the trial, and practically everyone had an opinion about the case. Law professor and legal commentator Douglas O. Linder cited the start of "a new type of 'immersion' journalism that still flourishes today." Other scholars noted the beginning of a new age of "telelitigation."

The criminal trial had all the makings of a Hollywood drama: a football legend, movie star, and jealous ex-husband; a seemingly perfect marriage gone sour; a beautiful ex-wife and her athletic young friend gruesomely murdered. Author Dominick Dunne called it "the Super Bowl of murder trials." A bloody glove, shoeprints, and other evidence collected from the scene seemed to point to O. J. Simpson. More than 140 million live television viewers watched, many in disbelief, as he was acquitted.

A civil trial followed, in which a jury found Simpson liable for battery against his ex-wife and the wrongful death of Goldman. Much can be and has been debated about the trial, but what remains indisputable is that the case forever changed the meaning of "the court of public opinion."

SEE ALSO Cameras in the Courts (1937).

O. J. Simpson tries on the infamous gloves at his murder trial in Los Angeles on June 21, 1995.

Limits on Punitive Damages

BMW of North America, Inc. v. Gore

Courts have long imposed punitive or exemplary damages on a defendant who has engaged in unlawful conduct in order to punish the defendant and also to deter repetition of the conduct. Originally, punitive damages served the additional interest of compensation as well as a substitute for revenge. Attorney Melvin Belli, famously known as the "King of Torts," observes that "ancient precursors to the concept of modern punitive damages may be found in the earliest collection of laws known to man," including the Code of Hammurabi, the Twelve Tables of Roman Law, and the Talmud.

Throughout the latter half of the twentieth century, the number and size of punitive damages verdicts steadily rose, with jury awards sometimes reaching hundreds of millions of dollars. Excessive awards became fodder for a growing tort reform movement. The beginnings of judicial limits on punitive damages emerged in 1996 with the Supreme Court's decision in *BMW of North America, Inc. v. Gore*. An Alabama jury had awarded Ira Gore Jr. $4 million in punitive damages (reduced to $2 million by the Alabama Supreme Court) after a BMW dealer sold Gore a new car without disclosing that it had been repainted after suffering minor damage during transportation from the factory. Gore prevailed on his claim for fraud under Alabama law and was also awarded $4,000 in compensatory damages.

The Supreme Court concluded that "the grossly excessive award imposed in this case transcends the constitutional limit." For the first time, the Court invoked the due process clause of the Fourteenth Amendment to strike a punitive damage award. In doing so, it offered guidelines to consider in evaluating the constitutional propriety of such awards. It enumerated the factors to consider as "the degree of reprehensibility of the defendant's conduct"; the ratio of the award "to the actual harm inflicted on the plaintiff" measured by what the plaintiff received as compensatory damages; and comparison to civil or criminal sanctions that might be imposed for comparable conduct. The decision laid the foundation for later cases that presumptively limited the ratio between compensatory and punitive damages to a single digit.

SEE ALSO The Code of Hammurabi (c. 1792 BCE); The Twelve Tables (450 BCE); The Talmud (c. 180); The Fourteenth Amendment (1868); Strict Products Liability (1941).

In the case of BMW of North America, Inc. v. Gore, *the Supreme Court struck down a punitive damage award for the first time, offering guidelines on evaluating the constitutional propriety of compensatory damages.*

South Africa's Constitution

Nelson Mandela (1918–2013)

In the more than forty years during which South Africa endured the formal strictures of apartheid, poverty and inequality—natural consequences of the country's colonial past—became even more deeply ingrained. After Nelson Mandela was elected president in 1994, he and the newly elected parliament drafted a permanent constitution, replacing the interim document that had paved their way by granting blacks the right to vote in the new elections and enumerating the socioeconomic rights that the government committed to recognizing and enforcing thenceforth.

The new constitution emerged in 1996 and came into force on February 4, 1997, upon certification by the South African Constitutional Court. Its preamble explains its purpose to "establish a society based on democratic values, social justice, and fundamental human rights" and to "improve the quality of life of all citizens and free the potential of each person."

In a 2013 address, Dikgang Moseneke, deputy chief justice of the country, described the new constitution as "emphatically" and "avowedly" transformative. He was referring to the constitution's bill of rights, patterned on the 1982 Canadian Charter of Rights and Freedoms, which obligates the state "to confront structural injustice caused by poverty, disease, and inequality." In response to citizen claims that one or more of their "socioeconomic rights" has been impinged, "the government bears the burden to demonstrate that it has taken legislative and other measures, within its available resources, to achieve the progressive realization of the right in issue."

South Africa's Constitutional Court has given meaning to the constitution's progressive ambition. It has found the constitution to require the state to provide access to adequate and affordable housing, to provide pregnant women and infants access to health services, and even to make available basic municipal services like electricity. Those progressive ambitions explain in part why the South African Constitution—along with the constitutions of Canada, Germany, and India—has become a model for other nations drafting new constitutions, including Kenya, Zimbabwe, South Sudan, and Zambia.

SEE ALSO Colonialism and Postwar Independence (1947); The Trial of Nelson Mandela (1963); The End of Apartheid (1990).

Nelson Mandela in Philadelphia in 1993, when he and F. W. de Klerk—the last president of apartheid-era South Africa—received America's Liberty Medal for effecting the transition to black-majority rule in their country.

Legalization of Marijuana

Historically, the use of marijuana for medical or recreational purposes has always generated polarized opinions. Although federal law continues to classify marijuana (*Cannabis sativa*) as an illegal substance, some states have decriminalized or legalized its possession for medicinal or recreational use.

In 1996, California became the first state to legalize marijuana for medical purposes when 56 percent of voters approved Ballot Proposition 215, eliminating criminal penalties on the use, possession, or cultivation of marijuana by patients whose physicians recommended it for medical treatment of a variety of conditions. As of April 2015, twenty-three states and the District of Columbia have enacted laws exempting medical marijuana users from penalties imposed under state law; four of those states have also legalized recreational marijuana use. These laws resulted from the efforts of physicians and lobbyists who argued convincingly that cannabis can provide effective treatment for various symptoms of AIDS, cancer, epilepsy, glaucoma, multiple sclerosis, and other serious diseases and conditions.

In November 2012, building on the momentum of legalization for medicinal use, Colorado and Washington became the first states to legalize possession of small quantities of marijuana for recreational use by those above age twenty-one. Alaska and Oregon followed in 2014.

Notwithstanding increased legalization, marijuana still remains a banned substance under the federal Controlled Substances Act, giving federal law enforcement agencies the legal basis to intervene. Despite the inconsistency between state and federal law, those state laws are legally irrelevant to federal prosecution. Indeed, in early 2012, federal prosecutors in California instituted a crackdown on lawful marijuana dispensaries to enforce the federal Controlled Substances Act.

More than a year later, it remained unclear whether or to what extent the federal government would continue to challenge marijuana use that comports with relevant state laws, although January 2013 news accounts reported that "President Obama has said the federal government has 'bigger fish to fry' and won't aggressively prosecute tokers in states where its use is legal."

SEE ALSO The Prohibition of Illegal Narcotics (1915); Prohibition (1918); The Repeal of Prohibition (1933); Public Health and Cigarettes (1970).

California became the first state to legalize the use of medical marijuana, and twenty-two other states and the District of Columbia followed suit. Washington, Colorado, Alaska, and Oregon went one step further, legalizing recreational use.

Presidential Immunity

Bill Clinton (b. 1946), **Paula Jones** (b. 1966), **Kenneth Starr** (b. 1946)

In 1982, the Supreme Court established that a president enjoyed absolute immunity from suits seeking to hold him liable for conduct in his official capacity. But could a sitting president be sued for unofficial conduct occurring prior to his presidency? In 1997, the Supreme Court unanimously held in *Clinton v. Jones* that such a suit was permissible because presidential immunity does not extend "beyond the scope of any action taken in an official capacity." The underlying suit, filed shortly after President Bill Clinton took office in 1993, stemmed from the claims of Paula Jones, a former Arkansas state employee, that Clinton had sexually harassed her in 1991 while he was governor of Arkansas.

Almost as important as the Court's legal holding rejecting absolute presidential immunity was the decision's impact on Clinton's legacy. In reviving Paula Jones's sexual harassment lawsuit, the Supreme Court set in motion a series of discoveries and events that ultimately led to the second impeachment of an American president.

During a 1998 deposition in the *Jones* case, President Clinton lied about the sexual nature of his relationship with White House intern Monica Lewinsky. Kenneth Starr, the independent counsel investigating Clinton's suspected involvement in the Whitewater real estate scandal, considered pressing perjury and obstruction of justice charges. When President Clinton testified before a grand jury—famously saying, "It depends on what the meaning of the word 'is' is"—he again denied having had a sexual relationship with Lewinsky.

Less than a month later, Starr presented his report to Congress, detailing grounds for impeachment. In December 1998, the House voted to impeach Clinton. In January 1999, the Senate began a trial on the two articles of impeachment voted by the House. Clinton was acquitted when the Senate couldn't achieve the constitutionally required two-thirds majority for conviction.

Before leaving office in January 2001, Clinton paid more than $800,000 to settle the Jones case. He also paid a $90,000 contempt fine for his perjury in that case. To avoid criminal prosecution for perjury and obstruction of justice after he left office, Clinton admitted to having lied under oath, paid an additional fine of $25,000, and surrendered his Arkansas law license for a period of five years.

SEE ALSO Impeaching President Andrew Johnson (1868); Presidential Subpoena Compliance (1974).

Two tickets, dated January 14, 1999, to the Senate Impeachment Trial of the President of the United States.

06TH CONGRESS—FIRST SESSION

United States Senate

Impeachment Trial of the
PRESIDENT OF THE UNITED STATES

R TO THE SENATE GALLERY

Sergeant-at-Ar

106TH CONGRESS—FIRST SESSION

United States Senate

Impeachment Trial of the
PRESIDENT OF THE UNITED STATES

ADMIT BEARER TO THE SENATE GALLERY

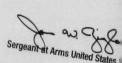

Sergeant-at-Arms United States

The Communications Decency Act

Reno v. American Civil Liberties Union

On multiple occasions in the latter half of the twentieth century, Congress and the Supreme Court teamed up to establish the government's right to regulate broadcast-radio and -television content. Doing so eroded a small portion of programmers' freedom of speech, but the government found the encroachment necessary to protect children from "low value" obscene content. In 1996, Congress continued its censorship crusade by sighting a new medium of communication in its crosshairs: the Internet.

The Communications Decency Act (CDA) made it a crime "to knowingly transmit obscene or indecent material to anyone under age eighteen or to display patently offensive material to minors" over the Internet. The motivation behind the Act exactly matched that of earlier laws enabling regulation of television and radio, but the question soon became whether online content was significantly different and therefore worthy of greater protection than other modes of electronic communication. This issue reached the Supreme Court in 1997 in *Reno v. American Civil Liberties Union*.

At the time, the Internet was considered a Wild West, with no government control on users' freedom of speech. The CDA, however, threatened to change that paradigm. In response, opponents of Internet regulation challenged the Act as an unconstitutional burden on speech. In *Reno*, the Supreme Court agreed, striking down the CDA as too broad, too vague, and nearly impossible to enforce. In its decision, the Court contrasted the Internet with broadcast television and radio, finding that the justifications used to regulate those media didn't apply online. The Internet, according to the Court, shouldn't be subject to government regulation except in extremely limited cases.

Reno stood poised to become a historic decision regardless of its outcome. Its importance, however, lies in the Court's guiding principles, which stand firm today. The Internet remains largely unregulated, making it one of the most unrestricted free-speech platforms in existence. Both the federal and state governments have tried repeatedly to craft online obscenity regulations narrow enough to satisfy the *Reno* standard, but few have withstood legal challenges.

SEE ALSO The Federal Communications Act (1934); The Fairness Doctrine (1969); A New Obscenity Standard (1973); The FCC and Filthy Words (1978).

Controlling and regulating content on the Internet has proven to be an elusive proposition—particularly in light of the competing values of free speech.

Physician-Assisted Suicide

Jack Kevorkian (1928–2011), *Cruzan v. Director, Missouri Department of Health*, **William Rehnquist** (1924–2005), *Vacco v. Quill, Washington v. Glucksberg*

In 1990, Dr. Jack Kevorkian invented a suicide device that mixed a lethal combination of medications to end a patient's life with the push of a button. He eventually helped more than one hundred terminal individuals painlessly end their own lives. In doing so, he knowingly broke the law. Supporters counted him an angel of mercy. Critics labeled him a serial killer, but various legal proceedings against him faltered.

Also in 1990, Chief Justice William Rehnquist noted in *Cruzan v. Director, Missouri Department of Health* that advances in medical technology resulted in a burgeoning of "cases involving the right to refuse life-sustaining treatment." The Court assumed, without deciding, that the Constitution affords a competent individual "a right to refuse lifesaving nutrition and hydration" but that the right—flowing from the liberty protection afforded by the Fourteenth Amendment's due process clause—wasn't absolute and had to be balanced against state interests.

Seven years later, the court considered the constitutional issues arising when physician assistance becomes necessary. In *Vacco v. Quill* and *Washington v. Glucksberg*, the Supreme Court rejected challenges under both the equal protection and due process clauses, holding that "everyone, regardless of physical condition, is entitled, if competent, to refuse unwanted lifesaving medical treatment; no one is permitted to assist a suicide."

In 1999, a *60 Minutes* broadcast showed Kevorkian injecting a lethal drug into a physically incapacitated would-be suicide. Michigan prosecutors pressed charges, Kevorkian was convicted of second-degree murder, and he was sentenced to ten to twenty-five years in prison. The sentencing judge exclaimed: "You had the audacity to go on national television, show the world what you did, and dare the legal system to stop you. Well, sir, consider yourself stopped."

Oregon, Washington, Vermont, the Netherlands, Luxembourg, and Switzerland have enacted legislation legalizing physician-assisted suicide. Kevorkian died of natural causes in 2011.

SEE ALSO The Fourteenth Amendment (1868); The Body and the Right of Privacy (1965); The Right to Die (1976).

Dr. Jack Kevorkian speaking at a press conference a few days after his release from prison.

The Line-Item Veto

Bill Clinton (b. 1946), *Raines v. Byrd, Clinton v. City of New York*

In his 1986 State of the Union Address, President Ronald Reagan made the following plea: "Give me what forty-three governors have: Give me a line-item veto this year. Give me the authority to veto waste, and I'll take the responsibility, I'll make the cuts." Reagan, like many prior presidents, wanted the power to reject individual provisions of a bill while permitting the remaining provisions to become law. Many legal scholars viewed the line-item veto as an effective way to cut congressional spending, enabling a president to veto certain appropriations—many involving pork-barrel and logrolling expenditures—without rejecting a bill entirely. Unfortunately for Reagan and his immediate predecessors, his pleas went unanswered. A decade later, however, when President Clinton renewed the call for a line-item veto, Congress finally complied. Amid great controversy, Congress enacted the Line-Item Veto Act in 1996.

Almost immediately, two lawsuits challenged the Act: *Raines v. Byrd*, brought by six members of Congress, and *Clinton v. City of New York*. The *Raines* plaintiffs initially succeeded in having the act declared unconstitutional. On appeal, however, the Supreme Court vacated the decision, finding that the members of Congress who had brought the case lacked standing to sue since none had suffered a personal injury. The *Clinton* plaintiffs—groups whose funding had been cut as a result of line-item vetoes—on the other hand, were found to have proper standing, spelling ultimate doom for the act.

In 1998, the Supreme Court declared the Line-Item Veto Act an unconstitutional violation of the presentment clause of Article I of the Constitution. Writing for the majority, Justice Stevens explained that the Act improperly granted "the President the unilateral power to change the text of duly enacted statutes." The decision made clear that a bill must be signed or vetoed in its entirety as passed by Congress.

In the years following *Clinton*, the call for a new line-item veto act has continued. As recently as 2012, the House of Representatives, with President Obama's support, passed such a bill, but the effort died in the Senate.

SEE ALSO The U.S. Constitution (1787); Presidential Subpoena Compliance (1974); Presidential Immunity (1997).

President Bill Clinton's official White House portrait, taken in 1993. Three years later he signed the Line-Item Veto Act into law; two years after that, the Supreme Court declared it unconstitutional.

Indictment of Augusto Pinochet

Augusto Pinochet (1915–2006)

Beginning in 1998, an international drama played out across South America and Europe as Chile, Spain, and Britain battled over the fate of a former military dictator, focusing the world's attention on sometimes arcane legal procedures.

After leading a 1973 military coup against President Salvador Allende of Chile, General Augusto Pinochet seized power. During his rule as president, more than three thousand people were killed or "disappeared." Thousands more were detained because of their political activities. Pinochet stepped down in 1990 but remained the commander in chief of the Chilean army and enjoyed the benefit of a 1978 amnesty law barring prosecution of military and government officials for certain criminal actions.

In 1998, he assumed the position of senator for life, a title that afforded him additional immunity from prosecution. That same year, a Spanish judge investigating human rights violations in Chile issued an international arrest warrant for Pinochet, who had traveled to London for surgery. An English magistrate supplied a provisional arrest warrant alleging that Pinochet had murdered Spanish citizens in Chile between 1973 and 1983. A subsequent warrant charged him with systematic torture and murder. Pinochet was arrested and held in custody as a battle ensued over the legality of extraditing him to Spain. At stake was the principle of whether a former head of state had immunity from prosecution for crimes of torture and murder. Britain's House of Lords twice rejected Pinochet's claim of immunity, finding that torture and genocide didn't form part of his "official duties as a head of state."

The Chilean Embassy persuaded the British home secretary that Pinochet's declining health made him unfit to stand trial. Pinochet was released and returned to Chile. Two years later, Chile's Supreme Court stripped him of immunity; he was indicted for kidnapping and murder and placed under house arrest. His health continued to decline—though skeptics questioned the veracity of those claims—and he never faced trial on those charges.

SEE ALSO The Nuremberg Trials (1945); The U.N. Convention on Genocide (1948); The Trial of Manuel Noriega (1991); Presidential Immunity (1997); The International Criminal Court (2002).

Chile's Paine Memorial—consisting of a 930-pole "forest" interspersed with 70 personalized mosaics— commemorates the lives of people abducted or unlawfully arrested and killed under the military dictatorship of Augusto Pinochet.

Copyright in the Digital Age

American copyright law has always been premised on the dual aims of increasing dissemination of creative works for the public benefit while financially incentivizing copyright owners to keep creating, but the power struggle between revenue-driven copyright holders and content-hungry consumers reached new heights as the world approached the twenty-first century.

In the 1990s, copyright holders saw the protection and earning potential of their works increase in various ways. For example, in 1992, Congress amended the Copyright Act to make all copyright renewals automatic, enabling copyright owners to keep their works legally protected and therefore profitable for longer periods of time. An even bigger windfall for copyright holders came in 1998, when Congress increased the term of copyright protection, through the Copyright Term Extension Act, for the lifetime of the author plus an additional seventy years.

In 1999, however, the rise of peer-to-peer file sharing platforms such as Napster marked the start of widespread digital piracy and substantial revenue losses for copyright holders. According to the Recording Industry Association of America, U.S. music sales dropped 53 percent, from $14.6 billion in 1999 to $7 in 2013. Even after a federal court shuttered Napster in 2001, the continued digitization of creative works by their creators and consumers, combined with the ever-expanding power and reach of the Internet, made it easier than ever to copy and disseminate files illegally.

Nor did the TV and movie industries remain immune from problems of piracy. Because of their enormous file sizes, digital videos enjoyed an inherent theft deterrent. But as Internet bandwidth, speed, and storage capacity increased, significant piracy began to emerge. Unlike the music industry, which challenged piracy in the courts through thousands of individual lawsuits, much of the video pirating was taking place in China and Russia, where judgments obtained in American courts had little effect. In any event, Hollywood responded by providing digital content affordably as part of a new business model that removed much of the bootlegging incentive. Congress has done little to address either situation, thus far ignoring calls from the legal community for another Copyright Act overhaul.

SEE ALSO America's First Copyright Law (1790); The Berne Convention (1878); The Copyright Act of 1976; Time-Shifting and Fair Use (1984); Expanded Copyrights (2001); Google Books and Fair Use (2010).

Copyright owners haven't yet been able to stifle the illegal copying and dissemination of works they are supposed to have control over.

Bush v. Gore

George W. Bush (b. 1946), Al Gore (b. 1948)

Article II of the Constitution, as modified by the Twelfth Amendment, provides for the election of the president by a "Number of Electors" appointed by each state. Since 1845, that body has been the electoral college. But in 2000, neither the electors of the electoral college nor the more than one hundred million voting Americans chose the president. That year, a 5–4 vote by the U.S. Supreme Court selected George W. Bush as president.

America went to the polls on November 7, 2000, to choose the nation's new leader. After the polls closed, it appeared that sitting vice president and Democratic candidate Al Gore had received the majority of the popular vote. But it looked as though his Republican opponent, George W. Bush, had carried Florida and with it the majority of electoral votes, which would make him president. After a recount required under Florida election law, Bush remained ahead by 327 votes.

Over the next thirty-six days came a flurry of lawsuits and court hearings as the country waited to learn who would sit as the next president. The final act of the riveting public drama unfolded in the U.S. Supreme Court between December 9—when it stayed a decision of the Florida Supreme Court—and December 12, when it released its own decision. The ultimate issue concerned the conduct of a statewide recount, which the Florida Supreme Court had ordered in part due to Miami-Dade County's failure to count nine thousand ballots not tabulated by machine because of incomplete punches of the voting cards (the infamous "hanging chad" issue). The U.S. Supreme Court's decision halted that recount, finding that the Florida court had violated the Fourteenth Amendment's equal protection clause by ordering a hand-recount to determine the "intent of the voter" without procedures or guidelines to ensure that all ballots be evaluated equally and receive "uniform treatment." On December 13, Vice President Gore conceded the election, and George W. Bush went on to become the nation's forty-third president.

SEE ALSO The U.S. Constitution (1787); The Power of Judicial Review (1803); The Fourteenth Amendment (1868).

Judge Robert Rosenberg of Broward County Canvassing Board using a magnifying glass to view a dimpled chad on a punch-hole ballot during a recount in Fort Lauderdale, Florida.

The Microsoft Monopoly

United States v. Microsoft Corporation

Founded by Bill Gates and Paul Allen in Albuquerque, New Mexico, in 1975, Microsoft became the world's largest software company in 1988. A decade later, its Windows operating system ran 90 percent of America's personal computers, and its corporate profits—approximately $4.5 billion—stood at twice those of any other corporation.

But great success invariably attracts attention. Ignoring the proverb that "you can't argue with success," the Department of Justice's Antitrust Division began investigating Microsoft's business practices in the early 1990s. Those investigations led to a 1998 lawsuit (joined by twenty states) and a trial described by *New York Times* journalists Joel Brinkley and Steve Lohr, who covered it gavel-to-gavel, as offering "an extraordinary window into the workings of one of the world's most important, influential and indisputably interesting companies—and into the often brilliant, sometimes foolish, always aggressive men who steered its ambitious course."

The government charged Microsoft with having monopolized the market for personal computer operating systems and having illegally excluded competition to protect its monopoly, all in violation of the Sherman Act. The trial court found Microsoft guilty of monopolization and ordered it broken into separate companies, one for operating systems and the other for software applications. The Court of Appeals for the D.C. Circuit unanimously upheld the monopolization finding but vacated the break-up order and directed consideration of alternative remedies.

Brinkley and Lohr observed that the case "stood to affect almost everyone who uses a computer" and as "likely to set rules that lay out the antitrust limits for the new economy." In 2007, antitrust law scholars William Page and John Lopatka agreed with that estimation, noting that "*Microsoft* was the defining antitrust case of our era, and will be the focus of scholarly discussion about the proper role of antitrust for years to come." Although Microsoft survived intact, it soon became the target of many private antitrust suits and faced major antitrust investigations from regulators in the European Union; it has been required to pay significant fines for its business practices there.

SEE ALSO The Sherman Antitrust Act (1890); Busting the Trusts (1911); The Clayton Antitrust Act (1914); Creation of the European Union (1993).

The U.S. government charged Microsoft, the target of numerous private antitrust suits, with violating the Sherman Antitrust Act and found the company guilty of monopolistic practices.

Golf Carts on the PGA Tour

Casey Martin (b. 1972), *PGA Tour, Inc. v. Martin*

When golfers complain about their handicap, they're usually not referring to a physical impairment. But professional golfer Casey Martin forever changed the rules of the game for the disabled when he successfully challenged the Professional Golfers' Association (PGA) Tour prohibition on using motorized golf carts while playing on tour.

Mark Twain once called golf "a good walk spoiled," but historically the PGA Tour required all golfers to walk the full course. During the standard eighteen-hole round, an average golfer walks approximately six miles. Martin—who suffers from a birth defect known as Klippel-Trenaunay-Weber syndrome, in which blood vessels fail to form properly resulting in limited circulation and intense pain—requested that he be allowed a golf cart during professional tournaments. The PGA denied his request, insisting that walking was a fundamental part of the game.

Martin filed suit under the Americans with Disabilities Act (ADA) claiming that the PGA Tour was a commercial enterprise, that golf courses constituted "public accommodations," and that the PGA failed to make a reasonable modification to its practices to accommodate his disability. The PGA countered that the play areas of its tournament golf courses weren't places of "public accommodation" within the scope of the ADA and that walking was a substantive rule of golf, waiver of which would fundamentally alter the nature of the competition.

The lower courts both agreed that Martin was entitled to reasonable accommodation and a cart. The Supreme Court also sided with Martin, holding that the denial of access to a golf cart during tournaments violated the ADA, rejecting the PGA argument that use of a cart would fundamentally alter tournament play. The Court reasoned that a fundamental alteration would occur only if an essential aspect of the game was changed or if an alteration gave a disabled competitor an advantage over nondisabled players. It concluded that because the essence of the game of golf involved shot-making, walking wasn't an essential attribute and that the trial court already had determined that use of a cart wouldn't unfairly advantage Martin.

SEE ALSO The Americans with Disabilities Act (1990).

A line of golf carts awaiting their battery charge before a day's rounds begin.

Expanded Copyrights

New York Times Co. v. Tasini

Throughout the 1990s, unprecedented technological growth gave rise to questions about how established legal principles would apply in the Age of Information. The proliferation of personal computers, the spread of Internet access, and the development of electronic publication platforms raised many issues implicating copyright law.

Traditionally, freelance journalists granted publishers the right to reproduce their articles in print publications. As technology progressed, however, publishers sought to provide additional access to these articles in digital format, a new medium. But who owned the right to electronic publication? Did the original freelance agreements, often silent on the subject of electronic rights, give publishers the right to control online publication in databases, or did the change in medium require new agreements with and additional compensation for freelance journalists?

Jonathan Tasini was the president of the National Writers' Union and one of six freelance writers who sued the *New York Times* and the proprietors of electronic databases that reproduced digital versions of the *Times*. The *Times* and the databases relied on section 201(c) of the Copyright Act, which allows a publisher of a collective work, like an issue of the *Times*, to reproduce and distribute that work but only as a collective work. Because the databases made available individual articles rather than entire newspaper issues, the collective-work privilege was inapplicable. The Supreme Court answered the ownership question in favor of freelance journalists. The ruling expanded copyright law because, instead of a single right to publication covering print and digital outlets, journalists now held two separate rights defined by an article's medium.

The impact of the *Tasini* decision remains evident. Today, all contracts involving the publication of copyrightable works explicitly address electronic publication separately from print publication. Meanwhile, electronic database users sometimes discover that articles published in print aren't available electronically. In most cases, these "missing" articles result from the lack of an explicit grant of electronic publication rights to a particular database.

SEE ALSO America's First Copyright Law (1790); The Berne Convention (1878); The Copyright Act of 1976; Copyright in the Digital Age (1999); Google Books and Fair Use (2010).

U.S. Supreme Court Justice Sonia Sotomayor ruled in favor of the New York Times Co. in 1997 when she served as a judge of the U.S. District Court for the Southern District of New York. The decision was reversed on appeal and the authors' victory was then upheld by the Supreme Court.

The USA PATRIOT Act

On September 11, 2001, four passenger planes hijacked by al-Qaeda terrorists crashed into the World Trade Center towers, the Pentagon, and a field near Shanksville, Pennsylvania, killing a total of 2,977 victims. In the wake of that horrific tragedy, Congress passed the Uniting and Strengthening America by Providing Appropriate Tools Required to Intercept and Obstruct Terrorism (USA PATRIOT) Act. For years it has polarized a nation struggling with concerns for security on the one hand and threats to privacy on the other.

Once described as "perhaps the longest, broadest, most sweeping piece of legislation in American history," the USA PATRIOT Act reflected unified congressional effort to combat terrorism by enhancing law enforcement agencies' surveillance and investigative powers. Congress passed it with overwhelming support: 357–66 in the House and 98–1 in the Senate, but critics have challenged the unorthodox nature of its passage. It had little federal agency review, no public hearings, no committee markup, no Conference Committee Report, little floor debate, and almost no time for review of the final bill before Congress voted, imparting a legacy of controversy to the legislation.

Two of the Act's core and most controversial provisions gave law enforcement agencies additional powers to monitor and intercept electronic communications that might relate to terrorist activities. This provision enhanced powers long available under the Foreign Intelligence Surveillance Act and the Electronic Communications Privacy Act. The new act permits electronic surveillance where a "significant purpose"—as opposed to the sole or primary purpose—is to gather foreign intelligence. Second, it permits "roving" surveillance of individuals, not limited to a single telephone or computer.

So as not to grant law enforcement officials a perpetual license to spy on whomever they wanted, the Act also included a four-year sunset stipulation. In 2005, Congress enacted the USA PATRIOT Improvement and Reauthorization Act, which made permanent most of the expiring provisions of the original act and adopted a new sunset date for the two most controversial sections. At time of press, the current expiration date for those sections was June 1, 2015. The debate over the Act is sure to persist as the nation continues to negotiate a balance between civil liberties and national security.

SEE ALSO The Right to Privacy (1890); Wiretaps (1928).

Sailors assigned to the guided-missile destroyer USS Michael Murphy salute the 9/11 Memorial on October 1, 2012.

The Sarbanes-Oxley Act

Paul Sarbanes (b. 1933), **Michael Oxley** (b. 1944)

Since passage of the securities acts in 1933 and 1934, the federal government has required full and accurate financial disclosure as the principal means of protecting investors and shareholders from corporate malfeasance. In 2001, the Enron Corporation collapsed after a long period of questionable record-keeping and poor financial reporting. It was the biggest corporate bankruptcy and auditing failure of its time, and the American energy company became a fixture in headlines worldwide.

Enron officials skirted their disclosure obligations through misleading accounting practices and by pressuring company auditors to remain silent. Doing so led not only to Enron's bankruptcy but also to the dissolution of Arthur Andersen LLP, at the time one of the five largest accounting and auditing firms in the world. A $40 billion investor lawsuit as well as criminal prosecutions followed, resulting in the imprisonment of high-ranking Enron officials.

In the aftermath of the Enron fiasco and other corporate scandals involving inaccurate financial reporting, the federal government intervened. In 2002, Congress passed the Sarbanes-Oxley Act, which set forth new rules on how companies were to maintain their records and report financial information publicly. The act required enhanced accounting oversight, prohibited auditors from furnishing non-audit services (to alleviate potential conflicts of interest), and restricted board membership on the audit committee to independent directors only. It also required personal attestation from CEOs and financial officers as to the accuracy of financial reports. These provisions were designed to protect shareholders against breaches of fiduciary duties by directors and to reassure investors of the safety of investing in American corporations.

Sarbanes-Oxley became law over a decade ago, but debate about its merits still rages. Supporters view it as promoting corporate responsibility and accountability. Opponents, however, point to the costs of full compliance with the act's complex requirements, estimated at about $2 million per company each year, as too high a burden, ultimately impacting all consumers through higher prices and also discouraging successful private ventures from going public.

SEE ALSO The Bubble Act (1720); Corporate Personhood and Liability (1897); Busting the Trusts (1911); Wall Street Regulation (1933); Wall Street Reform (2010).

Enron's logo sculpture in front of the company's corporate headquarters in Houston, Texas.

The International Criminal Court

Following the Nuremberg trials, the United Nations International Law Commission contemplated creating a permanent tribunal to handle similar international criminal cases in the future. At the time, the General Assembly was involved in ongoing negotiations that led to the 1948 Convention on the Prevention and Punishment of the Crime of Genocide. Those negotiations included debate over universal jurisdiction for international crimes, but the final convention failed to achieve agreement on that point. The Cold War then impeded further progress.

Renewed efforts began in the early 1980s and continued into the 1990s as the U.N. confronted the criminality of South African apartheid. In 1994, the U.N. Security Council established the International Criminal Tribunal for the Former Yugoslavia (ICTY) and the International Criminal Tribunal for Rwanda. Former Yugoslavian dictator Slobodan Milošević was indicted in 1999 and stood trial before the ICTY beginning in 2002, becoming the first head of state ever to face trial before an international criminal tribunal. He died in his cell in 2006, before the trial ended. International law scholar William Schabas notes that these "so-called ad hoc tribunals became a kind of laboratory for international criminal justice."

In 1995, the General Assembly created a Preparatory Committee on the Establishment of an International Criminal Court, which led to a 1998 diplomatic conference in Rome. At the conclusion of the conference, twenty-six countries signed what became the Rome Statute, creating the International Criminal Court. After ratification by sixty member nations, the Rome Statute entered into force on July 1, 2002. As of January 2015, 123 states had become parties.

Headquartered at The Hague, the court is independent and not a U.N. body. It prosecutes and tries those accused of genocide, crimes against humanity, and war crimes but only in cases where a member nation's judicial system hasn't itself pursued a prosecution. A little more than a decade into its existence, though, the court has yet to achieve the hoped-for results. Trials have been protracted, nations haven't always cooperated fully, and America thus far has refused to become a signatory.

SEE ALSO The Geneva Convention (1864); The Nuremberg Trials (1945); The U.N. Convention on Genocide (1948); The European Court of Human Rights (1959).

The International Criminal Court in The Hague, Netherlands.

Public Purpose and Eminent Domain

Kelo v. City of New London, **Susette Kelo** (b. 1956), **John Paul Stevens** (b. 1920)

In 1998, New London, Connecticut, embarked on a downtown waterfront redevelopment plan to create jobs, increase tax revenues, and revitalize the economically distressed city. The plan called for the purchase of private land. Although many residents willingly sold their land, Susette Kelo and eight other longtime property owners resisted, seeking a judicial ruling that the city's exercise of eminent domain constituted unlawful "takings" under the Constitution.

The Fifth Amendment holds that private property shall not be taken "for public use without just compensation." Because the land would be owned and operated by private parties and wasn't slated for public use, the Supreme Court examined whether the city's development plan served a "public purpose." Stressing the importance of federalism and the respect owed to state legislatures and courts in discerning local public needs, it found that the New London development plan fell within a traditionally broad understanding of "public purpose."

The Court concluded by noting that states could adopt legislative restrictions on local-government eminent domain. As constitutional scholar Jonathan L. Entin observed, "States accepted this invitation with alacrity," partly because the high court's decision generated a public furor. In a 2011 speech, retired justice John Paul Stevens acknowledged that *Kelo* was "the most unpopular opinion that I wrote during my thirty-four-year tenure on the Supreme Court." Legal scholars Robert Levy and William Mellor point out that "one year after *Kelo*, thirty-four states had enacted legislation that placed limits on previously unbridled authority."

Susette Kelo testified before the House Judiciary Committee Subcommittee on the Constitution and Civil Justice in April 2013 that, in a final insult, no development has taken place on the site, which "to this day remains a barren field, home to weeds and feral cats."

SEE ALSO The Superiority of Possession (1805); Rent Control (1946).

Susette Kelo in front of the famous little pink house in New London, Connecticut.

The Legality of Gun Control

District of Columbia v. Heller, McDonald v. Chicago

After the assassinations of President Kennedy, Malcolm X, Martin Luther King Jr., and Senator Robert Kennedy in fewer than five years, Congress passed the Gun Control Act of 1968, setting important restrictions on gun purchases. The confluence of these factors triggered a gun control debate that would continue for decades.

Between 1988 and 1992, notwithstanding that it had one of the strictest gun control laws in the country, the District of Columbia was called the murder capital of the United States, averaging roughly seventy-two murders per one hundred thousand residents in each of those years. It held that status again in 1996, 1998, and 1999. Dick Heller, a security officer authorized to carry a gun but not keep it at home, challenged the constitutionality of the D.C. statute. The Court of Appeals for the District of Columbia Circuit struck down the law. Hearing the case, the Supreme Court observed that "few laws in the history of our Nation have come close to the severe restriction of the District's handgun ban," which it found unconstitutional in that it violated the "inherent right of self-defense . . . central to the Second Amendment right." The Court's decision vindicated the individual-rights view of the Second Amendment, which, it held, protected an individual's right to own a gun for personal protection.

Two years later the Court ruled in *McDonald v. Chicago* that the Second Amendment applies to the states, thereby requiring state gun control laws to accommodate Second Amendment rights. But since the *Heller* and *McDonald* decisions, America has witnessed an unimaginable spree of mass shootings, many involving schools and children. A December 2012 report from *ABC News,* days after twenty-seven people were shot and killed at Sandy Hook Elementary School in Newtown, Connecticut, noted that since the 1999 massacre of thirteen people at Columbine High School, there have been thirty-one school shootings in the U.S. There were an additional eight school shootings in 2013 and 2014, with a total of thirteen deaths. Those events have heightened the gun debate, prompting new laws, which likely will lead to new legal challenges. Whether the Supreme Court will revisit the meaning of the Second Amendment remains to be seen.

SEE ALSO The U.S. Constitution (1787); The Bill of Rights (1791); Militias and the Right to Bear Arms (1939).

Supreme Court precedents that uphold citizens' rights to own and possess firearms in the face of restrictive state statutes haven't ended the debate over the Second Amendment.

Google Books and Fair Use

Authors Guild v. Google

The Internet has revolutionized our world. From communication to commerce, education to entertainment, it has transformed and continues to transform everything, including what we read and how we read it. Google Books stands at the forefront of that transformation. As James Grimmelmann, a noted scholar of copyright law in the digital age, explains, "We're living through the biggest shift in publishing since the invention of printing, and the biggest shift in copyright since the invention of copyright. The law is going to play a huge role in how we manage the transition."

In 2004, Google partnered with major academic libraries to scan and digitize their collections to develop an online corpus of books accessible to users through Internet searches. Although the entirety of each book is searchable, only bibliographic information about books still copyrighted, along with short excerpts or snippets, is displayed. Searchers have the option to buy the book or borrow it from a local library, which Google facilitates through online links. Only books by consenting authors or with expired copyrights—therefore in the public domain—are available in their entirety.

In 2005, the Authors Guild and the Association of American Publishers filed a class action lawsuit alleging that Google Books was infringing thousands of copyrights. Google argued that it was engaging in "fair use" under the copyright laws and therefore not infringing. In 2008, the parties announced a proposed settlement agreement, which required court approval. The court rejected the agreement in 2011.

By mid-2013, Google had scanned more than thirty million books. Later that year, U.S. Circuit Judge Denny Chin dismissed the suit, finding that the Google Books project comports with fair-use criteria. In December 2013, the Authors Guild appealed the ruling to the U.S. Second Circuit and the appeal was argued on December 3, 2014. It's unclear what the ultimate result will be or when it will arrive, but there's no question that it will have a far-reaching impact on the further development of copyright law.

SEE ALSO The Statute of Anne (1710); America's First Copyright Law (1790); The Berne Convention (1878); Copyright Act of 1976; Time-Shifting and Fair Use (1984); Copyright in the Digital Age (1999); Expanded Copyrights (2001).

The Google Books search engine offers access to scanned pages of more than thirty million books, although only books with consenting authors or expired copyrights can be viewed in their entirety. Whether Google Books is infringing on copyrights will depend on how the U.S. Second Circuit defines "fair use."

Google™
Book Search BETA

earch: ⦿ All books ○ Full view books

earch the full text of books and discover new ones

Wall Street Reform

Christopher Dodd (b. 1944), **Barney Frank** (b. 1940), **Barack Obama** (b. 1961)

During the Great Depression, Congress enacted laws designed to regulate the financial services industry and to foreclose even the possibility that the country's economic stability could crumble again. That regulatory scheme proved relatively satisfactory for nearly eighty years. But a series of financial disruptions in fall 2008 propelled the entire system to the brink of collapse.

Years of ballooning housing prices spurred riskier lending, resulting in a subprime mortgage market and then an unimaginable number of defaults. Financial firms suffered multiplying losses: Lehman Brothers disintegrated; Fannie Mae and Freddie Mac went into government conservatorship; Merrill Lynch and AIG barely averted bankruptcy by a fire sale and an $85 billion Federal Reserve loan respectively. The regulatory system had failed, and the Great Recession had begun.

In July 2009, Treasury Secretary Timothy Geithner issued a regulatory reform plan, which Congress used as a template to supply new bulwarks. A year later, President Obama signed into law the Dodd-Frank Wall Street Reform and Consumer Protection Act, the most sweeping financial reform legislation since the 1930s. The 848-page document dwarfed the three principal post-Depression enactments. Even more daunting were the rules it required to be developed and enforced by the SEC, the CFTC, the FDIC, the Federal Reserve, and two new agencies: the Financial Services Oversight Council (FSOC) and the Consumer Financial Protection Bureau (CFPB).

Dodd-Frank created the FSOC to subject "systemically significant" firms to increased "prudential" regulation, including limits on leverage, increased capital standards, and checks on forms of risky trading; created the CFPB to oversee consumer protection; required more derivatives to be cleared and traded on regulated exchanges; imposed new registration and reporting requirements for hedge funds; required credit rating agencies to provide greater disclosure and subjected them to legal liability provisions; prohibited proprietary trading by U.S. banks; regulated executive compensation; and mandated new standards governing investment services for retail customers.

By mid-2013, regulators had published close to fourteen thousand pages of rules, but they still hadn't finished issuing the called-for regulations.

SEE ALSO The Federal Reserve Act (1913); Wall Street Regulation (1933); The Securities Exchange Act (1934).

Heavily armed NYPD officers stand guard at the New York Stock Exchange near Wall Street.

The Future of Juvenile Punishment

John DiIulio (b. 1958), *Roper v. Simmons, Graham v. Florida, Miller v. Alabama*

Through the latter half of the twentieth century, America witnessed an increase in violent juvenile crime. The escalation certainly merited concern, but some painted the situation as a full-blown epidemic. In 1995, then Princeton professor John DiIulio coined the term "superpredators" to describe a "new breed" of juvenile criminals who "had absolutely no respect for human life and no sense of the future." His strident theory frightened the public, who looked to lawmakers for protection. A 2011 Department of Justice Office of Juvenile Justice and Delinquency Prevention report details that by the late 1990s "legislatures in nearly every state expanded transfer laws that allowed or required the prosecution of juveniles in adult criminal courts." These transfer laws exposed juveniles to the threat of life imprisonment and the death penalty.

But as new research began to undermine the superpredator myth and the doomsday projections about juvenile crime, a societal backlash followed. States began to turn away from trying juveniles as adults, and many (including Connecticut, Massachusetts, North Carolina, and Wisconsin) introduced legislation raising the maximum age of juvenile court jurisdiction. Even DiIulio himself acknowledged having an "epiphany." In a 2001 *New York Times* article, he conceded that his superpredator theory had been discredited.

Then, from 2005 to 2012, the Supreme Court handed down three milestone decisions that reflected society's change of heart in regard to juvenile sentencing. In *Roper v. Simmons* (2005), the Court held that imposing the death penalty on juveniles constituted cruel and unusual punishment. Building on *Roper*, the Court went further in *Graham v. Florida* (2010) and *Miller v. Alabama* (2012), declaring it unconstitutional to sentence juveniles to life imprisonment without the possibility of parole. In each opinion, the Court relied on psychological studies that proved juveniles lack the maturity to understand fully the consequences of their actions.

DiIulio now takes part in efforts to help misguided youths, and in light of these three decisions, the juvenile sentencing paradigm for the twenty-first century has shifted from punishment and retribution to rehabilitation.

SEE ALSO Banning the Death Penalty (1972); The Death Penalty Returns (1976).

Psychological studies suggesting that juveniles lack the maturity to understand the full consequences of their actions played a role in the shift away from punishment and toward rehabilitation in juvenile sentencing.

The Affordable Care Act

Barack Obama (b. 1961), **John Roberts** (b. 1955), *King v. Burwell*

Myriad cases have gone before the U.S. Supreme Court since, in 1849, Chief Justice Roger Taney limited oral argument to two hours per side (halved in 1925 and again in 1970). The Court has allowed only a handful of exceptions. The nearly six hours allotted for argument in the Patient Protection and Affordable Care Act (ACA) case in February 2012 represents the longest exception in over half a century.

Broadly, the ACA sought to increase Americans' access to health insurance coverage and to expand Medicaid coverage, laudatory goals that proved spectacularly controversial. President Obama signed the ACA into law on March 23, 2010, just before noon. Seven minutes later, thirteen states filed suit to challenge the law's constitutionality. Another thirteen states later joined, along with several business interests. The district court and the Eleventh Circuit Court of Appeals both struck down the act as unconstitutional (on different grounds), but, in a decision that surprised and perplexed pundits, the Supreme Court upheld the law. Constitutional scholars Nathaniel Persily, Gillian Metzger, and Trevor Morrison wrote that "no one foresaw the strange coalition of justices and rationales that would uphold some parts of the law, strike down others, and offer new interpretations to four different constitutional sources of federal power."

Chief Justice John Roberts's majority opinion held that the mandate—that all individuals obtain health insurance—fell within Congress's power to levy taxes. The same didn't hold true, however, with respect to the commerce clause or the necessary and proper clause. Those clauses, the Court found, had limits exceeded by a statute through which Congress wasn't regulating commerce but rather ordering "individuals to engage in it." The Court also found the act's coercion of states to expand Medicaid as a condition to receiving federal funds invalid under the Constitution's spending clause.

A fundamental tenet of medicine is the principle "do no harm," often attributed erroneously to Hippocrates. Ironically, the most trenchant criticism that the ACA has attracted is the harm it would cause and has caused to the health care system. Efforts to undo the ACA likely will continue, but in June 2015 the Supreme Court again upheld the act's validity despite finding it to contain "more than a few examples of inartful drafting."

SEE ALSO Congressional Regulation of Commerce (1824); Congressional Power to Tax Income (1909); Health Care and the Duty to Warn (1976); Stem Cell and Cloning Legislation (1995).

President Obama's campaign for reelection heavily stressed the benefits of the Affordable Care Act. Here the Obama and Biden families embrace onstage following Obama's speech at the 2012 Democratic National Convention in Charlotte, North Carolina.

The Legal Fight for Gay Marriage

Goodridge v. Department of Public Health, Obergefell v. Hodges

In June 2003, the Supreme Court in *Lawrence v. Texas* struck down Texas's sodomy law, thereby decriminalizing consensual sexual activity between gay male adults nationwide. Five months later, the Massachusetts Supreme Judicial Court became the first state high court to declare denying gay couples the right to marry unlawful under its state constitution. For the gay community, the Massachusetts decision in *Goodridge v. Department of Public Health* came after more than three decades of fighting for legal recognition of what they considered a fundamental civil right.

The Court construed civil marriage as "the voluntary union of two persons as spouses, to the exclusion of all others," which it called a "reformulation" that "furthers the aim of marriage to promote stable, exclusive relationships," thereby advancing legitimate state interests. The Massachusetts court found support in *Lawrence*'s references to the Fourteenth Amendment, which precluded "government intrusion into the deeply personal realms of consensual adult expressions of intimacy."

The Massachusetts court stayed its decision to give the legislature time to achieve a resolution. It also issued an advisory opinion rejecting a proposed compromise making gay civil unions lawful. Despite vigorous efforts, the legislature didn't put forward a legislative solution. At 12:01 A.M. on May 17, 2004, Cambridge City Hall opened to applicants for marriage licenses and issued them that morning to more than 260 couples, making Massachusetts the first state to legally solemnize gay marriage.

Critics lambasted the decision for containing "virtually no legal analysis" and for reflecting "judges' personal policy preferences." Nevertheless, the ruling dramatically impacted the gay marriage debate, inspiring thousands of gay couples to apply for marriage licenses. But it also galvanized opponents to seek political relief through state constitutional amendments that limited marriage to the union of a man and a woman.

On the anniversaries of *Lawrence v. Texas* and *United States v. Windsor*, the latter of which required federal recognition of state-licensed same-sex marriages, the Supreme Court ruled in *Obergefell v. Hodges* that the right to marry is a "fundamental right inherent in the liberty of the person" and that the due process clause of the Fourteenth Amendment guarantees gay couples the right to marry.

SEE ALSO The First Ban on Gay Marriage (1973); The First Gay Marriage Laws (1989).

In 2008, protesters in Sacramento voiced their objections to the passage of Proposition 8, which banned gay marriage in California with a referendum-based state constitutional amendment. A federal court later overturned the legislation.

Acknowledgments

To paraphrase Oliver Wendell Holmes Jr., the life of this book has not been logic; it has been experience—and what an experience it's been. It began with my dear cousin and agent, Al Zuckerman, who offered me the opportunity to submit the proposal for this book to Sterling. His favorable reaction to it both gratified and inspired me, and I remain immensely grateful for his steadfast support thereafter.

Many others deserve acknowledgment for their help in making this book happen. I was fortunate to have the enthusiastic assistance of a number of now-former New York Law School students working as research assistants. Their talents were many, and they all provided invaluable help with early research and drafting. I am indebted especially to Meghan Lalonde, Taylor Morris, and Lauren Majchrowski. They each cheerfully poured their hearts and souls into their respective efforts, all of which I deeply appreciate. My sincere thanks as well to Rena Malik and Gillad Matiteyahu for their important contributions.

I am fortunate to have been able to draw upon the rich resources of the Mendik Library at New York Law School, under the direction of Camille Broussard, and many other libraries as well, including the New York State Library, the Library of Congress, the Olin Library at Washington University in St. Louis, and countless others. Additional thanks to my current and former Mendik Library colleagues who answered questions, helped me find or borrow what I required, and stood in for me when needed. More than that, they tolerated my occasional mental absence. A special thanks goes to Farrah Nagrampa, who was there from the very beginning, often on her own time, undertaking whatever task was at hand, always with her usual alacrity and adeptness.

Two exceptional editors at Sterling Publishing, James Jayo and Melanie Madden, deserve special praise and sincere thanks. James—whose wide-ranging knowledge and expertise spared me more than one potentially embarrassing error—was an astute and thoughtful editor, uncluttering my prose, sharpening its focus, and generally righting whatever unbalanced phrases I had left behind. Melanie championed this project from the very beginning, artfully guiding it with a steady hand all the way. I also thank copyeditor Katherine Furman and photo editor Alexandra Brodsky for their significant contributions.

Many friends and close family members provided much needed fortification throughout the process. They never tired of asking how it was going and supplied inspiration and encouragement when it was needed most. I am immensely grateful for their friendship, love, and support. I'm especially grateful to Howard and Rita for their affection and generosity.

My daughter, Jillian, about to enter law school herself, helped research and draft early versions of two entries. Her words of encouragement, including those she memorialized on the face of a clock that looks down at me every day—*Write Now*—eased the process and always brought a smile to my face. My son, Ben, our resident photographer, provided images and expert suggestions for many entries as well as deliverance from technological purgatory. For all of their efforts, interest, and so much more, I will always be indescribably proud. I look forward to all of their many milestones yet to come. Finally, I am singularly indebted to my wife, Susan, in more ways than imaginable. Only her patience and understanding exceed her insights and judgment. Without her, none of this would have been possible.

Notes and Further Reading

From the numerous books, articles, journals, court cases, legal documents, online publications, and more consulted during the writing of this book, here are the best and most frequently used sources.

General Reading

Aitken, Robert, and Marilyn Aitken. *Law Makers, Law Breakers and Uncommon Trials*. Chicago: American Bar Association, 2007.

Chiasson, Lloyd, ed. *The Press on Trial: Crimes and Trials as Media Events*. Westport: Greenwood Press, 1997.

Ciment, James, ed. *Encyclopedia of American Immigration*. Armonk: M.E. Sharpe, 2001.

Dickler, Gerald. *Man on Trial: History-Making Trials from Socrates to Oppenheimer*. Garden City: Doubleday, 1962.

Encyclopædia Britannica Online; www.britannica.com.

Hall, Kermit, and James W. Ely Jr. *The Oxford Guide to United States Supreme Court Decisions*. New York: Oxford University Press, 2009.

Harris, Brian. *Injustice: State Trials from Socrates to Nuremburg*. Stroud: Sutton Publishing, 2006.

Hutchinson, Allan. *Is Eating People Wrong? Great Legal Cases and How They Shaped the World*. Cambridge: Cambridge University Press, 2011.

Johnson, Dennis. *The Laws That Shaped America: Fifteen Acts of Congress and Their Lasting Impact*. New York: Routledge, 2009.

Katz, Stanley, ed. *The Oxford International Encyclopedia of Legal History*. Online edition, 2012.

Knappman, Edward, ed. *Great American Trials*. 2 vols. Detroit: Gale Group, 2002.

Lieberman, Jethro Koller. *A Practical Companion to the Constitution*. Berkeley, CA: University of California Press, 1999.

Linder, Douglas. *Famous Trials*. http://law2.umkc.edu/faculty/projects/ftrials/ftrials.html.

Mikula, Mark, and L. Mpho Mabunda, eds. *Great American Court Cases*. 4 vols. Farmington Hills: Gale Group, 1999.

Seagle, William. *Men of Law, From Hammurabi to Holmes*. New York: Macmillan, 1947.

Shaffern, Robert. *Law and Justice from Antiquity to Enlightenment*. Lanham: Rowman & Littlefield Publishers, 2009.

Tanenhaus, David, ed. *Encyclopedia of the Supreme Court of the United States*. Detroit: Macmillan Reference, 2008.

VerSteeg, Russ. *Law in the Ancient World*. Durham: Carolina Academic Press, 2002.

White, G. Edward. *Law in American History: Volume 1: From the Colonial Years through the Civil War*. New York: Oxford University Press, 2012.

Zane, John Maxcy. *The Story of Law*. 2nd ed. Indianapolis: Liberty Fund, 1998.

2550 BCE, The Oldest Written Will

Harris, Virgil. *Ancient, Curious and Famous Wills*. Boston: Little Brown. 1911.

New York Times. "Oldest of Known Wills: Unearthed at Kahun, in Egypt, by Mr. Petrie." February 2, 1890, p. 14.

2100 BCE, The Code of Ur-Nammu

Feldbrugge, F. J. M., ed., *The Law's Beginnings*. Leiden: Martinus Nijhoff, 2003. See p. 137, Veenhof, K., "Before Hammurabi of Babylon. Law and the Laws in Early Mesopotamia."

Kramer, S. N. "The Ur-Nammu Law Code: Who Was Its Author?" *Orientalia*, vol. 52 (1983): 453–56.

1792 BCE, The Code of Hammurabi

Harper, Robert Francis. *The Code of Hammurabi King of Babylon*. Chicago: University of Chicago Press, 1904.

Miller, William. *Eye for An Eye*. Cambridge: Cambridge University Press, 2006.

1300 BCE, The Ten Commandments

Dershowitz, Alan. *The Genesis of Justice*. New York: Warner Books, 2000.

621 BCE, The Draconian Code

Freeman, Morton. *A New Dictionary of Eponyms*. Oxford Reference Online, 2012.

von Dornum, Deirdre Dionysia. "The Straight and the Crooked: Legal Accountability in Ancient Greece." *Columbia Law Review*, vol. 97, no. 5 (1997): 1483–1518.

594 BCE, The Laws of Solon

Maine, Henry. *Ancient Law*. New Brunswick, NJ: Transaction Publishers, 2002.

Pharr, Ralph. "Solon and the Greek Legal System." *Mercer Law Review*, vol. 20 (1969): 443.

480 BCE, The Gortyn Code

Gagarin, Michael. "The Organization of the Gortyn Law Code." *Greek, Roman, and Byzantine Studies*, vol. 23 (1982): 129–46.

Roby, H. J., "The Twelve Tables of Gortyn." *Law Quarterly Review*, vol. 2 (1886): 135–52.

450 BCE, The Twelve Tables

Madden, M. Stuart. "Integrating Comparative Law Concepts into the First Year Curriculum: Torts." *Journal of Legal Education*, vol. 56, no. 4 (2006): 560–77.

Maine, Henry. *Ancient Law*. New Brunswick, NJ: Transaction Publishers, 2002.

399 BCE, The Trial of Socrates

D'Amato, Anthony. "Obligation to Obey the Law: A Study of the Death of Socrates." *Southern California Law Review* (1976): 1079.

Hermann, Donald. "Socrates on Justice and Legal Obligation." *Seton Hall Law Review*, vol. 11 (1981): 663.

180, The Talmud

Glenn, H. Patrick. *Legal Traditions of the World*. Oxford: Oxford University Press, 2000.

Hecht, N. S., et al., *An Introduction to the History and Sources of Jewish Law*. Oxford: Oxford University Press, 1976.

250, The First Law School

Chroust, Anton-Hermann. "Legal Education in Ancient Rome," *Journal of Legal Education*, vol. 7 (1955): 509.

Lawler, Andrew. "Rebuilding Beirut." *Archaeology*, vol. 64, no. 4 (2011).

McNamee, Kathleen. "Another Chapter in the History of Scholia." *The Classical Quarterly*, vol. 48, no. 1 (1998): 269–88.

250, The Brehon Laws of Ireland

Ginnell, Laurence. *The Brehon Laws: A Legal Handbook*. London: T. Fisher Unwin, 1894.

Gorman, M. J. "The Ancient Brehon Laws of Ireland." *University of Pennsylvania Law Review*, vol. 61, no. 4 (1913): 217–33.

529, The Justinian Code

Berman, Harold. "The Origins of Western Legal Science." *Harvard Law Review*, vol. 90 (1976): 894.

Merryman, John, and Rogelio Perez-Perdomo. *The Civil Law Tradition: An Introduction to the Legal Systems of Europe and Latin America*. 3rd ed. Stanford: Stanford University Press, 2007.

561, The Irish Copyright War

Adamnan, St. *The Historians of Scotland, Vol. VI*. Edinburgh: Edmonston and Douglas, 1874. See esp. "Life of Saint Columba, Founder of Hy."

Menzies, Lucy. *Saint Columba of Iona*. London: J.M. Dent & Sons, Ltd., 1920.

624, The Tang Code

Johnson, Wallace. *The T'ang Code, Vols. I and II*. Princeton: Princeton University Press, 1979.

652, The Quran

Bhala, Raj. *Understanding Islamic Law*. New Providence: Matthew Bender & Co., 2011.

Hallaq, Wael. *An Introduction to Islamic Law*. Cambridge: Cambridge University Press, 2009.

1140, Canon Law and the *Decretum Gratiani*

Berman, Harold. "The Origins of Western Legal Science." *Harvard Law Review*, vol. 90 (1976): 894.

Coughlin, John. *Canon Law: A Comparative Study with Anglo-American Legal Theory*. Oxford: Oxford University Press, 2011.

1166, The Assize of Clarendon

Helmholz, Richard. "The Early History of the Grand Jury and the Canon Law." *University of Chicago Law Review*, vol. 50 (1983): 613–27.

Schiappa, Susan. "Preserving the Autonomy and Function of the Grand Jury: *United States v. Williams*." *Catholic University Law Review*, vol. 43 (1993): 311.

1200, *Lex Mercatoria*

Basile, Mary Elizabeth, ed. and trans., et al., *Lex Mercatoria and Legal Pluralism: A Late Thirteenth-Century Treatise and Its Afterlife*. Cambridge: The Ames Foundation, 1998.

Donahue Jr., Charles. "Medieval and Early Modern *Lex Mercatoria*: An Attempt at the *Probatio Diabolica*." *Chicago Journal of International Law*, vol. 5 (2005): 21.

1215, The Magna Carta

Howard, A. E. Dick. *Magna Carta, Text and Commentary*. Charlottesville: University Press of Virginia, 1964.

Podgers, James. "The 800-Year Reunion." *ABA Journal*, vol. 98 (2012): 60.

1275, The Statutes of Westminster

Plucknett, Theodore. *Studies in English Legal History*. London: The Hambledon Press, 1983.

Stubbs, William. *The Constitutional History of England in Its Origin and Development*. 4th ed. Oxford: Clarendon Press, 1896.

1350, The Star Chamber

Barnes, Thomas. "Star Chamber Mythology." *The American Journal of Legal History*, vol. 5, no. 1 (1961): 1–11.

Clapp, James, et al., *Lawtalk: The Unknown Stories Behind Familiar Legal Expressions*. New Haven: Yale University Press, 2011.

1431, The Trial of Joan of Arc

Frank, John P. "The Trial of Joan of Arc." *Litigation*, vol. 23 (1996): 51.

Tiefenbrun, Susan. "Why the Medieval Trial of Joan of Arc Is of Particular Interest Today." *Journal of Law and Religion*, vol. 21 (2005/2006): 469.

1481, Littleton's *Tenures*

Bracton, Gascoigne, Fortescue, and Littleton. "Notices of Early English Lawyers." *Law Magazine or Quarterly Review of Jurisprudence*, vol. 26 (1841): 267.

Luther, Peter. "Littleton and the Poets, A Literary Footnote to a Legal Text." *Nottingham Legal Journal*, vol. 5 (1996): 21.

1492, The Alhambra Decree

Ajami, Fouad. "The Other 1492: Jews and Muslims in Columbus's Spain." *The New Republic*, April 6, 1992, 22–25.

Katz, William. "Columbus and the American Holocaust." *The New York Amsterdam News*, October 9–15, 2003.

1527, *Les Termes de la Lay*

Cowley, J. D. "Some Early Dictionaries of English Law." *Juridical Review*, vol. 36 (1924): 165.

Yates, Sarah. "Black's Law Dictionary: The Making of an American Standard." *Law Library Journal*, vol. 103 (2011): 175–98.

1601, An Act for the Relief of the Poor

Fowle, T. W. *The Poor Law*. Littleton: F.B. Rothman, 1980.

Rosenheim, Margaret. "Vagrancy Concepts in Welfare Law." *California Law Review*, vol. 54 (1966): 511.

1616, Compulsory Education Law

Soysal, Yasemine Nuhoglu, and David Strang. "Construction of the First Mass Education Systems in Nineteenth-Century Europe." *Sociology of Education*, vol. 62 (1989): 277–88.

World Heritage Encyclopedia Online, "School Establishment Act 1616."

1625, *On the Law of War and Peace*

Dugard, John. "Grotius, the Jurist and International Lawyer: Four Hundred Years On." *South African Law Journal*, vol. 100 (1983): 213.

Reeves, Jesse. "The Life and Work of Hugo Grotius." *American Society of International Law Proceedings*, vol. 19 (1925): 48.

1629, The First Blue Laws

Boswell, Brown Hill. "Note, Sunday Laws." *North Carolina Law Review*, vol. 43 (1964): 123–54.

Clapp, James, et al., *Lawtalk: The Unknown Stories Behind Familiar Legal Expressions.* New Haven: Yale University Press, 2011.

1648, Peace of Westphalia

Croxton, Derek. "The Peace of Westphalia of 1648 and the Origins of Sovereignty," *International History Review,* vol. 21 (1999): 569.

Gross, Leo. "The Peace of Westphalia, 1648–1948." *American Journal of International Law,* vol. 42 (1948): 20–41.

Rowen, Herbert. "The Peace of Westphalia Revisited." *Journal of Modern History,* vol. 33 (1961): 53–56.

1651, *Leviathan*

Hobbes, Thomas. *Leviathan, or The Matter, Form and Power of a Commonwealth, Ecclesiastical and Civil.* 2nd ed. London: George Routledge and Sons, 1886.

Medina, Loreta. *The Creation of the U.S. Constitution.* Farmington Hills: Greenhaven Press, 2003.

1670, Bushel's Case

Mason, Wilmer. "The Four Jurors in Bushell's Case." *American Bar Association Journal,* vol. 51, no. 6 (1965): 543–47.

Nager, Barry. "The Jury That Tried William Penn." *American Bar Association Journal,* vol. 50 (1964): 168–70.

1679, The Habeas Corpus Act of 1679

Duker, William F. *A Constitutional History of Habeas Corpus.* Westport: Greenwood Press, 1980.

White, Edward G. *Law in American History, Vol. 1.* New York: Oxford University Press, 2012.

1685, The Black Code of Louis XIV

Palmer, Vernon Valentine. *The Louisiana Civilian Experience.* Durham: Carolina Academic Press, 2005.

Rodriguez, Junius P., ed. *The Historical Encyclopedia of World Slavery, Vol. 1.* Santa Barbara: ABC-CLIO, 1997. See esp. Chew, W. "Code Noir," 168–69.

1692, The Salem Witchcraft Trials

Louis-Jacques, Lyonette. "The Salem Witch Trials: A Legal Bibliography." *University of Chicago Library News Online,* October 29, 2012.

1695, Lapse of the Licensing Act

Hargreaves, Robert. *The First Freedom: A History of Free Speech.* Gloucestershire: Sutton Publishing Limited, 2002.

Siebert, Fredrick. *Freedom of the Press in England 1476–1776: The Rise and Decline of Government Control.* Urbana: University of Illinois Press, 1965.

1710, The Statute of Anne

Bently, Lionel., et al., *Global Copyright: Three Hundred Years Since the Statute of Anne, from 1709 to Cyberspace.* Cheltenham, UK: Edward Elgar Publishing Limited, 2010.

Patry, William F. *Copyright Law and Practice.* Washington, DC: Bureau of National Affairs, 2011.

1720, The Bubble Act

Patterson, Margaret, and David Reiffen. "The Effect of the Bubble Act on the Market for Joint Stock Shares." *Journal of Economic History,* vol. 50 (1990): 163.

Watzlaff, R. H. "The Bubble Act of 1720." *Abacus,* vol. 7 (1971): 8–28.

1735, The Trial of John Peter Zenger

Rutherford, Livingston. *John Peter Zenger: His Press, His Trial, and a Bibliography of Zenger Imprints.* New York: Dodd, Mead & Co., 1904.

1751, The Gin Act of 1751

Johnson, Frederic, and Ruth Kessler. "The Liquor License System: Its Origin and Constitutional Development." *New York University Law Quarterly Review,* vol. 15 (1937/1938): 210.

Randall, H. J. "The Evolution of the 'Pub'—A Sketch of the Earlier History of the Licensing Laws." *Law Quarterly Review,* vol. 20 (1904): 316.

1761, The Writs of Assistance Case

Stephens, Otis, and Richard Glenn. *Unreasonable Searches and Seizures: Rights and Liberties under the Law.* Santa Barbara: ABC-CLIO, Inc., 2006.

Trasewick, E. W. "Search Warrants and Writs of Assistance." *Criminal Law Quarterly,* vol. 5 (1962): 341.

1765, Blackstone's *Commentaries*

Lee, Duncan Campbell. "Blackstone." *American Bar Association Journal,* vol. 10 (1924): 395.

Lockmiller, David. "Sir William Blackstone." *Brief,* vol. 68 (1972/1973): 26.

1787, The U.S. Constitution

Beeman, Richard. *Plain, Honest Men: The Making of the Constitution.* New York: Random House, 2010.

Medina, Loreta. *The Creation of the U.S. Constitution.* Farmington Hills: Greenhaven Press, 2003.

1789, The Judiciary Act of 1789

Carp, Robert, and Ronald, Stidham. *The Federal Courts.* 4th ed. Washington, DC: Congressional Quarterly Press, 2001.

Marcus, Maeva., ed., *Origins of the Federal Judiciary, Esssays on the Judiciary Act of 1789.* New York: Oxford University Press, 1992.

1789, The Declaration of the Rights of Man

The French Declaration of the Rights of Man and of Citizen and the American Bill of Rights, A Bicentennial Issued Pursuant to S.J. Res. 317 100th Congress. Washington, DC: U.S. Congress, Senate, 1989.

Johnson, Vincent Robert. "The Declaration of the Rights of Man and of Citizens of 1789, the Reign of Terror, and the Revolutionary Tribunal of Paris." *Boston College International & Comparative Law Review,* vol. 1 (1990): 1.

1790, America's First Copyright Law

Patry, William. *Copyright Law and Practice.* Washington, DC: Bureau of National Affairs, 2011.

1791, The Bill of Rights

Powell Jr., Lewis. "Our Bill of Rights." *Indiana Law Review,* vol. 25 (1992): 937.

1792, The Coinage Act of 1792

Hepburn, Barton. *History of Coinage in the United States and the Perennial Contest for Sound Money.* New York: Macmillan, 1903.

Phillips Jr., Henry. *The Coinage of The United States of America.* Philadelphia: Horace Wemyss Smith, 1883.

1798, The Triple Assessment (Income Tax)
Grossfeld, Bernhard, and James Bryce. "A Brief Comparative History of the Origins of the Income Tax in Great Britain, Germany and the United States." *American Journal of Tax Policy*, vol. 2 (1983): 211.
Seligman, Edwin. *The Income Tax: A Study of the Theory and Practice of Income Taxation at Home and Abroad.* 2nd ed. New York: MacMillan Company, 1914.

1803, The Power of Judicial Review
Graber, Mark, and Michael Perhac, eds. *Marbury versus Madison: Documents and Commentary.* Washington, DC: CQ Press, 2002.
Hamilton, Alexander. "The Federalist, No. 78." 1788.

1804, The Napoleonic Code
Lobingier, Charles. "Napoleon and His Code." *Harvard Law Review*, vol. 32 (1918): 114–34.
Schwartz, Bernard. *The Code Napoleon and the Common-Law World.* New York: New York University Press, 1956.

1805, The Superiority of Possession
Pierson v. Post, 3 Cai. R. 175, 2 Am. Dec. 264 (N.Y. Sup. Ct. 1805).
Popov v. Hayashi, 2002 WL 31833731 (Cal. Sup. Crt. San Francisco City., Dec. 18, 2002).

1819 The Supremacy of Federal Law/ 1821 The Supremecy of Federal Courts
Cohens v. Virginia, 19 U.S. 264 (1821).
Johnson, Herbert A. Gibbons v. Ogden: *John Marshall, Steamboats, and the Commerce Clause.* Lawrence: University Press of Kansas, 2010.

1824, Congressional Regulation of Commerce
Gibbons v. Ogden, 22 U.S. 1 (1824).
Johnson, Herbert A. Gibbons v. Ogden: *John Marshall, Steamboats, and the Commerce Clause.* Lawrence: University Press of Kansas, 2010.

1824, Administering Native Peoples
Dudas, Jeffrey. *The Cultivation of Resentment: Treaty Rights and the New Right.* Stanford: Stanford University Press, 2008.

Smith, Paul, and Robert Allen Warrior. *Like a Hurricane: The Indian Movement from Alcatraz to Wounded Knee.* New York: New Press, 1996.
Strickland, Rennard, ed. *Felix S. Cohen's Handbook of Federal Indian Law.* Charlottesville, VA: Michie Bobbs-Merrill, 1982.

1839, *The Amistad*
Davis, David. *Inhuman Bondage: The Rise and Fall of Slavery in the New World.* New York: Oxford University Press, 2006.

1842, Recognition of Labor Unions
Commonwealth v. Hunt, 45 Mass. 111, 4 Metcalf 111 (1842).
Nelles, Walter. *Commonwealth v. Hunt.* Columbia Law Review, vol. 32 (1932): 1128–69.

1843, The M'Naghten Rule
Aitken, Robert, and Marilyn Aitken. "The M'Naghten Case: The Queen Was Not Amused." *Litigation*, vol. 36 (2010): 53–56.
Townsend, William Charles. *Modern State Trials.* London: Longman, Brown, Green, and Longmans, 1850.

1850, The Field Code
Field, Henry. *The Life of David Dudley Field.* New York: Charles Scribner's Sons, 1898.
LaPiana, William. "Just the Facts: The Field Code and the Case Method," *New York Law School Law Review*, vol. 36 (1991): 287.
Subrin, Stephen. "David Dudley Field and the Field Code: A Historical Analysis of an Earlier Procedural Vision." *Law and History Review*, vol. 6 (1988): 311–73.

1854, The Measure of Contract Damages
Conway-Jones, Hugh. "The Historical Setting for *Hadley v. Baxendale.*" *Texas Wesleyan Law Review*, vol. 11 (2004): 243.
Linzer, Peter, "*Hadley v. Baxendale* and the Seamless Web of Law." *Texas Wesleyan Law Review*, vol. 11 (2004): 225.

1857, The *Dred Scott* Decision
Dred Scott v. Sandford, 60 U.S. 393 (1857)
Finkelman, Paul. *Dred Scott v. Sandford.* Boston: Bedford Books, 1997.

1861, The Government Printing Office
Government Printing Office. *100 GPO Years 1861–1961: A History of United States Public Printing*, Sesquicentennial Edition 2010. Washington DC: 2010.

1863, The Emancipation Proclamation
Guelzo, Allen. *Lincoln's Emancipation Proclamation: The End of Slavery in America.* New York: Simon & Schuster, 2004.
National Archives. "The Meaning and Making of Emancipation." http://www.archives.gov/publications/ebooks/emancipation.html.

1864, The Geneva Convention
Bossy, Sanda. "The International Red Cross." *International Journal*, vol. 7 (1951): 204.
Dunant, Henry. *A Memory of Solferino.* Reprinted by the International Committee of the Red Cross (1959).

1865, The Abolition of Slavery
Daily National Republican. "The Official Announcement of the Adoption of the Constitutional Amendment: Opinions of the Leading Press," December 21, 1865.
Tsesis, Alexander. *The Thirteenth Amendment and American Freedom.* New York: New York University Press, 2004.

1866, The Civil Rights Act of 1866
Foner, Eric, and Henry Steele Commager. *Reconstruction: America's Unfinished Revolution 1863–1877.* New York: Harper & Row, 1989.
Franklin, John Hope. "The Civil Rights Act of 1866 Revisited." *Hastings Law Journal*, vol. 41 (1989): 1135.

1868, Impeaching President Andrew Johnson
Lewis, H. H. Walker. "The Impeachment of Andrew Johnson: A Political Tragedy." *American Bar Association Journal*, vol. 40, no. 1 (1954): 15.
Vicente, Jason. "Impeachment: A Constitutional Primer." *Texas Review of Law & Politics*, vol. 3 (1998): 117.

1868, The Fourteenth Amendment
Foner, Eric. "The Civil War, Reconstruction, and the Origins of Birthright Citizenship." *Marquette Lawyer Magazine* (Summer 2013): 32–42.

1869, Prohibition of Racial Voter Discrimination
Stephenson, Grier D. "The Supreme Court, the Franchise, and the Fifteenth Amendment: The First Sixty Years." *UMKC Law Review*, vol. 57 (1988): 47.
Wang, Xi. "Black Suffrage and the Redefinition of American Freedom, 1860–1870." *Cardozo Law Review*, vol. 17 (1995): 2153.

1870, The Law School Revolution
Alton, Stephen R. "Roll Over Langdell, Tell Llewellyn the News: A Brief History of American Legal Education." *Oklahoma City University Law Review*, vol. 35 (2010): 339.
Spencer, A. Benjamin. "The Law School Critique in Historical Perspective." *Washington and Lee Law Review*, vol. 69 (2012): 1949.

1872, Law Reporting and Legal Publishing
Brenner, Susan. *Precedent Inflation*. New Brunswick, NJ: Transaction Publishers, 1992.
Friedman, Lawrence. *A History of American Law* 3rd ed. New York: Touchstone, 2007.

1873, Obscenity and the Comstock Act
Blanchard, Margaret A. "The American Urge to Censor: Freedom of Expression versus the Desire to Sanitize Society— From Anthony Comstock to 2 Live Crew." *William and Mary Law Review*, vol. 33 (1991): 741.
Comstock, Anthony. *Frauds Exposed; or, How the People Are Deceived and Robbed, and Youth Corrupted*. New York: J. Howard Brown, 1880.

1873, Admission of Women to the Bar
Bradwell v. Illinois, 83 U.S. 130 (1873).
Gilliam, Nancy. "A Professional Pioneer: Myra Bradwell's Fight to Practice Law." *Law and History Review*, vol. 5 (1987): 105–33.

1876, Legal Aid Societies
Rhode, Deborah. *Access to Justice*. New York: Oxford University Press, 2004.
Smith, Reginald Heber. *Justice and the Poor*. New York: Charles Scribner's Sons, 1919.

1878, The Berne Convention
Bently, Lionel, et al., eds. *Global Copyright: Three Hundred Years since the Statute of Anne, from 1709 to Cyberspace*. Cheltenham, UK: Edward Elgar Publishing Limited, 2010.
Goldstein, Paul, and Bernt Hugenholtz. *International Copyright: Principles, Law, and Practice*. New York: Oxford University Press, 2010.

1881, The Insanity Defense
Rosenberg, Charles. *The Trial of the Assassin Guiteau*. Chicago: University of Chicago Press 1968.

1882, The Chinese Exclusion Act
Daniels, Roger. *Guarding the Golden Door: American Immigration Policy and Immigrants since 1882*. New York: Hill and Wang (2004).
Gyory, Andrew. *Closing the Gate: Race, Politics, and the Chinese Exclusion Act*.
Lee, Erika. *At America's Gates: Chinese Immigration during the Exclusion Era, 1882–1943*. Chapel Hill: University of North Carolina Press, 1998.

1883, The Civil Rights Cases
The Civil Rights Cases, 109 U.S. 3 (1883).
Rutherglen, George. *Civil Rights in the Shadow of Slavery*. New York: Oxford University Press, 2013.

1886, Equal Protection against Discrimination
Yick Wo v. Hopkins, 118 U.S. 356 (1886).

1887, The Interstate Commerce Act
Marquette Lawyer Magazine. "125 Years Since the Interstate Commerce Act." Fall 2012: 24.

1888, The Brazilian Slave Emancipation Act
Conrad, Robert. *The Destruction of Brazilian Slavery 1850–1888*. Berkeley University of California Press, 1972.

Davis, David. *Inhuman Bondage: The Rise and Fall of Slavery in the New World*. New York: Oxford University Press, 2006.

1890, The Right to Privacy
Brandeis, Louis, and Samuel Warren. "The Right to Privacy." *Harvard Law Review*, vol. 4 (1890): 193.
Kramer, Irwin R. "The Birth of Privacy Law: A Century Since Warren and Brandeis," *Catholic University Law Review*, vol. 39 (1989): 703.

1890, The Sherman Antitrust Act
Dewey, Donald. *The Antitrust Experiment in America*. New York: Columbia University Press, 1990.
Walker, Albert Henry. *History of the Sherman Law of the United States*. New York: Equity Press, 1910.

1893, New Zealand Women's Suffrage
Daley, Caroline, and Melanie Nolan, eds. *Suffrage and Beyond: International Federal Perspectives*. New York: New York University Press, 1994.
Douglas, Sir Arthur Percy. *The Dominion of New Zealand*. Boston: Little, Brown, & Co., 1909.

1896, *Plessy v. Ferguson*: Separate but Equal
Medley, Keith. *We as Freemen*. Gretna, LA: Pelican Pub. Co., 2003.

1897, Corporate Personhood and Liability
Butler, Henry. "General Incorporation in Nineteenth Century England: Interaction of Common Law and Legislative Processes." *International Review of Law and Economics*, vol. 6 (1986): 169.
Halpern, Paul, et al., "An Economic Analysis of Limited Liability in Corporation Law." *University of Toronto Law Journal*, vol. 30 (1980): 117.

1900, The German Civil Code
Freckmann, Anke, and Thomas Wegerich. *The German Legal System*. London: Sweet & Maxwell, 1999.
Lowey, Walter, trans. *The Civil Code of the German Empire*. Boston: The Boston Book Co., 1909.

1901, The Cuban Constitution of 1901
D'Zurilla, William. "Cuba's 1976 Socialist Constitution and the Fidelista Interpretation of Cuban Constitutional History." *Tulane Law Review*, vol. 55 (1981): 1223.

Hart, Bushnell, ed. *The American Nation: A History*. New York: Harper & Brothers Publishers, 1907.

1909, Congressional Right to Tax Income
Joseph, Richard. *The Origins of the American Income Tax: The Revenue Act of 1894 and Its Aftermath*. Syracuse, New York: Syracuse University Press, 2004.

Waltman, Jerold L. *Political Origins of the U.S. Income Tax*. Jackson: University of Mississippi Press, 1985.

1910, The White-Slave Traffic Act
Langum, David. *Crossing Over the Line: Legislating Morality and the Mann Act*. Chicago: University of Chicago Press, 1994.

Seagle, William. "The Twilight of the Mann Act." *American Bar Association Journal*, vol. 55 (1969): 641.

1910, Workers' Compensation Law
Eastman, Crystal. *Work-Accidents and the Law*. New York: Russell Sage Foundation, 1910.

Witt, John Fabian. *The Accidental Republic: Crippled Workingmen, Destitute Widows, and the Remaking of American Law*. Cambridge: Harvard University Press, 2004.

1911, Busting the Trusts
Meese, Alan. "Standard Oil as Lochner's Trojan Horse." *Southern California Law Review*, vol. 85 (2012): 783–813.

1911, The Triangle Shirtwaist Fire
Martin, Douglas. "Rose Freedman, Last Survivor of Triangle Fire, Dies at 107." *New York Times*, February 17, 2001.

Stein, Leon. *The Triangle Fire*. Ithaca: Cornell University Press, 2001.

1913, The Federal Reserve Act
Meltzer, Allan. *A History of the Federal Reserve, Vol. I: 1913–1951*. Chicago: University of Chicago Press, 2003.

1914, The Exclusionary Rule
Bradley, Gerald. "Present at the Creation? A Critical Guide to *Weeks v. United States* and Its Progeny." *St. Louis University Law Journal*, vol. 30 (1986): 1031.

1914, The Clayton Antitrust Act
Kintner, Earl. *An Antitrust Primer*. 2nd ed. New York: Macmillan, 1973.

Terry, Gene. "Clayton Act—Section 7—History and Amendment." *University of Kansas City Law Review*, vol. 24 (1956): 177.

1915, The Prohibition of Illegal Narcotics
Belenko, Steven, ed. *Drugs and Drug Policy in America: A Documentary History*. Westport: Greenwood Press, 2000.

Gray, James. *Why Our Drug Laws Have Failed and What We Can Do About It*. Philadelphia: Temple University Press, 2001.

1916, The Child Labor Act of 1916
Hindman, Hugh D. *Child Labor: An American History*. Armonk, New York: M.E. Sharpe, 2002.

Schmidt, James D. *Industrial Violence and the Legal Origins of Child Labor*. Cambridge: Cambridge University Press, 2010.

1916, The Expansion of Consumer Rights
Clarke, Sally. "Unmanageable Risks: *MacPherson v. Buick* and the Emergence of a Mass Consumer Market." *Law and History Review*, vol. 23 (2005): 1.

Probert, Walter. "Applied Jurisprudence: A Case Study of Interpretive Reasoning in *MacPherson v. Buick* and Its Precedents." *University of California Law Review*, vol. 21 (1988): 789.

Rabin, Robert, and Stephen Sugarman, eds. *Torts Stories*. New York: Foundation Press, 2003. See Henderson Jr., James A. "MacPherson v. Buick Motor Co.: Simplifying the Facts While Reshaping the Law."

1918, Prohibition
Asbury, Herbert. *The Great Illusion: An Informal History of Prohibition*. Garden City: Doubleday & Company, 1950.

Kyvig, David. *Repealing National Prohibition*. Kent: Kent State University Press, 2000.

1919, Women's Right to Vote
Clift, Eleanor. *Founding Sister and the Nineteenth Amendment*. Hoboken: John Wiley & Sons, 2003.

Pendergast, Tom, et al., *Constitutional Amendments*. Detroit: UXL, 2001.

1919, Yelling "Fire!" in a Crowded Theater
Schenck v. United States, 249 U.S. 47 (1919).

1920, New York State Legalizes Boxing
Mitchell, Kevin. "Fights, Camera, Action," *The Observer Sport Monthly*, July 3, 2005.

Spivey, Donald, ed. *Sport in America: New Historical Perspectives*. Westport, CT: Greenwood Press, 1985. See 95–128, Riess, Steven A. "In the Ring and Out: Professional Boxing in New York, 1896–1920"

1921, The Chicago "Black Sox" Trial
Asinof, Eliot. *Eight Men Out: The Black Sox and the 1919 World Series*. New York: Holt, Rinehart, and Winston, 1963.

1921, Censorship and the Hays Office
Ayer, Douglas, et al., "Self-Censorship in the Movie Industry: An Historical Perspective on Law and Social Change." *Wisconsin Law Review*, (1970): 791.

Vaughn, Stephen. "Morality and Entertainment: The Origins of the Motion Picture Production Code." *Journal of American History*, vol. 77 (1990): 39.

1921, The Emergency Quota Act
Silber, Rachel. "Eugenics, Family & Immigration Law in the 1920s." *Georgetown Immigration Law Journal*, vol. 11 (1996): 859.

Pula, James. "American Immigration Policy and the Dillingham Commission." *Polish American Studies*, vol. 37 (1980): 5.

1925, The Scopes "Monkey" Trial
University of Minnesota Law Library, The Clarence Darrow Digital Collection. "The Scopes Trial." http://darrow.law.umn.edu/trials.php?tid=7.

1926, The United States Code

Lee, Frederic, and Middleton Beaman. "Legal Status of the New Federal Code." *American Bar Association Journal*, vol. 12 (1926): 833–36.

Dwan, Ralph, and Ernest Feidler. "The Federal Statutes: Their History and Their Use." *Minnesota Law Review*, vol. 22 (1938): 1008.

1928, The Danger Zone in Tort Law

Manz, William. H. *The Palsgraf Case Courts, Law, and Society in 1920s New York*. Newark, NJ: Matthew Bender & Company, 2005.

Prosser, William. "Palsgraf Revisited." *Michigan Law Review*, vol. 52 (1953): 1.

1928, Wiretaps

Olmstead v. United States, 277 U.S. 438 (1928).

1933, Hitler's Rise to Power

Davidson, Eugene. *The Making of Adolf Hitler: The Birth and Rise of Nazis*, ch. 9. Columbia: University of Missouri Press, 1997.

Muller, Ingo, and Deborah Lucas Schneider, trans. *Hitler's Justice: The Courts of the Third Reich*. Cambridge: Harvard University Press, 1991.

1933, Wall Street Regulation

Brinkley, Alan. "When Washington Took On Wall Street." *Vanity Fair*, June 10, 2010.

Perino, Michael. *The Hellhound of Wall Street: How Ferdinand Pecora's Investigation of the Great Crash Forever Changed American Finance*. New York: Penguin Press, 2010.

1933, Censorship and *Ulysses*

Moscato, Michael, and Leslie LeBlanc, eds. *The United States of America v. One Book Entitled* Ulysses *by James Joyce*. Frederick, MD: University Publications of America, 1984.

Younger, Irving. "*Ulysses* in Court." The Irving Younger Collection. Chicago: American Bar Association, 2010.

1933, The Repeal of Prohibition

Asbury, Herbert. *The Great Illusion: An Informal History of Prohibition*. Garden City: Doubleday & Company, 1950.

Kyvig, David. *Repealing National Prohibition*. Kent: Kent State University Press, 2000.

1934, The Federal Communications Act

Figliola, Patricia Moloney. *The Federal Communications Commission: Current Structure and Its Role in the Changing Telecommunications Landscape*. Congressional Research Service Report, RL32589, November 18, 2013.

Shooshan III, Harry M. "A Modest Proposal for Restructuring the Federal Communications Commission." *Federal Communications Law Journal*, vol. 50 (1998): 637.

1934, The Securities and Exchange Act

Berle Jr., A. A. "New Protection for Buyers." *New York Times*, June 4, 1933.

Cornell University Law School, Legal Information Institute. "Securities Law History." https://www.law.cornell.edu/wex/securities_law_history.

1935, The National Labor Relations Act

Ray, Douglas, et al., *Understanding Labor Law*, 3rd ed. New Providence, NJ: Matthew Bender & Co., 2011.

1935, The Nuremberg Laws

Gutman, Israel, ed. *Encyclopedia of the Holocaust, Vol. 3*. New York: Macmillan, 1990.

Muller, Ingo, and Deborah Lucas Schneider, trans. *Hitler's Justice: The Courts of the Third Reich*. Cambridge: Harvard University Press, 1991.

1935, The Social Security Act

Dobelstein, Andrew. *Understanding the Social Security Act: The Foundation of Social Welfare for America in the Twenty-First Century*. Oxford: Oxford University Press, 2009.

Official Social Security Website. "Historical Background and Development of Social Security." http://www.ssa.gov/history/briefhistory3.html, accessed 09/14/2013.

1936, The *Federal Register*

Griswold, Erwin. "Government in Ignorance of the Law–A Plea for Better Publication of Executive Legislation." *Harvard Law Review*, vol. 48 (1934): 198.

Newman, Frank. "Government and Ignorance–A Progress Report on Publication of Federal Regulations." *Harvard Law Review*, vol. 63 (1950): 929.

1937, FDR and the Court-Packing Plan

Casebeer, Kenneth, ed. *American Labor Struggles and Law Histories*. Durham: Carolina Academic Press, 2011.

1937, Cameras in the Courts

Barber, Susanna. *News Cameras in the Courtroom: A Free Press–Fair Trial Debate*. Norwood: Ablex Publishing Corp., 1987.

Goldfarb, Ronald. *TV or Not TV: Television, Justice, and the Courts*. New York: New York University Press, 1998.

1938, Rule 23 and Modern Class Action

Hensler, Deborah, et al., *Class Action Dilemmas*. Santa Monica: RAND Corporation, 2000.

Rubenstein, William. *Newberg on Class Actions*. 5th ed. Eagan, MN: Thomsom Reuters, 2011.

1938, The Food, Drug and Cosmetic Act

Curtis, Patricia. *Guide to Food Laws and Regulations*. Ames: Blackwell Publishing, 2005.

Hilts, Philip. *Protecting America's Health: The FDA, Business, and One Hundred Years of Regulation*. New York: Alfred A. Knopf, 2003.

1938, The Fair Labor Standards Act

Linder, Marc. *The Autocratically Flexible Workplace: A History of Overtime Regulation in the United States*. Iowa City: Fanpihua Press, 2002.

Miller, Scott. "Revitalizing the FLSA." *Hofstra Labor and Employment Law Journal*, vol. 19 (2001): 1.

1939, Militias and the Right to Bear Arms

Utter, Glenn H. *Encyclopedia of Gun Control and Gun Rights*. Phoenix: Oryx Press, 2000.

Winkler, Adam. *Gunfight: The Battle Over the Right to Bear Arms in America*. New York: W.W. Norton & Co., 2011.

1940, The Alien Registration Act

Finan, Christopher. *From the Palmer Raids to the Patriot Act: A History of the Fight for Free Speech in America*. Boston: Beacon Press, 2007.

Oshinsky, David. *A Conspiracy So Immense: The World of Joe McCarthy*. New York: Free Press, 1983.

1941, Strict Products Liability

Escola v. Coca Cola Bottling Co., 24 Cal. 2d 453 (1944).

Rabin, Robert, and Stephen Sugarman, eds. *Torts Stories*. New York: Foundation Press, 2003. See Geistfeld, Mark. *"Escola v.Coca Cola Bottling Co.*: Strict Products Liability Unbound."

1941, California's Anti-Okie Statute

Edwards v. California, 314 U.S. 160 (1941).

1942, Internment of Japanese Americans

Greenaway Jr., Joseph. "Judicial Decision Making and the External Environment." *Rutgers Law Review*, vol. 51 (1998): 181.

Korematsu v. United States, 323 U.S. 214 (1944).

1944, The G.I. Bill

Kiester Jr., Edwin. "The G.I. Bill May Be the Best Deal Ever Made by Uncle Sam." *Smithsonian*, vol. 25 (Nov. 1994): 131.

United States Department of Veterans Affairs. "The GI Bill's History." http://www.gibill. va.gov/benefits/history_timeline.

1945, The Nuremberg Trials

Knappman, Edward, ed. *Great World Trials*. Detroit: Gale Research, 1997. See Golay, Michael. "Nuremberg Trial: 1945–46," 266–73.

Lewis, Andrew, and Michael Lobban, eds. *Law and History*. Oxford: Oxford University Press, 2004. See Douglas, L. "The Holocaust, History, and Legal Memory," 405–12.

1946, Rent Control

Keating, Dennis W., et al., *Rent Control: Regulation and the Housing Market*. New Brunswick, NJ: Center for Urban Policy Research, 1998.

Willis, John. "A Short History of Rent Control Laws." *Cornell Law Quarterly*, vol. 36 (1950): 54.

1946, The Protection of Trademarks

McCarthy, J. Thomas., *McCarthy on Trademarks and Unfair Competition* 4th ed., ch. 5. St. Paul, MN: West Group, 1996.

Phleger, D. "The Lanham Act's Contribution to Trademark Rights." *Journal of Contemporary Legal Issues*, vol. 12 (2001): 141.

1947, Colonialism and Postwar Independence

"The Atlantic Charter," *Department of State Bulletin*, August 16, 1941.

Laing, Edward. "The Contribution of the Atlantic Charter to Human Rights Law and Humanitarian Universalism." *Willamette Law Review*, vol. 26 (1990): 113.

1948, General Agreement on Tariffs and Trade

Hudec, Robert. *Enforcing International Trade Law: The Evolution of the Modern GATT Legal System*. Salem: Butterworth Legal Publishers, 1993.

U.S. Department of State, Office of the Historian. "Bretton Woods–GATT, 1941–1947." https://history.state.gov/ milestones/1937-1945/bretton-woods.

1948, The U.N. Convention on Genocide

Gaeta, Paola, ed. *The UN Genocide Convention: A Commentary*. Oxford: Oxford University Press, 2009.

Kiernan, Ben. *Blood and Soil: A World History of Genocide and Extermination from Sparta to Darfur*. New Haven: Yale University Press, 2007.

1948, The Hollywood Ten

Finan, Christopher. *From the Palmer Raids to the Patriot Act: A History of the Fight for Free Speech in America*. Boston: Beacon Press, 2007.

Oshinsky, David. *A Conspiracy So Immense: The World of Joe McCarthy*. New York: Free Press, 1983.

1948, Universal Declaration of Human Rights

Cheng, Tai-Heng. "The Universal Declaration of Human Rights at Sixty: Is It Still Right for the United States?" *Cornell International Law Journal*, vol. 41 (2008): 251.

Glendon, Mary Ann. "Knowing the Universal Declaration of Human Rights. *Notre Dame Law Review*, vol. 73 (1998): 1153.

1948, The Displaced Persons Act

Daniels, Roger. *Guarding the Golden Door: American Immigration Policy and Immigrants Since 1882*. New York: Hill and Wang, 2004.

Presidential Executive Order 10,003, Oct. 4, 1948, 13 Fed. Reg. 5819 (Oct. 6, 1948).

1951, Rejection of the Alien Registration Act

Oshinsky, David. *A Conspiracy So Immense: The World of Joe McCarthy*. New York: Free Press, 1983.

Sheft, Mark A. "The End of the Smith Act Era: A Legal and Historical Analysis of Scales v. United States," *American Journal of Legal History*, vol. 36 (1992): 164.

1951, The Rosenberg Trial

Radosh, Ronald, and Joyce Milton. *The Rosenberg File, 2nd ed.* New Haven: Yale University Press, 1997.

1951, The E.U. and the Treaty of Paris

McCormick, Michael. "A Primer on the European Union and Its Legal System." *Army Lawyer*, vol. 1 (2002).

1954, *Brown v. Board of Education*

Brown v. Board of Education, 347 U.S. 483 (1954).

1954, The Communist Control Act

McAuliffe, Mary. "Liberals and the Communist Control Act of 1954." *Journal of American History*, vol. 63 (1976): 351.

1956, The Interstate Highway Act

Levin, David. "Federal Aspects of the Interstate Highway Program." *Nebraska Law Review*, vol. 38 (1959): 377.

Lewis, Tom. *Divided Highways: Building the Interstate Highways, Transforming American Life*. Ithaca: Cornell University Press, 2003 e-book edition.

1957, The Limits on Obscenity

Ross v. United States, 354 U.S. 476.

Fahringer, Herald Price, and Michael J. Brown. "The Rise and Fall of Roth–A Critique of the Recent Supreme Court Obscenity Decisions," *Kentucky Law Journal*, vol. 62 (1973): 731.

1957, The Wolfenden Report and Gay Rights

Chesser, Eustace. *Live and Let Live: The Moral of the Wolfenden Report*. London: Heinemann, 1958.

The Wolfenden Report: Report of the Committee on Homosexual Offenses and Prostitution. New York: Stein and Day, 1963.

1959, The European Court of Human Rights

European Court of Human Rights, http://www.echr.coe.

O'Boyle, Michael. "The Future of the European Court of Human Rights." *German Law Journal*, vol. 12 (2011): 1862.

1959, No Man's Land

British Antarctic Survey. "The Antarctic Treaty Explained." http://www.antarctica.ac.uk/about_antarctica/geopolitical/treaty/explained.php.

Secretariat of the Antarctic Treaty. "The Antarctic Treaty." http://www.ats.aq/e/ats.htm.

1961, States and the Exclusionary Rule

Mapp v. Ohio, 367 U.S. 495 (1961).

Fitzpatrick, Daniel. "Should the Criminal Go Free Because the Constable Has Blundered?" *Criminal Justice Quarterly*, vol. 2 (1974): 73–87.

1961, The Eichmann Trial

Lipstadt, Deborah. *The Eichmann Trial*. New York: Schocken Books, 2011.

Rogat, Yosal. *The Eichmann Trial and the Rule of Law*. Santa Barbara: Center for the Study of Democratic Institutions, 1961.

1963, The Trial of Nelson Mandela

Joffe, Joel. *The State v. Nelson Mandela: The Trial That Changed South Africa*. Oxford: Oneworld Publications, 2007.

"U.N. Security Council Condemns Apartheid in South Africa; Sets Up Committee to Study Sanctions." *Department of State Bulletin*, vol. 51 (1964): 29–33.

1963, The Right to Counsel in State Court

Lewis, Anthony. *Gideon's Trumpet*. New York: Random House, 1964.

Gideon v. Wainwright, 372 U.S. 335 (1963).

1964, Limits on Libel Laws

N.Y. Times v. Sullivan, 376 U.S. 254 (1964).

Hall, Kermit, and Melvin Urofsky. New York Times v. Sullivan: *Civil Rights, Libel Law, and the Free Press*. Lawrence: University Press of Kansas, 2011.

1964, The Civil Rights Act of 1964

Lovey, Robert. *The Civil Rights Act of 1964: The Passage of the Law That Ended Racial Segregation*. Albany: State University of New York Press, 1997.

Patterson, Charles. *The Civil Rights Movement*. New York: Facts on File, 1995.

1965, The Voting Rights Act

May, Gary. *Bending Toward Justice: The Voting Rights Act and the Transformation of American Democracy*. New York: Basic Books, 2013.

McCrary, Peyton. "How the Voting Rights Act Works: Implementation of a Civil Rights Policy." *South Carolina Law Review*, vol. 57 (2006): 785–825.

1965, Conscientious Objection

Fogarty, John. "The Right Not to Kill: A Critical Analysis of Conscientious Objection and the Problem of Registration." *New England Law Review*, vol. 18 (1982): 655.

United States v. Seeger, 380 U.S. 163 (1965).

1965, The Body and the Right of Privacy

Johnson, John. Griswold v. Connecticut: *Birth Control and the Constitutional Right of Privacy*. Lawrence: University Press of Kansas, 2005.

Wawrose, Susan C. Griswold v. Connecticut: *Contraception and the Right of Privacy*. New York: Franklin Watts, 1996.

1966, The Freedom of Information Act

Davis, Charles, and Sigman L. Splichal, eds. *Access Denied: Freedom of Information in the Information Age*. Ames: Iowa State University Press, 2000.

Hitchcock, Cornish F. ed., *Guidebook to the Freedom of Information and Privacy Acts, Vol. 1*. Thomson Reuters/West, 2013.

1966, Miranda Warnings

Stuart, Gary. *Miranda: The Story of America's Right to Remain Silent*. Tucson: University of Arizona Press, 2004.

Lieberman, Jethro Koller. *Milestones! 200 Years of American Law*. New York: Oxford University Press, 1976.

1967, Interracial Marriage

Loving v. Virginia, 388 U.S. 1 (1967).

Maillard, Kevin, and Rose Villazor, eds. Loving v. Virginia *in a Post-racial World: Rethinking Race, Sex, and Marriage*. New York: Cambridge University Press, 2012.

1967, The Vietnam-Era Draft Laws

Flynn, George. *The Draft, 1940–1973*. Lawrence: University Press of Kansas, 1993.

Hershey, Lewis B. "Changes in the Draft: The Military Selective Service Act of 1967." *Columbia Journal of Law and Social Problems*, vol. 4 (1968): 120.

1969, No-Fault Divorce

Halem, Lynne. *Divorce Reform: Changing Legal and Social Perspectives*. New York: Free Press, 1980.

Wardle, Lynn D. "No-Fault Divorce and the Divorce Conundrum." *Brigham Young University Law Review* (1991): 79.

1969, Free Speech and Threats of Violence

Brandenburg v. Ohio, 395 U.S. 444 (1969).

1969, The Fairness Doctrine

Gray, Karen. "Fairness Doctrine Termination: Extinction of an Unenforceable Theory." *Suffolk University Law Review*, vol. 22 (1988): 1057.

Red Lion Broadcasting Co. v. FCC, 395 U.S. 367 (1969).

1970, The National Environmental Policy Act

Alm, Alvin. "NEPA: Past, Present, and Future." *Environmental Protection Agency Journal*, vol. 14 (1988): 32.

Clingham, James H. "NEPA: Birth and Infancy." *Catholic University Law Review*, vol. 20 (1971): 184.

1970, The Court-Martial of William Calley Jr.

Calley v. Callaway, 519 F.2d 184 (5th Cir. 1975).

Taylor, Telford. *Nuremberg and Vietnam: An American Tragedy*. New York: Quadrangle Books, 1970.

1970, Public Health and Cigarettes

Jacobson, Peter D., et al., "Historical Overview of Tobacco Legislation and Regulation." *Journal of Social Issues*, vol. 53 (1997): 75.

Parker-Pope, Tara, *Cigarettes: Anatomy of an Industry from Seed to Smoke*. New York: New Press, 2001.

1970, The RICO Act

Blakey, G. Robert, and Brian Gettings, "RICO: Basic Concepts—Criminal and Civil Remedies," *Temple Law Quarterly*, vol. 53 (1980): 1009.

Hall, Kermit, ed. *The Oxford Companion to American Law*. Oxford University Press, 2002.

1970, Baseball's Reserve Clause

Goldman, Robert. *One Man Out: Curt Flood versus Baseball*. Lawrence: University Press of Kansas, 2008.

Minan, John. *The Little White Book of Baseball Law*. Chicago: American Bar Association, 2009.

1970, The Occupational Safety and Health Act

Meeds, Lloyd. "A Legislative History of OSHA." *Gonzaga Law Review*, vol. 9 (1973): 327.

Mintz, Bejanmin W. *OSHA: History, Law, and Policy*. Washington, DC: Bureau of National Affairs, Inc., 1984.

1970, The Trial of Charles Manson

Gentry, Curt, and Vincent Bugliosi. *Helter Skelter: The True Story of the Manson Murders*. New York: W.W. Norton & Co., 1974.

1971, Enfranchising Eighteen-Year-Olds

Karlan, Pamela. "Ballots and Bullets: The Exceptional History of the Right to Vote." *University of Cincinnati Law Review*, vol. 71 (2002): 1345–72.

Lowering the Voting Age to 18, S. Rep. No. 92–26 (Feb. 17, 1971).

1971, The *Pentagon Papers*

New York Times Co. v. United States., 403 U.S. 713 (1971).

1971, Employment Discrimination

Griggs v. Duke Power Co., 401 U.S. 424 (1971).

1971, Court-Ordered School Busing

Schwartz, Bernard. *Swann's Way: The School Busing Case and the Supreme Court*. New York: Oxford University Press, 1986.

Swann v. Charlotte-Mecklenburg Board of Education, 402 U.S. 1 (1971).

1972, Banning the Death Penalty

Furman v. Georgia, 408 U.S. 238 (1972).

Blume, John H., and Jordan M. Steiker. *Death Penalty Stories*. New York: Foundation Press, 2009. See Steiker, Carol. "*Furman v. Georgia*: Not an End, but a Beginning."

1972, The Equal Employment Opportunity Act

EEOC. "35 Years of Ensuring the Promise of Opportunity." http://webharvest.gov/peth04/20041017193448/http://www.eeoc.gov/abouteeoc/35th/history/index.html.

Lindemann, Barbara, and Paul Grossman, eds. *Employment Discrimination Law*. Arlington: BNA Books, 2007.

1972, The Equal Rights Amendment

Lee, Rex E. *A Lawyer Looks at the Equal Rights Amendment*. Provo: Brigham Young University Press, 1980.

Schenken, Suzanne O'Dea, and Ann W. Richards. *From Suffrage to Senate: An Encyclopedia of American Women in Politics*. Santa Barbara: ABC-CLIO, 1999.

1972, The Trail of Broken Treaties

Bacigal, Ronald J. "Judicial Reflections upon the 1973 Uprising at Wounded Knee." *Journal of Contemporary Legal Issues*, vol. 2 (1989): 1–12.

Smith, Paul, and Robert Allen Warrior. *Like a Hurricane: The Indian Movement from Alcatraz to Wounded Knee*. New York: New Press, 1996.

1973, The Endangered Species Act

Bauer, Donald, and William Irvin, eds. *Endangered Species Act: Law, Policy, and Perspectives* 2nd ed. Chicago: American Bar Association, 2010.

Houck, Oliver. "Reflections on the Endangered Species Act." *Natural Resources & Environment*, vol. 10 (1996): 9.

1973, The First Ban on Gay Marriage

Conaway v. Deane, 932 A.2d 571 (Md. 2007).

Grossman, Joanna, and Lawrence M. Friedman. *Inside the Castle: Law and the Family in 20th Century America*. Princeton: Princeton University Press, 2011.

1973, A New Obscenity Standard

Harrison, Maureen, and Steve Gilbert, eds. *Obscenity and Pornography Decisions of the United States Supreme Court*. Carlsbad, NM: Excellent Books, 2000.

Miller v. California, 413 U.S. 15 (1973).

1973, *Roe v. Wade*

Roe v. Wade, 410 U.S. 113 (1973).

1973, The War Powers Act of 1973

Grimmett, Richard. *The War Powers Resolution*. New York: Novinka Books, 2002.

Perkins, Gerald, and Richard Grimmet, eds. *The War Powers Resolution After 30 Years*. New York: Novinka Books, 2005.

1974, Presidential Subpoena Compliance

United States v. Nixon, 418 U.S. 683 (1974).

1975, Attorneys' Fee Awards

Malson, Robert A. "In Response to *Alyeska*—The Civil Rights Attorney's Fees Awards Act of 1976." *St. Louis University Law Journal*, vol. 21 (1978): 430.

1975, Restrictions on Involuntary Commitment

Donaldson, Kenneth. *Insanity Inside Out*. New York: Crown Publishers, 1976.

Schopp, Robert. *Competence, Condemnation, and Commitment: An Integrated Theory of Mental Health Law*. Washington, DC: American Psychological Association, 2001.

1975, Racism and U.N. Resolution 3379

Troy, Gil. *Moynihan's Moment: America's Fight against Zionism as Racism*. New York: Oxford University Press, 2013.

U.S. Department of State Dispatch. "UN Repeals Zionism-Is-Racism Resolution." December 23, 1991.

1976, The Right to Die

Cantor, Norman L. "Quinlan, Privacy, and the Handling of Incompetent Dying Patients." *Rutgers Law Review*, vol. 30 (1977): 243–66.

Coburn, Daniel. R. "In Re Quinlan: A Practical Overview." *Arkansas Law Review*, vol. 31 (1978): 59–74.

In re Quinlan, 355 A.2d 647 (N.J. 1976).

1976, Health Care and the Duty to Warn

Rabin, Robert, and Stephen Sugarman, eds. *Torts Stories*. New York: Foundation Press, 2003. See Schuck, Peter H., and Daniel J. Givelber, "*Tarasoff v. Regents of the University of California*: The Therapist's Dilemma."

Tarasoff v. Regents of the Univ. of Cal., 551 P.2d 334 (Cal. 1976).

Thomas, Michael. "Expanded Liability for Psychiatrists: *Tarasoff* Gone Crazy?" *Journal of Mental Health Law* (Spring 2009): 45.

1976, The Copyright Act of 1976

"Copyright Basics," United States Copyright Office Circular 1, http://www.copyright.gov/circs/circ01.pdf.

Samuels, Edward. *The Illustrated Story of Copyright*. New York: St. Martin's Press, 2000.

1976, The Death Penalty Returns

Gregg v. Georgia, 428 U.S. 153 (1976).

Mandery, Evan. *A Wild Justice: The Death and Resurrection of Capital Punishment in America*. New York: W.W. Norton & Co., 2013.

1977, Palimony

Myricks, Noel. "'Palimony: The Impact of *Marvin v. Marvin*." *Family Relations*, vol. 29 (1980): 210.

Marvin v. Marvin, 122 Cal. App. 3d 871 (1981).

Marvin v. Marvin, 134 Cal. Rptr. 815, 577 P.2d 106 (1976).

1977, Attorney Advertising

Bates v. Arizona, 433 U.S. 350 (1977).

Meyer, Tiffany, and Robert Smith. "Attorney Advertising: *Bates* and a Beginning." *Arizona Law Review*, vol. 20 (1978): 427.

Smolla, Rodney. *Law of Lawyer Advertising*. Eagan, MN: Thomson West, 2006.

1978, Affirmative Action

Kellough, Edward. *Understanding Affirmative Action: Politics, Discrimination, and the Search for Justice*. Washington, DC: Georgetown University Press, 2006.

Regents of University of California v. Bakke, 438 U.S. 265 (1978).

1978, The FCC and Filthy Words

FCC v. Pacifica, 438 U.S. 726 (1978).

Harrison, Maureen, and Steve Gilbert, eds. *Obscenity and Pornography Decisions of the United States Supreme Court*. Carlsbad, NM: Excellent Books, 2000.

1978, The Son of Sam Law

Herrera, Tanya. "Dubious Victory for the Right of Free Speech—*Simon & Schuster, Inc. v. Members of the New York State Crime Victims Board*." *Harvard Civil Rights-Civil Liberties Law Review*, vol. 28 (1993): 567.

Simon & Schuster v. Members of the New York State Crime Victims Board, 502 U.S. 105 (1991).

Yager, Jessica. "Investigating New York's 2001 Son of Sam Law: Problems with the Recent Extension of Tort Liability for People Convicted of Crimes." *New York Law School Law Review*, vol. 48 (2004): 433.

1978, The Entrapment Defense

Blecker, Robert. "Beyond 1984: Undercover in America—Serpico to Abscam." *New York Law School Law Review*, vol. 28 (1983): 823.

Roffer, Michael H. "Pleading the Entrapment Defense: The Propriety of Inconsistency." *New York Law School Law Review*, vol. 28 (1983): 1025.

1983, The McMartin Molestation Case

Butler, Edgar, et al., *Anatomy of the McMartin Child Molestation Case*. Lanham: University Press of America, 2001.

Eberle, Paul. *The Abuse of Innocence: The McMartin Preschool Trial*. Buffalo: Prometheus Books, 1993.

Nathanson, Paul. *Legalizing Misandry: From Public Shame to Systemic Discrimination against Men*. Montreal: McGill-Queens University Press, 2006.

1984, The First Mandatory Seat-Belt Law

Aronson, Peter. "New York Pioneered Passage of Belt Laws Across the Country." *Sun Sentinel*, June 29, 1986.

Clarke, Sally H. "Unmanageable Risks: *MacPherson v. Buick* and the Emergence of a Mass Consumer Market," *Law and History Review*, vol. 23 (2005): 11.

N.Y. Veh. & Traf. L. § 1229-c.

Roberts, Sam. "John D. States Dies at 89; Doctor Helped Create New York's Seatbelt Law." *New York Times*, April 1, 2015 (online edition).

1984, Administrative Agency Determinations

Chevron U.S.A. v. Natural Resources Defense Council, 467 U.S. 837 (1984).

Elliott, E. Donald. "Chevron Matters: How the Chevron Doctrine Redefined the Roles of Congress, Courts and Agencies in Environmental Law." *Villanova Environmental Law Journal*, vol. 16 (2005): 1.

1984, Parody and the First Amendment

Hustler Magazine Inc. v. Falwell, 485 U.S. 46 (1988).

1984, Time-Shifting and Fair Use

Electronic Frontier Foundation. "The Betamax Case." https://w2.eff.org/legal/cases/betamax/.

Litman, Jessica. "The Sony Paradox." *Case Western Reserve Law Review*, vol. 55 (2005): 917.

Sony v. Universal City Studios, Inc., 464 U.S. 417 (1984).

1986, Peremptory Challenges to Jury Selection

Batson v. Kentucky, 476 U.S. 79 (1986).

Gertner, Nancy, and Judy Mizner. *The Law of Juries*. 2nd ed. Eagan, MN: Thomson West, 2009.

Sand, Leonard B. "Batson and Jury Selection Revisited." *Litigation*, vol. 22 (1996): 3.

1987, The First Evidentiary Use of DNA

The Innocence Project, http://www.innocenceproject.org/.

Levy, Harlan. *And the Blood Cried Out*. New York: Basic Books, 1996.

Lewontin, R. C., and Daniel L. Hartl. "Population Genetics in Forensic DNA Typing." *Science*, vol. 254 (December 20, 1991): 1745–50.

1987, Pregnancy Discrimination
California Federal Savings & Loan Ass'n v. Guerra, 479 U.S. 272 (1987).
Schneider, Elizabeth, and Stephanie Wildman, eds. *Women and the Law Stories*. New York: Foundation Press, 2011. See "Pregnant and Working: The Story of *California Federal Savings & Loan Association v. Guerra*."

1987, Robert Bork's Supreme Court Nomination
Epstein, Lee, and Jeffrey A. Segal. *Advice and Consent: The Politics of Judicial Appointments*. Oxford: Oxford University Press, 2005.
Miner, Roger J. "Advice and Consent in Theory and Practice." *American University Law Review*, vol. 41 (1992): 1075.
Wittes, Benjamin. *Confirmation Wars: Preserving Independent Courts in Angry Times*. Lanham: Rowman & Littlefield Publishers, 2006.

1988, Surrogate Motherhood
Cahn, Naomi. *Test Tube Families*. New York: New York University Press, 2009.
Dolgin, Janet. *Defining the Family*. New York: New York University Press, 1997.
In Re Baby M., 537 A.2d 1227 (N.J. 1988).

1988, Women's Admission to Private Clubs
Lapidus, Lenora, et al., *The Rights of Women*. New York: New York State Press, 2009.
New York State Club Association v. City of New York, 487 U.S. 1 (1988).
Speyer, Katherine. "*New York State Club Association v. City of New York*: The Demise of the All-Male Club." *Pace Law Review*, vol. 10 (1990): 273.

1989, The Fatwa against *The Satanic Verses*
Bhala, Raj. *Understanding Islamic Law*. New Providence, NJ: Matthew Bender & Co., 2011.
Levy, Leonard. *Blasphemy: Verbal Offense against the Sacred, from Moses to Salman Rushdie*. New York: Alfred A. Knopf, 1993.

Slaughter, M. M. "The Salman Rushdie Affair: Apostasy, Honor, and Freedom of Speech." *Virginia Law Review*, vol. 79 (1993): 153.

1989, Celebrity Tax Prosecution
Dershowitz, Alan. *Taking the Stand: My Life in the Law*. New York: Crown Publishers, 2013.
Hammer, Richard. *The Helmsleys: The Rise and Fall of Harry and Leona Helmsley*. New York: NAL Books, 1990.
Moss, Michael. *Palace Coup: The Inside Story of Harry and Leona Helmsley*. New York: Doubleday, 1989.

1990, The First Gay Marriage Laws
Badgett, M. V. *When Gay People Get Married: What Happens When Societies Legalize Same-Sex Marriage*. New York: New York University Press, 2009.
Broberg, Morten. "The Registered Partnership for Same-Sex Couples in Denmark." *Child and Family Law Quarterly*, vol. 8 (1996): 149.
Patterson, Nicholas. "The Repercussions in the European Union of the Netherlands' Same-Sex Marriage Law." *Chicago Journal of International Law*, vol. 2 (2001): 301.

1990, The Americans with Disabilities Act
Kidwell, Brent. "The Americans with Disabilities Act of 1990: Overview and Analysis." *Indiana Law Review*, vol. 26 (1993): 707.
Mayerson, Arlene. "The Americans with Disabilities Act—An Historic Overview." *The Labor Lawyer*, vol. 7 (1991): 1–9.
Rothstein, Laura. *Disabilities and the Law*. 4th ed. Eagan: West Publishing, 2009.

1990, The End of Apartheid
Abel, Richard L., *Politics by Other Means: Law in the Struggle against Apartheid, 1980–1994*, London: Routledge, 1995.
Ebrahim, Hassan. *The Soul of a Nation: Constitution-Making in South Africa*. Oxford: Oxford University Press, 1998.
Lapierre, Dominique. *A Rainbow in the Night: The Tumultuous Birth of South Africa*. Translated by Kathryn Spink. Cambridge: Da Capo Press, 2009.

1991, Confirming Clarence Thomas
Epstein, Lee, and Jeffrey A. Segal. *Advice and Consent: The Politics of Judicial Appointments*. Oxford: Oxford University Press, 2005.
Ragan, Sandra, et al., eds. *The Lynching of Language: Gender, Politics, and Power in the Hill-Thomas Hearings*. Urbana: University of Illinois Press, 1996.
Wittes, Benjamin. *Confirmation Wars: Preserving Independent Courts in Angry Times*. Lanham: Rowman & Littlefield Publishers, 2006.

1991, The Trial of Manuel Noriega
Noriega, Manuel, and Peter Eisner. *The Memoirs of Manuel Noriega*. New York: Random House, 1997.

1992, Smoking Litigation
Cipollone v. Liggett Group, 505 U.S. 504 (1992).
Mollenkamp, Carrick, et al., *The People vs. Big Tobacco: How the States Took on the Cigarette Giants*. Princeton: Bloomberg Press, 1998.
Parker-Pope, Tara. *Cigarettes: Anatomy of an Industry from Seed to Smoke*. New York: New Press, 2001.

1992, The Rio Conference
Baker, Bryan. "Environmental Controversies and Compromises at the Rio Conference." *Currents, International Trade Law Journal*, vol. 2 (1993): 45.
Segger, Marie-Claire Cordonier. "The Role of International Forums in the Advancement of Sustainable Development." *Sustainable Development Law & Policy* (Fall 2009): 5–18.
Silveira, MaryPat Williams. "International Legal Instruments and Sustainable Development: Principles, Requirements, and Restructuring." *Willamette Law Review*, vol. 31 (1995): 239.

1993, Creation of the European Union
Carolan, Bruce. "The Birth of the European Union: US and UK Roles in the Creation of a Unified European Community." *Tulsa Journal of Comparative & International Law*, vol. 16 (2009): 51.
European Union. "The European Union Explained: How the European Union Works," http://europa.eu/index_en.htm.

McCormick, Michael J. "A Primer on the European Union and Its Legal System." Department of the Army Pamphlet 27-50-358 (December 2002).

1994, The Hot Coffee Case

Bogus, Carl. *Why Lawsuits Are Good for America*. New York: New York University Press, 2001.

Diamond, Shari Seidman. "Truth, Justice, and the Jury." *Harvard Journal of Law & Public Policy*, vol. 26 (2003): 143.

Koenig, Thomas, and Michael Rustad. *In Defense of Tort Law*. New York: New York University Press, 2001.

1995, Stem Cell and Cloning Legislation

Feder, Jodey. "State Laws on Human Cloning." Congressional Research Service Report RS21517, May 14, 2003.

"Stem Cell Research Around the World." Pew Research Center, July 17, 2008, http://www.pewforum.org/2008/07/17/stem-cell-research-around-the-world/.

United Nations Declaration on Human Cloning, A/RES/59/280, March 8, 2005.

1995, The O.J. Simpson Murder Trial

Coffey, Kendall. *Spinning the Law: Trying Cases in the Court of Public Opinion*. New York: Prometheus Books, 2010.

Linedecker, Clifford. *O.J. A to Z: The Complete Handbook to the Trial of the Century*. New York: St. Martin's Griffin, 1995.

Schuetz, Janice, and Lin S. Lilley, eds. *The O.J. Simpson Trials: Rhetoric, Media, and the Law*. Carbondale: Southern Illinois University Press, 1999.

1996, Limits on Punitive Damages

Belli Sr., Melvin. "Punitive Damages: Their History, Their Use and Their Worth in Present-Day Society." *UMKC Law Review*, vol. 49 (1981): 1.

BMW of North America, Inc. v. Gore, 517 U.S. 559 (1996).

Colby, Thomas. "Clearing the Smoke from *Philip Morris v. Williams*: The Past, Present, and Future of Punitive Damages." *Yale Law Journal*, vol. 118 (2009): 392.

1996, South Africa's Constitution

Ebrahim, Hassen. *The Soul of a Nation: Constitution-Making in South Africa*. Cape Town: Oxford University Press, 1999.

Klug, Heinz. *The Constitution of South Africa: A Contextual Analysis*. Oxford: Hart Publications, 2010.

Moseneke, Dikang. "Remarks: The 32nd Annual Philip A. Hart Memorial Lecture: A Journey from the Heart of Apartheid Darkness Towards a Just Society: Salient Features of the Budding Constitutionalism and Jurisprudence of South Africa." *Georgetown Law Journal*, vol. 101 (2013): 749.

1996, Legalization of Marijuana

Bronstad, Amanda. "Federal Crackdown Continues against Marijuana Dispensaries." *National Law Journal*, January 19, 2012.

Kamin, Sam. "Marijuana at the Crossroads: Keynote Address." *Denver University Law Review*, vol. 89 (2012): 977.

Rabin, Roni Caryn. "Legalizing of Marijuana Raises Health Concerns." *New York Times*, January 7, 2013.

1997, Presidential Immunity

Hunter, Nan D. *The Power of Procedure: The Litigation of* Jones v. Clinton. New York: Aspen Law & Business, 2002.

Leibowitz, Arnold, and Herman Schwartz. *An Historical-Legal Analysis of the Impeachments of Presidents Andrew Johnson, Richard Nixon, and William Clinton: Why the Process Went Wrong*. Lewiston, NY: The Edwin Mellen Press, 2012.

1997, The Communications Decency Act

Harrison, Maureen, and Steve Gilbert, eds. *Obscenity and Pornography Decisions of the United States Supreme Court*. Carlsbad, NM: Excellent Books, 2000.

Rappaport, Kim L. "In the Wake of *Reno v. ACLU*: The Continued Struggle in Western Constitutional Democracies with Internet Censorship and Freedom of Speech Online." *American University International Law Review*, vol. 13 (1998): 765.

Reno v. American Civil Liberties Union, 512 U.S. 844 (1997).

1997, Physician-Assisted Suicide

Cruzan v. Director, Missouri Department of Health, 497 U.S. 261 (1990).

State-by-State Guide to Physician-Assisted Suicide, ProCon.org, http://euthanasia.procon.org/view.resource.php?resourceID=000132.

Vacco v. Quill, 521 U.S. 793 (1997).

Washington v. Glucksberg, 521 U.S. 702 (1997).

1998, The Line-Item Veto

Petrilla, Antony. "The Role of the Line-Item Veto in the Federal Balance of Power." *Harvard Journal on Legislation*, vol. 31 (1994): 469.

Rappaport, Michael B. "Veto Burdens and the Line Item Veto Act." *Northwestern University Law Review*, vol. 91 (1997): 771.

1998, Indictment of Augusto Pinochet

McHale, Laura. "The Case against General Augusto Pinochet." *Litigation*, vol. 27 (2001): 49.

Roht-Arriaza, Naomi. *The Pinochet Effect: Transnational Justice in the Age of Human Rights*. Philadelphia: University of Pennsylvania Press, 2005.

1999, Copyright in the Digital Age

Karjala, Dennis. "'Copying' and 'Piracy' in the Digital Age." *Washburn Law Journal*, vol. 52 (2013): 245.

Walker, Carson. "A La Carte Television: A Solution to Online Piracy?" *CommLaw Conspectus*, vol. 20 (2012): 471.

2000, *Bush v. Gore*

Bush v. Gore, 531 U.S. 98 (2000).

Wells, Charley. *Inside* Bush v. Gore. Gainesville: University Press of Florida, 2013.

2000, The Microsoft Monopoly

Brinkley, Joel. U.S. v. Microsoft: *The Inside Story of the Landmark Case*. New York: McGraw-Hill, 2001.

Page, William, and John Lopatka. *The Microsoft Case: Antitrust, High Technology, and Consumer Welfare*. Chicago: University of Chicago Press, 2007.

2001, Golf Carts on the PGA Tour

Johnson, Bradley. "*PGA Tour, Inc. v. Martin*: The U.S. Supreme Court Misses the Cut on the Americans with Disabilities Act." *The Labor Lawyer*, vol. 18 (2003): 47–78.

PGA Tour, Inc. v. Martin, 532 U.S. 661 (2001).

2001, Expanded Copyrights

Gordon, Wendy. "Fine-Tuning *Tasini*: Privileges of Electronic Distribution and Reproduction." *Brooklyn Law Review*, vol. 66 (2001): 473.

New York Times Co. v. Tasini, 533 U.S. 483 (2001).

2001, The USA PATRIOT Act

Foerstel, Herbert N. *The Patriot Act: A Documentary and Reference Guide.* Westport: Greenwood Press, 2008.

Gonzalez, Tracy Topper. "Individual Rights Versus Collective Security: Assessing the Constitutionality of the USA Patriot Act." *University of Miami International and Comparative Law Review*, vol. 11 (2003): 75.

Liu, Edward C. "Reauthorization of the FISA Amendments Act." *Congressional Research Service Report* R42725 (April 8, 2013).

2002, The Sarbanes-Oxley Act

Dunn, Catherine. "Still Debating the Merits of Sarbanes-Oxley, 10 Years Later." *Corporate Counsel Online* (October 4, 2012).

Fanto, James. "A Social Defense of Sarbanes-Oxley." *New York Law School Law Review*, vol. 52 (2007/2008):517.

Keneally, Kathryn. "The Sarbanes-Oxley Act: A Primer." *Tax Practice & Procedure* (December 2002/January 2003).

2002, The International Criminal Court

Bellelli, Roberto, ed. *International Criminal Justice: Law and Practice from the Rome Statute to Its Review.* Surrey: Ashgate Publishing Limited, 2010.

Schabas, William. *The International Criminal Court: A Commentary on the Rome Statute.* Oxford: Oxford University Press, 2010.

2005, Public Purpose and Eminent Domain

Kelo v. City of New London, 545 U.S. 469 (2005).

Levy, Robert, and William Mellor. *The Dirty Dozen: How Twelve Supreme Court Cases Radically Expanded Government and Eroded Freedom.* New York: Penguin Group, 2008.

Robson, Gregory. "*Kelo v. City of New London*: Its Ironic Impact on Takings Authority." *Urban Lawyer*, vol. 44 (2012): 865.

2008, The Legality of Gun Control

Utter, Glenn H. *Encyclopedia of Gun Control and Gun Rights.* Phoenix: Oryx Press, 2000.

Urbina, Ian. "Washington Officials Try to Ease Crime Fear." *New York Times* (online), July 13, 2006.

Winkler, Adam. *Gunfight: The Battle Over the Right to Bear Arms in America.* New York: W. W. Norton & Co., 2011.

2010, Google Books and Fair Use

Band, Jonathan. "The Long and Winding Road to the Google Books Settlement." *John Marshall Review of Intellectual Property Law*, vol. 9 (2009): 227.

Grimmelmann, James. "The Elephantine Google Books Settlement." *Journal of the Copyright Society*, vol. 58 (2010): 497.

2010, Wall Street Reform

"The Dodd-Frank Act: Too Big Not to Fail." *The Economist*, February 18, 2012.

Dodd-Frank Wall Street Reform and Consumer Protection Act, Public Law No. 111–203, July 21, 2010.

Webel, Baird. "The Dodd-Frank Wall Street Reform and Consumer Protection Act: Issues and Summary." *Congressional Research Service Report* R41350, July 29, 2010.

2012, The Future of Juvenile Punishment

Becker, Elizabeth. "As Ex-Theorist on Young 'Superpredators,' Bush Aide Has Regrets." *New York Times* (online), February 9, 2001.

Howell, James. *Preventing and Reducing Juvenile Delinquency: A Comprehensive Framework* 2nd ed. Thousand Oaks, CA: SAGE Publications, 2009.

2012, The Affordable Care Act

National Federation of Independent Business v. Sebelius, 132 S. Ct. 2566 (June 28, 2012).

Shapiro, Ilya. "Like Eastwood Talking to a Chair: The Good, the Bad, and the Ugly of the Obamacare Ruling." *Texas Review of Law & Politics*, vol. 17 (2013): 1.

Persily, Nathaniel, et al., eds. *The Health Care Case: The Supreme Court's Decision and Its Implications.* New York: Oxford University Press, 2013.

Redhead, C. Stephen, et al., "ACA: A Brief Overview of the Law, Implementation, and Legal Challenges." *Congressional Research Service Report* R41664, July 3, 2012.

2015, The Legal Fight for Gay Marriage

Goodridge v. Department of Public Health, 798 N.E.2d 941 (Mass. 2003).

Klarman, Michael. "Brown and Lawrence (and Goodridge)." *Michigan Law Review*, vol. 104 (2006): 431–89.

Wardle, Lynn. "Goodridge and 'The Justiciary' of Massachusetts." *Boston University International Law Journal*, vol. 14 (2005): 57.

Image Credits

Alamy: © Everyday Images 311; Heritage Image Partnership Ltd 247; © Frances Roberts 503; © The San Diego Union-Tribune/ZUMAPRESS.com 159; © Jim West 475

Courtesy Alyeska Pipeline Service Company: 391

Art Resource: HIP 173

Associated Press: 195, 317, 367, 497; © Mike Derer 397; © Greg English 321; © Douglas Pizac 417

Brian A Browne: 53

Bridgeman Art: 33, © Look and Learn / Elgar Collection 89

The British Museum: 91

Corbis Images: © Bettmann 259, 277, 291, 337, 339, 409; © Lorenzo Ciniglio 241; © O. J. Rapp 327; © Tony Savino 271

CPS-IRRI: Ram Cabrerra 429

Getty Images: © AFP 447; Archive Photos 69; © Galerie Bilderwelt 279; © Bloomberg 501; © Vince Bucci 463; © Ron Galella Ltd 441; © Gamma-Rapho 455; © Dirck Halstead 431; © Ken Howard 411; © Hulton Archive 405; © Peter Keegan 385; © Robert King/Newsmakers 483; © Mansell 19; © Behrouz Mehri 439; New York Public Library 201; © James Nielsen 493; © Paul J. Richards 275; © Sports Illustrated/Walter Iooss Jr 357; Universal Images Group 243; © Wally McNamee 377; © WIN-Initiative 85; Universal Images Group 243

The J. Paul Getty Museum: 43

Courtesy of Glenbow Archives: 171

Courtesy Google Books: 61

The Harry Ransom Center The University of Texas at Austin: 309

iStockphoto: © Alptraum 267; © Yuri Arcurs 433; © Belterz 469; © Bob Canon 379; © ClarkandCompany 343; © Duncan1890 63; © Pete Flyer 485; © A. Greenhill 365; © Isitsharp 381; © Jorisvo 457; © James Margolis 17; © Aleksandar Nakic 435; © Sedmak 55; © Seraficus 35; © Davis Turner 363; © Upheaval 393; © Wragg 261; © Stephan Zabel 401; © Zodebala 347

Adam Jones/adamjones.freeservers.com: 351

© Aggie Kenny: 415

Library of Congress: 21, 25, 49, 51, 75, 81, 97, 101, 103, 105, 117, 121, 123, 127, 131, 137, 139, 143, 145, 149, 151, 163, 165, 169, 177, 179, 189, 191, 197, 199, 205, 207, 211, 213, 215, 217, 219, 221, 223, 225, 227, 229, 231, 235, 249, 295, 297, 299, 303, 305, 325, 355, 369, 375, 383, 467

Metropolitan Museum of Art/Catharine Lorillard Wolfe Collection, Wolfe Fund, 1931: 27

National Archives and Records Administration: 167, 253, 265, 273, 281, 293, 323, 341, 387, 389, 419, 445

© National Portrait Gallery, London: 11, 95

National Portrait Gallery, Washington: 147

New York Public Library: 57, 213, 437

Steve Petteway, Collection of the Supreme Court of the United States: 449, 489

Shutterstock: © Helder Almeida 473; © Ari N 209; © Bikeriderlondon 427; © Bikeworldtravel 443; © Sascha Burkard 505; © Mikele Dray 407; © Lane V. Erickson 155; © Everett Historical 237, 331; © f8grapher 31; © GTS Productions 487; © Leonid Ikan 203; © Jdwfoto 335; © Barbara J. Johnson 333; © Jsp 15; © Maksim Kabakou 481; © Leonid Karchevsky 425; ©Trevor Kittelty 41; © Levent Konuk 459; © Koya979 301; © Jan Kranendonk 495; © Pan Kung 349;

© Karin Hildebrand Lau 509; © Teddy Leung 465; © Marzolino 39; © Stuart Monk 283; © Nagel Photography 403; © Netfalls - Remy Musser 107; © Nick Nick 67; © Pieter 287; © Gabor Racz 193; © Bruce Raynor 421; © Scott Richardson 233; © Fesus Robert 307; © Peggy Woods Ryan 185; © Luis Santos 359; © Stason4ik 133

United States Marine Corps: 499

The United States National Archives: 255

Courtesy Wikimedia Foundation: 29, 73, 135, 157, 175, 181, 187, 251, 263, 269, 345, 395, 86th AW Public Affairs 353; Bibliothèque Nationale de France 141; Bonhams 109; Carnavalet Museum 99; Charlottenburg Palace 113; Musée Condé 79; Defense Imagery 373; Gerald R. Ford Presidential Museum 471; Jimmy Flynt 423; Biswarup Ganguly 285; Tristan Harward 399; HoboJones 37; Lee Honeycutt 371; Infrogmation 183; Israel National Photo Collection 319; Louvre Museum 13; Lyndon Baines Johnson Library and Museum 329; Louvre Museum, 13; Chuck Kennedy/The White House 507; Bob McNeely/The White House 477; Museum Herrenhausen Palace 93; Museum of Memory and Human Rights 479; National Gallery London 71; National Portrait Gallery of Eminent Americans 119; Nikater 23; Dave Pape 315; PerSona77 289; John Phelan 153; Portraits of Territorial Governors 161; Prado Museum 59; Radio Corporation of America 245; Ryddragyn 461; Saforrest 45; Fred Schaerli 313; Tate Britain 87; Kim Traynor 65; United States Air Force 451; United States Navy 491; Fritz Wagner 47; The Weiss Gallery 77; Wellcome Library 453; Wellcome Trust 83, 129; The White House Historical Association 257

The White House Collection: 111

Yale Center for British Art: 115

Yale University Art Gallery: 125

© Ze Carrion: 361, 413

Index

Abolition of slavery, 142. *See also* Slavery
Abortion, legality of, 384–385
Act for the Relief of the Poor, 62–63
Adams, John, 92, 110
Administrative agency determinations, 420–421
Affirmative action, 408–409
Affordable Care Act (ACA), 506–507
Alhambra Decree, 58–59
Alien Registration Act, 268–269, 296–297
Alyeska Pipeline Service Co. v. Wilderness Society, 390
Americans with Disabilities Act (ADA), 444–445
Anderson, Margaret, 240
Anthony, Susan B., 216
Anti-Okie statute, 272–273
Apartheid, end of, 446–447
Arms. *See* Gun laws
Assize of Clarendon, 44–45, 76
Attlee, Clement, 284
Attorney advertising, 406–407
Attorneys' fee awards, 390–391
Authors Guild v. Google, 500

Baby M, 434
Baker, Richard John, *Baker v. Nelson*, 380
Bakke, Allan, 408–409
Baseball reserve clause, 356–357
Bates v. State Bar of Arizona, 406
Batson v. Kentucky, 426
Berkowitz, David, 412
Berne Convention, 162–163
Bill of Rights, 88, 100, 104–105, 148
Black Code of Louis XIV, 78–79
Black, Hugo, 274, 364
Blackstone, William, 24, 44, 74, 94–95, 152
Blakey, G. Robert, 354
Blue Laws, first, 68–69
BMW of North America v. Gore, 464–465
Body, privacy rights, 332–333
Bonaparte, Napoleon, 78, 108, 112–113
Bonsack, James, 352
Bork, Robert, 430–431
Boxing legalization, 220–221
Boyle, David, 7th Earl of Glasgow, 180
Bradwell v. Illinois, 158–159
Brandeis, Louis, 176–177, 234
Brandenburg v. Ohio, 344
Brazilian Slave Emancipation Act, 174–175
Brecht, Bertolt, 290
Brehon laws of Ireland, 32–33
Brennan, William J., Jr., 308
Briesen, Arthur von, 160
Brown, Henry Billings, 182
Brown, Linda, 302
Brown v. Board of Education, 182, 302–303, 368
Bryan, William Jennings, 228
Bubble Act, 86–87
Buchanan, James, 136
Buckey, Peggy McMartin, 416–417
Bugliosi, Vincent, 360
Burger, Warren E., 366–367, 382
Burn, Harry Thomas, 216

Bushel's Case, 74–75
Bush, George W., *Bush v. Gore*, 482–483
Busing, court-ordered, 368–369

California, Anti-Okie statute, 272–273
California Federal Savings & Loan Association v. Guerra, 428–429
Calley, William, Jr., court-martial, 350–351
Cameras in courts, 258–259
Caminetti v. United States, 194
Canon law and the *Decretum Gratiani*, 42–43
Capote, Domingo Méndez, 188
Cardozo, Benjamin, 204–205, 212, 232, 272
Carlin, George, 410–411
Censorship, 224–225, 240–241. *See also* Obscenity limits/standards
Chafee, Zechariah, Jr., 268
Chandler v. Florida, 258
Chevron U.S.A. v. Natural Resources Defense Council, Inc.*, 420–421
Chicago "Black Sox" trial, 222–223
Child Labor Act of 1916, 210–211
China, 38–39, 364, 480
Chinese Exclusion Act, 166–167
Churchill, Winston, 284
Cigarettes, legal issues, 352–353, 452–453
Cipollone v. Liggett Group., 452
Civil Rights Act of 1866, 142, 144–145, 148
Civil Rights Act of 1875, 168
Civil Rights Act of 1964, 326–327, 366, 372, 408
Civil Rights Cases (1883), 168–169
Class action, 260–261
Clayton Antitrust Act, 206–207
Clinton, Bill, 274–275, 460, 470, 476–477
Clinton v. City of New York, 476
Cloning laws, 460–461
Coca-Cola, products liability and, 270–271
Code of Hammurabi, 14–15
Code of Ur-Nammu, 12–13
Coffee, hot, litigation, 458–459
Coinage Act of 1792, 106–107
Colonialism, postwar independence and, 284–285
Columba, St., 36
Columbus, Christopher, 58, 152, 188
Comiskey, Charles, 222
Commentaries (Blackstone), 94–95
Commerce, congressional regulation of, 120–121
Commitment, involuntary, restrictions, 392–393
Commonwealth v. Hunt, 126
Communications Decency Act, 472–473
Communist Control Act, 304–305
Compulsory education laws, 64–65
Comstock Act, 156–157
Comstock, Anthony, 156–157
Congress, commerce regulation, 120–121
Conscientious objection, 330–331
Constantine the Great, 68

Constitution, Cuban, 188–189
Constitution, South African, 466–467
Consumer rights, 212–213
Copyrights, 36–37, 102–103, 400–401, 480–481, 488–489
Cormac, King, 32
Corporate personhood and liability, 184–185
Cosby, William, 88
Costello, Frank, 354–355
Counsel, right to, 322–323
Court of Star Chamber, 52–53, 82
Court-packing plan, FDR and, 256–257
Cruzan v. Director, Missouri Department of Health, 474
Cuban Constitution of 1901, 188–189

Damages, measure of, 132–133
Darrow, Clarence, 228
Day, William R., 204
Death penalty, 370–371, 402–403
Death, right to die, 396–397
Decency, communications, 472
Declaration of the Rights of Man, 100–101
Decretum Gratiani, canon law and, 42–43
de Klerk, F. W., 446
De Jure Belli ac Pacis (Grotius), 66–67
Dictionary, *Les Termes de la Ley* (Rastell), 60–61
DiIulio, John, 504
Dillingham, William P., 226
Disabilities act, 444–445
Discrimination: affirmative action and, 408–409; Chinese Exclusion Act, 166–167; employment, 366–367; Equal Employment Opportunity Act and, 372; equal protection against, 170–171; Equal Rights Amendment and, 374–375; Fair Labor Standards Act and, 264–265; gay marriage laws and, 442; gender. *See* Women; interracial marriage and, 338; Interstate Commerce Act and, 172; pregnancy, 428–429; prohibition of racial voter discrimination, 150–151; racism and U.N. Resolution 3379 and, 394–395; separate but equal (*Plessy v. Ferguson*), 182–183; Voting Rights Act of 1965 and, 328
Displaced Persons Act, 294–295
District of Columbia v. Heller, 498
Divorce, no-fault, 342–343
DNA, as evidence, 432–433
Dodd, Christopher, 502
Donaldson, Kenneth, 392
Draco, 18, 20
Draconian Code, 18–19
Draft laws, Vietnam-era, 340–341. *See also* Conscientious objection
Dred Scott Decision, 134–135
Drugs, prohibition of illegal, 208–209
Drummond, Edward, 128
Dunant, Jean-Henri, 140
Dwight, Theodore, 152

Earth Summit (Rio Conference), 454–455
Edict of Expulsion (Alhambra Decree), 58–59

Education, compulsory, 64–65
Edward I, King of England, 48, 50
Edwards v. California, 272
Eichmann, Adolf (trial), 318–319
Eighteen-year-olds, enfranchising, 362–363
Eisenhower, Dwight, 306
Elizabethan Poor Law, 62
Elizabeth I, Queen of England, 62–63, 82
Ellsberg, Daniel, 364
Emancipation Proclamation, 136, 138–139, 142
Emergency Quota Act, 226–227
Emerson, Irene, 134
Eminent domain, public purpose and, 496–497
Employment discrimination, 366–367
Endangered Species Act, 378–379
Entrapment defense, 414–415
Environmental policy act, 348–349
Equal Employment Opportunity Act (and Commission), 326, 372–373, 448
Equal Rights Amendment, 374–375
Escola, Gladys, *Escola v. Coca-Cola Bottling Co.*, 270
Estes v. Texas, 258
European Coal and Steel Community (ECSC), 300
European Court of Human Rights, 312–313
European Union, creation of, 456–457
European Union, Treaty of Paris and, 300–301
Evolution, Scopes "Monkey" Trial and, 228–229
Exclusionary Rule, 204–205, 316–317
Expositiones Terminorum Legum Anglorum (Rastell), 60–61

Fair Labor Standards Act, 264–265
Fairness Doctrine, 346–347
Fair use laws, 400, 424–425, 500–501
Falwell v. Flynt, 422
Fatwa, *Satanic Verses*, 438
Faubus, Orval, 302
FCC v. Pacifica Foundation, 410
Federal administrative agency determinations, 420–421
Federal Communications Act, 244–245
Federal Communications Commission (FCC), 244, 346, 410–411
Federal law, supremacy/jurisdiction, 116–117, 118–119
Federal Register, 254–255
Federal Reserve Act, 202–203
Ferdinand II, King of Spain, 58
Field Code, 130–131
Field, David Dudley, 130–131
Fifteenth Amendment, 150–151
Finnian of Moville, 36
"Fire!," yelling in crowded theater, 218–219
Flood, Curtis, *Flood v. Kuhn*, 356
Flynt, Larry, 422–423
Food, Drug, and Cosmetic Act, 262–263
Ford, Gerald, 400, 424
Fortas, Abe, 322
Fourteenth Amendment, 148–149

Frank, Barney, 502
Franklin, Benjamin, 100
Frederick William I, King of Prussia, 64
Freedom of Information Act, 334–335
Furman v. Georgia, 370, 402
Fyfe, David Maxwell, 310

Gandhi, Mohandas, 284
Garfield, James, 164
Garland, Lillian, 428
Gay marriage, 380–381, 442–443, 508–509
Gay rights, 310–311
General Agreement on Tariffs and Trade (GATT), 286–287
General Regulations for Village Schools, 64
Geneva Convention, 140–141
Genocide, U.N. Convention on, 288–289
George II, King of England, 92
German Civil Code, 186–187
Gibbons, Thomas, 120
Gibbons v. Ogden, 120
G.I. Bill, 276–277
Gideon, Clarence Earl, *Gideon v. Wainwright*, 322
Gilmore, Gary, 402
Gin Act of 1751, 90–91
Goldman, Ron, 462
Golf carts, on PGA tour, *PGA Tour, Inc. v. Martin*, 486–487
Goodridge v. Department of Public Health, 508–509
Google Books and fair use, 500–501
Gore, Al, 482
Gortyn Code, 22–23
Government Printing Office (GPO), 136–137
Graham v. Florida, 504
Gratian, 42
"Great Writ," 76
Green, William, 248
Gregg v. Georgia, 402
Griggs, Estelle, *Griswold v. Connecticut*, 332, 396
Grotius, Hugo, 66–67, 318
Guiteau, Charles, 164–165
Gun laws, 266–267, 498–499
Gutenberg, Johannes, 82

Habeas Corpus Acts, 52, 76–77
Hadley v. Baxendale, 132
Haeberle, Ronald, 350
Halsbury, Lord, 184
Hamilton, Alexander, 96, 98, 106, 120, 202
Hamilton, Andrew, 88
Hammurabi, 14–15
Hand, Learned, 296
Harding, Warren, 226
Harlan, John Marshall, 182, 382
Harper & Row, Publishers, Inc. v. Nation Enterprises, 424
Harrison, Francis Burton, 208
Hayes, Will H. (Hays Code), 224–225
Health care, ACA, 506–507
Health care, duty to warn, 398–399
Helmsley, Leona, 440–441
Henry I, King of England, 48, 260
Henry II, King of England, 44, 192
Henry VIII, King of England, 62

Hersh, Seymour, 350
Hill, Anita, 448
Hill, Henry, 412
Hindenburg, Paul von, 326
Hitler, Adolf, 236–237, 250–251, 318
Hobbes, Thomas, 72
Hogarth, William, 90, 128
Hollywood Ten, 290–291
Holmes, Oliver Wendell, Jr., 108, 218–219, 296, 344
Howard, Jacob M., 148–149
Hughes, Charles Evans, 196
Hugo, Victor, 162
Human rights, court of, 312–313
Human rights, universal declaration, 292–293
Humphrey, Hubert, 304
Hustler magazine, First Amendment and, 422

Immigration: Alien Registration Act rejection, 296–297; Chinese Exclusion Act, 166–167; Displaced Persons Act, 294–295; Emergency Quota Act, 226–227
Impeaching Andrew Johnson, 146–147
Income tax, Congressional right to levy, 192–193
Indians (native peoples), administering, 122–123. *See also* Trail of Broken Treaties
Insanity defense, 164–165
International Criminal Court, 494–495
Internment of Japanese Americans, 274–275
Interracial marriage, 338–339
Interstate Commerce Act, 172–173
Interstate Highway Act, 306–307
Ireland: Brehon laws of, 32–33; copyright war, 36–37
Isabella, Queen of Spain, 58
Isabel, Princess Imperial of Brazil, 174
Islamic (Sharia) law, 40

Jackson, "Shoeless" Joe, 222–223
Japanese Americans, internment of, 274–275
Jaworski, Leon, 388
Jeanne d'Arc, trial of, 54–55
Jefferson, Thomas, 100, 104, 110
Jeffreys, Alec, 432
Jéquier, Gustave, 14
Joan of Arc, trial of, 54–55
John, King of England, 48
Johnson, Andrew, 144, 146–147
Johnson, Lyndon, 326–327, 328–329, 340, 372, 418
Jones, Paula, 470
Joyce, James, 240
Juan Carlos, King of Spain, 58
Judiciary Act of 1789, 98–99
Jurisdiction of federal law, 118–119
Jury selection, peremptory challenges to, 426–427
Justinian Code, 10, 34–35
Justinian I, 30, 34
Juvenile punishment, future of, 504

Kagan, Elena, 420–421
Kelo v. City of New London, 496
Kennedy, John F., 326, 372, 498
Kevorkian, Jack, 474–475
Khomeini, Ruhollah, 438

King, Martin Luther, Jr., 324–325, 328–329, 334, 498
King v Penn and Mead (Penn), 74
Korematsu, Fred, 274–275
Kuhn, Bowie, 356
Ku Klux Klan, *Brandenburg v. Ohio*, 344

Labor unions, recognition of, 126–127
Lafayette, marquis de, 100
Landis, Kenesaw Mountain, 222
Langdell, Christopher Columbus, 152
Langton, Stephen, 48
Lanham, Fritz Garland, 282
Lapse of Licensing Act, 82–83
Lardner, Ring, Jr., 290
Law reporting and legal publishing, 154–155
Law school, first, 30–31
Law school revolution, 152–153
Laws of Solon, 20–21
Lawson, John Howard, 290
Legal aid societies, 160–161
Les Termes de la Ley (Rastell), 60–61
Leviathan (Hobbes), 72–73
Lex Mercatoria, 46–47
Libel laws, limits on, 324–325
Licensing Act, lapse of, 82–83
Liebeck, Stella, *Liebeck v. McDonald's Restaurants*, 458–459
Lincoln, Abraham, 138, 142, 192
Line-item veto, 476–477
Littleton's *Tenures*, 56–57
Littleton Thomas de, 56
Locke, John, 82, 100, 114
Louis X, King of France, 78
Louis XIV, King of France, 78
Loving, Richard and Mildred Jeter, *Loving v. Virginia*, 338–339

MacPherson v. Buick Motor Co., 212, 270
Madison, James, 104, 110
Magna Carta, 44, 46, 48–49, 92, 104, 160
"Magna Carta of humanity," 292
"Magna Carta of the electronic age," 424
Maine, Sir Henry, 24, 32
Mandela, Nelson, 320–321, 446, 466–467
Mann Act, 194
Mann, James R., 194
Manson, Charles, trial, 360–361
Mapp, Dollree, *Mapp v. Ohio*, 316–317
Marbury v. Madison, 110, 388
Marbury, William, 110
Maria Cristina Queen Regent of Spain, 188
Marijuana, legalization of, 468–469
Marriage, gay, 380–381, 442–443, 508–509
Marriage, interracial, 338–339
Marshall, John, 110, 116, 118–119, 120, 122
Marshall, Thurgood, 388
Martin, Casey, 486
Marvin, Lee and Michelle, *Marvin v. Marvin*, 404–405
Mary I, queen of England, 84
Mather, Cotton, 80
McCarthy, Joseph, 304
McConnell, James Michael, 380

McCorvey, Norma, 384
McCulloch, James W., *McCulloch v. Maryland*, 116, 118
McDonald v. Chicago, 498
McKinley, William, 188
McMartin molestation case, 416–417
McMartin, Virginia, 416
McNamara, Robert, 364
Mental health, involuntary commitment and, 392–393
Microsoft monopoly, 484–485
Miller v. Alabama, 504
Miller v. California, 382
Miranda, Ernesto, Miranda Warnings, 336–337
Mishnah, 28
Mitchell, Charles, 238
M'Naghten, Daniel, 128
M'Naghten Rule, 128–129, 164
Monroe, James, 122
Moses, 16
Moss, John E., 334
Motier, Gilbert du, 100
Mott, Lucretia, 216
Muhammad, 40–41, 438
Müller, Mary Ann, 180
Muller v. Oregon, 190

Napoleonic Code, 112–113, 186
Narcotics, prohibition of illegal, 208–209
National Environmental Policy Act (NEPA), 348–349
National Labor Relations Act, 248–249, 256
National Labor Relations Board v. Jones & Laughlin Steel Corp., 256
Native peoples, administering, 122–123
New Jersey v. Bruno Richard Hauptmann, 258
New York State Club Association v. City of New York, 436
New York Times Co. v. Tasini, 488
New York Times Co. v. United States, 364
New York Times v. Sullivan, 324
New Zealand Women's Suffrage, 180–181
Nixon, Richard, 340, 348, 350, 360, 362, 364–365, 386, 388–389, 424
No-fault divorce, 342–343
Noriega, Manuel, 450–451
Nuremberg Laws, 250–251
Nuremberg Trials, 278–279, 288, 494

Obama, Barack, 460, 468, 476, 502, 506–507
Obscenity limits/standards, 156–157, 308–309, 382–383
Occupational Safety and Health Act, 358–359
O'Connor v. Donaldson, 392
Ogden, Aaron, 120
Olmstead, Roy, *Olmstead v. United States*, 234
On the Law of War and Peace (Grotius), 66–67
Otis, James, Jr., 92
Outer Space, treaties on, 314–315
Oxley, Michael, 492

Palimony, 404–405
Palsgraf v. Long Island Railroad Co., 232

Parody, First Amendment and, 422–423
Patrick, St., 32
PATRIOT Act, 490–491
Paul, Alice, 374
Peace of Münster, 70–71
Peace of Westphalia, 70–71
Pecora, Ferdinand, 238
Penn, William, 74
Pentagon Papers, 364–365
Peremptory challenges to jury selection, 426–427
Peters, Samuel, 68
Petrie, Flinders, 10
Phips, William, 80
Physician-assisted suicide, 474–475
Pierson, Jesse, *Pierson v. Post*, 114
Pinochet, Augusto, indictment of, 478–479
Pitt, William the Younger, 108–109, 192
Platt, Orville (Platte Amendment), 188
Plessy, Homer, 182
Plessy v. Ferguson, 182–183, 302
Plutarch, 18, 20
Poor, act for relief of, 62–63
Popov v. Hayashi, 114
Possession, superiority of, 114–115
Post, Ludowick, 114
Powell, Lewis F., Jr., 104, 430
Pregnancy discrimination, 428–429
Presidential immunity, 470–471
Presidential subpoena compliance, 388–389
Privacy, right to, 176–177, 332–333
Privy Council's School Establishment Act, 64
Products liability, 270–271
Profanity, FCC and, 410
Prohibition, 214–215; Gin Act of 1751 and, 90–91; repeal of, 242–243
Public purpose and eminent domain, 496–497
Publishing. *See also* Copyrights: Government Printing Office (GPO), 136–137; law reporting and legal publishing, 154; obscenity, Comstock Act and, 156–157
Punitive damages, limits on, 464–465

Quinlan, Karen, 396
Quran, The, 40–41, 438

Racism and U.N. Resolution 3379, 394–395
Raines v. Byrd, 476
Randolph, Jennings, 362
Rastell, John, 60
Reagan, Ronald, 164, 290, 430, 476
Red Lion Broadcasting Co. v. FCC, 346–347
Regents of the University of California v. Bakke, 408–409
Rehnquist, William, 388, 422, 474
Reno v. American Civil Liberties Union, 472
Rent control, 280–281
Reserve clause, MLB, 356–357
RICO Act, 354–355
Right to privacy, 176–177
Rio Conference, 454–455
Roads, Interstate Highway Act, 306–307
Roberts, John, 506
Robespierre, Maximilien, 78
Robinson, Harriet, 134

Roe v. Wade, 384–385
Roosevelt, Eleanor, 292–293
Roosevelt, Franklin Delano (FDR), 238, 248, 252, 254, 255–256, 264, 268, 274, 276–277, 280, 284, 362, 400
Roosevelt, Theodore, 198–199, 388, 400
Roper v. Simmons, 504
Rosenberg Trial (Julius and Ethel), 298–299
Roth, Samuel, *Roth v. United States*, 308
Rule 23, 260–261
Rushdie, Salman, 438

Salem witchcraft trials, 80–81
Salomon, Edward, 160–161
Salomon v. A. Salomon & Co., 184
Sarbanes-Oxley Act, 492–493
Sarbanes, Paul, 492
Satanic Verses, fatwa against, 438–439
Saypol, Irving, 298
Schenck v. United States, 218
Schlafly, Phyllis, 374–375
School of law, first, 30–31
Scopes, John, 228–229
Scopes "Monkey" Trial, 228–229
Scott, Dred, 134–135
Seat-belt law, 418–419
Securities Exchange Act, 246–247
Seeger, Daniel, 330
Separate but equal, 182–183
Sharia law, 40
Shaw, George Bernard, 156
Shaw, Lemuel, 126
Shenck, Charles, 218
Sheppard, Kate, 180
Sherman Antitrust Act, 178–179
Sherman, John, 178–179
Simpson, Nicole Brown, 462
Simpson, O. J. murder trial, 462–463
Sirica, John, 388
Slavery: abolition of, 142–143; *The Amistad* and, 124–125; Black Code of Louis XIV, 78–79; Brazilian Slave Emancipation Act, 174–175; Civil Rights Act of 1866 and, 144; Dred Scott Decision and, 134–135; Emancipation Proclamation and, 136, 138–139, 142; Fourteenth Amendment and, 148–149; Gortyn Code and, 22; Laws of Solon and, 20; Twelve Tables and, 24; White-Slave Traffic Act, 194–195
Smith, Howard W., 268, 296
Smoking. *See* Cigarettes, legal issues
Sobell, Morton, 298
Social Security Act, 252–253
Socrates, trial of, 26–27
Solon, 20
Son of Sam Law, 412–413
Sony v. Universal City Studios, Inc., 424
Sotomayor, Sonia, 488–489
South Africa, Constitution, 466–467
Speech, freedom of, violence threats and, 344–345
Stanton, Edwin, 146
Stanton, Elizabeth Cady, 216
Star Chamber, 52–53, 82
Starr, Kenneth, 470
Statute of Anne, 84–85, 102
Statutes of Westminster, 50–51
Steinsaltz, Adin, 28

Stem cell laws, 460–461
Stevens, John Paul, 420–421, 476, 496
Stewart, Potter, 382
Stocks: Bubble Act, 86–87; Securities Exchange Act, 246–247; Wall Street regulation, 238–239
Subpoena compliance, presidential, 388–389
Suicide, physician-assisted, 474–475
Sullivan, Lester Bruce, 324
Superiority of possession, 114–115
Supremacy of federal law, 116–117
Supremacy of Supreme Court, 110–111
Supreme Court: Bork nomination, 430–431; Declaration of the Rights of Man and, 100–101; exclusionary rule and, 204–205, 316–317; FDR and court-packing plan, 256–257; Judiciary Act of 1789 and, 98–99; supremacy of, 110–111; Thomas confirmation, 448–449
Surrogate motherhood, 434–435
Swain v. Alabama, 426
Swann v. Charlotte-Mecklenburg Board of Education, 368–369

Taft, William Howard, 192, 234–235
Talmud, The, 28–29
Taney, Roger, 134, 506
Tang Code, 38–39
Tarasoff v. Regents of the University of California, 398
Tate, Sharon, 360
Taxes: celebrity prosecution, 440–441; Congressional right to tax income, 192–193; Triple Assessment, 108–109, 192
Ten Commandments, 16–17
Tenures (Littleton), 56–57
Terry, Luther, 352
The Amistad, 124–125
The Philadelphia Spelling Book (Barry), 102
Thomas, Clarence, 448–449
Thomas, J. Parnell, 290
Time-shifting, fair use and, 424–425
Tindal, Nicholas Conyngham, 128
Tort law, danger zone, 232–233
Trademarks, protection of, 282–283
Trail of Broken Treaties, 376–377
Traynor, Roger, 270
Treaty of Münster, 70
Treaty of Osnabrück, 70
Treaty of Paris, E.U. and, 300–301
Triangle Shirtwaist Fire, 200–201
Tribonian, 34
Triple Assessment, 108–109, 192
Truman, Harry S., 268, 282, 294
Trumbull, J. Hammond, 68
Trumbull, Lyman, 144
Trustees of Dartmouth College v. Woodward, 184
Trusts, busting, 198–199
Twelve Tables, 10, 24–25, 34, 464

Ulysses, censorship and, 240–241
U.N. Convention on Genocide, 288–289
United States Code (U.S.C.), 230–231
United States v. E. C. Knight Co., 198
United States v. Guiteau, 164
United States v. Helmsley, 440
United States v. Microsoft Corporation, 484–485

United States v. Miller, 266
United States v. Seeger, 330
Universal Declaration of Human Rights, 292–293
University of Bologna, first law school, 30–31
U.N. Resolution 3379, racism and, 394–395
U.N. treaties on Outer Space, 314
Ur-Nammu, 12
USA PATRIOT Act, 490–491
U.S. Constitution, 96–97. *See also* Bill of Rights

Vacco v. Quill, 474
Vaughan, John, 74
Veto, line-item, 476–477
Victoria, Queen of England, 128
Video, time-shifting, 424–425
Vietnam-era draft laws, 340–341
Volstead, Andrew (Volstead Act), 214
Voting: enfranchising eighteen-year-olds, 362–363; prohibition of racial voter discrimination, 150–151; rights for women, 216–217; Voting Rights Act of 1965, 328–329

Wade, Henry, 384
Wagner, Robert F., 248
Waldron, Francis, 296
Walker, James J., 220
Wallace, George, 302
Wall Street regulation/reform, 238–239, 502–503
War Powers Act of 1973, 386–387
Warren, Earl, 336, 338
Warren, Samuel, 176
Washington, George, 98, 102, 106
Washington v. Glucksberg, 474
Webster, Daniel, 120
Weeks v. United States, 204
Welfare programs, early basis if, 62
West, John Briggs, 154
Westminster, statutes of, 50–51
Westphalia, Peace of, 70–71
White, Byron, 436
White-Slave Traffic Act, 194–195
Wiley, Harvey, 262
Williams, Harrison A., Jr., 358, 414
Will, oldest written, 10–11
Wilson, Woodrow, 202, 206, 214
Wiretaps, 234–235
Witchcraft trials, Salem, 80–81
Wolfenden Report (Sir John Wolfenden), 310–311
Wolf v. Colorado, 316
Women: admission to private clubs, 436–437; admission to the bar, 158–159; Equal Rights Amendment, 374–375; in factories, 190–191; Fair Labor Standards Act and, 264–265; New Zealand Women's Suffrage, 180–181; right to vote, 216–217; *Roe v. Wade* and, 384–385; surrogate motherhood, 434–435
Wood, Leonard, 188
Woolsey, John M., 240
Workers' compensation law, 196–197
Writs of assistance case, 92–93

Yick Wo v. Hopkins, 170

Zenger, John Peter, 88–89